[対訳] 実務家のための
欧州特許条約

The European Patent Convention for Japanese Patent Practitioners

Hoffmann Eitle ［編著］
ホフマン アイトレ

日本評論社

推薦の言葉

　本書は、欧州特許実務を日本の実務家のために解説している。

　条文やケースローを学術的に解説するものではなく、欧州特許実務に精通した欧州弁理士により、日本の特許実務との違いに着目して欧州の特許実務が解説されており、欧州で特許を取得し活用しようとする日本企業にとって有用な情報が豊富に含まれた書となっている。

　日本企業としては、新たに導入され得る「欧州単一効特許」と「統一特許裁判所」との関連においても、欧州特許実務を習得する意義がある。現行の「欧州特許」を取得するべきか、「欧州単一効特許」を取得すべきか、それとも各国ごとに「国内特許」を取得すべきか、判断に迷うこともあろう。

　このような状況において、欧州特許条約とそれに関連する特許実務を理解することは必須であろう。

　各執筆者の原稿とその翻訳文が見開きで掲載されている点で、本書は原文を理解し欧州弁理士とディスカッションをする場においても役立つだろう。

日本知的財産協会副理事長
シスメックス株式会社

2016年9月
井上　二三夫

はしがき

　すでに日本特許庁やJETRO等により、欧州特許条約や欧州特許庁審査基準に関する翻訳物が刊行されています。また、日本の特許実務家等により、欧州特許実務について解説された書籍もいくつか出版されています。日本で特許実務に従事する方々が欧州特許実務にも関心を寄せていることがわかります。

　本書は、『［対訳］実務家のための欧州特許条約』と題し、欧州特許条約とそれに関連する実務を日本の特許実務家に向けて解説するものです。日本の特許実務との相違点に着目して欧州特許条約とそれに関連する実務について解説する書をご提供したいという願いで本書は企画されました。

　本書の原稿は、2015年春から、弊所の欧州弁理士により英語で執筆されました。日本語での解説書を希望される読者のために、英語の原文に日本語訳をつけました。日本語訳が不明な個所は原文をご参照ください。

　本書の第Ⅰ部から第Ⅳ部では、最初に、そこで参照されている欧州特許条約の条文を抜粋し、日本語訳を添えました。この日本語訳は、日本特許庁ウェブサイトから利用可能な欧州特許条約仮訳に基づき、弊所でわずかな修正を加えて作成したものです。巻末付録の「欧州特許庁の審判部の規則（関連規則の抜粋）」の日本語訳は、弊所でオリジナルに作成しました。公式的な翻訳物ではないことをご了承ください。

　第1章～第16章の各章冒頭では、欧州特許実務に特徴的な点を強調する目的で、メモ書きを添えました。メモ書きには、参照セクションを括弧書きで加えてあります。

本書の原稿には、欧州特許庁の最新版のガイドライン及び審決に合わせてアップデートされていない箇所が含まれていることをご了承ください。

　本書が、欧州特許実務を理解するための一助となることを願っております。

2016年9月

松澤 美恵子

Table of Contents

目 次

Recommendation Words	Fumio Inoue	iii
Preface	Mieko Matsuzawa	v
Introduction	Joachim Renken	xxxv

Part I Substantive Requirements   1

Legal Text   2

Chapter 1 Disclosure Concepts and Novelty
Martin Bachelin & Stephan Disser   11

1 The Law 14
2 Fundamental Concepts of Disclosure 18
   2.1 Public   18
   2.2 Direct and Unambiguous Disclosure   20
   2.3 Whole Content Approach and Combinations of Disclosure   20
   2.4 Enabling Disclosure   20
   2.5 Implicit Disclosure   22
   2.6 Disclosure by Public Prior Use   22
   2.7 Degree of Individualization   24
3 Novelty Assessment 24
4 Novelty by Selection 26
   4.1 General Considerations   26
   4.2 Selection from Generic Term   26
   4.3 Selection from List   28
   4.4 Selection from Numerical Range   28
   4.5 Partial Overlap with Known Numerical Range   30
   4.6 Selection of Sub-Genus from Generically Defined Area   30

推薦の言葉　　　　　　　　　　　　　　　　　　　井上二三夫　　iii
はしがき　　　　　　　　　　　　　　　　　　　　松澤美恵子　　v
序　　　　　　　　　　　　　　　　　　　　Joachim Renken　xxxv

第 I 部　　実体的要件　　　　　　　　　　　　　　　　　　　　　1

　　法規　　3

第 1 章　　開示概念と新規性
　　　　　　　　　　　　　　Martin Bachelin & Stephan Disser　11

　1　法律 ……………… 15
　2　開示の基本的概念 ……………… 19
　　　2.1　公衆　　19
　　　2.2　直接的かつ一義的な開示　　21
　　　2.3　内容全体によるアプローチ及び開示の組合せ　　21
　　　2.4　実施可能な程度の開示　　21
　　　2.5　黙示的な開示　　23
　　　2.6　先の公然使用による開示　　23
　　　2.7　個別化の程度　　25
　3　新規性の判断 ……………… 25
　4　選択により見出される新規性 ……………… 27
　　　4.1　概論　　27
　　　4.2　包括的用語からの選択　　27
　　　4.3　リストからの選択　　29
　　　4.4　数値範囲の選択　　29
　　　4.5　公知の数値範囲との部分的重複　　31
　　　4.6　包括的に定義された領域からの狭い範囲の選択　　31

    4.7 Selection of Purity Level   32

5 Novelty by Use Indication ·················· 34

    5.1 Use Indication in Non-Medical Product Claim   34
    5.2 Use Indication in Medical Product Claim   34
    5.3 Medical Use-Type Claims   36
    5.4 Non-Medical Use-Type Claims   36

6 Special Cases ··················· 38

    6.1 Negative Features   38
    6.2 Unclear Features   42
    6.3 Parameter Ranges and Error Margins   42
    6.4 Non-Technical Features   44

Chapter 2   Inventive Step   Declan Mulhern   47

Introduction   50

1 Legal Basis for Inventive Step ·················· 50

2 State of the Art ·················· 52

3 Person Skilled in the Art ·················· 54

4 Not Obvious? ··················· 56

5 Problem-Solution Approach ··················· 58

    5.1 Stage 1: The Closest Prior Art   58
        5.1.1 Conceived for the Same Purpose / 60
        5.1.2 Similar Technical Problem / 62
        5.1.3 Most Relevant Technical Features in Common / 62
        5.1.4 More than One Closest Prior Art? / 64
    5.2 Stage 2: The Objective Technical Problem   66
        5.2.1 Distinguishing Technical Features / 66
        5.2.2 Establishing a Technical Effect / 68
        5.2.3 Formulating the Objective Technical Problem / 70

  4.7　純度レベルの選択　33
5　用途の表示による新規性 ……………… 35
  5.1　非医薬発明における用途の表示　35
  5.2　医薬発明における用途の表示　35
  5.3　医薬用途タイプのクレーム　37
  5.4　非医薬用途タイプのクレーム　37
6　特別なケース ……………… 39
  6.1　ネガティブな特徴　39
  6.2　不明確な特徴　43
  6.3　パラメータの範囲と許容誤差　43
  6.4　非技術的特徴　45

第2章　進歩性　　　　　　　　　　Declan Mulhern　47

  はじめに　51
1　進歩性の法的根拠 ……………… 51
2　技術水準 ……………… 53
3　当業者 ……………… 55
4　自明なものではない？ ……………… 57
5　課題解決アプローチ ……………… 59
  5.1　第一段階：最も近い先行技術　59
    5.1.1　同一の目的で着想された発明／61
    5.1.2　類似の技術的課題／63
    5.1.3　関連する技術的特徴を最も共有すること／63
    5.1.4　最も近い先行技術が2つ以上ある？／65
  5.2　第二段階：客観的な技術的課題　67
    5.2.1　相違する技術的特徴／67
    5.2.2　技術的効果の確定／69
    5.2.3　客観的な技術的課題の設定／71

    5.3 Stage 3: Would It have been Obvious? 74
        5.3.1 Could-Would Approach / 74
        5.3.2 Reasonable Expectation of Success / 76
        5.3.3 Bonus Effect / 78
        5.3.4 Other Considerations / 80
6 Problem Inventions 80
7 Summary 82

Chapter 3 Prior Art   Jan-Hendrik Spilgies   85

1 Definition of the State of the Art 88
    1.1 Date of Disclosure   88
    1.2 Availability   90
        1.2.1 Public Information / 92
        1.2.2 Confidential Information / 94
    1.3 Types of Disclosure   96
        1.3.1 Written Disclosure / 96
        1.3.2 Oral Disclosure / 98
        1.3.3 Public Prior Use / 98
        1.3.4 Other Forms of Disclosure: Internet Disclosure / 100
    1.4 Scope of Disclosure   102
        1.4.1 Inherent Disclosure / 104
        1.4.2 Enabling Disclosure / 104
        1.4.3 Erroneous Disclosure / 106
2 Prior Rights under Art. 54(3):
   Discussion According to EPC 2000 Only 108
    2.1 Requirements   108
    2.2 Scope   108
    2.3 Poisonous Priority Applications and Divisional Applications   110
3 Non-Prejudicial Disclosure 110

5.3　第三段階：自明なものか？　75
　　　　　5.3.1　could-would アプローチ／75
　　　　　5.3.2　成功への合理的な期待／77
　　　　　5.3.3　ボーナス効果／79
　　　　　5.3.4　他の考慮事項／81
6　課題についての発明 ……………… 81
7　まとめ ……………… 83

第3章　先行技術　　　　　　　　　　　Jan-Hendrik Spilgies　　85

1　技術水準の定義 ……………… 89
　　1.1　開示の日付　　89
　　1.2　利用可能性　　91
　　　　　1.2.1　公の情報／93
　　　　　1.2.2　秘密情報／95
　　1.3　開示の種類　　97
　　　　　1.3.1　書面による開示／97
　　　　　1.3.2　口頭による開示／99
　　　　　1.3.3　先の公然使用／99
　　　　　1.3.4　他の形式での開示：インターネットによる開示／101
　　1.4　開示の範囲　　103
　　　　　1.4.1　内在する開示／105
　　　　　1.4.2　実施可能な開示／105
　　　　　1.4.3　誤った開示／107
2　第54条(3)の先願としての権利：
　　EPC 2000に基づく考察 ……………… 109
　　2.1　要件　　109
　　2.2　範囲　　109
　　2.3　有害な基礎出願及び分割出願　　111
3　不利とならない開示 ……………… 111

3.1 Evident Abuse   112
3.2 International Exhibition   112
3.3 Time Limit   114

Chapter 4 Sufficiency of Disclosure   Joachim Renken   117

Introduction   120

1 Legal Basis   120
2 The Person Skilled in the Art and Common General Knowledge   124
3 Reproducibility   128
4 Claim Scope   130
5 Parameter Claims and Functional Features   130
6 Pharmaceutical Inventions   132
7 Deposit of Biological Material and Antibodies   134
8 Evidence   138
9 Conclusion   140

Chapter 5 Patentable Subject-Matter I   Andreas Stefferl   143

Introduction   146

1 Inventions That Contravene "Ordre Public or Morality" (Art. 53(a) EPC)   150
   1.1 Art. 53(a) EPC in the Context of Biotechnological Inventions   152
   1.2 Patentability of Human Embryonic Stem (ES) Cells   154
   1.3 Suffering of Experimental Animals vs. Benefit to Mankind   158

3.1 明らかな濫用　113
3.2 国際博覧会　113
3.3 期限　115

第 4 章　　開示の十分性　　Joachim Renken　117

はじめに　121

1　法的根拠 ……………… 121

2　当業者及び技術常識 ……………… 125

3　再現性 ……………… 129

4　クレームの範囲 ……………… 131

5　パラメータクレーム及び機能的特徴 ……………… 131

6　医薬発明 ……………… 133

7　生物学的材料及び抗体の寄託 ……………… 135

8　証拠 ……………… 139

9　結論 ……………… 141

第 5 章　　特許の対象 I　　Andreas Stefferl　143

はじめに　147

1　「公の秩序又は善良の風俗」に反する発明
　（第53条(a)）……………… 151

　1.1　生物工学的発明との関連における第53条(a)　153
　1.2　人間胚性幹（ES）細胞の特許性　155
　1.3　実験動物の苦痛と人類の利益　159

2   Plant or Animal Varieties or Essentially Biological Processes for the Production of Plants or Animals (Art. 53(b) EPC) ·············· 160
    2.1 The Exclusion of Plant and Animal Varieties   160
    2.2 The Exclusion of Breeding Processes Including Sexual Crossing / Selection   164
    2.3 No Exclusion of Microbiological Processes   168
3   The Exclusions of Medical Methods under Art. 53(c) EPC ················ 170
    3.1 Methods of Treatment of the Human or Animal Body by Surgery   170
    3.2 Exclusion of Methods of Therapy of the Human or Animal Body   176
    3.3 Pharmaceutical Inventions can be Protected by Product and Purpose-Limited Product Claims   178
    3.4 Exclusion of Diagnostic Methods Practices on the Human or Animal Body   182

Chapter 6   Patentable Subject-Matter II
Michele Baccelli & Rainer E. Zangs   187

1   Software Patents at the EPO: A Quick Guide ················ 190
2   Legal Provisions and Definitions ················ 192
3   What Makes a Subject Matter Technical? ················ 194
4   Examination of CIIs ················ 198
5   The First Stage of Examination: Eligibility ················ 198
6   The Second Stage of Examination: Inventive Step and the Modified Problem Solution Approach (PSA) ················ 200
7   Types of Claims ················ 206
8   Certain Aspects Relating to the Search Phase ················ 208
9   Some Recommendations ················ 208

- 2 植物若しくは動物の品種又は植物若しくは動物を生産する本質的に生物学的な方法（第53条(b)）……… 161
  - 2.1 植物及び動物の品種の除外　161
  - 2.2 交配／選択を含む繁殖方法の除外　165
  - 2.3 微生物学的方法は除外されない　169
- 3 第53条(c)に基づく医療方法の除外 ………… 171
  - 3.1 手術による人間又は動物の体の処置方法　171
  - 3.2 人間又は動物の体の治療方法の除外　177
  - 3.3 医薬発明は、物のクレーム及び用途を限定した物のクレームによって保護される　179
  - 3.4 人間又は動物の体の診断方法の除外　183

第6章　特許の対象 II
Michele Baccelli & Rainer E. Zangs　187

- 1 欧州特許庁におけるソフトウェアの特許：概要 ………… 191
- 2 法の規定と定義 ………… 193
- 3 主題を技術的とするものは何か？ ………… 195
- 4 CII の審査 ………… 199
- 5 審査の第一段階：適格性 ………… 199
- 6 審査の第二段階：進歩性及び修正された課題解決アプローチ ………… 201
- 7 クレームの類別 ………… 207
- 8 調査段階に関連する特定の側面 ………… 209
- 9 提案事項 ………… 209

Part II Prosecution of EP Applications 213

Legal Text   214

Chapter 7 Filing of EP Applications
Leonard L. Werner-Jones   239

Introduction   242
1. Filing of Direct EP Applications   242
2. Filing of Euro-PCT Application   252
3. Filing of Divisional Application   258

Chapter 8 Claims   Matthias Wolf   265

Introduction   268
1. Requirements of EPC   268
   1.1 The Claims shall Define the Matter for Which Protection is Sought   270
   1.2 The Claims shall be Clear   272
   1.3 The Claims shall be Concise   276
   1.4 The Claims shall be Supported by the Description   276
   1.5 Procedural Matters   282
2. Kinds of Claims   284
   2.1 Categories   284
   2.2 One Independent Claim per Category   284
   2.3 Dependent Claims   286
   2.4 Alternatives and Options   288

第 II 部　欧州特許出願の手続　　　　　　　　　　213

　　法規　　215

第 7 章　　欧州特許出願
　　　　　　　　　　　　　　　　　　Leonard L. Werner-Jones　239

　　はじめに　243
1　直接的な欧州特許出願 ……………… 243
2　Euro-PCT 出願 …………… 253
3　分割出願 ……………… 259

第 8 章　　クレーム　　　　　　　　　Matthias Wolf　265

　　はじめに　269
1　欧州特許条約の要件 ……………… 269
　　1.1　クレームは保護が求められている事項を特定する　　271
　　1.2　クレームが明確であること　　273
　　1.3　クレームの記載が簡潔であること　　277
　　1.4　クレームが明細書により十分に裏付けされていること　　277
　　1.5　手続的事項　　283
2　クレームの種類 ……………… 285
　　2.1　カテゴリー　　285
　　2.2　各カテゴリーごとに 1 つの独立クレーム　　285
　　2.3　従属クレーム　　287
　　2.4　選択肢及び任意な特徴　　289

3   Claim Interpretation by EPO ·········· 288
4   Summary ············ 294

Chapter 9   Priority   James M. Ogle   297

Introduction   300

1   Basic Requirements for Claiming Priority under the EPC ············ 300

   1.1   Basic Formal Requirements   302
   1.2   Applicant Identity and the Transfer of Priority Rights   304
   1.3   Same Invention   308
   1.4   First Application   308

2   Procedural Formalities ············ 310

3   Partial Priority ············ 312

   3.1   Legal Basis, Currently Unresolved Issues, and the Problem of "Toxic" Priority Entitlement   312
   3.2   Best-Practice Measures to Safeguard Substantive Priority Rights   320

Chapter 10   European Search   Georg Siegert   331

Introduction   334

1   The Extended European Search Report ············ 334

   1.1   The European Search Report   334
   1.2   Search Opinion   350

2   Supplementary European Searches ············ 352

3   Response to the Extended European Search Report ············ 354

  3 欧州特許庁によるクレーム解釈 ……………… 289

  4 まとめ ……………… 295

第9章 優先権   James M. Ogle 297

  はじめに 301

  1 欧州特許条約による優先権主張の基本的な要件 ……………… 301

   1.1 基本的な方式要件 303

   1.2 出願人の同一性及び優先権の移転 305

   1.3 同一の発明 309

   1.4 最初の出願 309

  2 手続的要件 ……………… 311

  3 部分優先 ……………… 313

   3.1 法的根拠、現時点で未解決の問題、及び「toxic な」優先権の問題 313

   3.2 優先権を実質的に確保するための最良の実務 321

第10章 欧州調査   Georg Siegert 331

  はじめに 335

  1 拡張欧州調査報告 ……………… 335

   1.1 欧州調査報告 335

   1.2 調査見解書 351

  2 補充欧州調査 ……………… 353

  3 拡張欧州調査報告に対する応答 ……………… 355

Chapter 11 Substantive Examination
Christiane Stein-Dräger 361

Introduction 364
1 Procedural Requirements 364
2 Substantive Requirements 366
3 Official Action: Reply of the Applicant 368
4 Several Sets of Claims 374
5 Final Stage of Examination Proceedings 376
6 Interacting with the Examiner 380
7 Ex Parte Oral Proceedings 382
8 Refusal of European Patent Applications 384
9 Appeal Procedure: Interlocutory Revision 386
10 Accelerated Prosecution 388
   10.1 PACE 388
   10.2 Patent Prosecution Highway (PPH) 390
11 Further Remarks: Reduction of Costs 392
12 Summary 394

Chapter 12 Amendments
Morten Garberg 397

Introduction 400
1 Art. 123(2) EPC: Prohibition of Added Matter 402
2 How to Compare Information Content? 404
   2.1 The Novelty Test 404
   2.2 The Principle of Direct and Unambiguous Derivability 406
3 Art. 123(3) EPC and Its Interplay with Art. 123(2) EPC 408

第11章　実体審査

Christiane Stein-Dräger　361

　　はじめに　365

1　手続的要件 ……………… 365
2　実体的要件 ……………… 367
3　庁通知：出願人の応答 ……………… 369
4　複数セットのクレーム ……………… 375
5　審査手続の最終段階 ……………… 377
6　審査官とのやりとり ……………… 381
7　査定系口頭審理 ……………… 383
8　欧州特許出願の拒絶 ……………… 385
9　審判手続：中間修正 ……………… 387
10　早期審査 ……………… 389

　　10.1　PACE　389
　　10.2　特許審査ハイウェイ（PPH）　391

11　追記：経費削減 ……………… 393
12　まとめ ……………… 395

第12章　補　正

Morten Garberg　397

　　はじめに　401

1　第123条(2)：新規事項追加の禁止 ……………… 403
2　情報量の比較方法 ……………… 405

　　2.1　新規性テスト　405
　　2.2　直接的かつ一義的に導き出せることの原則　407

3　第123条(3)と第123条(2)との相互関係 ……………… 409

4	Numerical Ranges		410
5	Feature Combinations		412
6	Intermediate Generalizations		414
7	Disclaimers		416
	7.1	Scenario 1: The Application as Filed Discloses the Preferred Absence of a Certain Feature	418
	7.2	Scenario 2: The Application as Filed does not at All Mention the Feature to be Disclaimed	418
	7.3	Scenario 3: The Feature to be Disclaimed is Disclosed in the Application as Filed, but Only Positively	422
8	Rule 139 EPC and Correction of Errors		422
9	Conclusion		424

Chapter 13 Remedies   Matthias Kindler   429

1	Area of Application		432
2	Further Processing		432
	2.1	General Outline	432
	2.2	Exceptions for Which No Further Processing is Available	436
	2.3	Examples	438
3	Re-Establishment of Rights		442
	3.1	General Outline	442
	3.2	Deposition of Biological Material	444
	3.3	Opposition Proceedings	446
	3.4	Substantiation of the Request	448
	3.5	Time Limit for the Request	448
	3.6	Due Care	450

4　数値範囲 ………… 411
5　特徴の組合せ ………… 413
6　中間概念化 ………… 415
7　ディスクレーマ ………… 417

　7.1　ケース１：当初の出願書類に、ある特徴の不在が
　　　　好ましいものとして開示されている場合　　419
　7.2　ケース２：当初の出願書類にディスクレーマの対象とする
　　　　特徴がまったく記載されていない場合　　419
　7.3　ケース３：ディスクレーマによる除外の対象となる特徴が
　　　　当初の出願書類に開示されているが、肯定的な開示のみである
　　　　場合　　423

8　規則139と誤りの訂正 ………… 423
9　結論 ………… 425

第13章　救済　　Matthias Kindler　429

1　救済の適用対象 ………… 433
2　手続の続行 ………… 433

　2.1　概要　　433
　2.2　手続の続行が適用されないもの　　437
　2.3　具体例　　439

3　権利の回復 ………… 443

　3.1　概要　　443
　3.2　生物学的材料の寄託　　445
　3.3　特許異議申立手続　　447
　3.4　請求の理由　　449
　3.5　請求期間　　449
　3.6　相当の注意　　451

Part III   Procedures after Grant   455

    Legal Text   456

Chapter 14   Opposition Procedure   Veit-Peter Frank   477

    Introduction   480
1. Formal Requirements   480
2. Grounds for Opposition   484
3. Written Proceedings   488
4. Oral Proceedings   492
5. Amendments   498
6. Intervention of the Assumed Infringer   500
7. Conclusion of the Opposition Procedure   502

Chapter 15   Appeals   Morten Garberg   507

    Introduction   510
1. The Boards of Appeal   510
2. Initiating an Appeal   514
   - 2.1 The Notice of Appeal   516
   - 2.2 The Grounds of Appeal   516
3. Subject and Scope of the Appeal   516
4. Parties to the Proceedings   518
   - 4.1 Relevance of Party Status: Prohibition of *Reformatio in Peius*   518
   - 4.2 Third Party Observations   520

第 III 部　特許付与後の手続　　　　　　　　　　　　　455

　　法規　　457

第14章　　特許異議申立手続　　　　　Veit-Peter Frank　477

　　はじめに　481
1. 方式要件 ……………… 481
2. 特許異議の申立ての理由 ……………… 485
3. 書面審理 ……………… 489
4. 口頭審理 ……………… 493
5. 補正 ……………… 499
6. 侵害者とされた者の参加 ……………… 501
7. 特許異議申立手続の終結 ……………… 503

第15章　　審　判　　　　　　　　　　　Morten Garberg　507

　　はじめに　511
1. 審判部 ……………… 511
2. 審判の開始 ……………… 515
   - 2.1　審判請求書　517
   - 2.2　理由記載書　517
3. 不服申立ての対象と範囲 ……………… 517
4. 手続の当事者 ……………… 519
   - 4.1　当事者適格の関連性：不利益変更の禁止　519
   - 4.2　第三者による意見書　521

        4.3   Intervention of the Assumed Infringer   520

5   How Appeal Proceedings are Conducted ⋯⋯⋯⋯⋯⋯⋯ 522

        5.1   Written and Oral Proceedings   522
        5.2   *Ex Parte* Appeals   522
        5.3   *Inter Partes* Appeals   526

6   Time and Cost of Proceedings ⋯⋯⋯⋯⋯⋯⋯ 534

        6.1   Time to Completion   534
        6.2   Acceleration   534
        6.3   Costs   536

7   Binding Effect of Previous Decisions ⋯⋯⋯⋯⋯⋯⋯ 536

8   The Enlarged Board of Appeal ⋯⋯⋯⋯⋯⋯⋯ 538

        8.1   Decisions of the Enlarged Board of Appeal   538
        8.2   Petitions for Review   540

Chapter 16 Central Limitation and Revocation Procedure

David Lethem   543

        Overview   546

1   Why Limit or Revoke a Granted Patent? ⋯⋯⋯⋯⋯⋯⋯ 548

2   What can and cannot be Limited by Amendment? ⋯⋯⋯⋯⋯⋯⋯ 550

3   When can Amendments be Made? ⋯⋯⋯⋯⋯⋯⋯ 552

4   How is a Request for Central Limitation or Revocation Made? ⋯⋯⋯⋯⋯⋯⋯ 552

5   How does the EPO Examine a Request for Central Limitation or Revocation? ⋯⋯⋯⋯⋯⋯⋯ 554

6   Obtaining Different Claims for Separate Contracting States ⋯⋯⋯⋯⋯ 558

7   Successful Request ⋯⋯⋯⋯⋯⋯⋯ 560

8   Unsuccessful Request ⋯⋯⋯⋯⋯⋯⋯ 560

4.3　被疑侵害者の参加　　521

5　審判手続はどのように行われるか …………… 523

　　　5.1　書面及び口頭審理　　523
　　　5.2　査定系審判　　523
　　　5.3　当事者系審判　　527

6　審判手続に関する時間と費用 ……………… 535

　　　6.1　完了までの時間　　535
　　　6.2　早期審理　　535
　　　6.3　費用　　537

7　先の審決の拘束力 ……………… 537

8　拡大審判部 ……………… 539

　　　8.1　拡大審判部の決定　　539
　　　8.2　再審理の申請　　541

第16章　一元的な限定・取消手続

David Lethem　543

概要　547

1　特許付与後に限定又は取消しを行う理由 ……………… 549
2　補正によって限定できるもの、できないもの ……………… 551
3　補正が可能な時期 ……………… 553
4　一元的な限定又は取消しの請求をする方法 ……………… 553
5　一元的な限定又は取消しの請求はどのように審査されるのか
　　……………… 555
6　各締約国ごとに異なるクレームの取得 ……………… 559
7　請求が認められる場合 ……………… 561
8　請求が認められない場合 ……………… 561

Part IV National and EU Law Related to EPC   563

Legal Text   564

Chapter 17 EPC and National Law   Klemens Stratmann   573

1 Rights Conferred by European Patents ·············· 574
2 Validation and Translation Requirement ·············· 576
3 The Prohibition of Double Patenting ·············· 586
4 Annuities ············· 588
5 National Jurisdiction and Applicability of EPC and EP Case Law ············ 590
6 Precedence of EPO Opposition Proceedings over National Invalidation Proceedings ············· 602

Chapter 18 The European Patent within the Future EU Patent Package   Thorsten Bausch   607

Introduction   610
1 Legal Basis ············· 610
2 How to Obtain an EP-UE ············· 612
3 The Territorial Scope of an EP-UE ············· 614
4 Unitary Effect ············· 620
5 Translations ············· 622
6 Renewal Fees ············· 624

第 IV 部　欧州特許条約に関連する国内法と欧州法　　　563

　　法規　　565

第17章　欧州特許条約と国内法　　Klemens Stratmann　573

1 欧州特許により与えられる権利 ……………… 575
2 国内有効化及び翻訳要件 ……………… 577
3 ダブルパテントの禁止 ……………… 587
4 年金 ……………… 589
5 国内裁判管轄、並びに欧州特許条約及びケースローの
  適用可能性 ……………… 591
6 国内無効手続に対する欧州特許庁異議申立手続の優先性
  ……………… 603

第18章　今後の EU 特許パッケージの
　　　　　枠組みにおける欧州特許　　Thorsten Bausch　607

　　はじめに　　611
1 法的根拠 ……………… 611
2 単一効特許の取得方法 ……………… 613
3 単一効特許の地域的範囲 ……………… 615
4 単一効 ……………… 621
5 翻訳 ……………… 623
6 更新手数料 ……………… 625

7   For Whom will an EP-UE Commercially Make Sence? 626
     7.1 Cost of an EP-UE Compared to National Validation   626
     7.2 Renewal Fees   628
     7.3 Translation Costs   628
     7.4 Enforcement Costs   630
8   The Other Side of the Equation: The Covered Territory 630
9   Further Factors 634
10   Conclusion: EP-UE, European Patent or National Patent? 634

Annex: Rules of Procedure of the Boards of Appeal of the EPO   639

Authors / Editors   651
Our Office   662

7 誰にとって単一効特許は採算に合うのか ……………… 627
   7.1 単一効特許ルートと国内有効化ルートの費用の比較　627
   7.2 更新手数料　629
   7.3 翻訳費用　629
   7.4 特許権行使にかかる費用　631

8 もうひとつの側面：保護対象となる地域 ……………… 631

9 その他 ……………… 635

10 結論：単一効特許、欧州特許、それとも国内特許か ……………… 635

   付録：欧州特許庁の審判部の手続規則　639

   執筆者／編者紹介　651
   事務所紹介　662

Introduction

序

Joachim Renken

Patent law in Europe is complex in that national patent laws co-exist with the European Patent Convention (EPC). Since the EPC allows obtaining patent protection in 38 countries through a single procedure for the grant of patents, the EPC granting authority, the European Patent Office (EPO), has become by far the most important patent office in Europe. Currently, all the member states of the European Union together with Albania, Croatia, Macedonia, Iceland, Liechtenstein, Monaco, Norway, San Marino, Serbia, Switzerland and Turkey are members of the EPC.

In the next few years, European patent law will possibly see its major change since the EPC was signed in 1973: a patent with unitary effect within the European Union will become available, and a new European patent court system will take up work. While both the corresponding Regulations creating the European Patent with Unitary Effect (EP-UE) and the Unified Patent Court Agreement (UPCA) will provide additional options to patent applicants, the basic principles

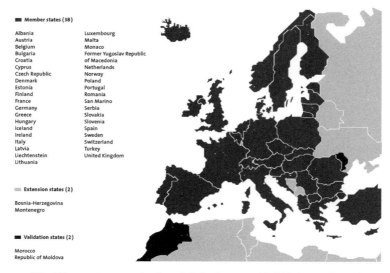

<http://documents.epo.org/projects/babylon/eponet.nsf/0/8C003885190F73D2C1257EEE002E4EBB/$File/European_patents_coverage_en.png> (May 20, 2016)

欧州の特許法は、各国の特許法と欧州特許条約とが併存している点で複雑である。欧州特許条約によれば、単一の特許付与手続によって、38カ国で特許による保護を求めることができるため、その付与官庁である欧州特許庁は、欧州において最も重要な特許庁となっている。現在のところ、欧州連合の全加盟国とアルバニア、クロアチア、マケドニア、アイスランド、リヒテンシュタイン、モナコ、ノルウェー、サンマリノ、セルビア、スイス及びトルコが欧州特許条約の締約国である。

　おそらく数年後には、欧州特許条約が1973年に署名されて以来の大きな変化が欧州特許法に起こり得る。具体的には、欧州連合内で単一の効果を持つ特許が利用可能となり、新たな欧州特許裁判制度の運用が始まることになろう。欧州単一効特許を創設する規則と統一特許裁判所協定を創設する規則の両方により、特許出願人には新たな選択肢が提供されることになるが、欧州特許条約に成文化され、かつ、欧州特許庁審判部のケースローによって整備されてきた欧

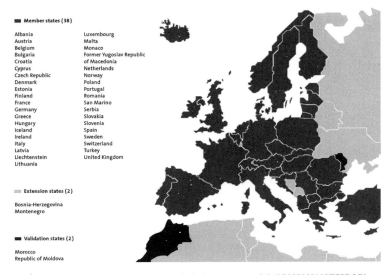

〈http://documents.epo.org/projects/babylon/eponet.nsf/0/8C003885190F73D2C1257EEE002E4EBB/$File/European_patents_coverage_en.png〉〈2016年5月20日〉

of European patent law, as codified in the EPC and further developed by the case law of the EPO's Boards of Appeal, will remain unchanged.

This book intends to provide an introduction to these basic principles for patent professionals in Japan. It is composed of four parts and a total of 18 chapters, each of them written by patent attorneys of the law firm Hoffmann Eitle. The basic patentability requirements are discussed in Part I. Part II guides the reader through the various stages of examination of a European patent application. Part III focusses on post-grant proceedings: oppositions, appeals and the central limitation and revocation procedure. Part IV looks at the interplay between the EPC and national law and provides an introduction to the EP-UE and the UPCA.

州特許法の基本原則は変わらない。

　本書は、日本の特許実務家のために、これらの基本原則を紹介する。本書は、計18の章からなる4部構成をとっており、Hoffmann Eitle の欧州弁理士により各章が執筆されている。第Ⅰ部では、基本的な特許要件を検討する。第Ⅱ部では、欧州特許出願をした後の様々な段階における手続について説明する。第Ⅲ部では、特許付与後の手続（特許異議申立手続、審判手続並びに一元的限定及び取消手続）に着目する。第Ⅳ部では、欧州特許条約と国内法との相互関係に目を向けて、欧州単一効特許及び統一特許裁判所協定を紹介する。

Part *I*

Substantive Requirements

実体的要件

Legal Text

Article 52   Patentable inventions

(1)   European patents shall be granted for any inventions, in all fields of technology, provided that they are new, involve an inventive step and are susceptible of industrial application.

(2)   The following in particular shall not be regarded as inventions within the meaning of paragraph 1:

   (a)   discoveries, scientific theories and mathematical methods;

   (b)   aesthetic creations;

   (c)   schemes, rules and methods for performing mental acts, playing games or doing business, and programs for computers;

   (d)   presentations of information.

(3)   Paragraph 2 shall exclude the patentability of the subject-matter or activities referred to therein only to the extent to which a European patent application or European patent relates to such subject-matter or activities as such.

Article 53   Exceptions to patentability

European patents shall not be granted in respect of:

   (a)   inventions the commercial exploitation of which would be contrary to "ordre public" or morality; such exploitation shall not be deemed to be so contrary merely because it is prohibited by law or regulation in

法規

第52条　特許を受けることができる発明

(1) 欧州特許は、新規性、進歩性及び産業上の利用可能性のあるすべての技術分野のあらゆる発明について与えられる。

(2) 次のものは、特に、(1)にいう発明とはみなされない。

   (a) 発見、科学の理論及び数学的方法

   (b) 美的創造物

   (c) 精神的行為、ゲーム又は事業を行うための計画、ルール及び方法、並びにコンピュータプログラム

   (d) 情報の提示

(3) (2)は、欧州特許出願又は欧州特許が(2)で言及される対象又は行為自体に関連する範囲においてのみ、その対象又は行為を特許の対象から除外する。

第53条　特許性の例外

欧州特許は、次のものについては与えられない。

   (a) その商業的利用が「公の秩序」又は善良の風俗に反するおそれのある発明。ただし、その利用が、一部又はすべての締約国において法律又は規則によって禁止されているという理由のみでは公の秩序又は善良の風

some or all of the Contracting States;

(b) plant or animal varieties or essentially biological processes for the production of plants or animals; this provision shall not apply to microbiological processes or the products thereof;

(c) methods for treatment of the human or animal body by surgery or therapy and diagnostic methods practised on the human or animal body; this provision shall not apply to products, in particular substances or compositions, for use in any of these methods.

Article 54 Novelty

(1) An invention shall be considered to be new if it does not form part of the state of the art.

(2) The state of the art shall be held to comprise everything made available to the public by means of a written or oral description, by use, or in any other way, before the date of filing of the European patent application.

(3) Additionally, the content of European patent applications as filed, the dates of filing of which are prior to the date referred to in paragraph 2 and which were published on or after that date, shall be considered as comprised in the state of the art.

(4) Paragraphs 2 and 3 shall not exclude the patentability of any substance or composition, comprised in the state of the art, for use in a method referred to in Article 53(c), provided that its use for any such method is not comprised in the state of the art.

(5) Paragraphs 2 and 3 shall also not exclude the patentability of any substance or composition referred to in paragraph 4 for any specific use in a

俗に反しているとはみなされない。

(b) 植物若しくは動物の品種又は植物若しくは動物を生産する本質的に生物学的な方法。ただし、微生物学的方法又は微生物学的方法により生産された物についてはこの限りでない。

(c) 人間又は動物の体を手術又は治療により処置する方法及び人間又は動物の体を診断する方法。ただし、この規定は、これらの方法のいずれかで使用するための物（特に物質又は組成物）には適用されない。

第54条　新規性

(1) 発明は、それが技術水準の一部を構成しない場合には、新規性を有するものとする。

(2) 欧州特許出願の出願日前に、書面若しくは口頭による陳述、使用又はその他のあらゆる方法によって公衆に利用可能になったすべてのものは技術水準を構成する。

(3) また、(2)にいう日の前に出願日を有し、かつ、その日以後に公開された欧州特許出願の出願時の内容も技術水準を構成するものとみなす。

(4) (2)及び(3)は、技術水準に含まれる物質又は組成物であっても第53条(c)にいう方法で使用するための物質又は組成物の特許性を排除するものではない。ただし、当該方法におけるその使用が技術水準を構成しない場合に限る。

(5) (2)及び(3)はまた、第53条(c)にいう方法で特定的に使用するための(4)にいう物質又は組成物の特許性を排除するものではない。ただし、その使用が

method referred to in Article 53(c), provided that such use is not comprised in the state of the art.

Article 55 Non-prejudicial disclosures

(1) For the application of Article 54, a disclosure of the invention shall not be taken into consideration if it occurred no earlier than six months preceding the filing of the European patent application and if it was due to, or in consequence of:

(a) an evident abuse in relation to the applicant or his legal predecessor, or

(b) the fact that the applicant or his legal predecessor has displayed the invention at an official, or officially recognised, international exhibition falling within the terms of the Convention on international exhibitions signed at Paris on 22 November 1928 and last revised on 30 November 1972.

(2) In the case of paragraph 1(b), paragraph 1 shall apply only if the applicant states, when filing the European patent application, that the invention has been so displayed and files a supporting certificate within the time limit and under the conditions laid down in the Implementing Regulations.

Article 56 Inventive step

An invention shall be considered as involving an inventive step if, having regard to the state of the art, it is not obvious to a person skilled in the art. If the state of the art also includes documents within the meaning of Article 54, paragraph 3, these documents shall not be considered in deciding whether there has been an inventive step.

技術水準を構成しない場合に限る。

第55条　新規性に影響を与えない開示

(1) 第54条の規定の適用上、発明の開示は、それが欧州特許出願前6月以内に行われ、かつ、それが次のものに起因するか又は次のものの結果である場合には、考慮されないものとする。

(a) 出願人又はその法律上の前権利者に対する明らかな濫用

(b) 出願人又はその法律上の前権利者が、1928年11月22日にパリで署名され、1972年11月30日に最後に改正された国際博覧会に関する条約にいう公の又は公に認められた国際的な博覧会で当該発明を展示したこと

(2) (1)(b)の場合については、出願人が欧州特許出願の際に、発明がそのように展示されたことを陳述し、かつ、施行規則に定める期限内に施行規則に定める要件に従ってこれを裏付ける証明書を提出した場合にのみ(1)の規定を適用する。

第56条　進歩性

発明は、その技術分野の専門家にとって技術水準からみて自明のものではない場合には、進歩性を有するものとする。第54条(3)に規定される欧州特許出願の書類が技術水準を構成する場合には、そのような書類は、進歩性の有無を判断する際には考慮されない。

Article 57 Industrial application

An invention shall be considered as susceptible of industrial application if it can be made or used in any kind of industry, including agriculture.

Article 83 Disclosure of the invention

The European patent application shall disclose the invention in a manner sufficiently clear and complete for it to be carried out by a person skilled in the art.

第57条　産業上の利用可能性

　発明は、農業を含む産業のいずれかの分野においてそれを生産し又は使用することができる場合には、産業上の利用可能性を有するものとする。

第83条　発明の開示

　欧州特許出願は、その技術分野の専門家が実施することができる程度に明確かつ十分に、その発明を開示する。

Chapter 1

Disclosure Concepts and Novelty

開示概念と新規性

Martin Bachelin
Stephan Disser

MEMO

▶ 新規性の判断の基になる開示の概念ですが、欧州では「直接的かつ一義的な開示」の概念が使われます（§2.2）。この概念は新規事項追加の判断にも使われています。

▶ パラメータにより物を特定する発明については、新規性の主張において日本の実務よりも立証責任が厳しいかもしれません（§3）。

▶ 選択発明については、その判断基準について欧州特許庁審判部により様々なアプローチが確立されてきました。「2リストの原則」や数値範囲の選択に使われる「3段階テスト」は、欧州実務に特有のものかと思われます。これらを含む欧州特許庁実務については、§4.3〜§4.7を参照してください。

▶ 第54条(4)及び(5)に「医薬発明」に関する明文の規定がある点で、日本の特許法と異なります。第54条(4)及び(5)で扱われているのは、いわゆる「第一医薬用途」のクレームと、第二及びそれ以降の医薬用途のクレームです。第54条(4)及び(5)によると、医薬発明は「物質又は組成物」という「物」の発明です。

▶ 欧州実務と日本の実務に違いはないようにも思われますが、クレームの記載方法が多少異なるかもしれません。日本の実務では「化合物Xを含む……薬剤」と記載するように推奨されていますが、第54条(5)による医薬発明は、通常、「……疾病Yを治療する方法で使用するための化合物X」というように記載されます（§5.2）。過去には「スイスタイプ」形式の医薬用途タイプのクレームがありまし

たが、第54条(5)が EPC2000に導入されたため使えなくなりました（§5.3）。

▶ 医薬発明でない物の発明で、用途限定により物を特定する場合の用途の表示は、表示された用途に適しているに過ぎないと解釈されます（§5.1）。新規性欠如の拒絶理由を解消することが難しければ、用途タイプ（使用）のクレームにクレームのカテゴリーを変えることが考えられます（§5.4）。

▶ 新規性を確立するためにディスクレーマが使える状況が日本の実務とは異なります。詳しくは§6.1を参照してください。

1 The Law

The novelty requirement stems from Article 52(1) EPC. This article reads as follows:

(1) European patents shall be granted for any inventions, in all fields of technology, provided that they are **new**, involve an inventive step and are susceptible of industrial application (emphasis added).

Hence, the novelty requirement is a fundamental requirement that must generally be fulfilled by all valid European patents at all stages of procedure. Novelty is defined in relation to the state of the art in subsection (1) of Article 54 EPC:

(1) An invention shall be considered to be new if it does not form part of the state of the art.

The above definition is noteworthy in so far as it is a negative definition. This means that there is an initial presumption that the invention of interest is novel unless there is specific state of the art that anticipates the invention. It is a direct consequence of this negative definition that the burden of proving lack of novelty initially rests on the examiner or opponent. The examiner is not entitled to assert lack of novelty without citing a specific piece of the state of the art that allegedly anticipates the invention of interest.

The state of the art is defined in the following subsections (2) and (3) of Article 54 EPC. While subsection (2) defines the normal state of the art, subsection (3) defines that post-published earlier EP applications constitute hypothetical prior art for the assessment of novelty only.

(2) The state of the art shall be held to comprise everything made available to the public by means of a written or oral description, by use, or in any other way, before the date of filing of the European patent application.

1　法律

新規性の要件は、第52条(1)に由来している。

(1)　欧州特許は、**新規性**、進歩性及び産業上の利用可能性のあるすべての技術分野のあらゆる発明について与えられる（強調付加）。

ゆえに、新規性の要件は、手続のあらゆる段階で、有効なすべての欧州特許に一般的に必要とされる基本的要件である。新規性は、技術水準との関連で第54条(1)に定義される。

(1)　発明は、それが技術水準の一部を構成しない場合には、新規性を有するものとする。

上記定義は、これが否定的な定義であるという点で特筆すべきである。これは、発明の新規性を喪失させる特定の技術水準がない場合は、対象となる発明は新規であると当初は推定されることを意味している。新規性の欠如を立証する責任が、当初は、審査官又は特許異議申立人にあることは、否定的な定義の直接の結果である。審査官は、対象となる発明の新規性を喪失させる特定の技術水準を引用することなしに、新規性の欠如を主張することはできないのである。

技術水準は、第54条(2)及び(3)で定義されている。(2)では、通常の技術水準が定義され、(3)では、先の欧州特許出願であれば後に公開された場合であっても、新規性の判断についてのみ、仮定の先行技術を構成すると定義されている。

(2)　欧州特許出願の出願日前に、書面若しくは口頭による陳述、使用又はその他のあらゆる方法によって公衆に利用可能になったすべてのものは技術水準を構成する。

(3) Additionally, the content of European patent applications as filed, the dates of filing of which are prior to the date referred to in paragraph 2 and which were published on or after that date, shall be considered as comprised in the state of the art

Regarding subsection (2), it should be considered that the listed types of disclosure are merely provided as examples since the wording "in any other way" covers any conceivable form of making the relevant information available to the public. For instance, internet disclosures may also form relevant state of the art. However, a stricter standard of proof compared to traditional documents is usually applied (Guidelines G-IV 7.5). Neither the meaning of "public" nor the standard for determining whether relevant information has indeed been "made available" are defined by law. The applicable standards established by case law are discussed below.

While subsection (2) expressly refers to the filing date of the European patent application, it should be kept in mind that a valid priority claim has the effect that this date is replaced by the priority date (Art. 89 EPC).

Two specific scenarios concerning medical inventions are dealt with in subsections (4) and (5) of Article 54 EPC. These subsections are intended to compensate pharmaceutical industry for the prohibition of obtaining patent protection for methods of treatment and the like in Article 53(c) EPC. Subsection (4) introduces the so-called "first medical use" claim, whereas subsection (5) provides a legal basis for claiming second and further medical uses:

(4) Paragraphs 2 and 3 shall not exclude the patentability of any substance or composition, comprised in the state of the art, for use in a method referred to in Article 53(c), provided that its use for any such method is not comprised in the state of the art.

(5) Paragraphs 2 and 3 shall also not exclude the patentability of any sub-

(3) また、(2)にいう日の前に出願日を有し、かつ、その日以後に公開された欧州特許出願の出願時の内容も技術水準を構成するものとみなす。

(2)では、開示の種類が具体例として列挙されているに過ぎないと考えるべきである。「他のあらゆる方法」の文言には、関連する情報が公衆に利用可能になると考えられるあらゆる形態が含まれるからである。例えば、インターネットによる開示が関連する技術水準を構成する場合がある。しかし、インターネットによる開示の証明については、通常、従来の文献の開示と比較して、厳格な基準が適用される（審査基準 G-IV 7.5）。「公衆」の意味も、関連する情報が実際に「利用可能になった」かどうかを判断する基準も、法律では定義されていない。適用可能な基準がケースローにより確立されており、これについては以下のセクションで考察する。

(2)は、欧州特許出願の出願日と明示しているが、優先権が有効に主張されるときは、出願日が優先日で置き換えられるという優先権の効果を念頭に置くべきである（第89条）。

医薬発明に関する特定のシナリオが2つ、第54条(4)及び(5)で扱われている。第53条(c)により、治療方法等については特許による保護が与えられないため、第54条(4)及び(5)は、製薬産業に対して埋め合わせをする意図を持つ。(4)は、いわゆる「第一医薬用途」クレームを扱い、(5)は、第二及びそれ以降の医薬用途をクレームする法的根拠を与える。

(4) (2)及び(3)は、技術水準に含まれる物質又は組成物であっても第53条(c)にいう方法で使用するための物質又は組成物の特許性を排除するものではない。ただし、その方法におけるその使用が技術水準を構成しない場合に限る。

(5) (2)及び(3)はまた、第53条(c)にいう方法で特定的に使用するための(4)にい

stance or composition referred to in paragraph 4 for any specific use in a method referred to in Article 53(c), provided that such use is not comprised in the state of the art.

Subsections (4) and (5) expressly refer to the patentability of any "substance or composition". Current case law interprets this wording as restricting the applicability of these subsections to inventions involving an active substance that undergoes a molecular interaction with a target substance (T 2003/08). Medical devices that are used in treatment methods based on purely mechanical interaction are thus not susceptible to protection by 1st or 2nd medical use claims (T 1069/11).

2 Fundamental Concepts of Disclosure

2.1 Public

The concept of "public" is applied in a broad manner in the case law of the EPO. Even a single person who is not bound by confidentiality and who can therefore freely pass on the information to other people will be regarded as "public". However, if the information is conveyed by oral disclosure (e.g. in a lecture), it is necessary that at least one member of the audience has sufficient skills to understand the information in order to be able to pass it on to others (T 877/90). Regarding disclosures via the internet, a test for public availability of a document stored on the World Wide Web and accessible via a specific URL was developed in decision T 1553/06. In summary, it was considered decisive in the decision whether the document could be found with the help of a public web search engine by using one or more keywords all related to the essence of the content of that document, and whether the document remained accessible at that URL for a period of time long enough for a member of the public to have direct and unambiguous access to it. For e-mails transmitted via the internet, the principle of confidentiality is deemed to apply, so that they are not considered to be publicly available. The technical possibility of getting to know the content of an e-mail by

う物質又は組成物の特許性を排除するものではない。ただし、その使用が技術水準を構成しない場合に限る。

(4)及び(5)は、あらゆる「物質又は組成物」の特許性に明確に言及している。現在のケースローは、ターゲットの物質と分子間相互作用を経る活性物質に関与する発明に対して、(4)及び(5)の適用を限定するものとし、この文言を解釈する（T 2003/08）。よって、治療方法において使用されるとしても、純粋に機械的な相互作用に基づく医療機器は、第一又は第二の医薬用途クレームによる保護を受けられない（T 1069/11）。

2　開示の基本的概念

2.1　公衆

「公衆」という概念は、欧州特許庁のケースローでは広い態様で適用される。秘密保持義務に拘束されず、他の人々に情報を自由に伝えられる者は、たった1人であっても「公衆」とみなされる。ただし、例えば、講義により情報が口頭で伝達される場合においては、聴衆の少なくとも1人が、他者にその情報を伝えられるよう、当該情報を理解できる十分なスキルを有していることが必要である（T 877/90）。インターネットによる開示に関しては、ワールド・ワイド・ウェブに蓄積され、特定のURLを介してアクセス可能な文献の公衆による利用可能性のテストが、T 1553/06審決で考案された。この審決では、文献の内容の要点にすべて関連する1つ以上のキーワードを用いて、公衆のウェブ検索エンジンの支援により当該文献が発見できたかどうか、かつ、公衆の1人の構成員が当該文献に直接的かつ一義的にアクセスするのに十分な期間にわたって当該文献がURLでアクセス可能であったかどうかが決定的とされた。インターネットにより送信される電子メールについては、秘密保持の原則が適用されるとみなされるため、電子メールは公衆に利用可能であるとは考えられない。ハッキングにより電子メールの内容を知るようになることが技術的に可能でも、秘密保持義務に違反して電子メールに含まれる情報が実際に開示

hacking does not change that principle, as long as an actual disclosure of the information contained in the e mail in breach of the confidentiality has not been proven. Therefore, the content of an e-mail does not become available to the public for the sole reason that it was transmitted via the internet (T 2/09).

2.2 Direct and Unambiguous Disclosure

When assessing the disclosure of a prior art document, the EPO applies a strict formalistic approach, according to which only that information has been disclosed, which the skilled person would derive **directly and unambiguously** using the common general knowledge at the time of its publication (G 2/98, G 2/10 and T 1363/12).

2.3 Whole Content Approach and Combinations of Disclosure

The whole content of the prior art document is to be considered for the novelty assessment, including especially definitions of technical terms provided in other parts of the same document. Even information provided in other "secondary" documents may be included in said disclosure of a "primary" document if there is a sufficiently clear cross-reference in the primary document to said information in the secondary document (Guidelines G-IV 8).

However, for raising a novelty objection, it is not possible to combine pieces of information that are disclosed in the same document but in a different technical context (Guidelines G-VI 1, T 305/87). Similarly, information provided in different documents must not be combined in the absence of a sufficiently clear cross-reference (Guidelines G-VI 1).

2.4 Enabling Disclosure

The disclosure of a prior art document is considered to be relevant state of the art only if said disclosure enables the skilled person to reproduce this disclo-

されたことが証明されない限り、この原則が適用される。よって、インターネットを介して送信されたという理由だけでは、電子メールの内容が公衆に利用可能とはならないと判断された（T 2/09）。

2.2 直接的かつ一義的な開示

先行技術文献の開示を検討する際に、欧州特許庁は、厳格な形式主義的アプローチを適用する（G 2/98、G 2/10、T 1363/12）。このアプローチによれば、開示の時点で当業者が技術常識に基づいて**直接的かつ一義的**に導き出すことができる情報だけが開示されたものとして扱われる。

2.3 内容全体によるアプローチ及び開示の組合せ

新規性の判断においては、先行技術文献の内容全体が考慮され、特に、同一文献の別の部分にある技術用語の定義も含まれる。他の「二次」文献で提供される情報であっても、当該情報についての相互参照が「主要」文献で十分に明確にされているときは、「主要」文献の当該開示に含めることができる場合がある（審査基準 G-IV 8）。

一方、同一文献であるが異なる技術的文脈で開示される複数の情報を組み合わせることで新規性欠如の拒絶理由を提起することはできない（審査基準 G-VI 1、T 305/87）。同様に、異なる文献で与えられる情報は、十分に明確な相互参照がない場合は、組み合わせることはできない（審査基準 G-VI 1）。

2.4 実施可能な程度の開示

先行技術文献の開示は、当該開示により当業者がこの開示を再現できる場合にのみ、関連する技術水準とみなされる（審査基準 G-IV 2 及び G-VI 4）。例え

sure (Guidelines G-IV 2 and G-VI 4). For instance, if a chemical compound mentioned in the prior art could not be produced since the starting materials and intermediates were unavailable, the compound does not belong to the relevant state of the art (T 206/83).

2.5 Implicit Disclosure

The disclosure of a prior art document is not restricted to what is expressly mentioned in said document. In addition to the express disclosure of a prior art document, the EPO also takes into account further information implied by said express disclosure. The concept of "implicit disclosure" encompasses all further information that is not expressly mentioned but follows as an inevitable consequence of the expressly mentioned prior art disclosure (Guidelines G-VI 6). When assessing implicit disclosures, the EPO applies a strict approach according to which it must be beyond all reasonable doubt that the information of interest is an **inevitable** consequence of the express teaching of the prior art document (T 793/93).

2.6 Disclosure by Public Prior Use

In cases of public prior use and in cases of implicit disclosure, the question sometimes arises which additional information on product characteristics has been made available if the product itself was publicly available. The EPO distinguishes between "intrinsic properties" and "extrinsic properties". Intrinsic properties are generally considered to be made available by a publicly available product irrespective of whether or not the skilled person would have had a motivation to analyze the product and/or whether the analysis would involve a significant effort (G 1/92). Intrinsic properties are product characteristics, which are inherent to the product of interest and not linked to external testing conditions. A typical example would be the chemical structure of a small organic molecule. Extrinsic properties, on the other hand, are generally not considered to be disclosed by a public availability of the product. These are properties that are exhibited by the

ば、出発原料及び中間体が利用可能でなかったために、先行技術で言及される化合物が生成できなかった場合は、その化合物は関連する技術水準には属さないとされた（T 206/83）。

2.5 黙示的な開示

先行技術文献の開示は、当該文献で明示的に言及されたものに限定されない。先行技術文献の明示の開示に加え、欧州特許庁は、前記明示的な開示が黙示するさらなる情報も考慮する。「黙示の開示」の概念は、明示的に言及されていないが、明示的に言及された先行技術の開示の必然的な結果として生じるすべての情報を網羅する（審査基準 G-VI 6）。黙示的な開示を判断する際に、欧州特許庁は、厳格なアプローチを適用する。このアプローチは、対象となる情報が、先行技術文献の明示的な教示の**必然的**な結果であることを、すべての合理的な疑いを超える程度に示すことを必要とする（T 793/93）。

2.6 先の公然使用による開示

先の公然使用の場合及び黙示的な開示の場合において、物そのものが公衆に利用可能となったときに、その物の特性について、どのような情報がさらに利用可能になったかという問題が生じる。欧州特許庁は、「内在的特性」と「外在的特性」を区別する。一般的に、物が公衆に利用可能になることによって、その物の内在的特性は公衆に利用可能になったと考えられ、当業者がその物を分析する動機付けがあったかどうかや、その物の分析に著しい努力を伴うかどうかに関わらない（G 1/92）。物の内在的特性はその物の特徴であり、対象となる物に内在し、外的試験条件とは関連しない。典型例は、小さな有機分子の化学構造である。他方で、物の外在的特性は、一般に、その物が公衆に利用可能になったことで開示されたとはみなされない。外在的特性とは、対象物が特定の試験条件下に置かれることによってのみ、その物により発揮される特性である。この典型例は、特定の疾病を治療することができる有機小分子の適合性

product of interest only if it is subjected to specific test conditions. A typical example would be the suitability of a small organic molecule for treating a particular disease.

2.7 Degree of Individualization

When assessing prior art disclosures, the EPO also considers the degree of individualization of the prior art disclosure and compares it to that of the claim of interest. A disclosure of a higher degree of individualization always takes away novelty of a claim, wherein the corresponding feature is specified at a lower degree of individualization. Conversely, novelty may or may not be established if the claim of interest characterizes a feature at a higher degree of individualization as compared to the degree of individualization of the corresponding prior art disclosure. For instance, the individualized disclosure of "copper" anticipates the more generic concept "metal". Conversely, the disclosure of the generic concept "metal" in the prior art does not anticipate a later claim with the individualized feature "copper" (Guidelines G-VI 5). The applicable approaches for assessing novelty by selection are explained in greater detail below.

3 Novelty Assessment

The assessment of novelty in proceedings before the EPO is usually carried out on a feature-by-feature basis. Novelty is normally denied only if it is established that the prior art document contains a direct and unambiguous disclosure of each and every feature in the claim. There are, however, some exceptions in examination practice before the EPO, mainly due to specific rules concerning the burden of proof. Exceptional situations are for instance as follows:

- Novelty objections can be raised against claims with parameter ranges if the parameter is an unusual parameter and if the prior art document does not provide any information on said parameter, provided that all other fea-

である。

2.7 個別化の程度

先行技術の開示を検討する際に、欧州特許庁は、先行技術の開示の個別化の程度も考慮し、これを対象となるクレームの個別化の程度と比較する。より高度に個別化された開示は、それに対応する特徴がそれより低度に個別化されてクレームに記載された発明の新規性を常に奪う。逆にいえば、対象となるクレームが、対応する先行技術の開示の個別化の程度と比較して、より高い程度の個別化で特徴付けられていれば、新規性が確立することもある。例えば、個別化された「銅」の開示は、より包括的な概念である「金属」の新規性を喪失させる。逆に、先行技術における包括的な概念である「金属」の開示は、個別化された特徴の「銅」を含む後願のクレームの新規性を喪失させない（審査基準G-VI 5）。選択発明の新規性を判断するために適用されるアプローチについては、後で詳細に説明する。

3　新規性の判断

欧州特許庁の手続における新規性の判断は、通常、特徴ごとに行われる。新規性は、通常、クレーム中のありとあらゆる特徴について先行技術文献が直接的かつ一義的に導き出せるように開示していることが確立される場合にのみ、その存在が否定される。しかし、立証責任に関する特別のルールを主に受けて、欧州特許庁での審査実務においては、いくつかの例外がある。例外的な状況は例えば、以下のとおりである。

- 特殊パラメータを使うクレームに対しては、先行技術文献が当該パラメータに関する情報をまったく提供していない場合であっても、クレームの他の特徴のすべてがこの文献に開示されているときは、新規性欠如の拒絶

tures of the claim are disclosed in this document. The burden of proving that the parameter features is not fulfilled by the prior art disclosure rests on applicant (Guidelines G-VI 6).

- Novelty objections can also be raised against claims with product-by-process features even if the prior art document does not mention the specified process. This is because product-by-process claims are construed at the EPO to protect the product *per se* (T 150/82) so that a similar product produced by a different process is also covered, provided the characteristics of the products are virtually indistinguishable. The burden of proving that the specified process imparts distinct product characteristics that are not found in the prior art product rests on applicant (Guidelines F-IV 4.12).

- Special rules also apply for use indications. These are discussed in section 5 below.

4   Novelty by Selection

4.1   General Considerations

The EPO acknowledges the concept of "novelty by selection". Depending on the factual scenario, different approaches have been developed by the EPO for assessing novelty of different types of selections. However, irrespective of the type of selection, the general rule applies that a novel selection is possible only if the prior art document does not contain an individualized disclosure, such as a specific example, falling within the selected area.

4.2   Selection from Generic Term

As noted above, a novel selection can be made from a general term or another type of general disclosure. In such a situation novelty is usually acknowledged in

理由が提起される。特殊パラメータの特徴が先行技術の開示によっては満たされないことを立証する責任は出願人にある（審査基準 G-VI 6）。

- プロダクト・バイ・プロセスの特徴を有するクレームに対して、先行技術文献が特定のプロセスに言及していない場合でも、新規性欠如の拒絶理由が提起される。プロダクト・バイ・プロセスクレームが物それ自体を保護すると欧州特許庁では解釈されるからである（T 150/82）。これにより、物の特徴をほとんど区別することができないことを前提に、当該クレームでは、異なるプロセスで製造された類似物もカバーされる。特定のプロセスが、先行技術の物にはない特徴をクレームされた物に与えることが明らかだと立証する責任は出願人にある（審査基準 F-IV 4.12）。

- 用途の表示については、特別のルールが適用される。これらについては後のセクション5で考察する。

4　選択により見出される新規性

4.1　概論

欧州特許庁は、「選択による新規性」の概念を肯定している。実際のシナリオに基づき、選択によって見出される新規性を判断するために、欧州特許庁では様々なアプローチが提案されてきた。ただし、選択のタイプに関わらず、先行技術文献が、選択された領域に属する特定の具体例など、個別化された開示を含んでいない場合にのみ、選択により新規性が見出されるという一般原則が適用される。

4.2　包括的用語からの選択

包括的用語又は他のタイプの一般的開示から新規な選択がなされることがあるのは上述のとおりである。このような状況では、通常、先行技術文献のより

the absence of a more specific (individualized) disclosure in the prior art document.

4.3 Selection from List

If a selection is made among alternatives that are disclosed in individualized form as members of a list in the prior art document, novelty is generally denied if said selection involves merely the selection of an individual feature from a single list. Conversely, if the claimed subject-matter can be derived from the prior art document only by means of a two-fold selection from two lists of some length, novelty is usually acknowledged (T 12/81, T 7/86, Guidelines G-VI 8(i)). The same conclusion applies also in cases where three or more selections from a corresponding number of lists are involved. This concept is sometimes referred to as the "two-lists principle". It applies if the individual selections involve a selection from a list of individualized alternatives (e.g., alternative substituent definitions in a Markush formula). The two-lists principle also applies if one or more of the individual selections involves another type of selection such as the selection of a numerical sub-range from a broader known numerical range.

4.4 Selection from Numerical Range

If there is a single selection of a sub-range from a broader known range, stricter rules apply. Usually, novelty is acknowledged in this situation only if the following 3 criteria are fulfilled (T 198/84, T 279/89 and Guidelines G-VI 8(ii)):

(a) the selected sub-range is narrow compared to the known range;

(b) the selected sub-range is sufficiently far removed from any specific examples, preferred sub-ranges or end-points of the known range;

(c) the selected range is not an arbitrary specimen of the prior art, i.e. not a

詳細な（個別化された）開示がない場合に新規性の存在が肯定される。

4.3　リストからの選択

　リストのメンバーとして先行技術文献に個別形式で開示された選択肢のなかから選択が行われる場合で、当該選択が単一のリストから個々の特徴を選択するに過ぎないときは、一般的に、新規性の存在が否定される。逆に、クレームの対象が、先行技術文献に開示された特定の長さを持つ２つのリストから二重の選択によってのみ導き出される場合は、通常、新規性の存在が肯定される（T 12/81、T 7/86、審査基準G-VI 8(i)）。これは、３つ以上のリストからの選択を伴う場合も同様に適用される。この概念は、「２リストの原則」と呼ばれる。この原則は、個々の選択が、個別化された選択肢（例えば、マーカッシュ形式で特定された置換基）のリストからの選択を伴う場合に適用される。さらに、２リストの原則は、個々の選択の少なくとも１つが、公知の数値範囲から狭い数値範囲を選択する等の他のタイプの選択を伴う場合にも適用される。

4.4　数値範囲の選択

　広い公知範囲（上位範囲）から狭い範囲（下位範囲）を単一に選択する場合には、より厳格な規則が適用される。通常、この状況では、以下の３つの基準が満たされる場合にのみ新規性の存在が肯定される（T 198/84、T 279/89、審査基準G-VI 8(ii)）。

(a)　選択された下位範囲は、公知範囲と比較して狭い。

(b)　選択された下位範囲は、公知範囲の実施例、好ましい範囲又はその端点から大きく離れている。

(c)　選択された下位範囲は、先行技術の任意のサンプルではなく、すなわち

mere embodiment of the prior art, but another invention (purposive selection, new technical teaching).

There has been some controversy in recent EPO case law whether the last criterion (c) is appropriate for the assessment of novelty. Some decisions (T 1233/05, T 230/07 and T 1130/09) held that said last criterion (c) is appropriate for the assessment of inventive step, but should not be applied for the assessment of novelty. Others (T 1827/08 and T 126/09) rejected this view. It thus remains to be seen whether discounting criterion (c) is a general trend. However, even the most recent version of the Guidelines still mentions criterion (c) as an essential precondition for novelty.

4.5 Partial Overlap with Known Numerical Range

Different criteria may apply in cases where a numerical range is selected from a known range such that the selected range partially overlaps with the known range. In this situation, it is frequently assessed whether the skilled person studying the prior art document would "seriously contemplate" working in the area of overlap (T 26/85 and Guidelines G-VI 8(iii)).

4.6 Selection of Sub-Genus from Generically Defined Area

A particularly difficult situation arises if a "selection" is made by a claim covering a generically defined area, which may be regarded as a sub-genus compared to the corresponding prior art disclosure (i.e. selections, wherein the selected area is defined in a similar but somewhat narrower manner compared to the prior art disclosure). In such situations, the EPO may decide on novelty by determining whether a "new technical element" is involved in the selection (T 12/90). In cases of families of chemical compounds characterized by generic Markush formulae, a new technical element may possibly be a particular chemical group not mentioned in individualized form in the prior art document, or a specific combination of two chemical groups that can be derived from the prior

先行技術の単なる実施形態ではなく、他の発明（意図的選択、新規な技術的教示）である。

最近の欧州特許庁のケースローでは、新規性の判断を行う際に、最後の基準(c)が適切かどうかについていくつかの論争がある。例えば、審決（T 1233/05、T 230/07、T 1130/09）では、最後の基準(c)は進歩性の判断にとって適切であるが、新規性の判断に適用されるべきではないと教示した。他の審決（T 1827/08及びT 126/09）は、この見解を認めなかった。よって、基準(c)を採用することが一般的な傾向であるか否かは依然として確かでない。最新版の欧州特許庁審査基準では、新規性にとって不可欠な前提条件として、基準(c)に依然として言及している。

4.5　公知の数値範囲との部分的重複

ある数値範囲を公知の数値範囲から選択する場合であって、選択された範囲が公知の範囲と部分的に重複するときは、違う基準が適用される。この状況では、先行技術文献を検討している当業者が重複範囲での実施を「真剣に考える」であろうか否かを判断する（T 26/85、審査基準G-VI 8(iii)）。

4.6　包括的に定義された領域からの狭い範囲の選択

包括的に定義された領域をカバーするクレームによって、対応する先行技術の開示と比較すると狭い範囲の「選択」がなされた場合、特に難しい状況が生じる。つまり、選択された領域が、先行技術の開示と比較して、類似する態様であるが若干狭い範囲で定義される「選択」である。このような状況では、欧州特許庁は、「新規な技術的構成要素」が選択に関与するか否かを判断することにより、新規性を判断することができる（T 12/90）。化合物ファミリーが一般的なマーカッシュ形式により特徴付けられる場合、新規な技術的構成要素は、先行技術文献に個別化された形式で言及されていない特定の化学基であるか、二重の選択によってのみ先行技術文献から導くことのできる2つの化学基の特定の組合せであってもよい。

art document only by means of a two-fold selection.

4.7 Selection of Purity Level

The characterization of a particular purity level in a small organic molecule normally does not permit to establish novelty by selection even if the prior art disclosure does not contain any information on the obtained purity level. Generally, the disclosure of a small organic compound is understood as the disclosure of said compound in any degree of purity that is available by applying conventional purification methods (T 990/96). Novelty is acknowledged only in special situations such as the following ones:

- conventional purification means at the priority date did not allow to accomplish the specified purity level (T 728/98);

- the claim at issue is directed to a manufacturing process and the purity level characterizes the starting material rather than the end product (T 786/00);

- the claim at issue is directed to a composition and the specified purity level characterizes an individual component of said composition (T 112/00) although this depends on the concrete technical context concerned (T 803/01); and

- the claim at issue is directed to a high molecular weight compound and the purity indication is a purposive selection essential for accomplishing the inventive technical effects and there was no desirability in the relevant prior art to obtain the claimed grade of purity (T 142/06).

4.7 純度レベルの選択

　特定の純度レベルで小さな有機分子を特徴付けることによっては、通常、選択により新規性をもたらすことはできない。先行技術の開示が、得られた純度レベルに関する情報をまったく含んでいない場合であってもである。一般に、小さな有機分子化合物の開示は、従来の精製方法を適用することにより得られるすべての純度を有する前記化合物の開示として理解される（T 990/96）。以下の状況など特定の状況でのみ、新規性の存在が肯定される。

- 優先日の時点で、従来の精製手段によっては、特定の純度レベルを達成することはできなかった（T 728/98）。

- 争点となるクレームは製造プロセスを対象とし、その純度レベルは、最終製品ではなく出発材料を特徴付けている（T 786/00）。

- 争点となるクレームは組成物を対象とし、特定の純度レベルは、前記組成物の個々の成分を特徴付ける（T 112/00）。ただしこれは関連する具体的な技術的内容に左右される（T 803/01）。

- 争点となるクレームは高分子化合物を対象としており、純度の表示は、発明に関する技術的効果の達成に不可欠な意図的な選択であり、かつ、関連する先行技術ではクレームされた純度を得ることが望まれていなかった（T 142/06）。

5 Novelty by Use Indication

5.1 Use Indication in Non-Medical Product Claim

A typical claim wording would be "Product X for (non-medical) use Y". The EPO treats use indications differently depending on the type of claim that is involved. If the claim of interest is a product claim in technical fields other than medicine, use indications are merely considered as specifying that the claimed product must be **suitable for** the indicated purpose (Guidelines F-IV 4.13). This means that novelty can be denied even if the intended use is not mentioned in the cited prior art document, provided that suitability for the indicated use is given for the prior art product.

5.2 Use Indication in Medical Product Claim

A typical claim wording would be "Compound X for use in a method for treating disease Y having the following features: …". Use indications in product claims in the field of medicine are treated differently as indications of non-medical uses. This different treatment is based on Article 54(5) EPC. For such second medical use-type claims, the indicated use is regarded as a functional technical feature similar to any other technical feature. Consequently, novelty of such claims can be denied only if the cited prior art document contains a direct and unambiguous disclosure of the specified medical use. All different aspects of the medical use may be relied on as distinguishing features, involving in particular the medical indication to be treated, the patient population to be treated, details of the treatment method, dosage regimen and the like (G 2/08).

A specific patient sub-population may establish novelty if there is a functional relationship between the features characterizing the selected patient group and the accomplished pharmacological effect, e.g. because the selected patient group benefits most from the inventive therapy (T 1399/04). The selection of a patient sub-population may also contribute to the establishment of novelty as one among

5 用途の表示による新規性

5.1 非医薬発明における用途の表示

典型的なクレームは、「Yに使用するための物X」というように記載される。欧州特許庁は、クレームのタイプに応じて、用途の表示を別々に処理する。対象となるクレームが、医薬以外の技術分野における物のクレームである場合には、用途の表示は、クレームされた物が、表示された用途に適していると特定するに過ぎない（審査基準 F-IV 4.13）。これは、引用された先行技術文献に意図された用途が言及されていない場合であっても、指摘された用途の適合性が先行技術の物に与えられていれば、新規性の存在が否定され得ることを意味している。

5.2 医薬発明におけるの用途の表示

典型的なクレームは、「以下の特徴を有する、疾病Yを治療する方法で使用するための化合物X」というように記載される。医薬分野では物についてのクレームでその用途を表示すると異なった扱いを受ける。この異なった扱いは、第54条(5)に基づいている。かかる第二の医薬用途タイプのクレームについては、表示された用途は、他の技術的特徴と同様に、機能的な技術的特徴とみなされる。結果として、かかるクレームの新規性は、引用された先行技術文献に、特定された医薬用途について直接的かつ一義的な開示がある場合にのみ否定される。医薬用途の異なる態様（特に、医学的適応、患者集団、処置方法の詳細、投与計画等を伴うもの）が相違点として依拠され得る（G 2/08）。

第二の医薬用途タイプのクレームの場合は、患者の母集団から特定の患者の部分集団を選択することにより、新規性を確立することもできるが、選択された患者のグループの特性と達成された薬理効果の特性との間に、（発明に関する治療方法から最も利益を得るのが当該選択された部分集団であるなどの理由により）機能的関係があるときに限られる（T 1399/04）。患者の部分集団の選択は、上

two or more individual selections according to the above-mentioned two lists principle (T 1805/09).

Discovery of a new therapeutic effect of a known treatment can form a basis for establishing novelty only if the newly discovered therapeutic effect establishes a new clinical situation that translates into a new industrial/commercial application (T 836/01, T 1642/06, T 1955/09).

5.3   Medical Use-Type Claims

Claims directed to medical uses as such ("Use of compound X for treating disease Y") are considered to be equivalent to claims directed to methods of treatment and they are therefore prohibited under Article 53(c) EPC. Claims drafted in the so-called "Swiss type" ("Use of compound X for manufacturing a medicament for treating disease Y") were introduced into patent practice of the EPO by the Enlarged Board of Appeal as a possibility for protecting 2nd and further medical uses before EPC 2000 came into force (G 1/83, G 5/83, and G 6/83). They are no longer available for protecting second and further medical uses under the EPC 2000 since they are no longer considered necessary in view of Article 54(5) EPC. An exception is made only for old patents and patent applications having an effective date earlier than January 29, 2011 (G 2/08). Even for such old patents and patent applications, the simultaneous presence of use-restricted product claims and Swiss-type claims is not generally allowed in the same application (T 1570/09) but may be allowed in a parent application/divisional application situation (T 1780/12).

5.4   Non-Medical Use-Type Claims

Non-medical use claims ("Use of product X for (non-medical) purpose Y") allow making the use indication an effective distinguishing feature. Hence, if the specified use is not disclosed in the prior art document, novelty should be acknowledged. It is even possible to establish novelty by specifying a use directed

述した２リストの原則に従い、２つ以上の個々の選択のうちの１つの選択として新規性の確立に寄与することもある（T 1805/09）。

既知の治療法における新しい治療効果の発見は、その新しく発見された治療効果が、産業上又は商業上での新しい応用につながる新たな臨床的症状を確立する場合に限り、新規性を確立する根拠になる（T 836/01、T 1642/06、T 1955/09）。

5.3 医薬用途タイプのクレーム

医薬用途そのものを対象とするクレームは、「疾病Ｙの治療のための化合物Ｘの使用」と記載され、治療方法を対象とするクレームに相当すると考えられる。このため、当該クレームは、第53条(c)により禁じられている。いわゆる「スイスタイプ」で作成されたクレーム（「疾病Ｙを治療する医薬物を製造するための化合物Ｘの使用」）は、欧州特許条約2000が発効する前に、第二及びそれ以降の医薬用途の保護を可能とすべく、拡大審判部により欧州特許実務に導入された（G 1/83、G 5/83、G 6/83）。欧州特許条約2000の下では、「スイスタイプ」のクレームは、第54条(5)の観点から必要とは考えられないため、第二及びそれ以降の医薬用途を保護するためにはもう利用できない。2011年１月29日より前に有効日を有する特許及び特許出願に関してのみ、例外が設けられている（G 2/08）。このような古い特許及び特許出願に関してであっても、用途が限定された物のクレームとスイスタイプのクレームとの同時存在は、同一出願では一般的に認められていないが（T 1570/09）、親出願／分割出願の立場では認められる場合がある（T 1780/12）。

5.4 非医薬用途タイプのクレーム

非医薬用途クレーム「（非医薬）用途Ｙのための物Ｘの使用」によれば、先行技術に係る物から相違させる点において、用途の表示が効果的に機能する。よって、特定の用途が先行技術文献で開示されていない場合には、新規性の存在が肯定される。新規な用途の実用的な実施が公知の用途の実用的な実施と異

to the accomplishment of a previously unknown technical effect if the practical implementation of the new use does not differ from the practical implementation of the known use (G 2/88 and G 6/88). This seemingly surprising view can be rationalized by considering that the new effect may provide the skilled person with new fields of application of the known use. Moreover, it may be kept in mind that the new effect is normally an extrinsic property, which is not made available by the known prior art use (see section 2.6 above).

A distinction must be made if there is a use indication in a process claim. If the new use characterizes the process itself (e.g. regarding the field of application), it must be regarded as a functional process feature, which is effective in distinguishing the claimed process from the known prior art process (T 848/93). Similarly, a new use is also effective in establishing novelty if the claim is directed to a process involving the use of a known substance and said new use pertains to the accomplishment of a newly discovered effect of said known substance (T 304/08). Conversely, if the process claim is directed to the manufacture of a product and the new use merely characterizes the product obtained by the specified process, it will not be effective in establishing novelty even if the prior art disclosure does not mention the obtained product characteristic (T 210/93).

6 Special Cases

6.1 Negative Features

Negative features may be used to establish novelty by expressly excluding certain embodiments from the claim scope, which are known from the prior art. Such negative features can be based on corresponding negative disclosures in the original application text (i.e. indications that the relevant embodiments are less desirable), they can be based on positive disclosures in the original application text (i.e. indications that the relevant embodiments are part of the disclosed invention) and, in some instances, they may be formulated without any basis in

ならない場合でも、以前は知られていなかった技術的効果の達成を対象とする用途を特定することにより、新規性を確立することが可能である（G 2/88及びG 6/88）。この見解は驚くに値するだろうが、当該新規な効果によって、公知の用途が新規な分野に適用される可能性を当業者に与えることを考慮すると合理的に説明できる。さらに新規な効果は、通常、公知の先行技術の用途からは利用可能とならない外在的な特性であることを念頭に置くとよい（上記セクション2.6参照）。

方法のクレームに用途の表示がある場合は、物のクレームに用途の表示がある場合と異なる。新規な用途が（例えば、適用分野に関して）方法それ自体を特徴付ける場合は、その用途は、機能的な方法の特徴とみなされ、クレームされた方法を先行技術の方法から区別するのに効果的である（T 848/93）。同様に、クレームの対象が既知の物質の新規な用途を伴う方法であり、その既知の物質に係る新たに発見された効果の達成に前記新規な用途が関与する場合は、新規性を確立するのに効果的である（T 304/08）。逆に、方法のクレームが物の製造に関連する場合であって、特定された方法から得られる物が新規な用途で特徴付けられるに過ぎないときは、当該得られた物の特徴についての言及が先行技術の開示になくとも、当該用途は、新規性を確立するには効果的ではない（T 210/93）。

6 特別なケース

6.1 ネガティブな特徴

先行技術から知られた特定の実施形態をクレームの範囲から明確に取り除くことによって新規性を確立するために、ネガティブな特徴を用いることができる。ネガティブな特徴は、当初の出願書類に対応するネガティブな開示（すなわち、特定の実施形態が好ましくないという指摘）を根拠とすることができるとともに、当初の出願書類におけるポジティブな開示（すなわち、特定の実施形態が開示された発明の一部であるという指摘）を根拠とすることもできる。場合によっては、当初の出願書類にまったく根拠がなくても、ネガティブな特徴を作

the original application (so-called "undisclosed disclaimers").

Negative features based on corresponding negative original disclosures are unproblematic.

Negative features based on positive original disclosures (so-called "disclosed disclaimers") may be allowed, provided that the exclusion of certain embodiments from the claim scope does not lead to the situation that the subject-matter remaining in the claim after the introduction of the disclaimer is not, be it explicitly or implicitly, directly and unambiguously disclosed to the skilled person using common general knowledge, in the application as filed (G 2/10). This means that the exclusion of individual examples should normally be allowed similar to the exclusion of individual features that are originally disclosed as specific alternatives in the form of a list among other alternatives. Added matter issues may arise if a disclosed disclaimer is formulated, wherein two or more features are isolated from the original disclosure and combined with each other to characterize the embodiments to be excised from the claim scope.

The formulation of undisclosed disclaimers is possible only in special circumstances, namely if one of the following situations is given (G 1/03):

- The disclaimer is used for establishing novelty over a post-published prior art reference under Article 54(3) EPC.

- The disclaimer is used for establishing novelty over an accidental anticipation. Thereby, the notion of "accidental anticipation" is construed narrowly and means a prior art disclosure that is so unrelated to and remote from the claimed invention that the person skilled in the art would **never** have taken it into consideration when making the invention. In such instances, disclaimers are available even if the accidental disclosure is pre-published prior art under Article 54(2) EPC.

成することができる。いわゆる「開示されていないディスクレーマ」である。

ネガティブな当初の開示に基づきネガティブな特徴を使うことは問題とならない。

ポジティブな当初の開示に基づきネガティブな特徴を使うこと（いわゆる「開示されたディスクレーマ」）は認められるが、クレームの範囲から特定の実施形態を除くディスクレーマを導入した後のクレームに残る対象が、明示的又は黙示的であるにせよ、技術常識を用いる当業者にとって直接的かつ一義的に出願当初の書類に開示されていない状況にならないことを条件とする（G 2/10）。これは、通常、個々の実施例を除くことが許容されるということである。選択肢間のリストの形式で特定の選択肢として当初開示されている個々の特徴を除くことと同様である。新規事項の問題は、開示されたディスクレーマが作成される場合に生じることがある。当初の開示では分離されていた２つ以上の特徴が互いに組み合わされて、クレームの範囲から除かれる実施形態を特徴付ける場合である。

開示されていないディスクレーマは、特別な場合にのみ使用できる。すなわち、以下の状況の１つに当てはまる場合である（G 1/03）。

- ディスクレーマは、第54条(3)に基づく後に公開された先行技術文献に対して新規性を確立する。

- ディスクレーマは、偶発的な新規性の喪失に対して新規性を確立するために使われる。ここで、「偶発的な新規性喪失」の概念は狭く解釈され、クレームに記載された発明とはあまりに関係なくかけ離れているために、当業者が発明する際にこれを決して考慮しなかったであろう先行技術の開示を意味する。かかる場合、ディスクレーマは、偶発的な開示が第54条(2)に規定する先に公開された場合であっても利用できる。

- The disclaimer is used for excluding subject-matter from the claim scope, which is excluded from patentability for non-technical reasons. For example, methods of treatment of the animal or human body might be qualified as "non-therapeutic" to avoid the prohibition of Article 53(c) EPC.

In all of the above situations, the disclaimer must fulfill the clarity requirement and it must not be relevant for the assessment of inventive step. Moreover, the disclaimer must not excise more than is necessary for establishing novelty unless a broader formulation of the disclaimer is appropriate in view of the clarity requirement (T 2130/11).

6.2 Unclear Features

It is normally difficult or even impossible to establish novelty on the basis of unclear features. Before grant the examiner will normally raise objections of lack of novelty and, additionally, lack of clarity (Guidelines F-IV 4.6). Both objections will need to be overcome independently of each other. While an unclear feature, for instance a relative term, might stay in the claim when there is no basis in the disclosure for a clear definition, it cannot be used by the applicant to distinguish his invention from the prior art, i.e. to establish novelty (Guidelines F-IV 4.6). After grant, the opposition division will normally interpret the claim in the broadest technically meaningful manner (T 686/96 and T 79/96). If this broadest technically meaningful interpretation encompasses prior art disclosures, novelty will be denied.

6.3 Parameter Ranges and Error Margins

Problems may also arise if the claim contains a feature characterizing a numerical range and if the corresponding prior art parameter value is outside the numerical range but very close to one of the limiting values of the claimed range since, as a rule, "technical equality" will be understood as having the meaning of "identity within inevitable measurement errors or manufacturing tolerances" (T

- ディスクレーマは、非技術的理由で特許の対象から除外される対象をクレームの範囲から取り除くために使われる。例えば、動物又は人間の体を処置する方法の場合に、第53条(c)に規定する特許性の例外を回避するために、「非治療的」とすることができる。

上記の状況では、そのすべてにおいて、ディスクレーマは明確性の要件を満たす必要があり、進歩性の判断に関連すべきでない。さらに、新規性を確立するために必要を超えてディスクレーマを用いるべきではないが、広い範囲でディスクレーマを作ることが明確性の要件の観点から適切であるときはこの限りでない（T 2130/11）。

6.2 不明確な特徴

不明確な特徴に基づいて新規性を確立することは、通常、難しいというか不可能である。特許を付与する前に、審査官は、新規性欠如の拒絶理由に加えて明確性欠如の拒絶理由を提起するのが通常である（審査基準F-IV 4.6）。出願人は、両方の拒絶理由を互いに独立して覆す必要がある。クレームに特定された不明確な特徴（例えば、相対的な用語）は、明確な定義の根拠が明細書に開示されていない場合は、そのままクレームに残しておいてもよいのであるが、出願人は、その不明確な特徴を使って、先行技術からクレームに記載された発明を区別して新規性を確立することはできない（審査基準F-IV 4.6）。特許が付与された後に、異議部は、クレームを最も広い技術的に意味のある態様で解釈するのが通常である（T 686/96、T 79/96）。この最も広い技術的に意味のある解釈により先行技術の開示を包括してしまうと、新規性は否定される。

6.3 パラメータの範囲と許容誤差

クレームに数値範囲を限定する特徴が含まれている場合であって、かつ、先行技術のパラメータ値がクレームされた数値範囲の外だが限界値の1つに非常に近接している場合についても問題が生じることがある。それは、原則として、「技術的品質」は、「必然的な測定誤差又は製作公差の範囲内にあるもの」を意味すると理解されるからである（T 605/97）。よって、クレームの範囲を

605/97). Hence, it may become necessary to specify the claimed range more narrowly such that there is no overlap even when taking measurement errors into account (Guidelines G-VI 8.1).

6.4 Non-Technical Features

Usually, for inventions that are partly or completely non-technical (e.g. business methods), the most critical obstacles are the general exclusion of non-technical subject-matter from patentability under Article 52 EPC, as well as the lack of contribution to inventive step under Article 56 EPC by non-technical features. In addition, non-technical features, to the extent that they do not interact with technical features to produce a technical effect, are also not effective for distinguishing a claimed invention from the cited prior art (T 154/04).

狭く特定することにより、誤差が考慮されても、重複が起こらないようにすることが必要となるだろう（審査基準 G-VI 8.1）。

6.4 非技術的特徴

完全に又は部分的に非技術的な発明（例えば、ビジネス手法）についての最大の障壁は、第52条の規定により、非技術的な対象は特許の対象から除外され、並びに、第56条の規定により、非技術的特徴が進歩性の存在に寄与しないことである。さらに、非技術的特徴は、技術的効果を生むようにそれが技術的特徴と相互作用しない範囲において、クレームに記載された発明を引用された先行技術から区別するのに有効ではない（T 154/04）。

Chapter 2

Inventive Step

進歩性

Declan Mulhern

MEMO

▶ 第56条によれば、技術水準からみて、当業者にとって、発明が「自明なものではない」場合は、進歩性の要件を満たすとされます。この点、当業者が「容易に発明をすることができた」かどうかを検討する日本の実務と異なります。発明が「自明なものではない」ことを決定的に確立することは不可能でしょう（§4）。欧州特許庁審判部は、クレームに記載された発明が自明なものであるかどうかを判断するための標準的アプローチである「課題解決アプローチ」を考案しました。

▶ 「技術水準」の定義については、§2及び第3章を参照してください。

▶ 欧州実務の進歩性判断における「当業者」については、§3を参照してください。この点、日本の実務との間に若干の差異があるかもしれません。日本特許庁審査基準によりますと、「当業者」とは、当該発明の属する技術分野の出願時の技術常識を有し、研究、開発のための通常の技術的手段を用いることができ、材料の選択や設計変更などの通常の創作能力を発揮でき、かつ、当該発明の属する技術分野の出願時の技術水準にあるものすべてを自らの知識とすることができ、発明が解決しようとする課題に関連した技術分野の技術を自らの知識とすることができる者、とあります（第Ⅲ部第2章第2節、2015年10月参照）。

▶ 「課題解決アプローチ」は、主に3段階に分けられます（§5）。

第一段階では、最も近い先行技術を選択し、クレームされた発明と先行技術との相違点を特定します。第二段階では、相違点に起因する技術的効果を考慮して、客観的課題を設定します。第三段階では、客観的な課題に鑑みて、当業者が最も近い先行技術を改変したであろうか、その結果としてクレームされた発明に到達したであろうかを検討します。

　日本の実務における進歩性の判断の基本的な考え方については、日本特許庁審査基準をご参照ください。

▶　欧州実務の第一段階は日本の実務と似ていますが、第二段階以降が日本の実務とは異なります。

Introduction

To be awarded a patent it is generally accepted that the underlying invention must be something more than a trivial modification of that which was already known. Each jurisdiction legislates for this in its own way but the fundamental approach is essentially the same: the invention in question must not be obvious to somebody who is presumed to have ordinary skill in the art. A number of questions naturally arise from this approach. Who is this person of ordinary skill? What information is available to them? And how exactly does one determine if the invention in question would not have been obvious to that person?

Courts in the various jurisdictions around the world have grappled with these and similar questions and over time have developed their own ways to answer them. In this chapter we will look at how the Boards of Appeal at the EPO deal with this issue and how that approach compares to the practice in Japan.

1   Legal Basis for Inventive Step

Whereas Japanese patent law invites one to consider if a person of ordinary skill *"would have been able to easily make the invention"* (Art. 29(2) JPA), the EPC requires the invention to *"involve an inventive step"* (Art. 52(1) EPC). The requirement to involve an inventive step is considered to be fulfilled if the invention is *"not obvious"* to the person skilled in the art having regard to the state of the art (Art. 56 EPC).

Since being *"not obvious"* leads to the recognition that an invention involves an *"inventive step"*, these and related terms are oftentimes used interchangeably in European patent practice. This may lead to some confusion, particularly for those who are perhaps more accustomed to dealing with the US requirement of *"non-obvious"* (35 U.S.C. §103). In proceedings before the EPO, it might be helpful to think of the expression *"involve an inventive step"* as one of the legal tests

はじめに

　特許が付与されるためには、発明は、すでに知られている事項の些細な改良では足りないということは一般的に受け入れられている。これは、各法域で、独自の方法で制定されているが、基本的なアプローチは実質的に同じである。クレームに記載された発明は、その技術分野の専門家と仮定される者（以下、当業者）にとって自明のものであってはならない。このアプローチから、いくつかの問題が当然のごとく生じる。当業者とは誰か。当業者にとっていかなる情報が入手可能か。そして、クレームに記載された発明が当業者にとって自明なものではないとはどう判断するのか。

　世界各国での管轄権を異にする裁判所は、上記の問題に面し、これらの問題に答えるために、長い時間をかけて独自の手法を開発してきた。本章では、欧州特許庁の審判部が上記の争点をどのように処理しているのかを考察する。また、日本の特許実務との比較にも触れる。

1　進歩性の法的根拠

　日本特許法では、当業者が「容易に発明をすることができた」かどうかを検討する（第29条第2項）。一方で、欧州特許条約は、発明が「進歩性を有する」ことを要件としている（第52条(1)）。技術水準からみて、当業者にとって、発明が「自明なものではない」場合は、進歩性の要件を満たすとされる（第56条）。

　「自明なものではない」ことにより、発明が「進歩性」を有することが肯定されるため、これら及び関連する用語は、欧州特許実務で交換可能に使用されることが多い。特に、「自明なものではない」というアメリカで必要とされる要件（第103条）に対応することに慣れている実務者にとっては、なんらかの混乱を招くことがある。欧州特許庁の手続では、「進歩性を有する」という表現を特許性の法的テストの1つとして、そして「自明なものではない」という

for patentability and the state of being "*not obvious*" as the way to pass that test. However, before assessing if an invention is "*not obvious*" we must first establish what is meant by the expressions "*state of the art*" and "*person skilled in the art*".

2   State of the Art

The state of the art is the body of public knowledge that the "*person skilled in the art*" is presumed to have access to when looking to solve technical problems. It is also the body of public knowledge from which a "*closest prior art*" will be chosen when performing the problem-solution approach (discussed in more detail later). Therefore, correctly establishing the state of the art is a key component before evaluating if an invention is "*not obvious*".

The state of the art comprises everything made available to the public (whether that is by written or oral description, by use, or by any other way) *before the date of filing* of the European patent application. If the application originates from a PCT application (EP-PCT), the filing date of the PCT application is decisive. Similarly, if a valid priority claim exists, then the filing date of the priority application is decisive. So-called Art. 54(3) prior art has not been made available to the public before the filing date and so is not considered prior art for the purpose of assessing inventive step under Art. 56 EPC. As in Japanese law (Art. 30(1) JPA), a public disclosure of the invention due to an abuse of some kind (e.g. a breach of confidence) is also not part of the state of the art provided that the EP or EP-PCT application (not the priority application!) is filed within six months of that disclosure (Art. 55 EPC).

Practitioners in Japan should note two important differences in how the state of the art is defined for the purposes of Art. 56 EPC and how it is defined in Arts. 29(1) and 29(2) JPA. Firstly, unlike Japan, public disclosures made earlier *on the same day* that an application is filed do not become part of the state of the art. Therefore, if a disclosure of the invention is inadvertently made there may still be

条件を、当該テストにパスするためのステップとして考えるとわかりやすい。発明が「自明なものではない」かどうかを判断する前に、まず、「技術水準」及び「当業者」という表現が何を意味するかをはっきりさせる必要がある。

2　技術水準

　技術水準は、技術的課題を解決しようと試みる際に、「当業者」がアクセスすると推定される公の知識の集まりである。また、技術水準は、課題解決アプローチを行う際に、「最も近い先行技術」が選択される公の知識の集まりでもある（後で詳細に述べる）。よって技術水準を的確に認定することは、発明が「自明なものではない」かどうかを検討する際に前提となる鍵である。

　技術水準は、欧州特許出願の出願日前に、書面若しくは口頭による陳述、使用又はその他のあらゆる方法によって、公衆に利用可能になったすべてのものから構成される。欧州特許出願がPCT出願から生じる場合、PCT出願の出願日が決定的である。同様に、優先権主張が有効に存在する場合は、先の出願の出願日が決定的である。いわゆる第54条(3)の先行技術は、出願日前に公衆に利用可能とはなっていないため、進歩性について判断する第56条の目的において先行技術とはみなされない。日本の特許法第30条第1項と同じく、ある種の濫用による発明の公衆への開示も、欧州特許出願又はEP-PCT出願が当該開示から6月以内に出願されていれば、技術水準の一部とはならない（第55条）。

　技術水準が、第56条の目的でどのように定義されているかについて、日本の特許法第29条第1項及び第2項との比較において、日本の実務家らは、2つの大きな違いに気づくだろう。第一に、日本とは違って、出願された日が「同日」であれば、（時間的に）先になされた公の開示は、技術水準の一部とはならない。よって発明の開示が不注意でなされた場合は、直ちに準備をして出願

enough time to quickly prepare and file an application and salvage patent rights in Europe. Secondly, unlike the six-month grace period afforded by Art. 30(2) JPA, the EPC *does not provide* any grace period for disclosures originating from the applicant. Practitioners in Japan should keep this in mind because such disclosures will be part of the state of the art for assessing novelty and inventive step at the EPO. It is therefore highly recommended that, if patent protection is to be pursued in Europe, a priority application is always filed before *any* public disclosure of the invention is made.

3 Person Skilled in the Art

The person skilled in the art – or the *"skilled person"* for short – plays a central role in determining if an invention involves an inventive step. After all, it is their knowledge and capability that is taken into account when assessing if an invention is *"not obvious"*.

Essentially, the skilled person is a hypothetical, experienced practitioner in the field where the invention solves a technical problem. He (or, once and for all, she) possesses no inventive capability but has at his disposal the means and capacity for normal routine work and experimentation. The skilled person is aware of the common general knowledge in the field which is usually established by disclosures in basic textbooks, handbooks, dictionaries, and the like. The skilled person is also presumed to have access to everything in the state of the art irrespective of its language, location, or time of disclosure. It is important to recognise that while *access* to the state of the art is absolute, this does not mean that the skilled person is familiar with everything in it, or that he will consider everything in it when looking to solve a problem. Rather, the skilled person will look to his own and neighbouring technical fields for solutions to any problems that he encounters. If the situation warrants, he may also look to more distant technical fields but only if he is prompted to do so. In cases where the solution to a problem spans multiple technical fields, the skilled person can be considered to be a

すれば、欧州での権利喪失を防ぐことができる。次に、日本の特許法第30条第2項で与えられる6月の猶予期間と違って、欧州特許条約は、出願人が行う開示については猶予期間を与えていない。日本の実務者らは、これを念頭に置くべきである。このような開示は、欧州特許庁では、新規性及び進歩性判断の技術水準の一部となるからである。よって、欧州で特許による保護を求める場合は、発明を公に開示する前に、常に、優先権の基礎となる先の出願をすることを強く勧める。

3　当業者

　その技術分野の専門家、すなわち「当業者」は、発明が進歩性を有するかどうかを判断するに際し、中心的な役割を果たす。発明が「自明なものではない」かどうかを判断する場合に考慮されるのが、当業者の知識及び能力である。

　実質的に、当業者とは、クレームに記載された発明が技術的課題を解決するその分野の架空の経験豊かな実務家である。当業者は、発明をする能力を持たないが、自分の裁量で通常の日常的作業及び実験を行う手段と能力を有する。当業者は、基礎的な教科書、ハンドブック、辞書等に載っている通常に確立された当該分野の技術常識を有している。当業者は、開示の言語、所在、時期とは関係なくすべての技術水準にアクセスするとも推定される。技術水準へのアクセスは絶対的である一方で、当業者が当該技術分野のすべてに通じていることや、課題解決に注力する際に当該技術分野のすべてを検討することを意味しているわけではない。むしろ、当業者は、自身が遭遇する任意の課題に対する解決手段に関して、自身の技術分野及び隣接する技術分野に目を向けるものである。状況によっては、当業者は、かけ離れた技術分野に目を向けるよう促される場合もある。課題を解決するための手段が複数の技術分野にわたる場合は、当業者は、各分野からの当業者で構成されるグループとも考えることができる。

group made up of a skilled person from each of the respective fields.

4 Not Obvious?

While it is comparatively straightforward to establish the state of the art and the appropriate skilled person, the next step of assessing if an invention is "*not obvious*" is not an easy task. In fact, one might say that it is impossible to *conclusively* establish that an invention is not obvious because there is always a possibility that some, as-yet, unconsidered prior art exists that renders the invention obvious.

In practice, rather than try to establish that an invention is *not obvious*, the burden initially rests with an examiner or an opponent to demonstrate that the invention *is obvious*. If this burden cannot be discharged then the invention is *presumed* to be not obvious in view of the available evidence. This is similar to the approach outlined in the Guidelines for Examination at the JPO where examiners are instructed to try and establish that the skilled person "*would have been able to easily make the invention*", and if that cannot be done, accept that the invention cannot easily be made.

As to what is meant by "*obvious*", the Boards of Appeal consistently refer to it as that which does not go beyond the normal progress of technology but merely follows plainly or logically from the prior art. In other words, something is obvious if it does not involve the exercise of any skill or ability beyond that which can be expected of the skilled person. This raises certain questions. For example, what starting point should be used when assessing if an invention is obvious? How much credence can we give to the inventor's own view of his invention and its merits when making that assessment? It was to address issues such as these that the Boards of Appeal developed the so-called "*problem-solution approach*" (or the "*PSA*" for short) which, although not coded in the law, is nevertheless the standard approach that is used at the EPO for assessing if an invention is obvi-

4　自明なものではない？

　技術水準及び適切な当業者を確立することは、比較的簡単である。一方、発明が「自明なものではない」ことを判断する次のステップは容易でない作業である。実際、発明を自明なものとする未考慮の先行技術が存在する可能性が常にあるため、発明が自明なものではないと決定的に確立するのは不可能であろう。

　実際には、出願人又は特許権者は、発明が自明なものではないことを確立する義務を最初は負わない。最初は、審査官又は特許異議申立人に、発明が自明なものであることを示す立証責任がある。この責任が転換されない場合は、利用可能な証拠からみて発明は自明なものではないと推定される。これは、日本の特許実務で行われるアプローチに類似する。日本の審査基準によると、審査官らは、当業者が「容易に発明をすることができた」ことを確立させようと務め、これができない場合は、容易に発明をすることができないことを推認するように概説されている。

　「自明」という用語の意味に関して、審判部は、一貫して、技術の通常の進歩を超えず、先行技術から明らかに又は論理的に起こるに過ぎないものとして、これに言及している。換言すれば、当業者の予測を超える熟練や能力の行使を伴わない発明は自明なものである。しかし、いくつかの問題がある。例えば、発明が自明なものであるかどうかを判断する場合に、どのような出発点が使われるべきか。かかる判断を行う場合に、発明についての発明者自身の見識をどの程度信頼すべきか。このような問題に対処するため、審判部は、いわゆる「課題解決アプローチ」を構築した。成文化はされていないものの、課題解決アプローチは、クレームに記載された発明が自明なものであるかどうかを判断するために欧州特許庁が使用する標準的アプローチである。

ous.

5 Problem-Solution Approach

Since an applicant generally discloses his invention in the context of a problem that he *perceives* to exist in the prior art, the applicant's problem and the proposed solution must be regarded from the outset as being *subjective* in nature. The purpose of the PSA is to provide an *objective* assessment if an invention is obvious having regard to the state of the art. The PSA consists of three main stages which are usually set out as shown below:

(1) determine the "*closest prior art*";

(2) establish the "*objective technical problem*" to be solved; and

(3) consider whether or not the claimed invention, starting from the closest prior art and the objective technical problem, would have been obvious to the skilled person.

Essentially, in stage (1) what is sometimes called "*the most promising springboard*" to the invention is determined. In stage (2) the technical contribution made by the invention in view of this closest prior art is established. Finally, in stage (3) one considers if it would have been obvious to the skilled person that this technical contribution could be achieved by something falling within the scope of the claim in question.

5.1 Stage 1: The Closest Prior Art

The choice of closest prior art is perhaps the most crucial aspect of the PSA since everything else flows from this. Not only does the choice of closest prior art directly affect how the "*objective technical problem*" in stage (2) is formulated,

5 課題解決アプローチ

出願人は、一般に、自己が認識する先行技術の課題との関連で自身の発明を開示するので、その特許出願で提示された課題及び提案された解決手段は主観的であるとみなされる。課題解決アプローチは、技術水準からみてクレームに記載された発明が自明なものであるかどうかについて、客観的な判断を提供することを目的とする。課題解決アプローチは、通常、以下に掲げる3つの段階から構成されている。

(1) 「最も近い先行技術」を特定する。

(2) 解決すべき「客観的な技術的課題」を設定する。

(3) 最も近い先行技術及び客観的な技術的課題からスタートして、クレームに記載された発明が当業者にとって自明であったかどうかを検討する。

第一段階では、特に、クレームに記載された発明に対して、「最も有望なスタート地点」とは何かを決定する。第二段階では、最も近い先行技術の観点から、どのような技術的貢献がクレームに記載された発明により成されたかを認定する。最後に、第三段階では、クレームで特定される事項により、その技術的貢献が達成できたことが、当業者にとって自明であったかどうかを検討する。

5.1 第一段階：最も近い先行技術

最も近い先行技術の選択は、おそらく、課題解決アプローチの最も重大な局面である。他のすべてがここから始まるからである。最も近い先行技術は、課題解決アプローチの第二段階で行う「客観的な技術的課題」の設定に直接に影

it is starting from this prior art in stage (3) that one considers if the invention is obvious. The choice of closest prior art is often the single most important factor leading to an invention being considered obvious at the EPO. Therefore, it will not surprise the reader to learn that in proceedings before the EPO, particularly in opposition proceedings, a great deal of time and effort is often spent debating whether a particular disclosure qualifies as the closest prior art.

5.1.1   Conceived for the Same Purpose

To qualify as the closest prior art, the first consideration is that the disclosure must be something *conceived for the same purpose* as the invention because otherwise it cannot lead the skilled person in an obvious way to the invention. The following example illustrates this point.

Imagine a claim to *a squash ball having a blue colour*. The description of the application (or patent) explains that the blue colour reduces visible markings on the white walls of the squash court. Furthermore, it is also explained that the blue colour allows a player to more easily track the ball against the white wall of the squash court as compared to a ball of any other colour. Now imagine different prior art disclosures: (i) a black squash ball that was widely used for over one hundred years; (ii) a more recently developed green squash ball that is said to leave less visible markings on the walls of a squash court; and (iii) a golf ball that is coloured blue for purely aesthetic reasons. Which of these prior art disclosures represents a suitable starting point for a development that will lead in an obvious way to the claimed invention?

The golf ball undoubtedly contains the core feature upon which the invention is based (i.e. the blue colour). However, it is not a realistic starting point for any development leading in an obvious way to the invention. Without hindsight of the invention, any development of a golf ball will lead to something that is still a golf ball. It is only with hindsight that one would argue that the skilled person, look-

響を与えるだけでなく、発明が自明なものであるかどうかを検討する第三段階もこの最も近い先行技術からスタートする。最も近い先行技術の選択は、欧州特許庁で、発明が自明なものであるとみなされることに繋がる最も重要なファクターとなることが多い。よって、欧州特許庁における手続、特に特許異議申立手続において、最も近い先行技術としてどの引用発明を採用すべきかの議論に多くの時間と労力が費やされて議論がされることは予想外のことではない。

5.1.1　同一の目的で着想された発明

先行技術の開示が最も近い先行技術として適格であるかどうかを考慮する際、まずは、その開示がクレームに記載された発明と同一の目的で着想されたものであるかどうかを考える。そうでなければ、当業者が自明の手法でクレームに記載された発明に導かれるとは想像できないからである。以下の例はこの点を記述している。

青色のスカッシュボールのクレームを想像されたい。出願（又は特許）の明細書には、スカッシュコートの白い壁上のマーキングが青色により減らされることが説明されている。また、当該明細書には、青色により、プレーヤーがスカッシュコートの白い壁に対して、他のどのような色のボールよりも容易にボールを追いかけることができるとも説明されている。ここで、(i)100年以上も広く使用されてきた黒色のスカッシュボールと、(ii)スカッシュコートの壁上のマーキングを減らすといわれる最近開発された緑色のスカッシュボールと、(iii)純粋に審美的理由で青色の色彩が付されたゴルフボールという先行技術の開示が別にあると想像されたい。これら先行技術の開示のうち、クレームに記載された発明に導かれることが自明であると展開するにあたって最も適切なスタート点を示しているのはどれだろうか？

ゴルフボールは疑いなく、クレームに記載された発明が根拠とする主な特徴（すなわち青色）を含んでいる。しかし、ゴルフボールは、クレームに記載された発明に自明な手法で導かれるための現実的なスタート点にはならない。発明の後知恵なしでは、ゴルフボールを開発しても、依然としてゴルフボールである何かに導かれる。スカッシュボールを製造することに注意を向ける当業者が

ing to make a squash ball, would start from a golf ball. This kind of hindsight is largely avoided by considering only those disclosures that are *conceived for the same purpose* as the invention in question. In this case the black squash ball or the green squash ball is objectively a better starting point and therefore a more suitable choice as the closest prior art.

5.1.2 Similar Technical Problem

When assessing if an invention is obvious it is reasonable to give some weight to the problem faced by the inventor when he conceived his invention. Therefore, another important consideration when choosing the closest prior art is whether it aims to solve the same or a similar technical problem which the application (or patent) addresses. Prior art disclosures that aim to solve the same or a similar problem will be considered more promising starting points than prior art disclosures which do not address the problem at all. This does not mean to say that the closest prior art must be something that was known to the inventor when he conceived his invention. An inventor cannot be expected to have complete knowledge of the state of the art and it might very well be that the problem faced by the inventor is best tackled (or indeed has been solved) from a starting point of which he was not aware. In the example above, the green squash ball addresses at least one of the problems mentioned in the application (less visible markings on the wall) and so arguably could be considered a more suitable choice as the closest prior art than the black squash ball.

5.1.3 Most Relevant Technical Features in Common

When faced with a number of prior art disclosures that address the same or a similar technical problem as the invention, a further approach that is widely adopted at the EPO is to choose the prior art that has the *most relevant technical features in common* with the invention. In other words, the closest prior art is that *single* piece of prior art which addresses the same or a similar technical problem as the invention and which requires the minimum of structural modifications to

ゴルフボールからスタートすることを議論するのは、後知恵の範囲に過ぎない。この種の後知恵は、クレームに記載された発明と同一の目的で着想された先行技術の開示のみを考慮することにより、大きく回避される。この場合、黒色のスカッシュボール又は緑色のスカッシュボールは、客観的に適切なスタート点であるため、最も近い先行技術として適切な選択と思われる。

5.1.2 類似の技術的課題

　発明が自明なものであるかどうかを判断する際に、発明者が自身の発明を着想したときに直面した課題になんらかの重きを置くことは妥当である。よって、対象とする出願（又は特許）と同一又は類似の技術的課題を解決することを目的とする先行技術の開示があるかどうかは、最も近い先行技術を選択する際に考慮される重要な要因の１つである。同一又は類似の課題を解決することを目的とする先行技術の開示は、課題にまったく対処しない先行技術の開示より有望なスタート点として考慮される。しかし、その発明を着想した際に、最も近い先行技術を発明者が知っていたに違いないと述べているわけではない。技術水準について完全な知識を有することは期待できず、発明者が直面する課題は、発明者が気づいていないスタート点からのほうがベストに対処できる（又は実際に解決されてきた）という可能性が十分にある。上記の例では、緑色のスカッシュボールは出願で言及された少なくとも１つの課題である壁のマーキングを減らすことに対処しているため、最も近い先行技術として、黒色のスカッシュボールより適切な選択とみなすことができる。

5.1.3 関連する技術的特徴を最も共有すること

　クレームに記載された発明と同一又は類似の技術的課題を有する先行技術の開示がいくつかある場合には、欧州特許庁では、クレームに記載された発明の技術的特徴に関連する特徴を最も共有する先行技術を選択することをさらなるアプローチとして広く採択している。換言すれば、最も近い先行技術は、クレームに記載された発明と同一又は類似の技術的課題に対処し、かつ、クレームに記載された発明に到達するために構造変更を最小限に必要とする単一の先行

reach the invention.

This approach is often adopted by examiners at the EPO for its practicality because there is a certain pressure to deal with each case as quickly and efficiently as possible. After all, if the invention is not obvious from this single closest prior art then the examiner can assume (whether rightly or wrongly) that he is unlikely to find the invention obvious from a disclosure that shares even less features in common with the invention.

5.1.4 More than One Closest Prior Art?

Two or more prior art disclosures are considered *equally* suited as the closest prior art if they address the same problem as the invention and each shares the same number of relevant technical features with the invention. In this situation it is widely accepted that stages (2) and (3) of the PSA should be performed for each of the disclosures in turn. Inventive step is then denied if the invention is found to be obvious starting from either disclosure.

Lengthy debates often occur if there are two or more prior art disclosures addressing the same problem as the invention where one leads in an obvious way to the invention but the other does not. Proponents of the "*most relevant features in common*" principle will argue that the closest prior art must be that which requires the minimum of structural modifications to reach the invention irrespective of the fact that it may not lead to the invention in an obvious way. This can lead to the strange scenario whereby the invention might have been considered obvious but for the discovery of that closest prior art. This is not a problem *per se* if one accepts as a matter of fact that the PSA must only be performed in view of a piece of prior art that is objectively chosen by some pre-defined criteria. However, it does seem to clash with the purpose of the exercise which is to determine, as best as possible, if the invention would have been obvious in the real world. Perhaps this approach places too much emphasis on the literal meaning of the

文献である。

　課題解決アプローチは、その実行性において、欧州特許庁で審査官により採択されることが多い。審査官は、可能な限り迅速、かつ、効率的に各ケースを処理するプレッシャーに瀕するからである。結局、最も近い先行技術からみてクレームに記載された発明が自明なものではない場合は、審査官は、発明と共通する特徴をそれ以上に共有しない他の引用文献の開示からみてクレームに記載された発明が自明なものであると認定しないであろう。

5.1.4　最も近い先行技術が2つ以上ある？

　最も近い先行技術として複数の先行技術の開示が同等に適していると考えられる場合がある。これらの開示がクレームに記載された発明と同一の課題に対処し、各々がクレームに記載された発明と同数の関連する技術的特徴を共有するときである。この状況では、課題解決アプローチの二段階目と三段階目が、各々について順番に実行される。いずれかの最も近い先行技術からスタートして、クレームに記載された発明が自明なものであると推認される場合には、進歩性の存在が否定される。

　先行技術の開示が2つ以上ある場合において、これらの開示がクレームに記載された発明と同一の課題に対処している場合において、1つは自明な方法でクレームに記載された発明に到達し、他方はそうでないという長丁場の議論が生じることが多い。「最も関連する技術的特徴が共有すること」の原理の提唱者は、最も近い先行技術は、クレームに記載された発明に導かれることが自明でないかもしれないという事実に関わらず、クレームに記載された発明に導かれるにあたって構造変更を最小限に必要とするものであると主張する。これは、当該先行技術の発見がなかったとしてもクレームに記載された発明が自明となったであろう奇妙なシナリオに至る可能性がある。それ自体は、実際いくつかの所定の基準により客観的に選択される1つの先行技術を考慮して課題解決アプローチを実行する必要があるに過ぎないことを受け入れる場合、問題ではない。しかし、発明が現実の世界で自明なものであったかどうかを可能な限り最善に判断するという実践の目的と衝突すると思われる。おそらくこのアプ

term "*closest*" in stage (1) of the PSA and not enough emphasis on the wording of the law itself which requires that one have regard to "*the state of the art*" (not just one or two pieces of it) when assessing if an invention is obvious.

Having said that, a number of decisions from the Boards of Appeal have accepted that if the skilled person has a choice of several workable routes which might lead to the invention, the rationale of the PSA requires that the invention be assessed relative to *each* of the workable routes. This approach appears to be more in line with the practice at the JPO.

5.2   Stage 2: The Objective Technical Problem

After a suitable closest prior art disclosure has been identified, the next stage of the PSA is to establish what technical contribution the invention makes in view of that disclosure. Once established, the contribution is formulated as the so-called "*objective technical problem*" – that is, the problem that the skilled person must attempt to solve by adapting or modifying the closest prior art. Since the technical contribution will depend on the choice of the closest prior art, the *objective* technical problem may not necessarily correspond to the perceived or *subjective* problem that the inventor initially considered his invention to solve.

Stage (2) of the PSA is generally performed in a number of discrete steps as outlined below.

5.2.1   Distinguishing Technical Features

First, the invention is compared with the closest prior art to identify the *distinguishing technical features* – namely, those technical features of the invention that are not present in the closest prior art. For the purpose of this exercise, features that qualify as technical features are those that contribute to the *technical character* of the invention. This includes features which, if taken in isolation, might not reveal a technical aspect but nevertheless contribute to the overall

ローチは、その一段階目で「最も近い」という用語の文言上の意味を過度に強調し、発明が自明か否かを判断する際に「技術水準」（単に１つや２つの先行技術でない）を考慮するよう要求する法律自体の文言を十分に強調していない。

そうはいっても、多くの審決において、発明に至るかもしれない複数の実行可能なルートの選択を当業者が有する場合、課題解決アプローチによると実行可能な各ルートについて発明が判断されるべきとされている。これは、日本特許庁の実務に沿っているかもしれない。

5.2　第二段階：客観的な技術的課題

課題解決アプローチの次の段階は、適切に特定された最も近い先行技術の内容からみて、どのような技術的貢献がクレームに記載された発明により成されるかを認定することである。これが認定されると、その貢献はいわゆる「客観的な技術的課題」（すなわち、当業者が最も近い先行技術を適用して又は変更することにより解決しようとする課題）として設定される。技術的貢献は、最も近い先行技術の選択に左右されるため、客観的な技術的課題は、発明者が解決するために当初考えた（又は主観的な）課題とは必ずしも一致しない。

課題解決アプローチの第二段階では、一般に、以下に概要する数々の個別のステップが実行される。

5.2.1　相違する技術的特徴

最初に、クレームに記載された発明と比較して最も近い先行技術に存在しない技術的特徴、すなわち、相違する技術的特徴を特定する。技術的特徴として参酌される特徴は、発明の技術的性質に貢献するものである。これには、分離して解釈した場合において技術的側面は明らかでないかもしれないが、技術的課題を解決するために他の特徴と相互作用することにより、全般的な技術的特性に貢献する特徴が含まれる。例えば、コンピュータプログラム、数学的方

technical character by interacting with other features of the invention to solve a technical problem (e.g. a computer program; a mathematical method; the colour blue in the example of the squash ball above, etc.). Naturally, the invention must contain at least one distinguishing technical feature otherwise it will already be deemed to have lacked novelty thus negating the need to consider inventive step at all.

5.2.2 Establishing a Technical Effect

Once the distinguishing technical features have been identified, a determination is made as to what technical effect, if any, can be attributed to those features and thus reflected in the objective technical problem to be solved.

First and foremost, any technical effect that is to be relied upon must be something that the skilled person can derive from the application as filed. A technical effect might be self-evident by how the distinguishing technical feature interacts with the rest of the invention, with or without further explanation in the description (as is more common in mechanical cases). Sometimes the technical effect requires a more concrete disclosure (as is more common in the fields of chemistry and biotechnology). For example, it is probably not self-evident that it is easier for the human eye to track a blue squash ball in flight than it is to track a black or green squash ball. Accordingly, this effect should be mentioned in the application as filed or at least be derivable there from if the effect is to be relied upon when formulating the objective technical problem.

Secondly, the skilled person must find it at least *plausible* from the application as filed that the effect to be relied upon can be achieved by the invention (e.g. from an explanation of how the invention works, from data in the application, using his common general knowledge having regard to the disclosure in the application, etc.). In cases where the technical effect is recited as something to be achieved in the claim language itself (e.g. in a second medical use claim), this plausibility requirement is usually discussed under the mantle of sufficiency of

法、上述したスカッシュボールの例の青色である。クレームに記載された発明は、少なくとも１つの相違する技術的特徴を当然に含んでいる必要がある。さもなければ、クレームに記載された発明は新規性を有しないとみなされるわけであり、進歩性を考慮する必要性は完全に否定される。

5.2.2　技術的効果の確定

　相違する技術的特徴が特定されると、技術的効果がある場合は、どのような技術的効果が相違する技術的特徴に起因するのかを決定することにより、解決すべき客観的な技術的課題に反映される。

　まず、技術的効果は、当業者が当初の出願書類から導くことができるものである必要がある。機械工学のケースでよく見られるように、技術的効果は、明細書の詳細な説明により、あるいはかかる説明がなくても、相違する技術的特徴が当該発明の他の部分とどのように相互作用するかにより明らかとなる場合がある。化学とバイオテクノロジーの分野でよく見られるように、技術的効果は、より具体的な開示を必要とすることもある。例えば、黒色又は緑色のスカッシュボールと比べて、青色のスカッシュボールが飛んでいるところを、人間の目でより容易く追跡することができるということは、おそらくわかりきったことではないだろう。よって、客観的な技術的課題を設定する際に、技術的効果が根拠とされる場合は、この効果は当初の出願書類に記載されているか、そこから導くことができるべきである。

　次に、クレームに記載された発明によってその技術的効果が達成されることが、当業者であれば、当初の出願書類から妥当であると認定する必要がある。例えば、出願書類の開示を考慮して、当業者の技術常識により、発明がどのように作用するかという説明から、又は出願書類中のデータから認定することができるということである。技術的効果が、クレーム自体において達成されるべきものとして記載されている場合（例えば、第二医薬用途クレーム）は、この妥当性の要件は、通常、開示十分性の要件の下に議論される。

disclosure.

The requirement that a technical effect is plausible does not mean that the application as filed must conclusively show that the effect *is* indeed achieved, or that the effect is something above and beyond that which is achieved by the closest prior art. If necessary, this can be demonstrated later with supplemental evidence (sometimes called *"post-published evidence"*). Supplementary evidence is most often required when the choice of closest prior art places the invention in a perspective that is different to that which was originally envisioned. This evidence, so long as it is timely filed, may be relied upon during prosecution, opposition and appeal proceedings at the EPO.

Finally, a technical effect needs to be established *across the whole scope* of the claim if it is to be taken into account when formulating the objective technical problem. In other words, all variants of the invention as claimed should be able to provide the effect. Objections that an effect has not been established across the whole scope of the claim are sometimes referred to as *"AgrEvo"* objections named after the appeal case that first decided the issue. These objections typically occur in the field of chemistry and biotechnology where it is common practice to claim a myriad of different variants (e.g. using Markush formulae) but provide experimental evidence for only a handful of those variants. If the extent of the effect is in doubt, and the applicant wishes to rely on the technical effect when formulating the objective technical problem, then there are basically two options available: (i) file supplementary evidence that establishes the effect across the whole scope of the claim, or (ii) limit the claim to those variants where the technical effect has been established.

5.2.3 Formulating the Objective Technical Problem

The final part of stage (2) of the PSA, and the part where practice at the EPO appears to differ from that of Japan, is to explicitly formulate the objective technical problem to be solved. Essentially, the skilled person is tasked with modifying

技術的効果に妥当性があることの要件は、効果が実際上達成されること、又は効果が最も近い先行技術により達成されるものをはるかに超えた何かであることを当初の出願書類に基づいて決定的に示す必要があることを意味しない。必要に応じて、これは、補足的証拠により後から実証できる。補足的証拠は、最も近い先行技術の選択が最初に想定したものとは異なる視点で発明を位置付ける際に要求される場合がほとんどである。この証拠は、タイムリーに提出される限り、欧州特許庁における審査、特許異議申立て及び審判手続の過程で根拠とすることができる。

最後に、客観的な技術的課題を設定するにあたって技術的効果を参酌する場合には、その技術的効果は、クレームの範囲全体にわたって存在する必要がある。換言すれば、クレームに記載された発明は、すべての変形において効果を有するべきということである。クレームの範囲全体にわたって効果が確立されていないことを理由とする拒絶は、最初に争点を判断した事案の審決を受けて"AgrEvo"拒絶と呼ばれることがある。当該拒絶は、種々の変形を無数にクレームする一方で、これらの変形の一握りのみの実験証拠を提示することが一般的な実務である化学とバイオテクノロジーで生じることが多い。例えば、マーカッシュ形式を利用してクレームした場合である。効果の範囲が未決定であり、出願人が客観的な技術的課題を設定する際に技術的効果を根拠とすることを望む場合は、利用できる選択肢が基本的に2つある。1つ目は、クレームの範囲全体にわたって効果を確立する補足的証拠を提出すること、2つ目は、技術的効果が確立された変形にクレームを限定することである。

5.2.3　客観的な技術的課題の設定

課題解決アプローチの第二段階の最終部分は、解決されるべき客観的な技術的課題を設定することである。この点で、欧州特許庁の実務は、日本の実務から異なるように思われる。本質的に、当業者は、クレームに記載された発明が

or adapting the closest prior art to provide the technical effect that the invention achieves over the closest prior art. Care should be taken at this stage not to include any pointers to the technical solution in the objective technical problem. For instance, in the squash ball example from above, a suitable objective technical problem might be to modify the green (or black) squash ball so that it can be tracked by the human eye more easily in flight. An inappropriately formulated problem would be, for example, to *modify the colour* of the black or green squash ball so that it can be tracked more easily in flight since this would then already contain a pointer to the solution (i.e. modify the colour).

If no technical effect has been demonstrated over the closest prior art, or if an effect has not been demonstrated over the *whole scope* of the claim, the objective technical problem to be solved is to provide an *alternative* to that which was already known from the closest prior art. The fact that the objective technical problem is to provide an alternative does not mean that a patent cannot be granted since it is not a requirement to show an improvement over the closest prior art. Alternative ways to solve problems that have already been solved are perfectly acceptable, provided of course that the proposed alternative solution is not obvious.

If a claim contains a mix of technical and non-technical features, any non-technical features (e.g. computer program, business method, aesthetic appearance, etc.) *that do not contribute* to the technical character of the invention may appear in the objective technical problem to be solved as a constraint that is to be met. This ensures that only the innovation in a technical field (as opposed to innovation in a non-technical field) is considered when assessing if an invention is obvious. For example, a claim to a new type of computer running an innovative business method contains technical features (the new computer) and non-technical features (a computer program for the innovative business method). In this case the objective technical problem to be solved might be formulated as the provision of a computer for running *that innovative business method*. Here, regardless of

最も近い先行技術を超えて奏する技術的効果を提供するように、最も近い先行技術を変更又は適用する任務を負う。ここで、技術的課題を解決するための技術的手段についてのヒントを、客観的な技術的課題に含めないよう注意する必要がある。例えば、上記のスカッシュボールの例では、緑色（又は黒色）のスカッシュボールが飛んでいるところを人間の目で容易に追跡できるように変更することを客観的な技術的課題として設定することが適切であろう。不適切に設定された客観的な技術的課題とは、例えば、黒色又は緑色のスカッシュボールが飛んでいるところを容易に追跡できるように、黒又は緑の色彩を変更することである。このように設定された課題はすでに解決手段についてのヒント（すなわち、色彩の変更）をすでに含んでいるからである。

最も近い先行技術と比較して有利な技術的効果が実証されなかった場合、又はクレームの範囲全体にわたって効果が存在することが実証されなかった場合は、解決すべき客観的な技術的課題は、最も近い先行技術においてすでに知られたものに代わる発明を提供することである。客観的な技術的課題が代替手段を提供することであるという事実は、特許が付与され得ないということを意味しない。最も近い先行技術を超えた改良を示すことが特許性の要件ではないからである。すでに解決された課題を解決するための代替的な解決手段でも、その解決手段が自明でないことを条件に認められる。

クレームが技術的特徴と非技術的特徴との組合せである場合に、発明の技術性に貢献しない非技術的特徴（例えば、コンピュータプログラム、ビジネス手法、審美的外観）でも、解決すべき客観的な技術的課題に表される場合がある。発明が自明なものであるかどうかを判断する際に、（非技術的分野の革新とは対照的に）技術分野の革新のみが確実に考慮されることになる。例えば、革新的なビジネス手法を実行する新しいタイプのコンピュータについてのクレームは、技術的特徴（新規なコンピュータ）及び非技術的特徴（革新的なビジネス手法のコンピュータプログラム）を含んでいる。この場合、解決すべき客観的な技術的課題は、当該革新的なビジネス手法を実行するコンピュータの提供と設定される。ここで、ビジネス手法は、商業分野でいかに革新的となり得るかに関わらず、技術的発明（すなわち新規なコンピュータ）が最も近い先行技術からみて

how innovative the business method might be in the field of commerce, it is not taken into account when assessing if the *technical* invention (i.e. the new computer) is obvious in view of the closest prior art.

5.3 Stage 3: Would It have been Obvious?

The third and final stage of the PSA is to consider if the claimed invention would have been obvious: that is, would the skilled person, looking to solve the objective technical problem, have adapted or modified the closest prior art in a way that leads to the claimed invention? When looking to solve the objective technical problem the skilled person generally looks to his own and neighbouring technical fields for solutions. The solution may be part of the common general knowledge, it may be derivable from the closest prior art itself, or it may be found in another prior art disclosure (usually a second prior art document). Regardless of where the potential solution might lie, the Boards of Appeal have long recognised that, once an invention is known, it can often be shown how the skilled person *could* have made it by combining different teachings in the prior art (an "*ex post facto*" analysis). This kind of analysis must be avoided since it draws on knowledge of the invention. Therefore, to avoid hindsight creeping in at the final stage of the PSA the so-called "*could-would*" approach is routinely applied to consider if an invention is obvious.

5.3.1 Could-Would Approach

Rather than ask if the skilled person *could* have carried out the invention, the "*could-would*" approach requires that one ask if the skilled person *would* have carried out the invention *in the expectation* of solving the objective technical problem. In essence, the point is not whether the skilled person *could* have arrived at the invention by modifying the closest prior art, but rather whether, in expectation of the technical effect to be achieved (i.e. in the light of the objective technical problem to be solved), the skilled person *would* have done so using his common general knowledge or because of promptings in some other prior art disclosure.

自明なものであるかどうかを判断する際には考慮されない。

5.3 第三段階：自明なものか？

課題解決アプローチの第三（最終）段階では、クレームに記載された発明が自明なものであったかどうかを検討する。すなわち、客観的な技術的課題を解決しようとする当業者は、クレームに記載された発明に至る手法で、最も近い先行技術を適用し又は変更したであろうか？ 客観的な技術的課題を解決しようとする際に、当業者は、一般的に、解決手段について自身の技術分野及び隣接する技術分野に関心を向ける。解決手段は、技術常識の一部であったか、最も近い先行技術それ自体から導くことができたか、あるいは、他の先行技術（通常は、「二次」文献）の開示に見出すことができたか。審判部は、発明を知った後であれば、可能性ある解決手段がどこにあるかにかかわらず、先行技術の様々な教示を組み合わせることにより、当業者がどのように発明し得たか（「事後」分析）を示すことが可能になると認識している。この種の事後分析は、発明の知識を利用するものであるため回避されるべきである。よって、後知恵が課題解決アプローチの最終段階に取り込まれることを避けるために、発明が自明なものであるかどうかを検討するには、いわゆる「could-would」アプローチが通常適用される。

5.3.1 could-would アプローチ

could-would アプローチは、当業者が発明を実施することができたかどうかを問うよりも、客観的な技術的課題を解決することを期待して当業者が発明を実施したであろうかを問う。実際は、当業者が最も近い先行技術を変更することにより発明に到達することができたかどうかではなく、達成される技術的効果を期待して、すなわち解決されるべき客観的な技術的課題の観点から、当業者が、技術常識を駆使して、又は他の先行技術文献にある開示に促されて先行技術を変更したであろうかがポイントである。

One important caveat to this general *"could-would"* approach at the EPO is where the objective technical problem is to provide an *alternative* to that which is already known from the closest prior art. In this case the alternative invention can be viewed as one variation among a number of possible variations of the closest prior art. The Boards of Appeal have repeatedly stated that the simple act of arbitrarily selecting one variation among any number of equally obvious alternative variations is devoid of inventive character. It follows that the *"could-would"* approach (which requires that some motivation be shown for why the skilled person would consider a particular solution) is not particularly suited to situations where the objective technical problem is to provide an alternative. Instead, for these situations an invention is considered to be obvious if the feature that is missing from the closest prior art is already conventional for the technical field in question. Of course, even if the feature is shown to be conventional there must be no teaching away or incompatibility issues as otherwise the skilled person would not have modified or adapted the closest prior art to include it. The reader will appreciate that where the objective technical problem is to provide an alternative, the reduced burden to provide motivation generally makes it easier to establish that the invention is obvious.

5.3.2   *Reasonable Expectation of Success*

An important factor in determining if the skilled person *would* consider modifying the closest prior art in view of another prior art teaching is that he has a *reasonable expectation* that the modification will solve the objective technical problem. A reasonable expectation of success is something more than a *"hope to succeed"* as arguably all developments are made in the hope that they succeed. At the same time, the skilled person can be expected to tolerate some failure and so does not need to be certain of success. Whether there is a reasonable expectation of success is very much dependent on the technical field in question and the case in hand. In comparatively unpredictable fields, such as chemistry or biotechnology, it is oftentimes more difficult to establish a reasonable expectation of success in the absence of a direct link between the feature in question and how it can help

この一般的な「could-would」アプローチに対して、重要な警告が1つある。それは、客観的な技術的課題が、最も近い先行技術で既知の発明に代わるものを提供する場合である。この場合、発明の代替手段は、多くの他の可能な変形のうち、最も近い先行技術について可能な変形の1つとみなされる。審判部は、等しく自明な代わりとなるあらゆる数の変形から1つの変形を任意に選択する単純な行為は発明性を欠いていると判断した。これにより、「could-would」アプローチは、当業者が特定の解決手段を考える根拠として、なんらかの動機付けを示すことを要求しており、客観的な技術的課題が代替手段を提供するという状況には特に適したものではないとされた。当該状況では、最も近い先行技術の発明から欠けている特徴が、争点となる技術分野においてすでに標準的である場合は、クレームに記載された発明は自明なものとみなされる。もちろん、当該特徴が標準的であることが示されていても、反教示や不適合性があってはならない。反教示や不適合性があれば、当業者は、欠けている特徴を含めるために、最も近い先行技術の発明を変更し又は適用することもしなかったであろう。客観的な技術的課題が、代替手段を提供することである場合は、動機付けを与えるという負担が軽減されることにより、クレームに記載された発明が自明であることの立証が、概して容易になる。

5.3.2　成功への合理的な期待

他の先行技術の教示を考慮して、最も近い先行技術の変更を当業者が検討するかどうかを判断する際に、最も重要な要因は、その変更により客観的な技術的課題が解決されると当業者が合理的に期待するかどうかである。成功への合理的な期待とは、おそらく、開発が成功すると期待して行われるような「成功への期待」を超えるものである。当業者は、失敗することが多少は予期されるため、成功を確信する必要はない。成功が合理的に期待されるかどうかは、その技術分野及びそのケースに大きく左右される。化学やバイオテクノロジーなど比較的に予測が難しい分野では、争点となる特徴が客観的な技術的課題をどう解決するかについて直接的なリンクがなければ、成功の合理的な期待を確定することは困難な場合が多い。

to solve the objective technical problem.

5.3.3 Bonus Effect

A surprising technical effect is generally indicative that an invention is not obvious and therefore can be considered as involving an inventive step. However, there are certain cases where the surprising effect is considered to be a *bonus effect* that arises naturally from that which is already obvious. For example, where it is considered obvious to modify the closest prior art to achieve a particular effect, the fact that the effect is achieved to a surprising degree is considered to be a bonus effect that does not make the invention any less obvious.

Furthermore, where it is obvious to modify the closest prior art to achieve a particular effect, and there is only one way to do this (the so-called *"one-way street"*), then any secondary effect arising from that modification is considered to be a bonus effect. Which effect is considered crucial and which is merely accidental (the *"bonus effect"*) requires a realistic approach to be taken that takes into account the relative technical and practical importance of those effects in the circumstances of a given case. For example, imagine that the application for the blue squash ball is primarily concerned with reducing visible markings on the white walls of a squash court, and that improved trackability is something that is discussed only briefly. If it could be shown that it is obvious to the skilled person that blue is the *only* colour other than green that reduces visible markings, then it could be argued that providing a blue squash ball is obvious and that the improved trackability of the blue ball is merely a bonus effect arising from that which is already obvious. However, if it could be shown that colours other than green and blue would also reduce visible markings (i.e. there is no one-way street but instead a choice of possible solutions to this particular problem) then the fact that the blue ball *additionally* leads to improved trackability is an effect that can be relied upon to argue that the invention is not obvious.

5.3.3 ボーナス効果

　一般に、予期しない技術的効果があると、発明は自明なものではなく、進歩性の存在を肯定するものとなる。しかし、予期しない技術的効果が、すでに自明である事項から自動的に生じるボーナス効果とみなされる場合がある。例えば、ある特定の効果を達成するために最も近い先行技術を変更することが自明とみなされる場合は、その効果が予期しない程度であるという事実は、発明を非自明にするものではないボーナス効果であるとみなされる。

　さらに、最も近い先行技術を変更して特定の効果を達成することが自明であり、これを達成する手段が1つしかない場合は、いわゆる「一方通行」と呼ばれ、当該変更から生じる二次的効果はすべてがボーナス効果とみなされる。どの効果が決定的とみなされ、どの効果が偶発的なボーナス効果に過ぎないかは、ケースの状況に応じて、技術的、かつ、実際上の重要性を比較して考慮する現実的なアプローチを必要とする。例えば、青色のスカッシュボールの出願が、スカッシュコートの白い壁のマーキングを減らすことに主に関連しており、改良された追従性は簡潔に議論されるに過ぎないものであることを想像してみる。マーキングを減らす色として青色が緑色以外の唯一の色であることが当業者にとって自明であると立証できる場合は、青色のスカッシュボールを提供することは自明であり、青色のボールが有する改良された追従性は、すでに自明なものから生じるボーナス効果に過ぎない。しかし、緑色と青色以外の色でもマーキングを減らせることが立証できる場合は、一方通行ではなく、その代わりにこの特定の課題に対して他の解決手段を選択することが可能なのであって、青色のボールがさらに改良された追従性に至るという事実は、クレームに記載された発明が自明なものではないことを主張するための根拠となる効果である。

5.3.4 Other Considerations

Secondary indications such as a providing a solution to a long-felt need or enjoying commercial success can be taken into account when assessing if an invention is obvious. However, secondary indications of this kind are only of importance in cases of doubt, i.e. when *objective evaluation* of the prior art teachings has yet to provide a clear picture as to whether an invention is obvious.

6 Problem Inventions

It is the normal task of the skilled person to be constantly occupied with eliminating deficiencies, overcoming drawbacks and improving known devices and/or products. Therefore, the appreciation of conventional technical problems which form the basis of the normal activities of the skilled person, such as the removal of shortcomings, the optimisation of parameters or the saving of energy or time, do not involve an inventive step. However, in certain cases the discovery of an unrecognised problem may give rise to patentable subject-matter even if the claimed solution is retrospectively trivial and in itself obvious. In the squash ball example from above, one might argue that squash had been played for over one hundred years with the same black ball but nobody had appreciated that tracking a black ball against a white wall could be improved. Therefore, even if it could be shown that it was retrospectively obvious to improve trackability by making the ball blue, discovery of the unrecognised problem itself may provide basis for a patentable invention. That does not mean to say, however, that the absence of a hint in the prior art that there might still be a desire for further improvement means that an unrecognised problem has been discovered. The appreciation of a technical problem only contributes to inventive step in very exceptional circumstances.

5.3.4　他の考慮事項

　長年にわたる要求に対応して解決手段を提供すること、又は商業的成功を享受すること等の二次的な示唆は、発明が自明のものであるかどうかを判断する際に考慮される。しかし、この種の二次的な示唆は、（先行技術の教示の客観的評価によって、発明が自明なものであるかどうかに関する明確な実態がいまだ提供されていない場合等の）疑義のあるケースにのみ重要である。

6　課題についての発明

　当業者は、通常の業務として、不備の解消、欠点の克服、公知の装置及び／又は製品の改良の達成に常に専念する。よって、欠点の除去、パラメータの最適化、労力と時間の節約等、当業者の通常の活動の基礎を形成する従来の技術的課題を認識することでは、進歩性の存在は肯定されない。しかし、特定のケースでは、認識されていない課題の発見により、クレームされた解決手段が過去に照らすと些細なことであってそれ自体は自明なものであるという事実に関わらず、特許性のある対象が生じる場合がある。スカッシュボールの例では、同じ黒色のボールで100年以上もスカッシュがプレーされているが、白い壁に対して黒色のボールを追跡することの改良を誰も評価しなかったと主張できる場合があるかもしれない。よって、青色のボールを製造することにより追従性を改良することが、過去に照らして自明であったと立証できても、認識されていない課題の発見自体は、特許可能な発明の根拠を与える。しかし、さらなる改良の願望が依然としてあり得ることが先行技術で示唆されていないことが、認識されていない課題の発見とされるわけではない。技術的課題を認識することが進歩性に貢献するのは、非常に例外的な状況に過ぎない。

7 Summary

There are many similarities between the practice in Japan and that at the EPO when it comes to assessing if an invention is obvious. Chief among these is the need to establish what contribution the invention makes in view of the closest prior art and to assess whether the skilled person is motivated by the state of the art to modify the closest prior art when seeking to provide that contribution. Where practice at the EPO diverges somewhat is in the structured way that this contribution is formulated as the objective technical problem to be solved. Supporters of this approach argue that it allows for an objective assessment of the invention which only takes into account the actual technical contribution that is made with respect to the closest prior art. Critics argue that the objective technical problem can be artificial (e.g. by choosing a single closest prior art) and is divorced from reality (e.g. by combining two pieces of prior art to reach the invention). Either way, there is no doubt that following the three stages of the PSA provides a reasonably efficient and predictable means by which to assess if an invention is obvious.

7　まとめ

　日本と欧州の特許実務では、発明が自明なものであるかどうかの判断に関しては、多くの類似点がある。主な類似点は、最も近い先行技術に鑑みて、いかなる貢献が発明によりもたらされるかを確定すること、そして、その貢献をもたらそうとする際に、技術水準により動機付けられて最も近い先行技術を当業者が変更するかどうかを判断することである。欧州特許実務が多少異なっているところは、解決すべき客観的な技術的課題としてこの貢献が設定されるという構造化された手法にある。課題解決アプローチの支持者らは、最も近い先行技術に対してなされる実際の技術的貢献を考慮して、クレームに記載された発明について客観的な評価ができると主張する。課題解決アプローチの批判者らは、客観的な技術的課題は、（例えば、単一の最も近い先行技術を選択する点で）人為的であり、現実（例えば、発明に到達するために２つの先行技術を組み合わせること）から解離していると主張する。どちらにしても、課題解決アプローチの３つの段階を踏むことにより、発明が自明なものであるかどうかを判断する効果的、かつ、予測可能な合理的な手段が提供されることは疑いない。

Chapter 3

Prior Art

先行技術

Jan-Hendrik Spilgies

MEMO

▶ 第54条(2)では、「欧州特許出願の出願日前に、書面若しくは口頭による陳述、使用又はその他のあらゆる方法によって公衆に利用可能となったすべてのもの」が技術水準を構成すると定義しています。つまり、当該出願の出願日と同日にされた情報の開示は、技術水準の一部を構成しないと推定されます（§1.1）。この点、出願の時分までも考慮する日本の実務（特許法第29条第1項「特許出願前」）と異なります。

▶ 第54条(3)は、特許出願の出願日より前に出願日（又は有効な優先日）を有する欧州特許出願で、当該特許出願の出願日以後に公開された他の欧州特許出願の内容も技術水準に含まれると規定します。よって、第54条(3)との関連では「先願としての権利」と呼ぶことにします。その要件と範囲については、§2.1及び§2.2を参照してください。

▶ 第54条(3)は、日本特許法第29条の2（拡大先願権）と比較されることがありますが、異なる重要な点がいくつかあります。日本の実務では、発明者同一と出願人同一の場合は他の出願が引例となりません。また、他の出願が分割出願の場合には、第29条の2の判断との関係では、他の出願の出願日は遡及せず、現実の出願日となります（第44条第2項）。このような規定は欧州特許法にはありません。よって、有害な（Poisonous/Toxic）分割出願の問題が発生することがあります（§2.3）。

▶ 第55条は、新規性喪失の例外規定に相当しますが、その適用は非

常に限られています。誤って発明を早期に開示してしまった（出願日前6月内であっても）という出願人を救済するものではありません（§3.1）。国際的な博覧会による展示も、その博覧会が限定されています（§3.2)。

1 Definition of the State of the Art

Under the EPC, the "state of the art", or prior art, is defined in connection with the novelty requirement. The intention of the EPC is to prevent anything from being patented which is already a part of the state of the art. Thus, paragraph (1) of Art. 54 considers an invention "to be new if it does not form part of the state of the art". Paragraph (2) then goes on to define the state of the art as comprising "everything made available to the public by means of a written or oral description, by use, or in any other way, before the date of filing of the European patent application".

In defining the state of the art, the EPC applies an <u>absolute concept</u>, i.e. there are no restrictions whatsoever as regards the place where the information concerned was made available to the public, or the language or manner in which this occurred. There is neither any restriction in time (age), provided the information was made available before the filing date of the patent application concerned.

There are two, or rather three, exceptions to this absolute concept. Firstly, a European prior right, even though published only after the filing date of the patent application concerned, will be deemed to be part of the state of the art (Art. 54(3)). Secondly, there are two types of non-prejudicial disclosure which, even though publicly available, are not to be taken into consideration for the definition of the state of the art, provided that certain conditions are met (Art. 55).

1.1 Date of Disclosure

As regards the cut-off date for what constitutes prior art, Art. 54(2) refers to the "date of filing of the European patent application". From the expression "date of filing", it is derivable that a <u>day</u> is the minimum unit of time. Hence, it can be assumed that any disclosure of information <u>on the same day</u> as the filing date of the application does <u>not</u> form part of the state of the art (even if, e.g., the disclosure occurred in the morning and the filing only took place in the afternoon of

1 　技術水準の定義

　欧州特許条約では、「技術水準」すなわち先行技術は、新規性の要件と関連して定義される。欧州特許条約の目的は、すでに技術水準の一部となっているものが特許されることを防止することである。よって、第54条(1)は、発明は「技術水準の一部を構成しない場合は、新規性を有する」とみなしている。そして、第54条(2)では、「欧州特許出願の出願日前に、書面若しくは口頭による陳述、使用又はその他のあらゆる方法によって公衆に利用可能となったすべてのもの」が技術水準を構成すると定義している。

　技術水準を定義する際に、欧州特許条約は、絶対的な概念を適用している。すなわち、関連する情報であれば、公衆に利用可能となった場所、言語若しくは方法に制限がない。さらに、時間（時代）にも制限がない。ただし、その特許出願日前に当該情報が利用可能となったことを条件とする。

　この絶対的な概念には、2つというより3つの例外がある。1つ目は、欧州特許出願の先願としての権利であり、審査対象の特許出願の出願日以後にはじめて公開された場合であっても、技術水準の一部とみなされる（第54条(3)）。2つ目は、新規性に影響を与えない開示であり、公に利用可能となった発明であっても特定の条件が満たされれば技術水準を認定する際に考慮されないもので、これには2つのタイプの開示がある（第55条）。

1.1 　開示の日付

　何が先行技術を構成するかの基準日に関しては、第54条(2)は「欧州特許出願の出願日」に言及している。「出願日」の表現から、日が時間の最小単位であることが導き出せる。当該出願の出願日と同日にされた情報の開示は、技術水準の一部を構成しないと推定される。例えば、開示が朝に生じて、同日の午後に出願がされた場合である。

the same day).

The "date of filing" as referred to in Art. 54(2) is the date on which the documents filed by the applicant contain (a) an indication that a European patent is sought, (b) information identifying the applicant, and (c) a description or reference to a previously filed application (Art. 80 and R. 40(1)). When priority of an earlier application has been claimed in a valid manner, the date of priority will count as the date of filing (Art. 89).

The EPO will generally accept an indication in a document of the date of its publication as correct, unless sound reasons for contesting this are given (Guidelines B-VI 5.6). If the date of disclosure cannot be identified precisely, e.g., "ca. 1960", such disclosure may still constitute prior art if it occurred far earlier than the relevant filing date (T 267/03).

If a document, such as a diploma thesis or a copy of a journal, is received by a library, the mere arrival in the library does not yet render the document part of the state of the art. Usually, at the time of arrival, the document is not yet catalogued or otherwise prepared for the public to gain knowledge of the existence of the document and its content. Thus, the exact date of availability to the public will depend on the library routine used (T 314/99 and T 1137/97).

1.2 Availability

Generally, only information which has been made available "to the public" can constitute prior art under Art. 54(2). At the same time, "made available" does not require that one or more persons actually became aware of the information. Instead, it is sufficient if the public had the possibility of accessing and, thus, gaining knowledge of the information.

第54条(2)にいう「出願日」とは、出願人が提出した書類に、(a)欧州特許を求める旨の表示、(b)出願人を特定する情報、及び(c)明細書又は先にした出願の参照が含まれる日である（第80条、規則40(1)）。先の出願の優先権が有効に主張されている場合は、優先日を出願日とみなす（第89条）。

欧州特許庁は、一般に、十分な反対理由がない限り、書面に記載された日の表示を正しいものと受け入れる（審査基準B-VI 5.6）。「1960年頃」のように開示の日が正確に判別できない場合には、かかる開示が当該出願日よりはるか前に生じていれば、依然として先行技術を構成する（T 267/03）。

学位論文や雑誌のコピー等の文献が図書館で受け取られる場合、図書館に単に届けられただけでは、文献が技術水準の一部になったとはいえない。通常、到着の時点で文献はまだ目録に入れられず、あるいは文献及びその内容の存在を公衆が知るような準備がされることもない。よって、公衆に利用可能となった正確な日付は、利用する図書館の日常業務に左右される（T 314/99及びT 1137/97）。

1.2　利用可能性

一般に、「公衆に」利用可能となった情報のみが第54条(2)の先行技術を構成し得る。同時に、「利用可能となった」ことは、1人以上の者がその情報を実際に知ったことを要件としない。その代わりに、公衆がアクセスしてその情報の知識を得られる可能性があったことで十分である。

1.2.1 Public Information

Public availability of subject-matter requires that members of the public were able to gain knowledge thereof and that there was no bar of confidentiality restricting the use or dissemination of such knowledge. For instance, the registration of German utility models in the Utility Model Register will be published (announced) in the Patent Bulletin. However, the content of a utility model can be viewed by the public via inspection of the Register already from the date of registration. As a result, a German utility model will belong to the state of the art as of its date of registration, and not only as of the date of announcement of the registration.

Information is deemed to be available to the public if <u>at least one member of the public</u> is in a position to (i) gain access to the information and (ii) disseminate it to others.

On the one hand, the word "public" does not necessarily refer to the man in the street. On the other hand, the member of the public gaining access to the information in question does not have to be a person skilled in the art, provided that the member is capable of further distributing the information to skilled members of the public.

Requirement (ii) does not mean that the information must actually have been disclosed to further members of the public; it is sufficient if the at least one member of the public was in a position to do so, i.e. not being under an obligation to maintain secrecy.

In the case of a written disclosure, requirements (i) and (ii) will usually be satisfied as soon as the document concerned can be picked up and disseminated further. In the case of an oral disclosure, there is another requirement, namely that the at least one member of the public is a skilled person, or at least understands the information. Only if this condition is satisfied will it be possible to di-

1.2.1　公の情報

　発明の対象が公衆に利用可能であるとは、公衆の構成員がその情報を得ることができたこと、及び当該情報を使用したり、広めたりすることを制限する秘密保持義務の制約がなかったことを要件とする。例えば、実用新案登録簿へのドイツ実用新案の登録は、特許公報で公開される（公示される）。しかし実用新案の内容は、登録の日からすでに登録簿の閲覧により公衆に閲覧可能である。その結果として、ドイツ実用新案は、登録の公示日の時点だけでなく、その登録日の時点で技術水準に属することとなる。

　<u>公衆の少なくとも１人の構成員</u>が、(ⅰ)情報へのアクセスを取得し、かつ、(ⅱ)これを他者に広めることができる立場にあれば、情報は公衆に利用可能であるとみなされる。

　「公衆」の文言は必ずしも、通りにいる人を指すのではない。他方、問題となっている情報にアクセスすることができる公衆の構成員は、当業者である必要はない。ただし、その構成員は、公衆の別の構成員に情報をさらに広めることができる者であることを条件とする。

　要件(ⅱ)は、その情報が公衆の別の構成員に実際に開示されたに違いないということまでは意味しておらず、公衆の少なくとも１人の構成員が開示を行うことができる立場にあれば、十分である。つまり、秘密を保持する義務を負っていないのであれば十分である。

　書面による開示の場合には、通常、当該書面が手に取られてさらに配布され得る状態に置かれた途端に、要件(ⅰ)及び(ⅱ)が満たされる。口頭による開示の場合には、他の要件がある。つまり、公衆の少なくとも一人の構成員が当業者であること、又はその情報を少なくとも理解できることである。この条件が満たされるときに限り、当業者を含む他の構成員に情報を明かすことが可能となろ

vulge the information to further members of the public, including skilled persons.

1.2.2 Confidential Information

Information can only be publicly available in the sense of Art. 54(2) in the absence of an obligation of confidentiality or to maintain its secrecy.

Subject-matter is not deemed to have been made available to the public if there is an <u>express</u> or <u>tacit</u> agreement on secrecy, or if the circumstances of the case are such that such secrecy derives from a relationship of good faith or trust (Guidelines G-IV 7.2.2). Good faith and trust are factors which may occur in contractual or commercial relationships. For example, the content of a business meeting is not deemed to have been made available to the public if the parties concerned understood it to be secret and no breach of secrecy has been established. An understanding of this kind may be reached at a business meeting in the context of a joint technical development if the parties are assumed to have parallel interests and if there is a secrecy proviso agreed verbally and based on a stamp on a drawing (T 830/90).

However, even an existing non-disclosure agreement may not necessarily prevent certain subject-matter from becoming prior art, namely if the subject-matter has been further disseminated to the public in violation of the agreement (see item 3.1 below as regards the exception of Art. 55(1)(a)).

Despite the above, it should be noted that information does not become confidential for the sole reason that it is offered only with an obligation not to further disseminate it, as it is the case with many literature databases today. In fact, it is not necessary that the information be supplied free of charge, or that the recipient should be entitled to disseminate it, <u>provided others can obtain the information for themselves from the original source</u> (T 50/02).

う。

1.2.2　秘密情報

情報は、秘密保持義務又は秘密を維持する義務がない場合に、第54条(2)の意味で公衆に利用可能なものになる。

秘密性に関する明示又は黙示の契約がある場合、又は当該秘密性が善意又は信頼関係から導かれるような状況では、発明の対象が公衆に利用可能になったとはみなされない（審査基準G-IV 7.2.2）。善意及び信頼は、契約又は契約取引関係で生じ得る要因である。例えば、関係当事者らがビジネス会議の内容を秘密事項であると理解し、守秘義務違反が確立されない場合は、そのビジネス会議の内容は公衆に利用可能になったとはみなされない。この種の理解は、共同技術開発に関連するビジネス会議で、当事者らが共通の利益を有するものと推定され、かつ、口頭及び検印に基づき秘密条項に合意がされた場合である（T 830/90）。

しかし、守秘義務契約があっても、その契約に違反してある対象が公衆に広められた場合などでは、その対象が先行技術となることは必ずしも妨げられない（第55条(1)(a)の例外に関しては、以下セクション3.1参照）。

上述のとおりではあるが、情報が提供されるときにさらに普及させない義務があるという理由だけでは、その情報は秘密事項とはならないことをここで指摘しておく（これは、今日の文献データベースのほとんどの場合に当てはまる）。実際には、他者が出典から自力で情報を入手できるのであれば、当該情報が無償で提供され、又は受け手がこれを広めることができる必要はない（T 50/02）。

1.3 Types of Disclosure

Art. 54(2) imposes no limitation on the means of disclosure, which is in line with the EPO's absolute concept of the state of the art. Thus, the disclosure could be in writing, by oral presentation, by display of an object, or by (public) use or conducting of a method or process.

1.3.1 Written Disclosure

The usual form of prior art is generally a written document, and ordinary examples of such documents include patent documents and scientific or technical papers. However, any other form of written disclosure will be accepted, for example brochures, newspaper articles, or even handwritten notes taken, e.g., during a presentation.

While the existence of a written disclosure as such may not be in dispute, this may not apply to the time of its publication, or the question of its public availability (see 1.1 and 1.2 above).

As regards patent documents, they usually contain an indication as to their date of publication, so that the time of public availability will not be at issue. The EPO will, however, clearly distinguish between the publication of an application (A1, A2, etc.) and the publication of the granted patent (B1, B2, etc.), as the patent specification may include information not yet contained in the underlying application text.

The language of a document has no relevance on whether or not it constitutes prior art. In case of a patent document in a non-EPO language, the EPO may accept or cite a patent family member in an EPO language (English, French and German) for reference purposes, but the authoritative text and disclosure will always be the original document.

1.3　開示の種類

第54条(2)は、開示の手段にいかなる制限も課しておらず、これは欧州特許庁による技術水準の絶対概念と一致する。よって、開示は、書面、口頭による発表、対象物の展示、（公然での）使用又は方法若しくはプロセスの実行によるものであってもよい。

1.3.1　書面による開示

一般に、先行技術の通常の形式は書面であり、かかる書面の通常の具体例としては、特許文献、科学的又は技術的な論文がある。しかし書面による開示の他のいずれの形式も認められ、カタログ、新聞記事、あるいはプレゼンテーション等の際に取られる手書きのメモであってもよい。

このような書面による開示の存在には争いがない一方で、その公開の時期や、公衆による利用可能性の問題が争われる場合がある（上記セクション1.1及び1.2参照）。

特許文献に関しては、公開の日付に関する表示を含むのが通常であるため、おそらく、公衆に利用可能となった時期は争点とはならない。一方、特許の明細書には、その出願の出願書類には含まれない情報が含まれることもあるため、欧州特許庁は、出願の公開（A1、A2等）と付与された特許の公開（B1、B2等）とを明確に区別している。

文献の言語は、これが先行技術を構成するか否かとは関係ない。特許文献が欧州特許庁の公用語ではない言語による場合には、欧州特許庁は参照目的で欧州特許庁の言語（英語、フランス語、ドイツ語）によるパテントファミリーの1つを受け入れ、又は引用することがあるが、正式な原本及び開示は、常に、原語による文献である。

1.3.2 Oral Disclosure

A lecture or presentation, if made prior to the relevant filing date, can provide prior art, even though it may be difficult to ascertain the exact content of disclosure. Likewise, relevant state of the art may be generated by means of radio or television broadcasts.

Sometimes information is made available both orally (for example in a public presentation at a conference) and in writing (such as a subsequent scientific paper or conference proceedings). If only the oral presentation occurred before the relevant date, it cannot be assumed as a rule that the subsequent written document is identical in content to the oral presentation (T 1212/97). Written notes taken by an attendee of a conference will not automatically be accepted as prior art, as they are usually not made available to the public and may not be an accurate account of what was in fact conveyed to the public. Similarly, the lecturer's script may not exactly reflect what was actually presented to the audience.

Finally, it may be disputed whether or not the oral disclosure was made unconditionally in public, i.e. such that arbitrary members of the public were able to take notice.

1.3.3 Public Prior Use

State of the art may also be generated by producing, offering, marketing or otherwise exploiting a product, or by offering or marketing a process or its application or by applying the process. In this regard, marketing may be affected by sale or exchange.

When an object is displayed on the occasion of a trade fair or similar event, it is generally accepted that only those features of the object are made available to the public which are visible from the outside. Internal features of the object which can be recognized only upon opening or even dismantling the object are

1.3.2 口頭による開示

講義やプレゼンテーションは、該当する出願日の前にされたものであれば、正確な開示内容を確かめることが難しい場合であっても、先行技術となることがある。同様に、関連する技術水準は、ラジオやテレビ放送によって生じる場合がある。

時には、口頭（会議での公衆の面前でのプレゼンテーション等）と書面（その後の科学論文又は会議の議事録等）の双方で、特定の情報が公衆に利用可能となることがある。口頭によるプレゼンテーションのみが該当する出願日前に行われた場合は、その後の書面は、原則として、口頭によるプレゼンテーションと内容的に同一であるとは推定されない（T 1212/97）。会議の出席者が取った書面によるメモは、自動的に先行技術としては認められない。そのようなメモは、通常は、公衆に利用可能とならず、公衆に実際に伝達されたことを正確に反映していないからである。同様に講演者の原稿は、実際に聴衆に発表されたものを正確に反映していない場合がある。

最後に、口頭による開示は、無条件に公衆の面前でされたか否か（すなわち、公衆の不特定の構成員が注意を払うことができたかどうか）が争われる場合がある。

1.3.3 先の公然使用

技術水準は、物を製造し、譲渡の申し入れをし、市場に出し、その他利用することにより、又は方法若しくはその活用の申し入れをし若しくは市場に出し、又はその方法を活用することによって生ずる場合がある。市場に出すことは、販売又は交換によって生じる場合がある。

対象物が見本市又はそれに類似するイベントに展示される場合は、外部から見える対象物の特徴のみが公衆に利用可能であることが一般には認められている。対象物を開けたり、分解したりすることによってのみ認識できるその内部の特徴は、これに反する証拠が入手できない限りは、非公開であるとみなされ

deemed to be non-public, unless proof to the contrary is available.

For the use of an object or process to constitute part of the state of the art, the EPO will usually determine the following details (see Guidelines G-IV 7.2):

(i) the date on which the alleged use occurred, i.e. whether there was any instance of use before the relevant date;

(ii) what has been used, in order to determine the degree of similarity between the object used and the subject-matter of the European patent or patent application; and

(iii) all the circumstances relating to the use, in order to determine whether and to what extent it was made available to the public, as for example the place of use and the form of use.

These matters are oftentimes summarized as the When, What, How, Where and by Whom, and a public prior use will usually be acknowledged only if there is proof beyond reasonable doubt (T 2010/08).

1.3.4 Other Forms of Disclosure: Internet Disclosure

More recently, disclosure of information on the internet or in online databases has become a relevant source of prior art. Such information is considered to be publicly available as of the date on which the information was publicly posted. The EPO has published a specific Notice[1] setting out the EPO practice when citing documents retrieved from the internet. In view of the transient nature of online information, as compared to, e.g., a written document, it may be more difficult to establish, under the standard of balance of probabilities, (i) when a certain

---

[1] OJ 2009, 456 <http://archive.epo.org/epo/pubs/oj009/08_09_09/08_4569.pdf>

る。

　対象物又は方法の使用が技術水準の一部を構成するか否かにつき、通常、欧州特許庁は以下の詳細について判断する（審査基準 G-IV 7.2参照）。

(i)　主張された使用が生じた日（すなわち、該当する日前になんらかの使用の例があったか否か）

(ii)　何が使用されたか（使用された対象物と欧州特許又は欧州特許出願の対象の類似の程度を判断するためである）

(iii)　使用に関連するすべての状況（例えば、使用の場所及び使用の形態等）（公衆に利用可能となったか、及び、どの程度が利用可能となったかを判断するためである）

　これらの事項は、いつ、何が、どのように、どこで、誰によって、というようにまとめられ、先の公然使用は、通常、合理的な疑いを超えた立証がある場合にのみ認められる（T 2010/08）。

1.3.4　他の形式での開示：インターネットによる開示

　最近、インターネット又はオンラインデータベースで開示された情報が、先行技術の適切な情報源となっている。このような情報は、その情報が公に掲載された日付をもって公衆に利用可能になったとみなされる。欧州特許庁は、特定の通知[1]を公表してインターネットから検索された文献を引用する際の欧州特許実務を明確にした。オンライン情報の一過性的性質を考慮すると、書面等と比較して、蓋然性の均衡の基準の下では、(i)特定の開示がいつ生じたか、及び、(ii)問題となる内容が実際にその日付をもって利用可能となったか否かを確

---

[1]　欧州特許庁公報2009, 456 〈http://archive.epo.org/epo/pubs/oj009/08_09_09/08_4569.pdf〉

disclosure occurred and (ii) whether the content in question was actually made available to the public as of that date.

Generally, unless there are specific indications to the contrary, computer-generated timestamps will be considered by the EPO as reliable publication dates, and the frequently used "last modified" date will be accepted as the publication date. Where an explicit indication of the publication date is not available, or is unreliable, evidence for publication may be derived from an internet archive service such as the so-called "Wayback Machine" <www.archive.org>.

If a web page is in principle available without any bar of confidentiality, neither restricting access to a limited circle of people (for instance via password protection) nor requiring payment for access will prevent said web page from constituting part of the state of the art (Guidelines G-IV 7.5.1).

Sometimes the internet publication of a scientific journal predates the printed paper publication, and the internet publication may deviate from the printed publication, for example lacking the final revision of the author. Thus, the EPO will usually treat the internet publication on the one hand and the printed publication on the other hand as separate documents having separate publication dates and possibly contents.

1.4 Scope of Disclosure

The content of a prior art document is to be interpreted with the eyes of the skilled person at the time the document was published. For instance, when the meaning of certain terminology changed over time, the terminology used in a prior art document must be given the meaning which it had at the time of publication.

立することがより困難となる場合がある。

　一般に、それに反する特定の指摘がなければ、コンピュータにより作成されたタイムスタンプは、信頼できる公開日として欧州特許庁により考慮され、頻繁に使用される「最終更新」日が公開日として認められる。公開日の明確な表示が入手できず、信頼できない場合は、公開の証拠は、いわゆる「Wayback Machine」〈www.archive.org〉等のインターネット・アーカイブサービスから導くことができる。

　原則として、（例えば、パスワードによる保護を介する）限定された人々のグループにアクセスを制限することなく、又はアクセスに支払いを要求することなしに、秘密保持義務の制約なくウェブページを利用できる場合には、当該ウェブページが技術水準の一部を構成することを妨げない（審査基準 G-IV 7.5.1）。

　科学雑誌のインターネットによる公開は、時折、刊行物より前の日付となることがあり、インターネットによる公開は、著者の最終更新がされていない等、刊行物から外れたものとなる場合がある。よって、欧州特許庁は、通常、インターネットによる公開と刊行物とは、別々の公開日を有するものとして扱い、また、その内容も異なる可能性がある。

1.4　開示の範囲

　先行技術文献の内容は、その文献が公開された時点で当業者の視点で解釈されるべきである。例えば、特定の用語の意味が時間とともに変わった場合は、先行技術文献で使用される用語には公開の時点でそれが有していた意味が与えられるべきである。

1.4.1 Inherent Disclosure

If an object is provided unconditionally to a member of the public, the public is allowed an unlimited access to any material aspect of the object, including knowledge of any of its properties. That is, not only those features of the object are publicly available which may be ascertained from an external examination, but also those which require further analysis or testing.

For example, public sale of a piston made from a specific alloy will also make available the inherent, specific composition of the alloy in terms of types and amounts of constituent elements, or its specific gravity. In contrast, if the piston is merely displayed at a public exhibition, and the public can only view the piston, but has no possibility of analyzing the underlying alloy (being barred from taking the piston with it), then the composition of the alloy will not be part of the state of the art.

A document disclosing a (low molecular) chemical compound and its manufacture normally makes available this compound to the public in all desired grades of purity, provided that such degree of purity could be accomplished with conventional purification methods in this field (T 990/96).

1.4.2 Enabling Disclosure

For a prior art disclosure to have been made available to the public, it is necessary that the information given to the skilled person is sufficient to enable him, at the relevant date, to carry out the technical teaching of the disclosure, taking into account the general knowledge at that time (the relevant date will be the date of publication or, in case of prior art under Art. 54(3), the date of filing). In other words, the disclosure belongs to the state of the art only if the skilled person can reproduce that subject-matter using common general knowledge.

For example (see Guidelines G-IV 2), a document may describe a chemical

1.4.1 内在する開示

ある対象物が公衆の構成員に無条件に提供された場合は、公衆には、その対象物の物質的側面（その対象物の特性についての知見を含む）に無制限のアクセスが認められる。すなわち、外部検査から確かめられる当該対象物の特徴だけでなく、分析や試験をさらに必要とする特徴を含めて公衆に利用可能となるわけである。

例えば、特定の合金から作られたピストンを公に販売することにより、その合金を構成する成分の種類と量又はその比重の観点から、その合金に特有の組成が利用可能となる。これとは対照的に、ピストンが公の展示会で展示されたに過ぎず、公衆がピストンをじっくりと見ることはできるが、ピストンを取り去ることは禁じられており、ピストンを作っている合金を分析できない場合は、合金の組成は先行技術の一部とはならない。

（低分子）化合物及びその製造法を開示する文献により、通常、当該化合物は、その技術分野で知られる慣習的な精製方法により所望の純度が達成できるときは、そのすべての純度で公衆に利用可能となる（T 990/96）。

1.4.2 実施可能な開示

公衆に利用可能となった先行技術の開示に関しては、当業者に与えられた情報が当該日付において、当該時点での技術常識を考慮すると、開示の技術的教示を当業者が実施できるようにするのに十分であることが必要である（当該日付は公開日であり、第54条(3)の先行技術の場合は、出願日である）。換言すれば、当業者が技術常識を用いて発明の対象を再現できる場合にのみ、その開示は技術水準に属することとなる。

例えば、化合物が名称又は構造式によって文献に記述され、その化合物は当

compound, either by name or structural formula, and indicate that the compound may be prepared by a process also described in that document. If the document does not indicate the details of the process, including starting materials and reaction conditions, and if the skilled person cannot get hold of the starting materials and suitable process conditions on the basis of his common general knowledge, e.g., relying on textbook knowledge, then the document would be regarded as providing an <u>insufficient</u> (non-enabling) disclosure with respect to said compound. Insofar, the chemical compound would not constitute part of the state of the art. If, however, the starting materials are commercially available, are well-known or described in reference text books, and if the skilled person can likewise identify suitable process conditions, using common general knowledge, the compound will be regarded as sufficiently disclosed. As a result, in this case, it would form part of the state of the art.

1.4.3 Erroneous Disclosure

If a prior art reference contains an error, such error will not affect its relevance as prior art provided that the skilled person, using common general knowledge, can (i) readily recognize that there is an error and (ii) identify what the only possible correction should be. In such case, the document can be regarded as including the correction, and its disclosure should be interpreted accordingly, i.e. in a corrected manner (T 591/90).

In contrast, if the literal disclosure of a document is erroneous and does not reflect the intended technical information, such disclosure will not be included in the state of the art (T 77/87). In similar manner, published information may not be counted as forming part of the state of the art if the skilled reader will reject it as erroneous because it is evidently implausible (T 412/91).

該文献に記載された方法によって製造されることも示されている場合がある（審査基準 G-IV 2 参照）。当該文献が、出発材料及び反応条件を含む方法の詳細を示していない場合において、当業者が教科書の知識に頼るなど技術常識に基づいて出発材料及び適切なプロセス条件を把握できないときは、当該文献は前記化合物に関して実施可能ではない<u>不十分な開示</u>を提供するものとみなされる。その開示不十分な程度において、その化合物は技術水準の一部を構成しない。しかし、出発材料が市販されている場合、周知の場合、又は参考となる教科書に記載されている場合であって、かつ、当業者が技術常識を用いて適切なプロセス条件を同様に特定できる場合は、その化合物は十分に開示されているとみなされる。この場合、当該化合物は先行技術の一部を構成する結果となる。

1.4.3　誤った開示

先行技術文献が誤りを含んでいる場合であっても、以下を条件として、先行技術としての関連性に影響を与えない。すなわち、当業者が技術常識を用いて、(i)誤りがあることを容易に認識でき、かつ、(ii)その誤りの訂正として唯一可能なものを特定できることである。このような場合は、当該文献はその訂正を含んでいるものとみなされ、その開示は訂正された様式で解釈されるものとする（T 591/90）。

これとは対照的に、文献の開示が文言上誤っており、意図した技術情報を反映していない場合は、かかる開示は技術水準には含まれない（T 77/87）。公開された情報が一見して信じ難いという理由で、専門家である読み手がこれを誤りとして受け入れない場合も、技術水準の一部を構成するものとはみなされない（T 412/91）。

2 Prior Rights under Art. 54(3): Discussion According to EPC 2000 Only

Under the EPC, the state of the art also comprises the content of other European patent applications which were filed (or validly claim a priority date) earlier than the relevant date of filing of the patent application concerned, but which were only published on or after said date. These European patent applications constitute prior art only in the assessment of novelty, but not when considering inventive step (Art. 56). The aim of this provision is to prevent double patenting, accounting for the fact that a later applicant could become aware of the content of such a "prior right" only at the time of its publication, and not already at its date of filing.

2.1 Requirements

For a European patent application to constitute prior art under Art. 54(3), it must have a filing date which is before the relevant date of filing of the application concerned, and its publication date must be on or after that date. In addition, it is important that the prior right was still pending at the time of publication (it might be published despite its earlier withdrawal, namely when the withdrawal occurred at a time when the preparations for publication were already complete and, thus, publication could no longer be prevented) (J 5/81). Any changes in the state of the application after publication have no bearing on its effect as a prior right.

2.2 Scope

The "content" of a prior right is the whole disclosure of the application, including its description, drawings and claims, but excluding the abstract or the content of a priority document (both of which not being part of the application). The effect under Art. 54(3) covers all contracting states, independent of payment of a designation fee or withdrawal of designations. The effect also covers PCT ap-

2 第54条(3)の先願としての権利：
EPC2000に基づく考察

　欧州特許条約によると、技術水準には、特許出願の出願日より先に出願され（又は有効に主張された優先権の優先日がこれより先で）、当該特許出願の出願日以後に公開された他の欧州特許出願の内容も含まれる。かかる欧州特許出願は、進歩性（第56条）を考慮する際ではなく、新規性の判断においてのみ先行技術を構成する。当該規定の目的は、二重特許の防止である。後の出願の出願人は、「先願としての権利」（第54条(3)の規定による先行技術としての権利）の内容を、先の出願の出願日でなく、その公開の時になって知得する事実による。

2.1 要件

　第54条(3)の規定により先行技術を構成する欧州特許出願としては、その出願日が該当する出願の出願日前であり、かつ、その公開日が該当する出願日以後である必要がある。また、先願としての権利は、その出願が公開の時点で依然として係属していることが重要である。ここで、出願は、それが公開される前に取り下げられていても、公開される場合がある。つまり、公開の準備がすでに完了している時点で取り下げられたため、公開をもはや取りやめることができない場合である（J 5/81）。出願が公開された後に出願内容が変更されたとしても、先願としての権利には影響しない。

2.2 範囲

　先願としての権利の「内容」は、明細書、図面、クレームを含む出願書類全体としての開示であるが、要約又は優先権書類の内容は除かれる（この双方とも出願の一部とはならない）。第54条(3)による効果は、すべての締約国に及び、これは指定手数料を支払っているか、指定の取下げを行っているかに関係ない。この効果はEPを指定するPCT出願にも及ぶ。ただしPCT出願人が必要

plications designating EP, provided that the PCT applicant paid the required filing fee and, where applicable, supplied a translation into one of the official languages (English, French and German) to the EPO (Art. 153 and R. 159(1)(c)).

National rights of an earlier date in a Contracting State can <u>not</u> constitute state of the art under Art. 54(3). However, they may constitute a ground for revocation under national patent law after grant (Art. 139(2)). For this reason, if a relevant prior national right exists, the applicant may be allowed to submit separate claims for the Contracting State concerned (see Guidelines H-III 4.5).

2.3 Poisonous Priority Applications and Divisional Applications

If a European patent application claims priority from an earlier application, and either (i) the earlier application is a European patent application and was published, or (ii) a divisional application was filed and published, the priority or divisional application may constitute prior art under Art. 54(3) under specific circumstances. Namely, if the claims of the European patent application are broader in scope and, thus, not fully supported by its priority application, the disclosure of a specific embodiment in the priority or divisional application might be cited as a novelty-destroying disclosure. With decision T 557/13[2] of July 17, 2015, an EPO Technical Board of Appeal has referred questions to the Enlarged Board of Appeal to resolve this issue. The referral is presently pending under case G 1/15.

3   Non-Prejudicial Disclosure

The EPC does not provide for any grace period which would allow an inventor to disclose his invention prior to the filing of a patent application without said disclosure becoming state of the art. As explained in item 1.1 above, as a last resort, if an own disclosure occurred one day, and if this was noticed sufficiently early,

---

[2] <http://www.epo.org/law-practice/case-law-appeals/recent/t130557ex1.html>

な出願手数料を支払っており、必要に応じて公用語（英語、フランス語、ドイツ語）の１つで翻訳文を欧州特許庁に提出したことが条件である（第153条及び規則159(1)(c)）。

締約国における先の国内の権利は、第54条(3)の技術水準を構成し得ない。しかし、付与後に国内特許法による取消しの理由とはなり得る（第139条(2)）。先の国内の権利が存在する場合は、当該締約国用に別個のクレームを提出することが出願人に認められる場合がある（審査基準 H-III 4.5参照）。

2.3 有害な基礎出願及び分割出願

欧州特許出願が先の出願の優先権を主張している場合において、(i)当該先の出願が欧州特許出願であり、かつ、公開されており、又は、(ii)出願の分割がされ、その分割出願が公開されているときは、基礎出願又は分割出願は特定の状況下で第54条(3)による先行技術を構成することがある。すなわち、欧州特許出願のクレームがより広い範囲であるため、その優先権主張の基礎となる先の出願により完全にサポートされていない場合は、基礎出願又は分割出願に含まれる特定の実施形態の開示を引用して新規性が否定される場合がある。2015年７月17日付の審決 T 557/13[2]で欧州特許庁技術審判部は、この争点を解決するように拡大審判部に問題を付託した。付託は現在、G 1/15として係属中である。

3 不利とならない開示

欧州特許条約は、技術水準を構成することなく自己の発明を出願前に開示することを許容する猶予期間を発明者に一切与えていない。発明者が、ある日自分の発明を開示し、そのことに十分早く気づいた場合は、原則として、セクション1.1で説明したように、特許出願を準備して同日に出願し、その開示が不

---

[2] 〈http://www.epo.org/law-practice/case-law-appeals/recent/t130557ex1.html〉

then it might in principal be possible to prepare and file a patent application still on the same day, so that the earlier disclosure does not constitute detrimental prior art.

There are only two exceptions to the EPO's absolute state of the art concept, thus excluding certain disclosures from the prior art, as explained below. However, they will not usually "save" an inventor who, of his own volition or by accident, disclosed his invention prior to filing a patent application. Hence, it is strictly advisable to make sure that any own disclosure of an invention be postponed until after the filing date.

3.1 Evident Abuse

According to alternative (a) of Art. 55(1), a disclosure will not be included in the state of the art if, subject to the 6-month time limit explained below, it was due to an evident abuse in relation to the applicant or his predecessor. This pertains in particular to any disclosure of the invention which occurred despite an express or tacit confidentiality agreement. An "evident abuse" will be established only if there was actual intent to cause harm or knowledge that harm would or could ensue from the unauthorized disclosure (T 173/83). Insofar, early publication of an invention as a result of an error may not necessarily satisfy the requirement of "evident abuse" (T 585/92).

3.2 International Exhibition

A second exemption of disclosure from the prior art is the display of the invention by the applicant (or his legal predecessor) at an officially recognized exhibition (Art. 55(1)(b)). "Recognized exhibitions" are published regularly in the EPO Official Journal. For validly making use of this exemption, a respective statement regarding the display of the invention is required at the time of filing of the application. In addition, the applicant has to file a supporting certificate within four months from the filing date (Art. 55(2) and R. 25).

利に先行技術を構成することがないよう努めることができる。

　欧州特許庁の絶対的な技術水準の概念に関して、例外が２つだけあり、以下で説明するように、特定の開示が先行技術から除外される。しかし、これらの例外は、通常は、特許出願前に自分の意思で又は不注意で自分の発明を開示した発明者を「救済」しない。よって、出願日が確定するまで発明の開示を延期することを強く勧める。

3.1　明らかな濫用

　第55条(1)に規定される選択肢(a)によると、以下に述べる６月の期限の制限を受けることを条件として、発明の開示が、出願人又はその法律上の前権利者に対する明らかな濫用による場合は、その開示された発明は技術水準に含まれない。この規定は、特に、明示又は黙示の秘密保持契約にもかかわらず発明が開示されたことに関するものである。「明らかな濫用」は、損害を生じさせるという実際の意図があった場合、又は許可されていない開示から損害が生じるであろう又は生じ得たという知識があった場合にのみ成立する（T 173/83）。誤って発明を早期に開示してしまったという程度の発明の開示は、必ずしも「明らかな濫用」の要件を満たさない（T 585/92）。

3.2　国際博覧会

　発明の開示が先行技術を構成しないという例外の２つ目は、その発明が、出願人又はその法律上の前権利者により、公の又は公に認められた国際的な博覧会で展示されたことによる（第55条(1)(b)）。「公の又は公に認められた国際的な博覧会」は、欧州特許庁の公報に定期的に掲載される。この例外を有効に利用するために、発明の展示についての説明が出願時点で要求される。また、出願人は、出願日から４月以内にこれを裏付ける証明書を提出する必要がある（第55条(2)及び規則25）。

3.3 Time Limit

Any disclosure to be excluded from the state of the art under Art. 55(1) must have taken place not earlier than six months preceding the filing of the application. For calculating the 6-month period, the relevant date is that of the actual filing of the European patent application, not the priority date (G 3/98 and G 2/99).

3.3 期限

第55条(1)の規定により技術水準から除外される開示は、出願日前6月以内に生じたものでなければならない。6月の期間は、優先日ではなく欧州特許出願の実際の出願日を基準に計算される（G 3/98及びG 2/99)。

Chapter 4

Sufficiency of Disclosure

開示の十分性

Joachim Renken

MEMO

▶ 第83条は、「欧州特許出願は、当該技術分野における専門家が実施することができる程度に明確かつ十分に発明を開示しなければならない」と規定し、出願の明細書だけでなく欧州特許出願全体に言及しています。よって、欧州特許出願の開示の十分性は、その明細書、クレーム、及び（存在する場合は）図面に基づいて判断されます（§1）。この点、日本特許法第36条第4項第1号の規定の仕方とわずかに異なりますが、発明の完全な開示は明細書（発明の詳細な説明）において行われるのが通常ですので、開示の十分性又は実施可能性を判断する原則が、日本の特許法におけるものと類似することが解せます。

▶ 第83条との関連で、欧州実務では「その技術分野の専門家（以下、当業者）」という架空の人物が、欧州特許出願に含まれる情報について、その者がその発明を実施することができる程度に明確かつ十分であるかを判断します。ここでいう当業者は、進歩性の評価で登場する者と同様ですが、例外として、開示の十分性を評価する際には、当該当業者は、先行技術の知識だけでなく開示された発明の知識も有しています（§2）。

▶ 日本特許庁審査基準によりますと、実施可能要件の判断との関係で想定される当業者は、その発明の属する技術分野において研究開発（文献解析、実験、分析、製造等を含む）のための通常の技術的手段を用い、通常の創作能力を発揮できる者とされ、この者が、明細書及び図面に記載した事項と出願時の技術常識とに基づき、クレームに記載された発明を実施することができるかを判断します（第

II 部第 1 章第 1 節参照)。進歩性の判断との関係で想定される当業者は、当該発明の属する技術分野の出願時の技術常識を有し、研究、開発のための通常の技術的手段を用いることができ、材料の選択や設計変更などの通常の創作能力を発揮でき、かつ、当該発明の属する技術分野の出願時の技術水準にあるものすべてを自らの知識とすることができる者であり、当該当業者は、発明が解決しようとする課題に関連した技術分野の技術を自らの知識とすることができる、とあります（第 III 部第 2 章第 2 節参照）。

▶ 欧州実務では、当業者の試行錯誤は必ずしも特許出願を開示不十分なものとはしません（§3）。日本の実務でも、「当業者に期待しうる程度を超える」試行錯誤は実施可能要件が満たされないと判断されます。

▶ 医薬発明に関しては、欧州実務では、薬理試験結果の記載が当初明細書等に存在することが必ずしも絶対的でない場合があります（§6）。この点、日本の実務とは多少異なるかもしれません。

Introduction

As in any other patent law, the European Patent Convention requires the patentee to make the subject matter of the invention available to the public in return to the grant of the monopoly right. It is thus unsurprising that the principles for the assessment of sufficiency of disclosure or enablement under the EPC are similar to those under Japanese Patent Law.

1   Legal Basis

The basic legal provision for sufficiency of disclosure in the EPC is Article 83:

> *The European patent application must disclose the invention in a manner sufficiently clear and complete for it to be carried out by a person skilled in the art.*

Since a European patent application may not be amended in such a way that it contains subject-matter which extends beyond the content of the application as filed (Art. 123(2) EPC), it is not permissible to add further information to the application at a later stage to rectify insufficiency issues. Hence, it is clear that the requirement of sufficiency of disclosure has to be met at the date of filing.

It should also be noted that Article 83 EPC not only refers to the description of the application, but to a European patent application as a whole. Therefore, European patent applications can be assessed for sufficiency of disclosure on the basis of their description, claims and their drawings, if any. In other words, it is not a requirement that any single part (e.g. claims) of the application should sufficiently disclose an invention.

Nevertheless, it is usually in the description that an invention is fully dis-

はじめに

他の法域の特許法と同様に、欧州特許条約は、特許権者に対し独占権の付与と引き換えに発明の対象を公衆に利用可能にするよう求める。よって、開示の十分性又は実施可能性を判断する欧州特許条約の原則が、日本の特許法におけるものと類似することは驚くに値しない。

1　法的根拠

欧州特許条約における開示の十分性についての基本的な法規定は、第83条である。

> 欧州特許出願は、当該技術分野における専門家が実施することができる程度に明確かつ十分に発明を開示しなければならない。

当初の出願書類の内容を超える対象を含めるように欧州特許出願の補正をしてはならないため（第123条(2)）、開示不十分の問題を解消するために後の段階で出願に新たな情報を追加することは許されない。そのため、開示の十分性の要件は出願日の時点で満たされていなければならないことが明らかである。

また、第83条が出願の明細書だけでなく欧州特許出願全体に言及していることにも留意すべきである。よって、欧州特許出願の開示の十分性は、その明細書、クレーム、及び（存在する場合は）図面に基づいて判断される。言い換えれば、出願のいずれか単独の部分（例えばクレーム）により発明が十分に開示されていることは要件ではない。

そうはいうものの、発明の完全な開示は通常は明細書において行われる。明

closed. The provisions relating to the content of the description are set out in Rule 42(1) EPC.

The description shall:

(a) specify the technical field to which the invention relates;

(b) indicate the background art which, as far as is known to the applicant, can be regarded as useful to understand the invention, draw up the European search report and examine the European patent application, and, preferably, cite the documents reflecting such art;

(c) disclose the invention, as claimed, in such terms that the technical problem, even if not expressly stated as such, and its solution can be understood, and state any advantageous effects of the invention with reference to the background art;

(d) briefly describe the figures in the drawings, if any;

(e) describe in detail at least one way of carrying out the invention claimed using examples where appropriate and referring to the drawings, if any;

(f) indicate explicitly, when it is not obvious from the description or nature of the invention, the way in which the invention is industrially applicable.

Since the examiner of a patent application does not have the means to test and verify statements made by the applicant, an applicant may obtain a patent without facing any objections as to lack of sufficient disclosure. This may change in opposition proceedings, and in fact very often does, at least in cases relating to inventions in chemistry or biotechnology, as lack of sufficient disclosure is a ground for opposition (Art. 100(b) EPC).

細書の内容に関係する規定である規則42(1)には以下のとおり定められている。

　明細書は、次のように記述する。

(a)　その発明が関連している技術分野を特定する。

(b)　出願人の知る限りにおいて、その発明を理解し、欧州調査報告を作成し、さらに、その欧州特許出願を審査するうえで有用であると思われる背景技術を表示し、また、できれば当該技術を反映している書類を引用する。

(c)　クレームに記載された発明を、その技術的課題（そのように明示的に陳述されていない場合を含む）及びその解決手段を理解することができるような表現で開示し、また、背景技術との関連においてその発明が有利な効果を有する場合は、その効果を記述する。

(d)　図面がある場合は図面の図について簡単に説明する。

(e)　クレームに記載された発明を実施するための少なくとも1つの方法を詳細に説明する。その場合は、適切なときは実施例を使用し、図面があるときはその図面を参照する。

(f)　発明の説明又は内容から明らかでない場合は、その発明が産業上利用可能である方法を明示的に指摘する。

　特許出願を審査する審査官は、出願人が記載した内容について試験及び検証を行う手段を持たない。そのため、出願人は、開示十分性の欠如の拒絶理由を受けることなく特許を取得できる可能性がある。一方で、開示十分性の欠如は特許異議の申立理由となっているので（第100条(b)）、この状況は特許異議申立手続においては異なり、実際のところ、少なくとも化学又はバイオテクノロジーに関連する発明の事案においては、当該状況が異なることが多い。

2 The Person Skilled in the Art and Common General Knowledge

Article 83 refers to "the person skilled in the art". This fictitious person determines whether the information as contained in the European patent application is sufficiently clear and complete to allow him or her to carry out the invention. The person skilled in the art is the same person that is used for assessing inventive step with the exception that when assessing sufficiency of disclosure, the person skilled in the art not only has knowledge of the prior art but also of the invention as disclosed (T 694/92).

The person skilled in the art is considered to resemble an ordinary practitioner aware of common general knowledge in the art at the relevant date, is capable of routine work and experimentation and is presumed to have access to everything in the state of the art, in particular handbooks and basic textbooks (*cf.* Guidelines for examination in the EPO, G-VII 3).

It should be borne in mind, however, that the person skilled in the art is not inventive (T 39/93) and is a captive of established prejudices in his field (T 455/91). In an invention entailing multiple technical fields where multiple skilled people are required to perform an invention, the person skilled in the art may be considered to be a group of people skilled in their respective fields (T 141/87; T 99/89).

The skilled person's common general knowledge will "automatically" be added to the described teaching. In other words, the assessment of sufficiency of disclosure must be based on both the written disclosure of the patent document as well as the common general knowledge available to the skilled worker.

The common general knowledge of the person skilled in the art has been defined by the Boards of Appeal as being normally represented by the content of encyclopedias, handbooks and dictionaries on the subject in question (T 766/91;

2　当業者及び技術常識

　第83条は、「その技術分野の専門家（以下、当業者）」に言及している。この架空の人物が、欧州特許出願に含まれる情報について、その者がその発明を実施することができる程度に明確かつ十分であるかを判断する。ここでいう当業者は、進歩性の評価で登場する者と同様であるが、例外として、開示の十分性を評価する際には、当該当業者は、先行技術の知識だけでなく開示された発明の知識も有している（T 694/92）。

　当業者は、該当する日におけるその分野の技術常識を把握し、通常の業務及び実験を行うことができ、当該技術水準のすべて、特に、ハンドブック及び基礎的な教科書にアクセスできると推定される通常の実務者にたとえられる（審査基準G-VII 3を参照）。

　一方、当業者に独創性はないこと（T 39/93）、当業者はその分野で確立された先入観にとらわれていること（T 455/91）を念頭に置く必要がある。発明を実施するために複数の当業者が必要とされる多技術分野にわたる発明においては、当業者は、各分野の当業者からなるグループであると考えられる（T 141/87、T 99/89）。

　当業者の技術常識は、明細書に記載された教示に「自動的に」追加される。言い換えれば、開示の十分性は、特許書類の書面による開示及び当業者に利用可能な技術常識の両方に基づいて判断される。

　審判部は、当業者の技術常識を、問題の対象について百科事典、ハンドブック、及び辞書で記載されている内容により通常代表されるものとして定義している（T 766/91、T 206/83、及びT 234/93）。研究分野が新しいためテキスト

T 206/83; and T 234/93). When a field of research is so new that technical knowledge is not yet available from textbooks, patent specifications and scientific publications have exceptionally been considered as belonging to the skilled person's common general knowledge (T 51/97; T 772/89).

Moreover, the content of databases may belong to the common general knowledge, provided the following requirements are met (T 890/02): Firstly, the database should be known to the skilled person as an adequate source to obtain the required information. Secondly, the database is one from which the required information may be retrieved without undue burden, without the need of a search strategy. Thirdly, the database must provide the required information in a straightforward and unambiguous manner without doubts or need for further research work. These criteria were held applicable to all types of information sources, not only databases.

In decision T 890/02, the Board considered the information provided in the ENZYME and EMBL databases to belong to the common general knowledge, as the skilled person knows beforehand which type of information will be retrieved and can do so readily by inputting the name or EC number of the enzyme or nucleotide sequence. On the other hand, the Chemical Abstracts database was held to fail these requirements as a search in this database is a search over the complete prior art and anybody looking for information there is required to use sophisticated search strategies. Moreover, the kind of information retrieved cannot be anticipated before the search is made and more often than not, the skilled person would need to further pursue the original published articles.

In addition to his common general knowledge, the person skilled in the art may also obtain information required to reproduce the invention from another document which is cited in the original description (T 267/91; T 611/89).

ブックから技術的な知識が入手できない場合には、特許明細書及び科学出版物が、例外的に、当業者の技術常識に属するものとみなされる（T 51/97、T 772/89）。

さらに、以下の要件が満たされることを条件に、データベースの内容も技術常識に属する可能性がある（T 890/02）。第一に、当該データベースは、必要な情報を得るための適切な情報源として当業者に知られていることである。第二に、当該データベースは、調査戦略を立てることなく、過度の努力なしに必要な情報を検索できるものであることである。第三に、当該データベースは、疑義又はさらなる研究作業の必要性を伴わずに、必要な情報をわかりやすく、かつ、はっきりとした方法で提供するものであることである。これらの基準は、データベースだけでなく、すべての種類の情報源に適用される。

審決 T 890/02において、審判部は、「ENZYME」及び「EMBL」のデータベースにより提供される情報を技術常識に属するものとした。どの種類の情報が検索されるかが予め当業者にわかり、酵素又はヌクレオチド配列の名称又はEC 番号を入力することで容易に検索が行えるためである。これに対して、「Chemical Abstracts」データベースは、前述の要件を満たさないとされた。このデータベースでの検索は先行技術全体の検索であり、このデータベースで情報を探そうとする者は洗練された検索方法を用いる必要があるためである。また、検索できる情報の種類を当業者が検索前に予め予測することはできず、当業者は公開されている原著論文をさらに追い求めることを強いられる。

当業者は、技術常識に加えて、明細書で引用された別の文献から当該発明を再現するために必要な情報を取得することもできる（T 267/91、T 611/89）。

3 Reproducibility

The European patent application must be sufficiently clear and complete to allow its reproduction.

According to Rule 42(1)(e) EPC, the description shall therefore *describe in detail at least one way of carrying out the invention claimed using examples where appropriate and referring to the drawings, if any.* Thus, examples are required where appropriate. However, if for example the patent specification gives precise instructions on what to do, examples may not be necessary (T 984/00).

The examples should confirm that the description of the patent application provides a coherent, convergent teaching enabling the skilled person to arrive at the goals of the claimed invention, and should thus make an extensive research programme superfluous. Examples should provide the person skilled in the art with all essential details necessary for the verification of their reported results (e.g. by repetition, if necessary), such as starting materials, process features and process conditions (T 1140/06).

If a specifically described example is not repeatable, this does not necessarily mean that the requirement of sufficiency of disclosure is not met (T 281/86). Rather, what is required is that the patent application describes the invention in sufficiently clear terms so that a person skilled in the art can reproduce it without "undue burden". Even occasional failures and the necessity of trial-and-error experimentation does not necessarily render a patent application insufficient. A certain amount of trial and error is acceptable as long as a course of action is described that points in the direction of how to perform the invention even if negative results are initially obtained (T 322/93). However, trial and error becomes unacceptable if, on receiving a suboptimum result, no further direction is given as to how to perform the invention (T 727/95).

3　再現性

欧州特許出願は、発明の再現をすることができる程度に明確かつ十分でなければならない。

規則42(1)(e)によれば、明細書は、「クレームに記載された発明を実施するための少なくとも1つの方法を詳細に説明する。その場合は、適切なときは実施例を使用し、図面があるときはその図面を参照する」。このため、適切と思われるときは、実施例が必要である。しかし、例えば、何を行うべきかについての詳細な指示が明細書に記載されている場合には、実施例が必要とされないこともある（T 984/00）。

実施例は、クレームに記載された発明のゴールに当業者が到達できるよう、特許出願の明細書が一貫した教示を与えることを確実にするものでなければならず、さらなる研究計画を不必要にするものでなければならない。実施例は、報告された結果を（例えば、必要な場合は、繰り返しにより）検証するために必要不可欠なすべての詳細（出発物質、方法の特徴、及び方法の条件等）を当該技術分野における当業者に提供しなければならない（T 1140/06）。

具体的に記述された実施例が反復不可能な場合でも、それは必ずしも開示の十分性の要件が満たされないことを意味するものではない（T 281/86）。むしろ、必要とされているのは、当業者がその発明を「過度の負担」なしに再現できるように、十分に明確な用語を使って当該発明が特許出願書類に記載されていることである。時折発生する失敗や試行錯誤の必要性は、必ずしも特許出願を開示不十分なものとはしない。一連の行為が記載されており、どのように発明を実施するかを方向付けるポイントが示されている限り、当初は否定的な結果が得られたとしても、ある程度の試行錯誤は許される（T 322/93）。一方、準最適な結果が得られても、当該発明を実施する方法についてさらなる方向が示されていない場合は、それに必要とされる試行錯誤は許されない（T 727/95）。

4 Claim Scope

The requirement of sufficiency of disclosure must be satisfied over the entire claim scope. The description of one way of performing the invention is thus sufficient only if it allows the invention to be performed in the whole range claimed. The question of whether one way is sufficient is a question of fact that must be answered on the basis of the available evidence, and on the balance of probabilities in each individual case (T 409/91).

When a claim covers a broad field or range, a patent application should not usually be regarded as satisfying the requirements of Article 83 EPC unless the description gives a number of examples or describes alternative embodiments or variations extending over the area protected by the claims (Guidelines F-III 1). In such a case, the fact that the claim also covers non-working embodiments may not be harmful, and it is neither necessary nor appropriate to disclaim such non-working embodiments (G 1/03).

5 Parameter Claims and Functional Features

A product may be characterized by its parameters when the invention cannot be adequately defined in any other way, provided that those parameters can be clearly and reliably determined either by indications in the description or by objective procedures which are usual in the art (Guidelines F-IV, 4.11; T 94/82). In other words, when an invention is defined by a physical parameter, the requirement of sufficiency of disclosure is fulfilled only if the skilled person knows how said parameter can be measured with an acceptably accurate result, to an extent that any skilled person carrying it out will produce essentially the same result (T 541/97). If the gap between the explicit information about the measurement method provided in the patent and the necessary information to obtain acceptably accurate results cannot be filled by the skilled person's common general knowledge or a cross-referenced document, the application fails for lack of suffi-

4 クレームの範囲

開示十分性の要件は、クレームの範囲全体にわたって満たされていなければならない。よって、発明を実施するための方法が1つ記載されていれば十分なのは、クレームに記載された範囲全体にわたる発明の実施がその記載により可能になる場合のみである。1つの方法で十分か否かは、入手可能な証拠及び個々の事案における蓋然性のバランスに基づいて回答すべき問題である（T 409/91）。

クレームが広い領域又は範囲をカバーする場合は、明細書にいくつかの実施例が示されているか又はクレームにより保護される範囲全体に及ぶ代替的実施形態若しくはバリエーションが記載されていない限り、通常、その特許出願は第83条の要件を満たしているとはみなされない（審査基準F-III 1）。このような場合において、機能しない実施形態をクレームがカバーしているという事実があっても不利にはならない可能性もあり、このような機能しない実施形態をディスクレームすることは必要とされず、また適切でもない（G 1/03）。

5 パラメータクレーム及び機能的特徴

物の発明において、他のあらゆる方法ではその発明を適切に特定できない場合に、パラメータによりそれを特徴付けることが可能であるが、明細書における記述又は当該技術分野で通常使われる客観的手段のいずれかにより、これらのパラメータを明確、かつ、確実に決定することができることを条件とする（審査基準F-IV 4.11、T 94/82）。言い換えれば、物理的パラメータにより発明を特定する場合は、どうすれば許容範囲の正確度でそのパラメータを測定できるか（当該測定を実施するすべての当業者が原則的に同じ結果を得る程度の正確度で測定できるか）を当業者が認識できるときに限って、開示の十分性の要件が満たされるということである（T 541/97）。その特許に示されている測定法についての明確な情報と、許容範囲の正確度で結果を得るために必要な情報との間のギャップを、当業者の技術常識又は相互参照文献により補充することができない場合には、当該出願は開示十分性の要件を満たしていないことになる

cient disclosure (see e.g. T 805/93). Such a cross-referenced document is oftentimes an industry standard such as a JIS standard. However, such reference to industry standards should be used with caution as industry standards oftentimes do not specify all measurement conditions either.

Applicants also often use functional claim language with the aim of maximizing the protective scope and sometimes try to define the invention by a result to be achieved. Such claims are usually not allowed, in particular if they only amount to claiming the underlying technical problem (Guidelines F-IV 4.10). However, they may be allowed if the invention either can only be defined in such terms or cannot otherwise be defined more precisely without unduly restricting the scope of the claims. Moreover, the result must be one which can be directly and positively verified by tests or procedures adequately specified in the description or known to the skilled person and which do not require undue experimentation (T 68/85).

A functional definition of a compound by means of its binding to a receptor ("reach through claims") lacks a sufficient disclosure if the identification of further compounds showing this function, besides those that are exemplified in the patent application, requires undue experimentation. If such further compounds can be prepared with routine methods (e.g. antibodies) or if there is a "selection rule" for these compounds (T 1063/06), there may be no undue burden. A selection rule can possibly be a structure-activity relationship on the basis of which the skilled person could identify from the outset suitable compound classes, or the indication of a specific compound class (e.g. nucleic acids; T 216/96) in combination with the functional definition.

6   Pharmaceutical Inventions

In applications relating to pharmaceutical inventions where the therapeutic effect, such as the treatment of a specific disease, is in the claim, the patent appli-

（例えば、T 805/93を参照）。かかる相互参照文献は、JIS規格等の業界規格であることが多い。ただし、業界規格はすべての測定条件を明記してはいないことが多いため、業界規格の参照は慎重に行うべきである。

出願人は、特許により保護する範囲を最大化するため、機能的なクレームの文言を用いることも多く、また達成するべき結果により発明の特定を試みることもある。かかるクレームは、通常は認められず、根本的な技術的問題をクレームしている場合は特に認められない（審査基準F-IV 4.10）。しかし、このような文言によってしか当該発明を特定できない場合、又はそれ以外ではクレームの範囲を不当に制限せずに発明を特定することができない場合は、かかるクレームは認められることもある。さらに、当該結果は、明細書で適切に詳述された又は当業者に周知の試験又は手順によって直接的かつ確実に検証可能なものでなければならず、かつ、過度の実験を必要としないものでなければならない（T 68/85）。

受容体に対する結合という手段を用いて化合物を機能的に特定すること（以下、「リーチスルークレーム」という）は、その特許出願において例示されたもの以外に当該機能を呈する追加的化合物を特定する目的で過度の実験が必要とされる場合には、開示の十分性を欠くとされる。かかる追加的化合物が常法により調製できる場合（例えば、抗体等）、又はこれらの化合物に「選択ルール」（T 1063/06）が存在する場合には、過度の負担が存在しないとされる可能性もある。「選択ルール」としては、構造活性相関であってそれに基づき当業者が適切な化合物クラスを最初から特定できるようなものや、機能的定義との組合せで具体的な化合物クラス（例えば、核酸：T 216/96）の表示が考えられる。

6　医薬発明

医薬発明に関連する出願で、特定の疾病の治療等の治療効果がクレームに含まれる場合、開示十分性の要件を満たすためには、当該特許出願はその効果を

cation must make said effect plausible to fulfill the requirement of sufficiency of disclosure. If the effect is not in the claim (e.g. in case of pure compound claims), the lack of plausibility is a question of inventive step, rather than one of sufficiency of disclosure (G 1/03). The patent application should thus provide some information in the form of, for example, experimental tests, to the effect that the claimed compound, administered as stated in the claims, has a direct effect on a metabolic mechanism specifically involved in the disease (T 491/08). This mechanism must be either known from the prior art or demonstrated in the application per se.

What kind of experimental data is necessary thus depends on the type of disease and the knowledge of the metabolic mechanism involved in the disease. The experimental data may be obtained with cell cultures or immobilized biological markers/receptors *in vitro* or *in silico* or with animal models regarded as appropriate for reasonably inferring the possibility of a treatment of human beings. Data obtained with human patients is only required, if no established animal model exists (see e.g. T 1001/01; T 158/96; T 715/03).

In exceptional cases, the therapeutic effect may be plausible even without experimental data (see e.g. T 108/09, where the application however contained a detailed protocol of a planned clinical trial).

7 Deposit of Biological Material and Antibodies

It is oftentimes difficult, if not impossible, to adequately describe how to reproduce certain biological material. If an applicant files a patent for an invention using such biological material that is not available to the public, this can lead to a lack of sufficient disclosure. He must deposit the biological material in a recognised publicly accessible depositary institute. The relevant law for applications before the EPO is Rule 31(1) EPC.

蓋然性あるものとしなければならない。効果がクレームに含まれない場合（例えば、純粋化合物クレームの場合など）は、蓋然性の欠如は開示十分性の問題ではなく、進歩性の問題である（G 1/03）。よって、特許出願は、クレームに記載された化合物をクレームに記載されたとおりに投与した場合に、その疾病に特異的に関係する代謝機序に対して直接的な効果があることを示すなんらかの情報を（例えば実験形式で）提供する必要がある（T 491/08）。この機序は、先行技術により知られているか、又は当該出願自体により説明されている必要がある。

どのような種類の実験データが必要とされるかは、疾病の種類及びその疾病に関与する代謝機序についての知識に依存する。実験データは、*in vitro* 若しくは *in silico* における細胞培養若しくは固定化された生物学的マーカー／受容体を用いて、又は人間の治療への可能性を合理的に推論するうえで適切と認められる動物モデルを用いて得ることができる。確立された動物モデルが存在しない場合は、人間患者についてのデータが要求される（例えば、T 1001/01、T 158/96、T 715/03を参照）。

実験データなしでも治療効果に蓋然性があるとされる例外的な場合もある（例えば、実験データはないが出願に臨床試験計画の詳細なプロトコルが記載されていた事案がある T 108/09を参照）。

7　生物学的材料及び抗体の寄託

特定の生物学的材料を再現して作る手順を適切に記載又は概説することは、不可能でないにしても、困難であることが多い。公衆に利用可能ではないこのような生物学的材料を用いる発明について出願人が特許出願をする場合には、開示の十分性に欠けるという結果に導かれる。出願人は、公衆がアクセスすることのできる承認された寄託機関にその生物学的材料を寄託しなければならない。欧州特許庁へ出願する場合、該当する法規定は、規則31(1)である。

According to this provision, the applicant should deposit cell lines and microorganisms under the Budapest Treaty at an international depositary authority such as the National Institute of Technology and Evaluation, Patent Microorganisms Depositary (NPMD) before the application's effective date. If this is not (properly) done, the application may be insufficiently disclosed, which cannot be cured at a later point.

Thus, the sufficiency of disclosure of an antibody may be established by reference to a deposited hybridoma cell line. However, applicants should pay attention to the fact that the reference to a single deposit may not be sufficient for a claim wherein the antibodies are defined by their function, e.g. their binding to a certain antigen, as in this case the requirement of sufficiency of disclosure may not be fulfilled over the entire claim scope (T 1466/05). If the function is the binding to a known antigen, the requirement of sufficient disclosure is however regularly met since the techniques for the production and selection of hybridomas are deemed to be common routine techniques.

Rule 31(1)(d) EPC regulates the conditions under which an invention involving the use of (deposited) biological material satisfies the requirements of sufficiency of disclosure when the depositor of such material does not correspond to the applicant of the patent application. If the depositor is a coapplicant of the EP application, then the provisions of Rule 31(1)(d) EPC do not apply. If the deposit was made by someone else, the requirements of this rule are fulfilled if the depositor has authorised one of the applicants (see Official Journal of the EPO 10/2010 par. 3.8).

For PCT applications published in an EPO official language (e.g., English), the indications of Rule 31(1)(d) EPC (name and address of the depositor, and the statement) must be furnished to the International Bureau (IB) within 16 months from the effective filing date. This time limit is deemed to have been met if the indication reaches the IB before the technical preparations for international publication have been completed (*i.e.* before entering the EP regional phase!) if they

この規定によれば、出願人は、ブダペスト条約に基づき、有効な出願日より前に、国際寄託機関（例えば、独立行政法人製品評価技術基盤機構、特許微生物寄託センター）に細胞株及び微生物を寄託しなければならない。寄託が（適切に）行われない場合、その出願は開示不十分とされることがあり、後の時点でこれを是正することはできない。

　よって、抗体についての開示の十分性は、寄託されたハイブリドーマ細胞株を参照することにより確立できる場合がある。一方、抗体がその機能により特定されているクレームについては、単一の寄託物を参照するだけでは十分でないことがあるという事実に出願人は注意を払うべきである。例えば、抗体がその機能（例えば、特定の抗原との結合）で特定されている事案では、開示の十分性の要件がクレームの範囲全体について満たされない可能性がある（T 1466/05）。けれども、当該機能が既知の抗原への結合であれば、ハイブリドーマの生産及び選択の手法が一般的な通常手法であるとみなされるため、開示の十分性の要件は通常満たされる。

　規則31(1)(d)は、（寄託された）生物学的材料の使用を含む発明において、当該材料の寄託者が特許出願の出願人と一致しない場合に、かかる出願が開示の十分性の要件を満たすための条件を定める特別の規定である。寄託者が欧州特許出願の共同出願人である場合には、規則31(1)(d)の規定は適用されない。それ以外の者による寄託の場合、寄託者が出願人の1人に承諾を与えているときに規則31(1)(d)が満たされる（欧州特許庁公報2010年10月号第3.8項参照）。

　欧州特許庁の公式言語（例えば英語）で公開されたPCT出願の場合は、有効な出願日から16月以内に、規則31(1)(d)の表示（寄託者の名称及び宛先、並びに証拠書類）を国際事務局に提出しなければならない。この提出期限は、当初提出された出願に当該表示が記載されていない場合でも、国際公開のための技術的準備が完了する前（すなわち、欧州領域段階への移行前）に当該表示が国際事務局に到達すれば、遵守されたものとみなされる。規則31(1)(d)の要件がこの期

are not present in the application as originally filed. As a consequence of not complying with the requirements of R. 31(1)(d) EPC within this time limit, the application could be refused by the EPO examiner for insufficiency of disclosure. Further information and an example of depositor's statement of authorisation and consent can be found in the Official Journal of the EPO 10/2010.

8 Evidence

The burden of proof to establish insufficiency of disclosure generally lies upon an opponent or the examiner. An insufficiency objection generally presupposes that there are serious doubts, substantiated by verifiable facts, regarding enablement (T 19/90). When the patent does not give any information of how a feature of the invention can be put into practice, only a weak presumption exists that the invention is sufficiently disclosed. In such case, the opponent can discharge his burden by plausibly arguing that common general knowledge would not enable the skilled person to put this feature in practice. The patent proprietor then has the burden of proof for contrary assertion that common general knowledge would indeed enable the skilled person to carry out the invention (T 63/06).

Sufficiency of disclosure is a requirement that the EP patent application must comply with from the filing date. The insufficiency cannot be cured *a posteriori*, since this would add matter (contravening Art. 123(2) EPC). Accordingly, evidence published after the filing date cannot establish sufficiency of disclosure. For instance, if the description in a patent specification provides no more than a vague indication of a possible medical use for a chemical compound yet to be identified, more detailed evidence cannot be used later to remedy the fundamental insufficiency of disclosure of such subject-matter (T 609/02).

Evidence published after the filing date can however be taken into account to back-up the findings in the patent application, e.g. in relation to the use of an ingredient as a pharmaceutical (T 609/02).

限までに遵守されなかった場合は、開示が不十分であるとの理由で欧州特許庁の審査官により出願が拒絶される可能性がある。承諾及び同意に関する寄託者の陳述書の詳細と具体例は、欧州特許庁公報2010年10月号に記載されている。

8　証拠

一般に、開示不十分を確立する立証責任は、異議申立人又は審査官にある。開示不十分の理由は、一般に、検証可能な事実に裏付けられた重大な疑義が実施可能性についてあることを前提としている（T 19/90）。発明の特徴をどのように実施するかについての情報を特許が提供していない場合は、その発明が十分に開示されているとの推定は弱いものでしかない。そのような場合には、異議申立人は、当業者が技術常識に基づいてこの特徴を実施することはできないという説得力のある議論を行うことにより立証責任を果たすことができる。そうすると立証責任が転換され、特許権者は、技術常識に基づいて、当業者であればたしかにその発明を実施することができると反論することになる（T 63/06）。

開示の十分性の要件は、欧州特許出願の出願日の時点で満たされていなければならない。不十分な開示を後から是正することは、出願内容の追加に該当するため第123条(2)の規定に違反することとなり不可能である。したがって、出願日の後に公開された証拠により開示の十分性を立証することはできない。例えば、まだ特定されていない化合物の潜在的医学的用途について、特許明細書には曖昧な示唆しか記載されていない場合、このような発明の対象についての根本的に不十分な開示を、さらに詳細な証拠を用いて後から是正することは不可能である（T 609/02）。

一方、ある成分が医薬として用いられることが発見された場合等、特許出願における発見を裏付けるために出願後に公開された証拠が考慮されることがある（T 609/02）。

9 Conclusion

Sufficiency of disclosure is a basic requirement for a European patent. While corresponding objections are not so common in examination proceedings, sufficiency of disclosure often plays a decisive role in opposition proceedings. This is particularly true in the fields of pharmacy and biotechnology, where most of the case law on this requirement has developed. This case law reveals differences with respect to approaches taken by other patent offices.

9　結論

　開示の十分性は、欧州特許の基本的要件である。出願段階では、開示の十分性の要件が満たされないことによる拒絶理由はそれほど頻繁にみられないが、特許異議申立手続においては開示の十分性が決定的役割を果たすことが多い。これは、薬事及びバイオテクノロジーの分野に特に当てはまり、当該要件についてのケースローは、ほとんどがこの分野で確立されたものである。当該ケースローによれば、他の特許庁のアプローチとは異なるアプローチが欧州特許庁で採用されていることがわかる。

Chapter 5

Patentable Subject-Matter I

特許の対象 I

Andreas Stefferl

MEMO

▶ 第53条は、法上の「発明」に該当しても特定の理由により特許の対象から除外される事項を規定しています。

▶ 第53条(a)の事由は、日本特許法第32条の不特許事由に相当します（§1参照）。

▶ 第53条(b)により植物の品種が特許の保護対象から除外されている理由は、日本と類似します。第53条(b)では、植物の品種以外にも特許の保護から除外される対象を列挙しています。

▶ 第53条(c)に規定される3つ方法の例外は、EPC1973の下では、産業上利用することができないという法的擬制に基づくものでした。改正後の欧州特許条約（EPC2000）では、この法的擬制を取り止め第53条(c)において特許性の例外として規定されました（§3）。

▶ 第53条(c)では「人間又は動物」というように規定され、拡大審判部により、特許権によって「医療及び獣医の活動」が制限されるのを防ぐことが第53条(c)の意図である（G 1/83、G 5/83及びG 6/83）と明確にされています。一方、日本では、手術、治療又は診断する方法の対象に人間が含まれないことが明らかでなければ、人間を手術、治療又は診断する方法として取り扱われる点で異なります（審査基準第III部第1章参照）。

Introduction

According to Art. 52(1) EPC, "European patents shall be granted for **any inventions**, in **all fields of technology**, provided that they are new, involve an inventive step and are susceptible of industrial application."

In principle, thus, the EPC provides broad access to patentability for "inventions" that provide a technical contribution to the art. The broad language of Art. 52(1) EPC is quite similar to Art. 27(1) of the TRIPS Agreement[1], which equally speaks of "any invention" in "all fields of technology".

However, there are important limitations to patentability of certain kinds of subject matter. In fact, therefore, not "any" invention in "all" fields of technology is eligible to patent protection. The legislator's motivation to exclude certain types of inventions from patent protection is as diverse as is the nature of the exclusions. It ranges from fundamental moral principles such as human dignity and the right to life, to more profane aspects like the avoidance of double protection for plant varieties under the EPC and plant variety protection acts. Other exclusions are motivated by socio-economic concerns, like the freedom of medical practitioners to treat patients, unimpeded by any patent rights.

In the EPC2000, the various exceptions to patentability are defined in Art. 53 EPC. The function of Art. 53 EPC is distinct from that of Art. 52(2) and (3) EPC. Whilst Art. 52(2) and (3) defines subject matter that is not considered an invention in the first place[2], Art. 53 EPC excludes subject matter *even though* it is considered an invention, i.e. a technical contribution to the art.

---

[1] The TRIPS Agreement dates from 1994, i.e. it is twenty years younger than the EPC. Its Art. 27(1) reads: *Patentable Subject Matter* 1. Subject to the provisions of paragraphs 2 and 3, patents shall be available for any inventions, whether products or processes, in all fields of technology, provided that they are new, involve an inventive step and are capable of industrial application.

はじめに

第52条(1)によれば、「欧州特許は、新規性、進歩性及び産業上の利用可能性のある**すべての技術分野のあらゆる発明**について与えられる」。

したがって、原則として、欧州特許条約は、先行技術に対して技術的貢献をもたらす「発明」に特許性があると幅広く規定している。第52条(1)の広範な文言は、TRIPS協定第27条(1)[1]と類似しており、TRIPS協定第27条(1)においても同様に、「すべての技術分野」における「あらゆる発明」と記載されている。

一方で、特定の対象については、その特許性に重要な制限が課されている。よって、「すべて」の技術分野における「あらゆる」発明に対して特許による保護が与えられないのが実際のところである。特定の発明を特許による保護から除外しようとする立法者の動機は、除外のタイプと同様に様々である。それは、基本的な道徳原則（例えば、人間の尊厳及び生命に係る権利）から、より世俗的な側面（例えば、欧州特許条約及び植物品種保護法下における植物品種の二重保護の防止）に及ぶ。その他は、社会経済的懸念（例えば、医療従事者が患者を治療する自由は、いかなる特許権によっても妨げられない）が動機となっている。

EPC2000は、第53条で特許性の例外を規定している。第53条の機能は、第52条(2)及び(3)の機能と明確に異なる。第52条(2)及び(3)は、発明に該当しない対象を定義しているのに対して[2]、第53条は、対象が発明（すなわち、先行技術に対する技術的貢献）と考えられる場合であっても、それを特許の対象から除外している。

---

[1] TRIPS協定は1994年から始まる。すなわち、TRIPS協定は、EPCよりも20年新しい。第27条(1)は特許を受けることができる対象を以下のように記載している：(2)及び(3)の規定に従うことを条件として、特許は、新規性、進歩性及び産業上の利用可能性のあるすべての技術分野のあらゆる発明（物であるか方法であるかを問わない）について与えられる。

Art. 53 EPC defines exclusions from patentability in three categories:

(a) inventions that contravene "ordre public" or morality

(b) plant or animal varieties or essentially biological processes for the production of plants or animals[3];

(c) methods for treatment of the human or animal body by surgery or therapy and diagnostic methods practised on the human or animal body[4].

These exceptions from patentability pursuant to Art. 53 EPC are similar, but not identical to the wording of Art. 27(2) and (3) of the TRIPS agreement[5].

In practical terms, the consequences of these exceptions to patentability are very different. They range from the severe consequence of completely excluding certain subject matter from patent claims (e.g. business methods, surgical methods), to the much milder consequence of finding acceptable claim wording for (essentially) the same subject matter (e.g. methods of treatment).

---

[2] Art 52(2) EPC lists the following (non-limiting) examples of subject matter that is not considered an invention: discoveries, scientific theories and mathematical methods; aesthetic creations; schemes, rules and methods for performing mental acts, playing games or doing business, and programs for computers; presentations of information. A common denominator of these types of subject matter is their "non-technical" nature. The EPO does not accept patentability of "business methods".

[3] **not** excluded are: microbiological processes or the products thereof.

[4] **not** excluded are: products, in particular substances or compositions, for use in any of these methods (Art. 54(4) and (5) EPC).

[5] Like Art. 53(a) EPC, Art. 27(2) TRIPS speaks of "ordre public or morality". The TRIPS agreement exemplifies this further, "including to protect human, animal or plant life or health or to avoid serious prejudice to the environment". Art. 53(b) EPC resembles Art. 27(3)(b) TRIPS, notably, however, TRIPS does not speak of "varieties" but more broadly of plants and animals. Art. 53(c)EPC resembles Art. 27(3)(a) TRIPS, "for the treatment of the human or animal body" is phrased "for the treatment of humans or animals" in TRIPS.

第53条は、特許の対象からの除外を3つのカテゴリで規定する。

(a) 「公の秩序」又は善良の風俗に反する発明

(b) 植物若しくは動物の品種又は植物若しくは動物を生産する本質的に生物学的な方法[3]

(c) 人間又は動物の体を手術又は治療により処置する方法及び人間又は動物の体を診断する方法[4]

第53条に規定する特許性の例外は、TRIPS協定の第27条(2)及び(3)の文言と類似しているが、同一ではない[5]。

実際、これらの特許性の例外はまったく異なる帰結をもたらす。クレームから特定の対象（例えば、ビジネス方法、手術方法）を完全に除くという厳しい結末から、（本質的に）同一の対象（例えば、処置方法）について、認められ得るクレームの文言を見つけ出すというマイルドな結末にわたる。

---

[2] 第52条(2)には、発明とみなされない対象について、以下の（非限定的な）例が列挙されている：発見、科学の理論及び数学的方法；美的創造物；精神的行為、ゲーム又は事業を行うための計画、ルール及び方法、並びにコンピュータプログラム；情報の提示。これらの種類の対象に共通する特徴は、「非技術的な」性質である。欧州特許庁は、「ビジネス方法」の特許性を認めていない。

[3] 微生物学的方法又は微生物学的方法による生産物は除外されない。

[4] これらの方法のいずれかで使用するための物（特に、物質又は組成物）は除外されない（第54条(4)及び(5)）。

[5] 第53条(a)のように、TRIPS第27条(2)には「公の秩序又は善良の風俗」について記載されている。TRIPS協定は、これについて「人間、動物若しくは植物の生命若しくは健康を保護し又は環境に対する重大な損害を回避することを含む」とさらに例示している。第53条(b)は、TRIPS第27条(3)(b)に特に似ているが、TRIPSには「品種」について記載されておらず、より広く植物及び動物について記載されている。第53条(c)は、TRIPS第27条(3)(a)に似ているが、「人間又は動物の体の処置のための」は、TRIPSでは「人間又は動物の治療のための」と表現されている。

The most frequently encountered exception from patentability concerns methods of treatment and diagnosis. As the EPC, however, allows patentability of products for use in methods of treatment/diagnosis (Art. 53(c) EPC, Art. 54(4) and (5) EPC), Applicants frequently have to adapt the claim language when prosecuting an application containing "US-style" language before the EPO. In certain constellations, finding appropriately amended language can be challenging.

In fact, the earliest decisions of Enlarged Board of Appeal (G 1/83, G 5/83, G 6/83) were an interpretation of the exception of therapeutic methods. Ever since then, and including some recent decisions, the Enlarged Board had to further clarify the various exceptions under Art. 53 EPC.

The three sub-paragraphs of Art. 53 EPC and their interpretation by the Enlarged Board of Appeal will now be discussed in more detail.

1 Inventions That Contravene "Ordre Public or Morality" (Art. 53(a) EPC)

In day-to-day practice, the exclusion of inventions contrary to "ordre public" or morality has, for a long time, been of little significance. The dogmatic discussion focused, for example, on products or devices with a "dual use", i.e. having potentially "immoral" as well as "moral" applications. For example, a chemical agent may have the potential to kill human beings, but, on the other hand, may have a morally acceptable use, e.g. as intermediates in a production process. Similarly, certain devices may have (potentially) immoral applications, as well as morally acceptable ones. According to EPO practice, such products or devices having "dual use" are considered patentable. In other technical fields, e.g. weapons of mass destruction, it is not common to seek for patent protection, in the first place.

最も頻繁に遭遇する特許性の例外は、処置及び診断方法に関するものである。一方で、欧州特許条約は、処置／診断方法に使用する物については特許性を認めている（第53条(c)、第54条(4)及び(5)）。そのため、「米国式」の文言を含む出願は、欧州特許庁での審査の際にクレームの文言を修正しなければならないことが多い。事案によっては適切に補正する文言を見つけることが難しい。

実際、拡大審判部の最初期の審決（G 1/83、G 5/83、G 6/83）は、治療方法の例外について解釈することであった。それ以来、最近の審決を含め、拡大審判部は、第53条の様々な例外をさらに明確にしてきた。

拡大審判部による解釈とともに、第53条に設けられた規定を以下で詳細に説明する。

1　「公の秩序又は善良の風俗」に反する発明（第53条(a)）

「公の秩序」又は善良の風俗に反する発明を特許の対象から除外することは、日常の実務では長い間あまり重要ではなかった。その議論は、例えば、「二重用途」（すなわち、潜在的に「非道徳的な」用途及び「道徳的な」用途）を有する物又はデバイスに集中していた。例えば、化学的薬剤は人間を殺す潜在性を有するが、道徳的に許容可能な用途（例えば、製造工程における中間体）も有し得る。同様に、特定のデバイスは、（潜在的に）「非道徳的な」用途とともに、道徳的に許容可能な用途も有し得る。欧州特許実務によれば、「二重用途」を有する上記のような物又はデバイスは、特許を受けることができるとみなされている。他の技術分野（例えば、大量破壊兵器）では、特許による保護を求めることがそもそも一般的ではない。

1.1 Art. 53(a) EPC in the Context of Biotechnological Inventions

More recently, however, with the advent of biotechnology, Art. 53(a) EPC and the respective rules in the Implementing Regulations have gained considerable attention. The field of biotechnology has been subject to – oftentimes controversial – public debate, and, on the level of the European Union, has lead to the issuance of the so-called "Biotech directive" 98/44/EC of July 6, 1998. The aim of the directive was to harmonize the approach to biotechnological inventions across the member states of the European Union. Following this political aim, the EPO has adopted key aspects of the directive, such as the definition of "biotechnological invention", into its Implementing Regulations (see definitions in Rule 26 EPC). The directive is to be used as a supplementary means to interpret the EPC (Rule 26(1) EPC).

Biotechnological inventions are such concerning "biological material" (Rule 26(2) EPC), which means material "containing genetic information and capable of reproducing itself or being reproduced in a biological system" (Rule 26(3) EPC). Biotechnological inventions, in principle, are patentable under the EPC (Rule 27 EPC), even though there are important exceptions.

As concerns the exception from patentability under Art. 53(a) EPC, explicit guidance can be found in Rule 28 EPC, that lists the following biotechnological inventions as un-patentable:

(a) processes for cloning human beings;

(b) processes for modifying the germ line genetic identity of human beings;

(c) uses of human embryos for industrial or commercial purposes.

The law-maker's concern as regards human beings is further reflected in Rule 29 EPC, which excludes from patentability the "human body and its ele-

1.1　生物工学的発明との関連における第53条(a)

一方、最近では、生物工学の出現により、第53条(a)及びそれに関連する施行規則に大きな注目が集まっている。生物工学の分野は（多くの場合に賛否両論がある）国民的な議論となっており、欧州連合レベルでは、1998年7月6日にいわゆる「生物工学的発明の法的保護に関する指令」98/44/EC が発行された。当該指令の目的は、欧州連合の加盟国全体で、生物工学的発明に対するアプローチを統一することであった。この政治的な目的に従って、欧州特許庁は、当該指令の重要な側面（例えば、「生物工学的発明」の定義）をその施行規則に採用した（規則26の定義を参照）。当該指令は、欧州特許条約を解釈するための補助的手段として使用すべきものである（規則26(1)）。

生物工学的発明は、「生物学的材料」に関するものである（規則26(2)）。「生物学的材料」とは、「遺伝子情報を含んでおり、それ自体で繁殖すること又は生物系において繁殖することが可能な」材料を意味する（規則26(3)）。重要な例外はあるものの、原則として、生物工学的発明は、欧州特許条約の下では特許を受けることができる（規則27）。

規則28は、第53条(a)の特許性の例外に関して明確なガイドラインを規定し、特許を受けることができない生物工学的発明として以下のものを列挙している。

(a)　人間をクローン化する方法

(b)　人間に係る生殖細胞系の遺伝子的同一性を変更する方法

(c)　工業目的又は商業目的での人間の胚の使用

人間に関する立法者の懸念は、規則29においてさらに反映されており、「人間の体及びその構成要素」を特許の対象から除外している。一方で、人間の体

ments". Not excluded, however, are elements isolated from the human body or produced by means of a technical process, even if these isolated elements are identical to that of a natural element (Rule 29(2) EPC). Thus, for example isolated (human) gene sequences may represent patentable subject matter under the EPC (Rule 29(2) EPC). The EPC imposes a limit, however, in so far as "the industrial application of a sequence or a partial sequence of a gene must be disclosed in the patent application" (Rule 29(3) EPC). This requirement follows suit from the restriction that the mere discovery of an element of the human body, such as a gene sequence, cannot constitute a patentable invention (Rule 29(1) EPC).

These exceptions in European practice do not, however, go as far as the current approach on natural products of the USPTO, following the controversial implementation of the decisions *Alice v. CLS Bank, Mayo and Myriad* into USPTO Examination Guidelines. In fact, Rule 27 EPC explicitly supports patentability of biological material isolated from its natural environment, even if it previously occurred in nature (Rule 27(a) EPC).

1.2 Patentability of Human Embryonic Stem (ES) Cells

The exception to patentability for moral reasons has been interpreted by the Enlarged Board of Appeal in its decision **G 2/06**. Also subject of this interpretation was the guidance of Rule 28 EPC, in particular the prohibition to "use human embryos for industrial or commercial purposes" (Rule 28(c) EPC).

In its decision G 2/06, the Enlarged Board of Appeal found that claims to human embryonic stem cells contravene Art. 53(a) EPC. The Enlarged Board reasoned that for the generation of human embryonic stem cells, it is necessary to destroy a human embryo, and that the destruction of a human embryo contravenes morality. More specifically, the Enlarged Board reasoned that the destruction of a human embryo to generate an ES cell line represents an industrial or commercial use, contrary to Rule 28(c) EPC. Some time after G 2/06, the Court of Justice of the European Union (CJEU) was considering patentability of human

から分離された構成要素や、技術的な方法によって生産された構成要素は、たとえ自然界に存在する構成要素と同一であっても、除外の対象ではない（規則29(2)）。よって、欧州特許条約の下では、例えば、分離された（人間）遺伝子配列は、特許の対象に相当し得る（規則29(2)）。ただし、欧州特許条約は、「遺伝子の配列又は部分的配列の産業上の利用は、特許出願において開示しなければならない」という制限を課している（規則29(3)）。この要件は、人間の体の構成要素（例えば、遺伝子配列）の単なる発見は、特許を受けることのできる発明を構成しないという制限（規則29(1)）に倣ったものである。

しかしながら、欧州特許実務における上述の例外は、天然物に関する米国特許商標庁の現行のアプローチ（これは、*Alice v. CLS Bank, Mayo and Myriad* 判決を USPTO の審査基準に組み入れた後のものである）ほどのものではない。規則27は、実際のところ、生物学的材料であって、自然界においてそれがすでに生じている場合であっても、自然環境から分離されているものの特許性を明確に支持している（規則27(a)）。

1.2 人間胚性幹（ES）細胞の特許性

道徳的な理由による特許性の例外は、拡大審判部によって審決 G 2/06で解釈された。この解釈の対象は規則28の指針であり、特に、「工業目的又は商業目的での人間の胚の使用」の禁止（規則28(c)）についてであった。

審決 G 2/06において、拡大審判部は、人間胚性幹細胞のクレームは第53条(a)に反すると認定した。拡大審判部は、人間胚性幹細胞を作製するためには人間の胚を破壊する必要があり、人間の胚の破壊は道徳に反すると判断した。より具体的には、拡大審判部は、人間の胚を破壊して ES 細胞株を作製することは工業目的又は商業目的での使用に相当し、規則28(c)に反すると判断した。G 2/06審決の後しばらくして、欧州連合司法裁判所（CJEU）は、いわゆる「*Brüstle*」判決（CJEU 判決 C-34/10）において、人間胚性幹細胞の特許性を検討した。CJEU は欧州特許庁よりもさらに制限的なアプローチをとり、以下を

embryonic stem cells in the so-called *"Brüstle"* decision (CJEU decision **C-34/10**). The CJEU took an even more restrictive approach than the EPO, in that it found that inventions are excluded that require.

> *"the prior destruction of human embryos or their use as base material, **whatever the stage at which that takes place** and even if the description of the technical teaching claimed does not refer to the use of human embryos."*

This reasoning excludes e.g. human embryonic stem cell lines, which were already established many years ago by destroying a human embryo.

Whereas the CJEU does not have formal jurisdiction over the EPO, the President of the EPO has decided to follow this decision, and has revised the EPO Guidelines for Examination (cf. G-II 5.3(iii); new part emphasised):

> *"A claim directed to a product, which at the filing date of the application could be exclusively obtained by a method which necessarily involved the destruction of human embryos from which the said product is derived is excluded from patentability under Rule 28(c), even if said method is not part of the claim (see G 2/06). **The point in time at which such destruction takes place is irrelevant.**"*

Thus, in the current practice of the EPO products exclusively prepared by the destruction of human embryos, independently of the point in time at which this takes place, are considered as *"contrary to 'ordre public' or morality"* pursuant to Art. 53(a) EPC.

It should be noted that uses that are to the benefit of the embryo, e.g. a treatment of the embryo with the purpose of curing a disease, are not excluded from patentability under Art. 53(a) EPC.

必要とする発明は特許の対象から除外されると認定した。

> 「人間の胚を前もって破壊すること又はそれを原料物質として使用することであって、**それが行われる段階がどの段階であれ**、そして、クレームされている技術的な教示の記載に人間の胚の使用について言及されていない場合であってもである。」

この論理付けによれば、人間の胚を破壊することによって何年も前にすでに樹立されたもの（例えば、人間胚性幹細胞株）が除外される。

CJEUは欧州特許庁に対する正式な管轄権を持たないが、特許庁長官はこの判決に従うことを決定し、審査基準を改訂した（G-II 5.3(iii)では新たな部分が強調されている）。

> 「クレームに記載の発明が物についての場合であって、特許出願の出願日において、人間の胚の破壊を必然的に伴う方法によってのみその物が得られるときは、その方法がクレームの一部でなくても、規則28(c)に基づき当該発明は特許の対象から除外される（G 2/06を参照）。**この破壊が起こる時点は重要ではない。**」

よって、現行の欧州特許実務では、人間の胚の破壊によって調製される物は、破壊が行われる時点に関係なく、第53条(a)にいう「『公の秩序』又は善良の風俗に反する」とみなされる。

第53条(a)の下では、胚の恩恵に関する用途（例えば、疾患の治療目的での胚の処置）は特許性から除外されないことに留意すべきである。

From a practical point of view it is noteworthy that the EPO accepts that after January 2008 it was technically feasible to generate human embryonic stem cells *without* destruction of the embryo. This provides a technical counter-argument against an objection under Art. 53(a) EPC, for inventions having an effective date after this cut-off date. In other words, inventions on human embryonic stem cells having an effective date after January 2008 are potentially no longer excluded from patentability under Art. 53(a) EPC. The impact on Applicants of the decisions G 2/06 and CJEU decision C-34/10 will therefore likely subside with time. Irrespective of patentability of the claims, the EPO will routinely request that the specification is adapted such that there is no reference to destruction of human embryos.

1.3 Suffering of Experimental Animals vs. Benefit to Mankind

Another landmark decision which concerned the exclusion of inventions *"contrary to 'ordre public' or morality"* is the so-called *"Oncomouse decision"* (T 19/90), dealing with the question whether a transgenic animal having an increased probability of developing cancer (or, in more general terms, a predisposition to a severe disease) is patentable under the EPC.

The relevant legal provision is the exclusion of *"processes for modifying the genetic identity of animals which are likely to cause them suffering without any substantial medical benefit to man or animal, and also animals resulting from such processes"*, pursuant to Rule 28(d) EPC.

The competent Board of Appeal came to the conclusion that decisions on the patentability of transgenic animals will have to be made by ***"careful weighing up of the suffering of animals and possible risks to the environment on the one hand, and the invention's usefulness to mankind on the other."*** (cf. Reasons for the decision, item 5; emphasis added).

This "careful weighing up" is clearly case sensitive, and an assessment has to

実務的な観点からすると、2008年1月より、胚を破壊せずに人間胚性幹細胞を作製することが技術的に可能であったことを欧州特許庁が認めていることは注目に値する。よって、この基準日よりも後に有効日を有する発明については、第53条(a)に基づく拒絶理由に対して技術的な反論の機会がある。換言すれば、2008年1月よりも後に有効日を有する人間胚性幹細胞に関する発明は、第53条(a)に基づき特許の対象からもはや除外されない可能性がある。よって、審決G 2/06及びCJEU判決C-34/10が出願人に及ぼす影響は、時間とともに弱まるであろう。クレームに記載の発明の特許性とは関係なく、欧州特許庁は、人間の胚の破壊に関する記述を明細書から除くよう出願人に求めることだろう。

1.3 実験動物の苦痛と人類の利益

「『公の秩序』又は善良の風俗に反する」発明を特許の対象から除外することについては、別の画期的な審決がある。それは、いわゆる「オンコマウス審決」（T 19/90）であり、がんを発症する確率が高い（又は、より一般的な観点では、重度の疾患に対する素因がある）トランスジェニック動物について欧州特許条約下で特許を受けることができるか否かという問題が取り上げられた。

これに関する規定は規則28(d)であり、「動物の遺伝子的同一性を変更する方法であって、人間又は動物に対する医学上の実質的な利益がなく、その動物に苦痛をもたらすおそれがあるもの、そして、当該方法から生じる動物」は特許の対象から除外されている。

上記審決を担当した審判部は、「**動物の苦痛及び起こり得る環境リスクと、人類に対して発明がもたらす有用性とを慎重に比較判断すること**」によって、トランスジェニック動物の特許性に関する判断をしなければならないという結論に達した（審決の理由、項目5を参照。強調は追加したもの）。

この「慎重に比較判断する」は事案に依存することが明らかであり、個々の

be made on a case-by-case basis.

2 Plant or Animal Varieties or Essentially Biological Processes for the Production of Plants or Animals (Art. 53(b) EPC)

Art. 53(b) EPC excludes *"plant or animal varieties or essentially biological processes for the production of plants or animals"* from patentability, with the exception of microbiological processes.

2.1 The Exclusion of Plant and Animal Varieties

The EPC distinguishes between "plant or animal *varieties*" – which are non-patentable (Art. 53(b) EPC), and "plants and animals" in a wider sense, which are patentable (Rule 27(b) EPC), provided the "technical feasibility of the invention is not confined to a particular plant or animal variety".

The scope of the exception to patentability is hence crucially dependent on the technical meaning of "variety". As concerns plant varieties, the Implementing Regulations contain a definition in Rule 26(4) EPC:

> *"Plant variety" means any plant grouping within a single botanical taxon of the lowest known rank, which grouping, irrespective of whether the conditions for the grant of a plant variety right are fully met, can be:*
>
> *(a) defined by the expression of the characteristics that results from a given genotype or combination of genotypes,*
>
> *(b) distinguished from any other plant grouping by the expression of at least one of the said characteristics, and*

2 植物若しくは動物の品種又は植物若しくは動物を生産する本質的に生物学的な方法（第53条(b)）

第53条(b)は、微生物学的方法を除く「**植物若しくは動物の品種又は植物若しくは動物を生産する本質的に生物学的な方法**」を特許の対象から除外している。

2.1 植物及び動物の品種の除外

欧州特許条約は、「植物若しくは動物の品種」（第53条(b)により特許を受けることができない）を、より広義の「植物及び動物」（規則27(b)により特許を受けることができる）から区別している。ここでは「発明の技術的な実現可能性は特定の植物若しくは動物の品種に限定されない」ことが前提である。

そのため、特許性の例外の範囲は、「品種」の技術的意味に大きく依存する。植物の品種については、規則26(4)にその定義が示されている。

> 「植物の品種」とは、既知の最下位級に属する単一植物分類群のなかでの植物群であって、植物の品種について権利付与を受けられる条件が完全に満たされているか否かを問わず、次の条件をすべて満たすものをいう。
>
> (a) 所与の遺伝子型若しくは遺伝子型の組合せに起因する特性の表現によって定義することができること。
>
> (b) 前記特性の少なくとも1つによる表現により他の植物群と識別することができること。

> *(c) considered as a unit with regard to its suitability for being propagated unchanged.*

This definition is essentially the same as that used in the EU Regulation on Community Plant Variety Rights (EC 2100/94)[6]. This is consistent with the legislator's intention to exclude parallel protection of plants a) as a plant variety, and b) in a patent. Thus, when the subject matter represents a plant variety, it can be protected as a plant variety right, when it is not a plant variety, it can be protected by a patent. This is sometimes referred to as a "seemless fit" between plant variety protection and patent protection.

Interestingly, whereas the law contains a clear definition of plant varieties, it does not with respect to animal varieties. Moreover, the exclusion of animal varieties requires a different justification, in so far as there is no codified protection for "animal varieties" that could lead to parallel protection.

In view of the economic significance of the plant breeding industry, the EPO had to decide on patentability of plant related claims on a number of occasions.

According to EPO practice, claims directed to a group of plants that may include, but is not identical to a plant variety, are allowable. This practice, set forth in **G 1/98**, is consistent with the EU biotech directive[7]. The Guidelines for examination reflect this principle:

> *"A claim wherein specific plant varieties are not individually claimed is not excluded from patentability under Art. 53(b) even though it may embrace plant varieties (see G 1/98, and G-II 5.4)."* (Guidelines, G-II 5.2(ii)).

---

[6] Art. 5(2) of Regulation EC 2100/94
[7] EU Dir. 98/44/EC, rec. 29

(c) 繁殖するための適合性に関して、変化しない単位と考えられること。

　この定義は、共同体植物品種権に関するEU規則（EC2100/94）[6]で使用されているものと基本的に同じである。これは、a)植物品種として、及び、b)特許により、植物を二重に保護することを防止しようとする立法者の意図と一致している。よって、対象が植物の品種に相当する場合は、植物品種権としてそれを保護することができ、それが植物の品種ではない場合は、特許によってそれを保護することができる。これは、植物の品種による保護と特許による保護との間の「シームレスフィット」と称されることもある。

　興味深いことに、法規定には植物の品種についての明確な定義が含まれているのに対して、動物の品種については定義されていない。また、二重保護につながり得る「動物の品種」について成文化された保護がない限りにおいて、動物の品種を特許の対象から除外するには様々な根拠が必要である。

　植物育種産業の経済的重要性の観点から、欧州特許庁は、何度にもわたって植物関連クレームの特許性を決定しなければならなかった。

　欧州特許実務によれば、植物の品種を含むとしても、それと同一ではない植物群を対象とするクレームは認められる。当該実務は審決 G 1/98に示されており、生物工学的発明の法的保護に関するEU指令[7]と一致している。審査基準では、この方針が反映されている。

> 「特定の植物の品種が個別化されてクレームされていない場合、そのクレームは、それが植物の品種を包含しているものであっても、第53条(b)により特許の対象から除外されない（G 1/98及びG-II 5.4参照）。」（審査基準、G-II 5.2(ii)）。

---

[6] 規則 EC2100/94の第 5 条(2)
[7] EU 指令96/44/EC, rec. 29

In other words, a claim directed to e.g. "chrysanthemum variety White Snowball V" would not be patentable. A broader claim, directed to chrysanthemum plants having e.g. a certain genetic modification, on the other hand would be patentable under Art. 53(b) EPC, even if this claim covers "chrysanthemum variety White Snowball V". Provided the correct claim wording is chosen, genetically modified plants are therefore patentable under Art. 53(b) EPC.

This approach has recently been confirmed in the parallel decisions **G 2/12** and **G 2/13**, even for the case where the claimed plants can *only* be obtained by a "classical" crossing and selection approach, which in itself is excluded from patentability as an "essential biological process".

As concerns animal varieties, much less case law is available. There is a consensus, however, that genetically modified animals do not represent an "animal variety", and are not as such excluded from patentability under Art. 53(b) EPC.

2.2 The Exclusion of Breeding Processes Including Sexual Crossing / Selection

Breeding processes for plants or animals based on sexual crossing and selection are typically not patentable. There has been recent debate whether such processes can be patentable, if they comprise *additional* steps of technical nature. This discussion hinged on the wording of Rule 26(5) EPC, which defines "*essentially biological processes*" as such that "*consist entirely of natural phenomena such as crossing or selection.*" The discrepancy between the terms "essentially" and "entirely" in the wording of Rule 26(5) EPC lead to the parallel decisions **G 2/07** and **G 1/08** of the Enlarged Board of Appeal (the "broccoli" and "tomato" decisions).

The discussion is of relevance in the context of modern breeding techniques that are e.g. assisted by genetic markers used in crossing/selecting. The Enlarged Board held that the process does not become patentable under Art. 53(b)

換言すれば、例えば、「菊の品種 White Snowball V」を対象とするクレームは、特許を受けることができないであろう。一方、例えば、特定の遺伝子組換えを有する菊植物を対象とするより広いクレームは、このクレームが「菊の品種 White Snowball V」を包含する場合であっても、第53条(b)により特許の対象から除外されない。正しいクレームの文言を選択すれば、遺伝子改変植物は、第53条(b)により特許の対象から除外されない。

当該アプローチは、最近、2つの平行する審決であるG 2/12及びG 2/13において確認された。クレームされている植物が「古典的な」交配及び選択方法（それ自体は「本質的に生物学的な方法」として特許の対象から除外されている）によってのみ得ることができる場合であってものことである。

動物の品種については、利用できるケースローが非常に少ない。その一方で、遺伝子組換え動物は「動物の品種」に相当せず、第53条(b)により特許の対象から除外されるものではないという合意がある。

2.2 交配／選択を含む繁殖方法の除外

交配及び選択に基づく植物又は動物の繁殖方法は、通常、特許を受けることができない。最近は、技術的な工程が当該方法に追加されて含まれる場合には特許を受けることができるか否かという議論がなされている。この議論は、「本質的に生物学的な方法」を「**全面的に交配又は選択等の自然現象によるものである**」と定義する規則26(5)の文言から生まれた。規則26(5)の文言における「本質的に」及び「全面的に」という用語間の矛盾が、拡大審判部の2つの並行する審決G 2/07及びG 1/08（「ブロッコリ」審決及び「トマト」審決）につながった。

この議論は、最新の繁殖技術（例えば、交配／選択に使用される遺伝子マーカーを利用するもの）の内容と関連する。拡大審判部は、当該方法は、技術的構成要件が単にクレームに追加されているという理由では特許の対象にならず、

EPC, merely because such additional technical elements are claimed, as follows from the second headnote of G 2/07:

> "2. **Such a process does not escape the exclusion of Art. 53(b) EPC merely because it contains**, as a further step or as part of any of the steps of crossing and selection, **a step of a technical nature which serves to enable or assist** the performance of the steps of sexually crossing the whole genomes of plants or of subsequently selecting plants."

Thus, processes "containing" a step of crossing/selecting are excluded from patentability, irrespective of additional technical elements. In justifying the exclusion, the Enlarged Board explained that the additional technical aspects may be elective to patent protection as such.

For example, a step of genetic modification, or the genetic marker suitable for assisting a crossing and selection process may be patentable subject matter in its own right, provided the claim does not include the sexual crossing and selection process[8]:

> "This is the case, for example, for **genetic engineering techniques applied to plants** which techniques differ profoundly from conventional breeding techniques as they work primarily through the purposeful insertion and / or modification of one or more genes in a plant (cf T 356/93 supra). **However, in such cases the claims should not, explicitly or implicitly, include the sexual crossing and selection process.**"

However, in cases where the additional "steps of technical nature" are performed *within* – rather than before or after – the crossing and selection step, they may lead to patentability, as follows from the third headnote of G 2/07:

---

[8] G 2/07, Reasons for the decision 6.4.2.3

第53条(b)により特許の対象から除外されると判断した。この点、G 2/07の第二の頭注に以下の記述がある。

> 「2．**このような方法は、**植物の全ゲノムを交配する工程又はそれに続く植物を選択する工程の実施を**可能にするか又は支援する技術的な工程を**交配及び選択の工程に追加的に含むか、又はその一部として含むだけでは、**第53条(b)による除外を免れない。**」

よって、技術的構成要件の追加にかかわらず、交配／選択の工程を「含む」方法は特許の対象から除外される。この除外の根拠として、拡大審判部は、そのような技術的な態様はそれ自体で特許により保護され得ると説明した。

例えば、遺伝子組換えの工程、又は交配及び選択の方法を適切に支援する遺伝子マーカーは、そのクレームが交配及び選択の方法を含まない限り、それ自体の権利として特許の対象であり得る[8]。

> 「これは、例えば、**植物に適用される遺伝子工学技術**に関する事例であり、遺伝子工学技術は、植物において１つ以上の遺伝子を意図的に挿入及び／又は改変することによって主に機能するので、従来の繁殖技術とは大きく異なる（前掲のT 356/93を参照）。**しかしながら、このような事例では、クレームは、交配及び選択の方法を明示的にも暗示的にも含んではならない。**」

一方、G 2/07の第三の頭注にあるように、「技術的な工程」が交配及び選択の工程中に（工程の前後ではなく）追加されて実施される事案では、それらの工程は特許性を導き得る。

---

[8] G 2/07、審決の理由6.4.2.3

"*3. If, however, such a process contains **within** the steps of sexually crossing and selecting **an additional step of a technical nature, which step by itself introduces a trait into the genome** or modifies a trait in the genome of the plant produced, so that the introduction or modification of that trait is not the result of the mixing of the genes of the plants chosen for sexual crossing, **then the process is not excluded from patentability under Article 53(b) EPC.*"

The Enlarged Board of Appeal stresses that such additional steps of technical nature must be *"performed **within** the steps of sexually crossing and selection ... Otherwise the exclusion of sexual crossing and selection processes from patentability under Article 53(b) EPC could be circumvented simply by adding steps which do not properly pertain to the crossing and selection process, being either upstream steps dealing with the preparation of the plant(s) to be crossed or downstream steps dealing with the further treatment of the plant resulting from such crossing and selection process"*[9]. To ensure this limitation, the Enlarged Board of Appeal reasons that steps performed either **before or after** the process of crossing or selection should be ignored for determining the exclusion under Art. 53(b) EPC[10].

2.3 No Exclusion of Microbiological Processes

For completeness sake it should be emphasized that the exclusion of essentially biological processes does not extend to *"a microbiological or other technical process, or a product obtained by means of such a process other than a plant or animal variety"* (Rule 27(c) EPC).

The term "microbiological process" means *"any process involving or performed upon or resulting in microbiological material"* (Rule 26(6) EPC). Hence, in the field of microbiology no exceptions to patentability in the sense of Art. 53 EPC

---

[9] G 2/07, Reasons for the decision 6.4.2.3
[10] G 2/07, Reasons for the decision 6.4.2.3

「3．しかしながら、このような方法が、**技術的な追加工程であって、それ自体が形質をゲノムに導入するか、又は生産される植物のゲノム中の形質を改変する工程を、その形質の導入又は改変が交配のために選択された植物の遺伝子を混合することにならないように、交配及び選別の工程の中に含む場合、その方法は第53条(b)により**特許の対象から除外されない。」

拡大審判部は、このような技術的な追加の工程が、「交配及び選択の工程中に実施」されなければならず、「そうでなければ、第53条(b)に基づき交配及び選択の方法を特許の対象から除外することは、交配及び選別の方法とは適切な関連がない工程（交配すべき植物の調製を扱う上流工程又はこのような交配及び選別の方法から得られる植物について追加の処理を扱う下流工程）を単に追加することによって回避されてしまう」と強調している[9]。この制限を確実にするために、拡大審判部は、第53条(b)による除外の決定については、交配又は選択の方法の**前後**いずれかに実施される工程を無視すべきであると説明している[10]。

2.3　微生物学的方法は除外されない

本質的に生物学的な方法の除外は、「微生物学的若しくはその他の技術的な方法、又は当該方法によって得られる生産物であって、植物若しくは動物の品種以外のもの」（規則27(c)）には及ばないことを強調しておかなければならない。

「微生物学的方法」という用語は、「微生物学的材料を含む、又はその材料について行われる、又はその材料を生じるすべての方法」（規則26(6)）を意味する。したがって、微生物学の分野では、第53条の意味での特許性の例外に遭遇

---

[9] G 2/07、審決の理由6.4.2.3
[10] G 2/07、審決の理由6.4.2.3

are encountered.

3 The Exclusions of Medical Methods under Art. 53(c) EPC

Art. 53 (c) EPC contains three different exceptions to patentability:

- methods for treatment of the human or animal body by **surgery**,

- methods for treatment of the human or animal body by **therapy**, and

- **diagnostic methods** practised on the human or animal body.

All exceptions under Art. 53(c) EPC serve to free the work of medical practitioners from patent constraints. Under the EPC1974, the exceptions were based on a legal fiction of lack of industrial applicability. This legal fiction was given up in the revised EPC (EPC2000). It is acknowledged that the methods referred to in Art. 53(c) EPC are industrially applicable inventions. However, their exception from patentability is justifiable for reasons of public health.

Each of these exceptions has been subject to interpretation by the Enlarged Board of Appeal. The scope of the exceptions, and possible ways of overcoming the exceptions are quite different. The three exceptions will be discussed separately in the following.

3.1 Methods of Treatment of the Human or Animal Body by Surgery

For a long time, the EPO followed a restrictive approach when assessing this exception from patentability. In brief, this – out dated – approach of the EPO could be summarized as follows: If a method included any step of breaching the physical integrity of a person or animal, irrespective of how significant the breach

しない。

3 第53条(c)に基づく医療方法の除外

第53条(c)には、3つの異なる特許性の例外が含まれる。

- **手術**による人間又は動物の体の処置方法

- **治療**による人間又は動物の体の処置方法

- 人間又は動物の体の**診断**方法

第53条(c)に規定されるすべての例外は、特許による制約から医療従事者の活動を自由にする役割を果たす。EPC1974の下では、これらの例外は、産業上の利用可能性の欠如という法的擬制に基づくものであった。改正後の欧州特許条約（EPC2000）では、この法的擬制を取りやめた。第53条(c)において言及される方法は、産業上利用可能な発明であることが認められている。一方で、これらの特許性の例外は、公衆衛生上の理由から正当化されている。

これらの各例外は、拡大審判部による解釈の対象となった。これらの例外は、その範囲と、それに対処する可能な克服手段とを異にする。以下、3つの例外を別々に論じる。

3.1 手術による人間又は動物の体の処置方法

長い間、この特許性の例外を判断する際、欧州特許庁は制限的なアプローチをしてきた。この（時代遅れの）アプローチを要約すると以下のようになる：ある方法が、人間又は動物の身体的な完全性を破壊する工程を含む場合、その破壊がどれほど重大であるかにかかわらず、その方法は特許の対象から除外さ

was, the method was excluded from patentability. This also applied to relatively minor, routine interventions that did not require the presence of a medical doctor, such as e.g. venous puncture to draw a blood sample.

This strict, but simple, approach was significantly revised by the Enlarged Board of Appeal in its decision **G 1/07**, which held that a narrower approach to the exclusion of treatments by surgery was required. According to this decision, the *nature and severity* of the surgical step is of significance.

Whether a method falls within the exclusion from patentability can be judged on the basis of the following criteria:

1. The physical intervention is **substantial**.

2. **Professional medical expertise** is required.

3. **Substantial health risk** is involved.

Accordingly, the decision whether a particular surgical method is excluded from patentability has to be made on a case-by-case basis. This new approach relieves many types of subject matter from exclusion under Art. 53 EPC, which were previously excluded. Simple, routine interventions that are not associated with a significant health risk no longer justify an exclusion from patentability. On the other hand, it may not always be easy to predict whether a given claim is excluded from patentability, given the relative nature of the criteria set forth by the Enlarged Board of Appeal. It will be up to case law to provide further guidance whether a given physical intervention or health risk is "substantial".

Importantly, a single step of surgical nature in a multi-step process may suffice to trigger the exclusion (in this respect, previous practice was maintained). It is also irrelevant for this exclusion whether the surgical step is for therapeutic purposes. In this respect, the Enlarged Board advocated a broad understanding

れていた。これは、医師の存在を必要としない比較的些細な手順の治療介入（例えば、血液サンプルを採取するための静脈穿刺）にも適用されていた。

審決 G 1/07では、拡大審判部によって、この厳格だが単純なアプローチが大幅に見直され、手術による処置の除外についてより限定的なアプローチが要求された。この審決によれば、手術工程の性質及び重大性が重要である。

以下の基準に基づいて、ある方法が特許の対象から除外される範囲に該当するか否かを判断することができる。

1. **身体的な治療介入が実質的**なものである。

2. **医療専門家の専門知識**が必要とされる。

3. **実質的な健康リスク**を伴う。

したがって、特定の手術方法が特許性から除外されるか否かの判断は、個々の事例に基づいてされるべきである。この新たなアプローチにより、これまでは除外されていた多くの種類の対象が、第53条に基づく除外から救済される。重大な健康リスクを伴わない簡単な日常的治療介入は、もはや特許の対象から除外する根拠とはならない。一方、拡大審判部が示した基準の相対的性質を考慮すると、所定のクレームが特許の対象から除外されるかを予測することは常に容易ではない。所定の身体的治療介入又は健康リスクが「実質的」であるかについては、ケースロー次第であり、それによりさらなる指針が提供されるだろう。

重要なことに、複数の工程を含む方法において手術的性質の工程が１つあれば、それは、この除外の要因となるのに十分であり得る（この点については、これまでの特許実務が維持された）。また、手術工程が治療目的であるか否かは、この除外とは無関係である。この点について、拡大審判部は、「手術による処

of "treatment by surgery", as referring to the nature of the treatment rather than its purpose.

When encountering an objection by the EPO, sometimes the claim can be reworded to avoid recital of a surgical method step. In case of a multi-step process, where only a single step is (allegedly) a surgical method step, it can be considered to define a particular patient group having received the surgical treatment, rather than the surgical method step as such. In the alternative, the omission of the surgical step has to be assessed. The concrete means of dealing with an objection against a surgical method step depend strongly on the nature of the invention, and on the relationship between the surgical step and the essential features defining the contribution to the art.

To give an example, a method may comprise a step of a) injecting a contrast agent into a patient, and b) obtaining an image from the patient. Such a claim could be reworded, such that it relates to taking an image from a patient, wherein the patient is characterized in that it has been administered with a contrast agent. In this wording, the claim does not comprise the injection step, but rather defines the appropriate patient group. This practice has been accepted by the EPO even under the stricter approach taken before G 1/07. Such amendment may not be possible, however, if the sole technical contribution resides in the way of performing surgery, as such.

Devices used in surgical methods are patentable as surgical devices (i.e. products) *per se*. Their use in a method of surgery, however, would not be patentable. Moreover, surgical devices cannot be protected by a "second surgical use" claim, when the invention resides in a new surgical use of a known device. In this respect, practice on surgical methods is more restrictive as compared to pharmaceutical inventions (see below). The EPO reasons that surgical devices are not encompassed by the term "substance or composition" used in Art. 54(5) EPC, and hence, devices are not eligible to purpose limited product claims. In principle, first or further surgical uses can be claimed for "substances or composi-

置」を、その目的ではなく処置の性質について幅広く理解すると主張した。

　欧州特許庁からの拒絶理由に対しては、手術方法の工程の記載を排除するようにクレームを補正することができるときもある。複数の工程を含む方法において、1つの工程のみが手術方法の工程である場合、手術方法の工程そのものではなく、手術的処置を受けた特定の患者群を定義することが考えられる。代替案では、手術工程の削除を検討しなければならない。手術方法の工程に対して拒絶理由が提起された場合の具体的な対応策は、先行技術に対する貢献を規定する本質的な特徴とその手術工程との間にある関係、及び発明の性質に大きく依存する。

　一例として、a) 造影剤を患者に注入する工程、及び、b) 当該患者から画像を取得する工程を含む方法が挙げられる。このようなクレームは、患者から画像を撮影する工程であって、患者に造影剤が注入されたことを特徴とするものとなるように補正することができる。この文言では、注入工程がクレームに含まれず、適切な患者群が定義されている。この特許実務は、G 1/07が出される前の厳格なアプローチの下であっても、欧州特許庁により認められていた。一方で、上記のような補正は、唯一の技術的貢献が手術の実施様式それ自体にある場合は不可能かもしれない。

　手術方法に使用されるデバイスは、手術デバイス（すなわち、物）それ自体として特許の対象である。その一方で、手術方法におけるそれらの使用は特許を受けることができない。また、発明が公知のデバイスの新たな手術用途である場合は、「第二の手術用途」のクレームによって手術用デバイスを保護することはできない。この点について、手術方法に関する実務は、医薬発明と比較してより制限的である（以下を参照）。欧州特許庁は、第54条(5)で使用されている「物質又は組成物」という用語には手術デバイスが含まれないので、デバイスは、用途を限定した物のクレームとして特許の対象にならないと判断している。原則として、第一の手術用途又はさらなる手術用途は、第一の医薬用途又

tions", analogously to first or further medical use claims (see below). However, such subject matter is only rarely encountered.

3.2 Exclusion of Methods of Therapy of the Human or Animal Body

In the field of pharmaceutical inventions, Art. 53(c) EPC makes a strict distinction between "methods of therapy", which are excluded from patentability, and "products, in particular substances or compositions" for use in such methods, which are patentable. The EPO considers use claims to be equivalent to method claims, such that use claims are equally excluded from patentability for pharmaceutical inventions. In a multi-step method, a single step that is of therapeutic nature is sufficient to trigger the exclusion under Art. 53(c) EPC.

The concept of "therapy" has to be understood broadly, and is not restricted to therapy for curative purposes. The Enlarged Board clarified in some of its earliest decisions that the intention of Art. 53(c) EPC was to prevent "*medical and veterinary activities*" from being restrained by patent rights (G 1/83, G 5/83 and G 6/83). This line of reasoning was maintained in G 1/07, confirming that the exclusion from patentability serves to protect the "*medical and veterinary practitioners' freedom to use the best available treatments to the benefit of their patients, uninhibited by any worry that some treatment might be covered by a patent*".

Only therapeutic methods are excluded from patentability, whereas for example cosmetic methods are not, i.e. the exclusion cannot be extended to treatments, which are not therapeutic in character. Where a treatment can have therapeutic or non-therapeutic effects, it may be necessary to clearly distinguish these in the claim, e.g. to explicitly direct the claim to a cosmetic method, to exclude therapy. Where the therapeutic and non-therapeutic use cannot be distinguished by the wording of the claim, a method claim will not be allowable.

Therapy generally relates to "the alleviation of the symptoms of pain and suf-

はさらなる医薬用途のクレームと同様に、「物質又は組成物」についてクレームすることができる（以下を参照）。しかしながら、このような対象は極めて珍しい。

3.2　人間又は動物の体の治療方法の除外

医薬発明の分野では、第53条(c)は、特許の対象から除外される「治療方法」と、このような方法に使用される「物、特に物質又は組成物」（これは特許の対象である）とを厳格に区別している。欧州特許庁は、使用クレームが方法クレームと同等であると考えているので、医薬発明については使用クレームも特許の対象から同様に除外される。複数の工程を含む方法において治療的性質の工程が１つあれば、それは、第53条(c)の除外の要因となるのに十分である。

「治療」の概念は広く理解すべきであり、治癒目的の治療に限定されない。最初期の審決のいくつかにおいて、拡大審判部は、第53条(c)の意図が、特許権によって「医療及び獣医の活動」が制限されるのを防ぐことであると明確にした（G 1/83、G 5/83及びG 6/83）。G 1/07でこの一連の判断が維持されたことから、特許の対象からの除外は、「患者の利益のために利用可能な最良の処置を使用する医療従事者及び獣医従事者が、一部の処置が特許に含まれるのではないかという懸念によって妨げられない自由」を保護する役割を果たすことが確認された。

治療方法のみが特許の対象から除外され、例えば、美容方法は除外されない。すなわち、この除外は、非治療的性質の処置にまで及ぶことはない。処置が治療効果又は非治療効果を有し得る場合はクレームにおいてこれらを明確に区別することが必要である。例えば、クレームから治療法を除き、クレームを明らかに美容方法にすることである。クレームの文言によって治療用途及び非治療用途を区別することができない場合、当該方法クレームは認められないであろう。

治療は、一般に、疾患の一般的又は治癒的処置だけではなく、「痛み及び苦

fering", as well as general or curative treatment of a disease. The concept of therapy also includes prophylactic treatment, aimed at maintaining health. In contrast, a method of contraception was not considered a method of therapy, as pregnancy is not an illness.

Whether prophylactic or curative, therapy must be "directed to the maintenance or restoration of health".

3.3 Pharmaceutical Inventions can be Protected by Product and Purpose-Limited Product Claims

In the case of a novel substance, a pharmaceutical invention can be protected by a product claim. In contrast, where the substance or composition is known from the art, the claim needs to be restricted to the novel technical contribution – the use as a medicament. However, the claim cannot be drafted as a method or use claim, because of the exclusion under Art. 53(c) EPC.

In order to reflect the importance of research in the pharmaceutical field for society, the EPC provides an exception from the principle of absolute novelty in the pharmaceutical field. Specifically, Art. 54(4) and (5) EPC provide for purpose-limited product protection.

Specifically, a "substance or composition, comprised in the state of the art" can be protected "**for use in a method of therapy**", provided that it has not been disclosed as a medicament in the art (Art. 54(4) EPC).

According to this provision, a composition or substance that has not previously been disclosed as a medicament can be patented in a so-called "first medical use" claim. According to the Guidelines for Examination, G-II 4.2, first medical use claims can have the format:

"Substance or composition X" followed by the indication of use, for instance "…

痛の症状の緩和」に関するものである。治療の概念には、健康の維持を目的とする予防的処置も含まれる。対照的に、避妊方法は、妊娠が病気ではないので、治療方法ではないと考えられた。

予防的か治癒的かにかかわらず、治療は、「健康の維持又は回復を対象」とする。

3.3 医薬発明は、物のクレーム及び用途を限定した物のクレームによって保護される

新規な物質の場合、医薬発明は、物のクレームによって保護することができる。対照的に、物質又は組成物が当技術分野で公知である場合は、クレームを新規な技術的貢献（医薬としての使用）に限定する必要がある。しかし、第53条(c)による除外により、当該クレームは方法クレームとしても使用クレームとしても起案することができない。

医薬分野における研究の重要性を社会貢献として反映させるために、欧州特許条約は、医薬分野において、絶対的な新規性の原則の例外を提供している。具体的には、第54条(4)及び(5)は、用途を限定された物の保護を提供する。

具体的には、「技術水準に含まれる物質又は組成物」であっても**「治療方法において使用されるもの」**は、それが当技術分野で医薬として開示されていない場合は保護され得る（第54条(4)）。

この規定によれば、医薬としてこれまでに開示されていない組成物又は物質は、いわゆる「第一医薬用途」クレームとして特許を受けることができる。審査基準のG-II 4.2によれば、第一医薬用途クレームは、以下の形式をとることができる。

「物質又は組成物X」とそれに続く用途の表示、例えば、「医薬として使用す

for use as a medicament" or "... for use in therapy".

This wording deviates from the practice required by the EPO immediately after the EPC2000 came into effect, where the indication of the use was to be worded "for use <u>in a method</u> of therapy ...".

If a substance or composition has already been disclosed for use in therapy, Art. 54(5) EPC provides for so-called second- or further medical use claims, for any (novel) "**specific** use" in a method of therapy. The Guidelines for examination recommend a wording such as:

"Substance or composition X" followed by the indication of the **specific** therapeutic use, for instance, "... for use in treating disease Y" (see G-VI 7.1).

Decision **G 2/08** of the Enlarged Board of Appeal gives guidance on the correct interpretation of the term "specific". The case underlying this decision was directed to the use of a known drug in a known treatment. The distinction over the art resided in a particular dosage regimen (*administration once per day prior to sleep*).

The Enlarged Board reasoned that a "specific" use in a method of therapy is not restricted to treating a novel disease, but extends to *any* "specific" aspect of treatment. This may be a particular way of treating the same illness, for example, a particular dosage regimen. It may also relate to a new patient group, within the more general teaching in the prior art, or, more generally, to a "new clinical situation".

Thus, G 2/08 opens a broad applicability of second/further medical indication claims under the novelty requirement. In practice, this oftentimes shifts the main challenge to patentability to the assessment of inventive step.

Additionally, decision **G 2/08** holds that the so-called *"Swiss-type claim"* (*"Use*

るための……」又は「治療に使用するための……」。

　この文言は、EPC2000施行直後に欧州特許庁から要求された特許実務（用途の表示を「治療の方法において使用するための」と記載すべきこととされていた）から逸脱している。

　物質又は組成物が治療用途についてすでに開示されたものである場合、第54条(5)は、治療方法における（新規な）**「特定の用途」**のための、いわゆる第二医薬用途クレーム又はさらなる医薬用途クレームを提供する。審査基準では、例えば、以下の文言が推奨されている。

　例えば、「疾患Yの治療に使用するための……」という**特定の**治療用途の表示が後に続く「物質又は組成物X」（G-VI 7.1を参照）。

　拡大審判部の審決G 2/08では、「特定の」という用語の正しい解釈について指針が示されている。この審決に係る不服審判事件の対象は、公知の治療における公知の薬物の使用であった。先行技術との差異は、特定の投与計画にあった（就寝前に1日1回投与）。

　拡大審判部は、治療方法における「特定の」用途は新規疾患の治療に限定されず、あらゆる「特定の」治療態様に及ぶと判断した。これは、同じ病気を治療する特定の方法（例えば、特定の投与計画）であり得る。また、これは、先行技術の一般的教示における新たな患者群や、より一般的には「新たな臨床状況」に関するものであり得る。

　よって、G 2/08は、新規性の要件において第二医薬用途クレーム／さらなる医薬用途クレームを広く起用可能にしている。実際のところ、これにより、特許性の主な課題が進歩性の判断にシフトされることが多い。

　さらに、審決G 2/08では、2011年1月28日よりも後の有効日を有する出願

of compound X for the manufacture of a medicament for treating disease Y") is no longer allowed for applications having an effective date after January 28 2011. Only the "purpose-limited product claims" as outlined above are allowable under the EPC2000.

3.4 Exclusion of Diagnostic Methods Practices on the Human or Animal Body

The final exclusion under Art. 53(c) EPC pertains to "diagnostic methods", when "performed on the human or animal body".

The Enlarged Board of Appeal gives guidance in **G 1/04** under which conditions a diagnostic method is *"practised on the human or animal body"*. Following this decision, a claim falls under the exclusion only when *all* of its steps are performed "on the human or animal body". When a claim comprises at least one (technical) step performed *in vitro*, it does not fall under the exclusion. Thus, diagnostic method claims that encompass the *in vitro* determination of a marker or specific diagnostic value do not fall under the exclusion. For this reason alone, the practical scope of the exclusion is limited.

The assessment of (multi-step) diagnostic methods and surgical- or therapeutic methods is hence significantly different. A *single* surgical or therapeutic step suffices for a multi-step method to fall under the exclusion. In contrast, *all* of the steps of a diagnostic method must be performed on the human or animal body, to be excluded.

G 1/04 in addition holds that, for a method to be excluded as a diagnostic method, it must also comprise the step of making the diagnosis in the stricter sense, or, in the words of the decision: *"the diagnosis for curative purposes stricto sensu representing the deductive medical or veterinary decision phase as a purely intellectual exercise"*. In contrast, methods that pertain to the steps preceding diagnosis, i.e. the data gathering or processing steps, but do not claim the diagnostic

については、いわゆる「スイスタイプクレーム」（「疾患Yを治療するための医薬を製造するための化合物Xの使用」）がもはや認められないと判断されている。EPC2000では、上述した「用途が限定された物のクレーム」のみが許可され得る。

3.4　人間又は動物の体の診断方法の除外

第53条(c)の最後の除外は、「人間又は動物の体に対して実施される」場合の「診断方法」に関するものである。

拡大審判部は、診断方法が「人間又は動物の体に対して実施される」ことになる条件について、G 1/04において指針を示している。この審決を受けて、その工程のすべてが「人間又は動物の体に対して」実施される場合にのみ、クレームはこの除外に該当する。クレームが、インビトロで実施される少なくとも１つの（技術的）工程を含む場合、そのクレームはこの除外に該当しない。したがって、マーカー又は特定の診断値をインビトロで決定することを含む診断方法クレームは、この除外に該当しない。この理由１つによっても、除外について実際の範囲が制限されている。

このため、（複数の工程を含む）診断方法及び手術方法又は治療方法の判断は大きく異なる。複数の工程を含む方法において手術工程又は治療工程が１つあれば、それは、この除外に該当するのに十分である。対照的に、診断方法については、その工程のすべてが人間又は動物の体に対して実施されなければ、それは除外されない。

加えて、G 1/04では、診断方法として除外されるべき方法について、より厳密な意味で診断を行う工程を含まなければならないと判断されている。厳密な意味での診断とは、審決の文言によれば「純粋な知力の行使としての演繹的な医療的又は獣医的判断段階を象徴する厳密な意味で治癒目的のための診断」である。対照的に、診断前の工程（すなわち、データ収集工程又はデータ処理工程）に関する方法であって、診断工程それ自体をクレームしていない方法は除

step as such, are not excluded. However, most diagnostic method claims are directed to the data gathering/processing aspect of the method, but do not necessarily include, as an essential feature of defining the contribution to the art, the *"purely intellectual exercise"* of *the "medical or veterinary decision phase"*, *i.e.* the diagnosis *stricto sensu*. For this additional reason, exclusions of diagnostic methods are quite rare in day-to-day practice.

Should an objection be raised, it can be assessed whether to omit the "medical or veterinary decision phase", and/or add a limitation to "in vitro" for at least one particular method step.

In principle, purpose-limited product claims are allowable pursuant to Art. 54(4) and (5) EPC, for the first- or second diagnostic use of substances or compositions. However, such purpose limited product claims are only allowable if, in the first place, the method claim as such is excluded under Art. 53(c) EPC. For the reasons outlined above, this is quite rarely the case. Hence, in most cases it will not be possible to utilize purpose limited product claims in the diagnostic field. In these cases, however, method and use claims are permissible.

外されない。その一方、ほとんどの診断方法のクレームは、その方法のデータ収集／処理の態様を対象とするものであり、先行技術に対する貢献を定義する本質的な特徴として、「医療的又は獣医的判断段階」の「純粋な知力の行使」（すなわち、厳密な意味での診断）を必ずしも含んでいない。このさらなる理由により、診断方法が除外されることは、日常の実務では非常に珍しい。

拒絶理由が提起された場合は、「医療的又は獣医的判断段階」を方法から削除すること、及び／又は少なくとも１つの特定の工程に「インビトロ」の限定を追加することを検討することができる。

原則として、物質又は組成物の第一診断用途又は第二診断用途については、用途を限定する物のクレームは、第54条(4)及び(5)の規定により認められ得る。一方、このような用途を限定した物のクレームは、方法のクレームそれ自体が第53条(c)に基づきそもそも除外される場合にのみ認められる。上記の理由により、これは非常に珍しい場合である。したがって、診断分野では、ほとんどの場合、用途を限定した物のクレームを利用することは不可能であろう。このような場合は、方法クレーム及び使用クレームが認められる。

Chapter 6

Patentable Subject-Matter II

特許の対象 II

Michele Baccelli
Rainer E. Zangs

MEMO

▶ コンピュータにより実施される発明(以下、CII)については、最近、「修正された課題解決アプローチ」の新バージョンが審査基準に導入されました。

▶ このアプローチによると、発明に照らして達成される技術的効果を根拠にして決められる「技術的性質に貢献する特徴」に着目することにより進歩性について審査されます。この分野の実務で使われてきた「修正された課題解決アプローチ」の旧バージョンとの違いについては、§4〜§6を参照してください。

▶ 新バージョンにおける「技術的性質に貢献する特徴」の認定手法は、「人為的取決め等とシステム化手法に分けて認定するのは適切ではなく、クレームに記載された発明を全体としてとらえる」という日本の実務に類似すると思われます。ただし、客観的課題の設定の仕方が欧州に特有です。

▶ この分野の発明について詳細な情報をご希望であれば、以下に示す文献を併せてご参照ください。

1 Baccelli Michele 著(平塚三好・日本国際知的財産保護協会事務局訳)「欧州特許条約の下でのコンピュータ実施発明」日本国際知的財産保護協会月報(AIPPI)53巻4号(2008年)202-219頁。

2 Baccelli Michele 著(平塚三好・日本国際知的財産保護協会事

務局訳)「ソフトウェアシミュレータの特許保護：欧州特許庁における実務と未解決の問題」日本国際知的財産保護協会月報（AIPPI）54巻4号（2009年）178-190頁。

3 Baccelli Michele, Muller Markus 著（平塚三好ほか訳）「ドイツにおけるコンピュータ実施発明及び欧州特許庁との比較検討」日本国際知的財産保護協会月報（AIPPI）55巻12号（2010年）836-848頁。

1 Software Patents at the EPO: A Quick Guide

Software inventions, or Computer Implemented Inventions (CIIs) as they are usually called at the EPO, are not excluded from patent protection if they are technical. However, inventive step of CII claims is acknowledged only on the basis of claim features providing a technical contribution.

Examination can be said to follow a two-stage approach. In the first stage, eligibility is affirmed if the claim defines at least a technical feature, without any reference to the state of the art and regardless of how trivial the technical feature is (in fact, a claim comprising a common computer would suffice to this effect). In the second stage, if novelty is established, inventive step is examined by focusing on those features which contribute to the technical character of the invention. Such features are determined on the basis of the technical effects achieved in the context of the invention. Features making no technical contribution, or any non-technical effect achieved by the invention, may instead appear in the formulation of the objective technical problem as a constraint that has to be met by the skilled person.

As a consequence of such an approach, overcoming the eligibility hurdle is relatively simple at the EPO. However, overcoming the inventive step hurdle may be relatively difficult in practice, since the claim may be stripped off of features not contributing to a technical effect.

While technical character is a central aspect to CIIs, there is no definition as to what is technical and what is not. Consolidated experience and in-depth knowledge of case law provide guidance in overcoming uncertainties and difficulties on a case-by-case basis.

1 欧州特許庁におけるソフトウェアの特許：概要

　ソフトウェア関連発明は、欧州特許庁ではコンピュータにより実施される発明（以下、CII）と概して呼ばれるが、技術性を有するCIIであれば特許による保護から除外されない。一方、CIIのクレームに進歩性が認められるのは、そのクレームの特徴が技術的貢献をもたらす場合のみである。

　CIIの審査は、2段階方式に則って行うとされる。第一の段階では、なんらかの技術的特徴が少なくとも1つクレームに特定されていれば、技術水準には一切言及されず、また、その技術的特徴が取るに足らないものであっても、適格性が認められる。実際のところ、ありふれたコンピュータを記載したクレームで十分である。第二の段階では、新規性が認められた場合は、発明の技術的性質に貢献する特徴に着目することにより進歩性について審査される。技術的性質に貢献する特徴は、発明に照らして達成される技術的効果に基づいて決められる。技術的にまったく貢献しない特徴、又は、発明によって達成される非技術的効果については、客観的な技術の課題を設定する際に当業者によって対処されるべき制約として現れる。

　こうしたアプローチをとる結果、欧州特許実務では、適格性の要件を満たすことは比較的容易である。しかし、進歩性については、技術的効果に貢献しない特徴が取り除かれたクレームに基づくので、実際のところ、進歩性の要件を満たすことは多少難しくなっている。

　CIIの中心は技術的性質にあるが、何が技術で何が技術でないかについての定義はない。経験を積み重ね、ケースローを深く理解することが不明確性や難題をケース・バイ・ケースで解消するための一助となる。

2 Legal Provisions and Definitions

While software related invention is a generally understood expression, we will use the term Computer Implemented Invention (CII) as defined by the EPO:

> "An invention whose implementation involves the use of a computer, computer network or other programmable apparatus, the invention having one or more features which are realized wholly or partly by means of a computer program is termed a computer implemented invention", EPO OJ, November 2007, pages 594–600.

Evidently, the definition covers a wide range of software based innovations ranging from business methods to Graphical User Interfaces (GUI), from computer games to simulation software, from software control of industrial processes to software control of shopping systems, and in general to any solution implemented at least partly by means of a computer.

The general patentability requirements applicable to CIIs are given in Article 52(1) EPC setting out that patents are granted to inventions. No definition for invention is explicitly given, though. However, Article 52(2) EPC defines an exclusion list of what shall not be considered inventions, and thus not eligible to patent protection: (a) discoveries, scientific theories and mathematical methods; (b) aesthetic creations; (c) schemes, rules and methods for performing mental acts, playing games or doing business, and programs for computers; (d) presentations of information.

It is important to note that not only programs for computers, but all above listed items are relevant to CIIs, as in fact a mathematical method, a mental rule, a game, a presentation of information or a business scheme may all be implemented on a computer.

2　法の規定と定義

「ソフトウェア関連発明」という表現が一般的に認識されているが、本章では、欧州特許庁が以下のように定義するコンピュータにより実施される発明（CII）という用語を用いる。

> 「その実施にコンピュータ、コンピュータネットワーク、その他プログラム可能な装置の使用を伴い、その１つ以上の特徴の全部又は一部がコンピュータプログラムによって実現される発明を、コンピュータにより実施される発明と呼ぶ」（欧州特許庁公報2007年11月号、594-600頁）。

明らかに、上記定義はソフトウェアをベースにした発明を広い範囲でカバーしている。その範囲は、ビジネス方法からグラフィカル・ユーザ・インターフェース（GUI）、コンピュータゲームからシミュレーションソフトウェア、工業プロセスのソフトウェア制御からショッピングシステムのソフトウェア制御、そして、少なくともその一部がコンピュータを使って実施される解決策までと多岐にわたる。

CIIには、一般的な特許要件（「欧州特許は、……発明について与えられる」）を規定している第52条(1)が適用される。ただし、この規定では発明についての明確な定義が一切されていない。一方、第52条(2)には、発明とはみなされず、よって、特許を受けることができない事項が挙げられた除外リストがある。つまり、以下の事項は発明とはみなされない：(a)発見、科学の理論及び数学的方法、(b)美的創造物、(c)精神的行為、ゲーム又は事業を行うための計画、ルール及び方法、並びにコンピュータプログラム、(d)情報の提示。

留意すべき点は、コンピュータプログラムだけでなく、上記除外リストにある事項のすべてがCIIに関連していることである。実際のところ、数学的方法、精神的行為、ゲーム、情報の提示又は事業計画は、おそらく、そのすべてがコンピュータ上で実施され得るものである。

The exclusions from patentability shall however not be absolute, but (narrowly) applied only to "patent applications or patents that relate to said subject matter or activities as such", Article 52(3) EPC.

The Boards of Appeal have clarified certain implicit requirements of an invention, namely that it should solve a technical problem and be defined by technical features. The EPO often uses the term *technicality* to refer to technical character of an invention or to technical considerations underlying an invention. Based on this, the meaning of the exclusion list and of "as such" can be exemplified as that:

> CIIs, even if directed to any item included in the exclusion list, can enjoy patent protection if they have technicality and if they are directed to a non-obvious technical solution.

3 What Makes a Subject Matter Technical?

As anticipated above, technicality plays a central role in establishing patent eligibility and inventive activity. The EPO has however refrained from giving a definition as to what "technical" means, on grounds that technological progress may soon render obsolete any such definition. Nevertheless, the following are examples elaborated from EPO case law, which could serve as guidance in assessing technicality of other cases:

- T 208/84, VICOM: "a method of digitally filtering a two-dimensional data array having elements arranged in rows and columns" is not regarded as technical since it is directed to mathematical expressions (for instance, applying the convolution to a data array). However, "a method of digitally filtering images in the form of a two dimensional data array" may be regarded as technical, since it is an industrial application and as such belonging to the technical world. According to the Board, a "method for obtaining

しかし、こうした特許性からの除外は絶対的ではなく、「欧州特許出願又は欧州特許が(2)で言及される対象又は行為それ自体に関連する範囲においてのみ」と（狭義に）適用される（第52条(3)）。

審判部は、発明における特定の黙示要件（すなわち、発明が技術的課題を解決し、かつ、技術的特徴によって特定されるべきものであること）を明らかにしてきた。欧州特許庁は、発明の技術的性質又は発明の背景にある技術的問題について言及する際、『技術的であること』という用語を頻繁に用いる。これに基づき、上記除外リスト及び「それ自体」の趣旨について、例えば、以下のように述べることができる。

「CIIは、除外リストに含まれる事項を対象にしているとしても、技術的であり、かつ、非自明な技術的解決手段を提供することを目的とするものであれば、特許による保護を受けることができる。」

3 主題を技術的とするものは何か？

上述したように、「技術的であること」は特許対象としての適格性と発明的活動とを確立する中心的役割を担う。一方、欧州特許庁は、技術の進歩により、およそ定義といったものはいずれ時代に合わなくなることを理由として、「技術的」の意味を定義することを控えている。以上の次第ではあるが、以下に、欧州特許庁のケースローから抜粋した事例を示す。これらの事例は、「技術的であること」を他の事例で判断する際に参考となり得る。

- T 208/84（VICOM）「行と列に配置した要素を有する2次元データ配列のデジタルフィルタ法」は、数式（例えば、データ配列を重畳積分する）を対象とするため、技術性を有するとはみなされない。しかし、「二次元データ配列形式の画像のデジタルフィルタ法」の場合、産業上の用途があり、それ自体は技術分野に属しているため、技術性があるとみなされる可能性がある。審判部によれば、「人工的に再現した対象（例えば、CAS/CAM）の画像をも含む物理的対象物の画像の取得及び／又は再現方法」

and / or reproducing an image of a physical object or even an image of a simulated object (as in CAS/CAM) may be used e.g. in investigating properties of the object or designing an industrial article". Also, while mathematical methods operate on an abstract level, a technical process is one that is "carried out on a physical entity by some technical means implementing the method and provides as a result a certain change in that entity", when noting that the entity can "be a material object but equally an image stored as an electric signal".

- T 110/90, IBM: a method "for transforming a source document cast in a first editable form which includes a plurality of input items therein, to a target document of a second form, comprising output items" would not be regarded as technical under EP practice, since this could also be exclusively executed mentally by a human being, possibly with the use of appropriate decision tables. Instead, an amended claim to a "method of transforming text which is represented in the form of digital data" comprising a step of "digitally processing the text" and further specifying that the input and output items refers to "input or output control items" may be considered technical. According to the Board, such a claim can "only be understood as meaning data in the form of digital electrical signals (bits and bytes)", and thus not performable mentally; and that it "must be understood as acting on items of hardware such as a printer", and not on abstract text items.

- T 769/92, SOHEI discusses a claim directed "a computer system for plural types of independent management including at least financial and inventory management", further defining different types of files and processing operations performed on data comprised in said files in order to produce output data to be visualized. While the financial and inventory management of such claim, when taken alone, could be regarded as being a business activity excluded from patentability, technicality is provided by the fact that the claim addresses technical considerations in that "the system allows data necessary for one type of processing … and data neces-

を、例えば、その対象物の特性調査、又は、産業製品の設計に用いることは可能である。また、数学的方法は抽象的に行われるが、ある物理的実体が「有形物であると同時に電気信号として保存される画像」であり得ることに注目すると、技術的プロセスとは「なんらかの技術的な方法実行手段を用いて、その物理的実体に対して実行され、結果として、その実体に一定の変化をもたらす」プロセスである。

- T 110/90（IBM）「複数の入力項目を含む第一の編集可能な様式で作成したソース文書を、出力項目を含む第二の様式の目標文書に変換する」方法は、専ら、人間が、おそらくは適当な決定表を用いて精神的に実行することができるため、欧州特許の慣例では技術性があるとはみなされない。一方、クレームを、「デジタルデータ様式で表したテキストを変換する方法であって、前記テキストをデジタル処理し」、さらに、前記入力及び出力項目は「入力又は出力制御項目」を指すことを特定するステップを含む「方法」と補正すると、技術性が認められる可能性がある。審判部によれば、このようなクレームは、「デジタル電気信号（ビット、バイト）形式のデータを意味するとしか理解できない」ため、精神的に遂行可能なものではなく、また、抽象的なテキスト項目ではなく、「プリンタのようなハードウェアの項目に作用すると理解する必要がある」と述べている。

- T 769/92（SOHEI）この事例では、「少なくとも財務・在庫管理を含む複数種類の独立管理用コンピュータシステム」であって、視覚化対象出力データを生成するために、異なる種類のファイルを定義し、かつ、前記ファイルに含まれるデータに演算処理を行うコンピュータシステムのクレームについて議論されている。このようなクレームの財務・在庫管理は、これのみを取り上げた場合、特許を受けることができないビジネス行為とみなされる可能性がある。しかし、「前記システムにより、ある種類の処理に必要なデータ、……独立して行う別の種類の処理に必要なデータ、……単一、かつ、共通の様式を用いて入力、……前記ユーザに表示する」とす

sary for another type of processing to be performed independently ... to be input using a single, common form ... displayed to the user".

Further to the above examples, the following can be regarded as rough indicators of the presence of technical character:

- the problem solved by a feature or by a combination of features is technical;

- the claimed solution provides technical improvement(s) to a technical device or process;

- technical features and means are necessary for carrying out a method or process;

- technical considerations are required, especially when solving a technical problem by means of a technical feature.

4 Examination of CIIs

It can be said that examination is carried out in a two-stage approach: first eligibility is determined; then, if novelty is established, inventive step is assessed. Technicality plays a role in both stages, as it can also be derived from the following.

5 The First Stage of Examination: Eligibility

When deciding whether an invention is patent eligible or not, Examiners analyse the claim as a whole and without taking the prior art into account.

ることで、このクレームは技術的問題を記載しており、この点により技術性がもたらされている。

上記に加えて、技術的性質の存在を大まかに示す表示と捉えることができるものを下に示す。

- ある特徴又は複数の特徴の組合せにより解決される課題に技術性があること。

- クレームに記載の解決手段が技術的なデバイス又はプロセスに技術的改善をもたらすこと。

- 方法又はプロセスを実施するために技術的特徴及び手段が必要であること。

- 技術的特徴を用いて技術的課題を解決するときはとりわけ、技術的考慮が必要とされること。

4　CIIの審査

審査は2段階に分かれるといえる。まず、適格性を判断する。その後、新規性が認められた場合は、進歩性を判断する。以下の説明からもわかるように、「技術的であること」は両段階において一翼を担っている。

5　審査の第一段階：適格性

発明が特許の対象として適格であるか否かを決める場合、審査官は、先行技術を考慮せず、そのクレームを全体的に分析する。

If the claim as a whole does not have technical character, then the claim is rejected as excluded from patent protection under Article 52(2) and (3) EPC. This can occur, for instance, if the claim defines a pure abstract mental activity or a business scheme without any explicit intervention of technical means.

Since the assessment is made independently of the prior art, the eligibility test is passed by including in the claim even the most trivial technical features like a computer or a pen. It is thus important for the application to provide support for the technical features necessary to the implementation of the invention.

From the above, it should be evident that the eligibility hurdle is relatively low at the EPO.

6   The Second Stage of Examination: Inventive Step and the Modified Problem Solution Approach (PSA)

The low eligibility hurdle shall however not be misleading: obtaining a patent for a CII may in fact still be difficult, since features not contributing to technicality can be decisive when assessing inventive step.

Case law has established that patents should be granted to inventions making a technical contribution over the prior art, or leading to technical improvements. As such, inventive step is based only on those features that make a technical contribution.

In view of the above, and of the fact that CII claims may present a combination of technical and non-technical features, the EPO has modified the PSA to ensure, as far as possible, that patents are granted to inventions providing an inventive contribution to technology.

クレームが全体的に技術的性質を備えていない場合、そのクレームは第52条(2)及び(3)により、特許の保護対象から除外される。これは、例えば、技術的手段が明示的に介在しない、純粋に抽象的な精神的行為や事業計画をクレームが定義している場合に起こり得る。

先行技術をまったく考慮せずに判断されるため、コンピュータやペンといった非常にありふれた技術的特徴が含まれているだけで、そのクレームは適格性審査をパスする。よって、発明の実施に必要な技術的特徴が出願書類に開示されていることが重要である。

上記から明らかであるが、欧州特許庁における適格性判断のハードルはさほど高くない。

6 審査の第二段階：
進歩性及び修正された課題解決アプローチ

適格性のハードルが低いとはいえ、誤解のないように言及しておくと、「技術的であること」に貢献しない特徴が進歩性を判断する際に決定的となり得るため、CIIにとって特許取得は依然として難しいといえる。

ケースローによると、先行技術に対して技術的貢献をもたらすか、又は、技術的改良をもたらす発明に対して特許が付与されるべきであることが確立されている。そのため、進歩性の判断は、技術的貢献をもたらす特徴を唯一の根拠としている。

上記の点、並びに、技術的特徴と非技術的特徴とが組み合わされてCIIクレームに存在することもある事実から考えて、欧州特許庁は、技術の発展に独創的な貢献をもたらす発明について可能な限り特許が与えられるようにするために、課題解決アプローチを修正したのである。

The modified objective technical problem (OTP) is schematically illustrated in the EPO Guidelines, which we have here slightly modified for illustrative purposes:

(i) To start with, the features which contribute to the technical character of the invention are determined "on the basis of the technical effects achieved in the context of the invention".

(ii) Based on the features identified as contributing to the technical character of the invention, the closest prior art is selected.

(iii) The distinguishing features over the closest prior art are determined, as well as the corresponding technical effects "in the context of the claim as a whole". At this point, when having in mind the determined technical effects, a discrimination is made between those features which make a technical contribution and those which do not.

(a) If there are no differences (not even a non-technical difference), an objection of lack of novelty is raised.

(b) If the differences do not make any technical contribution, an objection under Art.56 is raised. The reasoning for the objection should be that the subject-matter of a claim cannot be inventive if there is no technical contribution to the prior art.

(c1) If the differences include features making a technical contribution, then the objective technical problem is formulated on the basis of the technical effect(s) achieved by these features.

(c2) In addition, if the differences include features making no technical contribution: these features may appear in the formulation of the objective technical problem as part of what is "given" to the skilled person, in partic-

欧州特許庁の審査基準には、修正された客観的な技術的課題の設定について概説されているが、本書では、説明のために若干の変更を加えている。

(i) まずはじめに、「発明によって達成される技術的効果に基づいて」発明の技術的性質に貢献する特徴を決定する。

(ii) 発明の技術的性質に貢献すると特定された特徴に基づき、最も近い先行技術を選択する。

(iii) 最も近い先行技術から相違する特徴を決定し、それに相当する技術的効果を「クレーム全体としての内容で」決定する。この時点で、その決定された技術的効果を念頭において、技術的貢献をもたらす特徴とそうでない特徴を区別する。

(a) 相違点（非技術的なものも含めて）が皆無の場合、新規性の欠如による審査官の拒絶理由が提起される。

(b) 相違点が技術的貢献をもたらすものではない場合、第56条に基づく拒絶理由が提起される。なぜなら、先行技術に対して技術的貢献がなければクレームの対象に進歩性があるとはいえないからである。

(c1) 相違点に技術的貢献をもたらす特徴が含まれている場合、その特徴により達成される技術的効果に基づいて客観的な技術的課題を設定する。

(c2) さらに、相違点に技術的貢献をもたらさない特徴が含まれている場合、その特徴は、客観的な技術的課題を設定する際に、当業者に「与えられた」もの（具体的には、対処すべき制約）として現れる。同様に、発明によ

ular as a constraint that has to be met. Similarly, any non-technical effect achieved by the invention may appear in the technical problem as a constraint to be met.

(c3) Once the technical problem is formulated, possibly taking into account the non-technical constraint(s), it is determined whether the claimed technical solution to the objective technical problem is obvious to the person skilled in the art. The presence or absence of inventive activity is thus established.

It can be said that including non-technical features, even if claimed, into the OTP is effectively applied in derogation to the general principle of avoiding hindsight, according to which the OTP should not comprise claim features or even pointers thereto. By way of the modified approach, however, the EPO ensures that even if a claim may easily pass the eligibility test, the same claim will lead to grant only if it provides a non-obvious technical solution.

It is also interesting noting that the modified PSA is in place since long time, but that it has been modified with the Guidelines of November 2015. In particular, the previous version of the modified PSA allowed Examiners to start examination by identifying the "non-technical aspects" as claimed or as derivable from the description, and by formulating a requirement specification on the basis of the non-technical aspects. Thereafter, Examiners were asked to consider the (remaining) technical aspects, and assess whether the (remaining) features are inventive.

The new version of the modified PSA has deleted any reference to "non-technical aspects", and apparently puts the initial examination focus on the features actually claimed, as well as their technical effect within the context of the invention. Only after the technical aim of the invention has been put into the spotlight, then it is possible to determine which are those features non contributing to technical character.

って達成される非技術的効果も、対処すべき制約として技術的課題に現れる。

(c3) 客観的技術的課題が設定されると（非技術的制約を考慮することによる場合もある）、その客観的技術的課題を解決するためにクレームに記載された技術的手段が当業者にとって自明であるか否かを判断する。このようにして、発明的活動の有無が確定される。

　クレームに記載された非技術的特徴を客観的技術的課題に含めれば、事実上、後知恵防止の一般的原則から逸脱することになる。この原則によれば、クレームの特徴はもとより、それを示唆するものを客観的な技術的課題に含むべきではない。欧州特許庁は、修正後の課題解決アプローチを用いることにより、適格性審査を簡単にパスできるクレームであっても、非自明な技術的解決手段を提供する場合にのみ特許が付与されることを確実にしている。

　また、興味深い点は、修正された課題解決アプローチは長きにわたって実施されてきたが、2015年の11月付け審査基準においてさらに修正が加えられたことである。特に、修正された課題解決アプローチの旧バージョンでは、審査官は、クレームに記載又は明細書から導き出せる「非技術的態様」を特定し、非技術的態様に基づいて要求仕様を設定することで審査を開始することができた。その後、審査官は、（残りの）技術的態様を検討し、（残りの）特徴に進歩性があるか否かを判断するよう求められた。

　修正された課題解決アプローチの新バージョンでは、「非技術的態様」への言及はすべて削除されており、審査の初期段階における焦点を、クレームに実際に記載された特徴とその技術的効果に絞っていると考えられる。発明の技術上の目的が明らかにされてはじめて、技術的性質に貢献しない特徴を決定することができる。

It can be said that the older version of the modified PSA allowed examination to start directly with depriving the claim from non-technical aspects. In contrast thereto, the new version of the modified PSA requires a higher initial attention to the claim features and their technical effect, before non-technical features can be stripped off from the same claim.

The amendments to the Guidelines can theoretically mean that Examiners need to be more careful before dismissing certain features as non-technical. Practice will show whether these amendments will lead to any change in practice, and more importantly whether it can lead to higher legal certainty and predictability in this field.

7 Types of Claims

A CII invention can and should be claimed in different forms, for instance as method, apparatus, system, signal, computer program, medium for storing the program as long as the set of claims complies with the requirements of Rule 43.

It is however noted that, for a computer program claim not to be excluded from patentability, it is necessary to show that it is capable of bringing about, when running on or loaded into a computer, a further technical effect going beyond the "normal" physical interactions between the program (software) and the computer (hardware) on which it is run, as presently defined in the EPO Guidelines. In practice, if a method claim is considered allowable, then also a computer program claim referring to the method or defining features corresponding to those of the method would be allowable.

修正された課題解決アプローチの旧バージョンでは、クレームから非技術的態様を取り除くことで、直ちに審査を開始することができたといえる。それとは対照的に、修正された課題解決アプローチの新バージョンでは、クレームから非技術的特徴を取り除く前に、まず、クレームの特徴及びその技術的効果について一層高い水準の注意を払うよう求めている。

　審査基準の改訂が理論的に意味するものは、ある特徴を非技術的なものとして片づけてしまう前に、審査官はより慎重を期すべきだということであろう。審査基準の改訂により実務になんらかの変化がもたらされるのか、さらに重要な点として、当該技術分野においてより高い法的確実性及び予見性がもたらされるのか、実務を通して明らかになるであろう。

7　クレームの類別

　CII 発明は、一連のクレームが規則43の要件に従う限り、異なる形式でクレームすることが可能であり、また、それが望ましい。例えば、方法、装置、システム、信号、コンピュータプログラム、プログラムを格納する媒体としてのクレームである。

　留意点として、コンピュータプログラムのクレームが特許の対象から除外されないためには、コンピュータプログラム（ソフトウェア）がコンピュータ上で実行され又はコンピュータに読み込まれた場合に、該プログラムとこれが実行されるコンピュータ（ハードウェア）との間で、「標準的」物理的相互作用の範疇を超えた、さらなる技術的効果が実現可能であることを示す必要がある。これは、欧州特許庁の審査基準の現行規定である。実際問題として、ある方法クレームが特許性ありと判断される場合、該方法に言及したコンピュータプログラムのクレームや、該方法の特徴に対応する特徴を特定したコンピュータプログラムのクレームも同様に、その特許性が認められると考えてよい。

8 Certain Aspects Relating to the Search Phase

When dealing with CII inventions, and especially those having abstract or business related aspects, it is not unusual receiving a notification that no search could be carried out. This can occur when the claims are considered to be devoid of technical character. In other situations, the Examiner may regard the claim as defining only trivial technical features, like a computer: in this case, no prior art may be cited.

The applicant has however the possibility, when entering examination, to amend the non-searched claims in order to specify features lending technical character, and/or to argue in favor of technicality.

If the examining division is of the opinion that the initial deficiencies have been corrected by amendment or by convincing arguments provided by the applicant, it can still perform an additional search which may result in new prior art relevant for the claimed subject matter. Also, it is not infrequent that Examiners cite new documents also in late stages of the procedure.

9 Some Recommendations

In an ideal world, and when wanting to maximize the chances of success, a CII invention for the EPO should be drafted in an EP application differently and independently from an application directed to the same solution and intended for other jurisdictions. In a real world where a single text is to be drafted for later prosecution in multiple jurisdictions, the following is worth noting.

Since amendments shall be based on the application as originally filed, it is very important to ensure that the application documents as originally filed clearly disclose the technical character of the invention, e.g. in terms of technical fea-

8 調査段階に関連する特定の側面

　CII 発明を取り扱う場合は、調査が不可能であった旨の通知を受けることが珍しくない。これは CII 発明（特に、抽象的又は事業に関連する態様を備えたもの）を取り扱う場合に当てはまる。この事態は、クレームが技術的特性を欠くと考えられるときに起こる。これ以外の状況では、審査官が、コンピュータ等のありふれた技術的特徴しかクレームに特定されていないとみなす場合である。この場合、先行技術が引用されないことがある。

　ただし、審査段階に入ると、出願人は、調査されなかったクレームについて補正をすることで、技術的特性をもたらす特徴を特定したり、「技術的であること」を主張して反論したりすることが可能である。

　出願人により提出された補正書又は反論により当初の不備が解消されたとの見解にいたれば、審査部は、追加の調査をするが、その結果として、クレームの対象に関連する新たな先行技術が見つかることもある。また、審査手続の後期に到って審査官が新たな文献を引用することも往々にしてある。

9 提案事項

　欧州特許庁において CII 発明について特許取得の可能性を最大限にしたい場合は、他の管轄地域向けに意図された同一の解決手段を、それとは別個、かつ、独立して欧州用として起案するのが理想的である。1 つの文書を作成して多数の管轄地域におけるその後の手続に対処する現実においては、以下の事項は注目に値する。

　当初の出願書類に基づいて補正をしなければならないので、出願当初の出願書類に発明の技術的性質を明確、かつ、確実に開示することが非常に重要である。例えば、技術的効果を提供する技術的特徴によって発明の技術的性質を開

tures providing a technical effect.

Also, it is recommendable under EP practice to be silent on possible non-technical benefits reached by means of the invention. Similarly, it is generally better not mentioning possible non-technical motivations behind the invention, like for instance the wish to provide an incentive to purchase by means of a better user interface.

Finally, particular care needs to be taken for inventions that can be regarded as a computer implementation of an idea stemming from pure non-technical considerations or motivations.

示する。

　また、欧州特許実務では、発明により達成される非技術的利益への言及は避けることが望ましい。同様に、発明の背景にある動機で考えられ得る非技術的なものへの言及も避けたほうがよい。例えば、改良したユーザインターフェースを用いて購入意欲を煽る等の動機である。

　最後に、純粋に非技術的な問題や動機に端を発した思想をコンピュータ上で実施するとみなされ得る発明については、特に注意が必要である。

Part *II*

Prosecution of EP Applications

欧州特許出願の手続

Legal Text

Article 75 Filing of a European patent application

(1) A European patent application may be filed:

   (a) with the European Patent Office, or

   (b) if the law of a Contracting State so permits, and subject to Article 76, paragraph 1, with the central industrial property office or other competent authority of that State. Any application filed in this way shall have the same effect as if it had been filed on the same date with the European Patent Office.

(2) Paragraph 1 shall not preclude the application of legislative or regulatory provisions which, in any Contracting State:

   (a) govern inventions which, owing to the nature of their subject-matter, may not be communicated abroad without the prior authorisation of the competent authorities of that State, or

   (b) prescribe that any application is to be filed initially with a national authority, or make direct filing with another authority subject to prior authorisation.

Article 76 European divisional applications

(1) A European divisional application shall be filed directly with the European Patent Office in accordance with the Implementing Regulations. It may be filed only in respect of subject-matter which does not extend beyond the content of the earlier application as filed; in so far as this requirement is complied with, the divisional application shall be deemed to have been

法 規

第75条　欧州特許出願

(1) 欧州特許出願は、次のいずれかに提出することができる。

　(a) 欧州特許庁

　(b) 締約国の法令が認める場合には、第76条(1)の規定に従うことを条件として、当該締約国の中央工業所有権官庁又は締約国の他の管轄当局（この手段で提出された出願は、同日に欧州特許庁に提出されたものと同一の効果を有する）

(2) (1)は、各締約国において、次のいずれかの立法又は規制規定が適用されることを妨げない。

　(a) その対象の本質からみて、当該締約国の管轄当局の事前の承認なしに外国に知らせてはならない発明を統治するもの

　(b) いずれの出願も国内当局に最初に提出しなければならないか、さもなければ事前に承認を受けたうえで他の当局に直接に出願することを規定するもの

第76条　欧州分割出願

(1) 欧州分割出願は、施行規則に従って、欧州特許庁に直接に提出する。欧州分割出願は、先の出願の出願時の内容を超えない対象についてのみ行うことができる。この要件を満たす場合に限り、分割出願は、当該先の出願の出願日に提出されたものとみなされ、優先権の利益を享受する。

filed on the date of filing of the earlier application and shall enjoy any right of priority.

(2) All the Contracting States designated in the earlier application at the time of filing of a European divisional application shall be deemed to be designated in the divisional application.

Article 78   Requirements of a European patent application

(1) A European patent application shall contain:

(a) a request for the grant of a European patent;

(b) a description of the invention;

(c) one or more claims;

(d) any drawings referred to in the description or the claims;

(e) an abstract,

and satisfy the requirements laid down in the Implementing Regulations.

(2) A European patent application shall be subject to the payment of the filing fee and the search fee. If the filing fee or the search fee is not paid in due time, the application shall be deemed to be withdrawn.

Article 79   Designation of Contracting States

(1) All the Contracting States party to this Convention at the time of filing of the European patent application shall be deemed to be designated in the request for grant of a European patent.

(2) 欧州分割出願の出願時に、先の出願において指定されているすべての締約国は、欧州分割出願においても指定されたものとみなす。

第78条　欧州特許出願の要件

(1) 欧州特許出願は、次のものを含むものとし、

(a) 欧州特許の付与を求める願書

(b) 発明の記載（明細書）

(c) １つ以上のクレーム

(d) 明細書又はクレームにおいて言及されている図面

(e) 要約書

かつ、施行規則に定める要件を満たすものとする。

(2) 欧州特許出願については、出願手数料及び調査手数料を納付しなければならない。出願手数料又は調査手数料が適時に納付されないときは、その出願は取り下げられたものとみなす。

第79条　締約国の指定

(1) 欧州特許出願の出願時における本条約のすべての締約国は、欧州特許の付与を求める願書において指定されたものとみなす。

(2) The designation of a Contracting State may be subject to the payment of a designation fee.

(3) The designation of a Contracting State may be withdrawn at any time up to the grant of the European patent.

Article 80 Date of filing

The date of filing of a European patent application shall be the date on which the requirements laid down in the Implementing Regulations are fulfilled.

Article 82 Unity of invention

The European patent application shall relate to one invention only or to a group of inventions so linked as to form a single general inventive concept.

Article 84 Claims

The claims shall define the matter for which protection is sought. They shall be clear and concise and be supported by the description.

Article 86 Renewal fees for the European patent application

(1) Renewal fees for the European patent application shall be paid to the European Patent Office in accordance with the Implementing Regulations. These fees shall be due in respect of the third year and each subsequent year, calculated from the date of filing of the application. If a renewal fee is not paid in due time, the application shall be deemed to be withdrawn.

(2) 締約国の指定については、指定手数料を納付しなければならない。

(3) 締約国の指定は、欧州特許が付与されるまでは、いつでも取り下げることができる。

第80条　出願日

欧州特許出願の出願日は、施行規則に定める要件が満たされた日とする。

第82条　発明の単一性

欧州特許出願は、1つの発明のみ又は単一の包括的発明概念を形成するように関連している一群の発明について行う。

第84条　クレーム

クレームには、保護が求められている事項を特定する。クレームは、明確かつ簡潔に記載されていなければならず、明細書により十分な裏付けがされていなければならない。

第86条　欧州特許出願の更新手数料

(1) 欧州特許出願の更新手数料は、施行規則に従って、欧州特許庁に納付する。更新手数料は、出願日から起算して第3年及びそれに続く各年につき納付しなければならない。当該更新手数料が期限どおりに納付されない場合は、その出願は取り下げられたものとみなす。

(2) The obligation to pay renewal fees shall terminate with the payment of the renewal fee due in respect of the year in which the mention of the grant of the European patent is published in the European Patent Bulletin.

Article 87 Priority right

(1) Any person who has duly filed, in or for

  (a) any State party to the Paris Convention for the Protection of Industrial Property or

  (b) any Member of the World Trade Organization,

  an application for a patent, a utility model or a utility certificate, or his successor in title, shall enjoy, for the purpose of filing a European patent application in respect of the same invention, a right of priority during a period of twelve months from the date of filing of the first application.

(2) Every filing that is equivalent to a regular national filing under the national law of the State where it was made or under bilateral or multilateral agreements, including this Convention, shall be recognised as giving rise to a right of priority.

(3) A regular national filing shall mean any filing that is sufficient to establish the date on which the application was filed, whatever the outcome of the application may be.

(4) A subsequent application in respect of the same subject-matter as a previous first application and filed in or for the same State shall be considered as the first application for the purposes of determining priority, provided that, at the date of filing the subsequent application, the previous application has been withdrawn, abandoned or refused, without being open to

(2) 当該更新手数料の納付義務は、欧州特許を付与する旨が欧州特許公報に掲載された年について納付すべき更新手数料が納付されれば消滅する。

第87条　優先権

(1) 次のいずれかの国において又はいずれかの国について、特許、実用新案登録又は実用新案証の出願を正規にした者又はその承継人は、最初の出願の日から12月の期間、同一の発明について欧州特許出願をすることに関し優先権を有する。

　(a) 工業所有権の保護に関するパリ条約の同盟国、又は

　(b) 世界貿易機関の加盟国

(2) 出願がされた国の国内法令又は本条約を含む二国間若しくは多国間の条約により正規の国内出願とされるすべての出願は、優先権を生じさせるものと認められる。

(3) 正規の国内出願とは、結果のいかんを問わず、出願をした日付を確定するために十分なすべての出願をいう。

(4) 先の最初の出願と同一の対象について同一の国において又は同一の国についてされた後の出願は、当該後の出願の出願日において、先の出願が公衆の閲覧に付されないで、かつ、いかなる権利をも存続させないで、取り下げられ、放棄され又は拒絶の処分を受けたこと、及びその先の出願がまだ優先権の主張の基礎とされていないことを条件として、優先権の決定を

public inspection and without leaving any rights outstanding, and has not served as a basis for claiming a right of priority. The previous application may not thereafter serve as a basis for claiming a right of priority.

(5) If the first filing has been made with an industrial property authority which is not subject to the Paris Convention for the Protection of Industrial Property or the Agreement Establishing the World Trade Organization, paragraphs 1 to 4 shall apply if that authority, according to a communication issued by the President of the European Patent Office, recognises that a first filing made with the European Patent Office gives rise to a right of priority under conditions and with effects equivalent to those laid down in the Paris Convention.

Article 88   Claiming priority

(1) An applicant desiring to take advantage of the priority of a previous application shall file a declaration of priority and any other document required, in accordance with the Implementing Regulations.

(2) Multiple priorities may be claimed in respect of a European patent application, notwithstanding the fact that they originated in different countries. Where appropriate, multiple priorities may be claimed for any one claim. Where multiple priorities are claimed, time limits which run from the date of priority shall run from the earliest date of priority.

(3) If one or more priorities are claimed in respect of a European patent application, the right of priority shall cover only those elements of the European patent application which are included in the application or applications whose priority is claimed.

(4) If certain elements of the invention for which priority is claimed do not appear among the claims formulated in the previous application, priority

するに際して最初の出願とみなされる。当該先の出願は、その後、優先権の基礎とすることができない。

(5) 先の最初の出願が工業所有権の保護に関するパリ条約又は世界貿易機関を設立するための協定に加入していない工業所有権当局になされた場合には、当該当局がパリ条約に定める要件と同等の条件の下に同等の効力を有する優先権を欧州特許庁になされた最初の出願について認めるときは、欧州特許庁長官による通知に従い、(1)から(4)までを適用する。

第88条　優先権主張

(1) 先の出願の優先権の利益を利用しようとする出願人は、施行規則に従って、優先権申立書及びその他の必要書類を提出する。

(2) 複合優先権は、これらの優先権が異なる国で発生した場合であっても、欧州特許出願について主張することができる。適切な場合には、いずれか1つのクレームについて複合優先権を主張することができる。複合優先権が主張される場合には、優先期間は、最先の優先日から起算される。

(3) ある欧州特許出願について一又は二以上の優先権が主張される場合には、当該欧州特許出願の構成部分のうちその優先権が主張されている一又は二以上の出願に含まれる部分についてのみ優先権が及ぶ。

(4) 優先権は、発明の構成部分で当該優先権の主張に係るものが先の出願においてクレーム内のものとして記載されていない場合においても認められ

may nonetheless be granted, provided that the documents of the previous application as a whole specifically disclose such elements.

Article 89 Effect of priority right

The right of priority shall have the effect that the date of priority shall count as the date of filing of the European patent application for the purposes of Article 54, paragraphs 2 and 3, and Article 60, paragraph 2.

Article 90 Examination on filing and examination as to formal requirements

(1) The European Patent Office shall examine, in accordance with the Implementing Regulations, whether the application satisfies the requirements for the accordance of a date of filing.

(2) If a date of filing cannot be accorded following the examination under paragraph 1, the application shall not be dealt with as a European patent application.

(3) If the European patent application has been accorded a date of filing, the European Patent Office shall examine, in accordance with the Implementing Regulations, whether the requirements in Articles 14, 78 and 81, and, where applicable, Article 88, paragraph 1, and Article 133, paragraph 2, as well as any other requirement laid down in the Implementing Regulations, have been satisfied.

(4) Where the European Patent Office in carrying out the examination under paragraphs 1 or 3 notes that there are deficiencies which may be corrected, it shall give the applicant an opportunity to correct them.

(5) If any deficiency noted in the examination under paragraph 3 is not cor-

る。ただし、先の出願に係る出願書類の全体により当該構成部分が明らかにされている場合に限る。

第89条　優先権の効力

　優先権の効果により、第54条(2)及び(3)並びに第60条(2)の規定の適用上は、優先日が欧州特許出願の出願日として扱われる。

第90条　出願時の審査及び方式要件についての審査

(1)　欧州特許庁は、施行規則に従って、出願日を付与するための要件を出願が満たしているか否かを審査する。

(2)　(1)の審査により出願日が与えられない出願は、欧州特許出願として取り扱われない。

(3)　欧州特許出願に出願日が与えられた場合には、欧州特許庁は、施行規則に従って、第14条、第78条及び第81条に定める要件が満たされているか否かを審査し、場合によっては、第88条(1)及び第133条(2)並びに施行規則に定める他の要件が満たされているか否かを審査する。

(4)　欧州特許庁は、(1)又は(3)の審査において、是正することができる欠陥を発見した場合には、出願人に対し、その欠陥を是正する機会を与える。

(5)　(3)の審査において発見された欠陥が是正されない場合には、別段の法的

rected, the European patent application shall be refused unless a different legal consequence is provided for by this Convention. Where the deficiency concerns the right of priority, this right shall be lost for the application.

Article 92 Drawing up of the European search report

The European Patent Office shall, in accordance with the Implementing Regulations, draw up and publish a European search report in respect of the European patent application on the basis of the claims, with due regard to the description and any drawings.

Article 94 Examination of the European patent application

(1) The European Patent Office shall, in accordance with the Implementing Regulations, examine on request whether the European patent application and the invention to which it relates meet the requirements of this Convention. The request shall not be deemed to be filed until the examination fee has been paid.

(2) If no request for examination has been made in due time, the application shall be deemed to be withdrawn.

(3) If the examination reveals that the application or the invention to which it relates does not meet the requirements of this Convention, the Examining Division shall invite the applicant, as often as necessary, to file his observations and, subject to Article 123, paragraph 1, to amend the application.

(4) If the applicant fails to reply in due time to any communication from the Examining Division, the application shall be deemed to be withdrawn.

帰結が本条約により定められている場合を除き、欧州特許出願は拒絶される。欠陥が優先権に関する場合には、その優先権は、当該出願については喪失する。

第92条　欧州調査報告の作成

　欧州特許庁は、明細書及び図面に適切な考慮を払ったうえで、クレームに基づき、施行規則に従って、欧州特許出願について欧州調査報告を作成し公開する。

第94条　欧州特許出願の審査

(1)　欧州特許庁は、施行規則に従って、請求により、欧州特許出願及びその出願に係る発明が本条約の要件を満たすか否かを審査する。審査手数料が納付されるまでは出願審査の請求があったものとはみなされない。

(2)　出願審査の請求が適時にされなかったときは、出願は取り下げられたものとみなす。

(3)　その出願又は出願に係る発明が本条約の要件を満たしていないことが審査によって明らかになったときは、審査部は、出願人に対し、必要に応じて何度でも意見書を提出し、かつ、第123条(1)に従い出願について補正をするよう求める。

(4)　出願人が審査部からの通知に対して適時に応答しないときは、当該出願は取り下げられたものとみなす。

Article 97   Grant or refusal

(1) If the Examining Division is of the opinion that the European patent application and the invention to which it relates meet the requirements of this Convention, it shall decide to grant a European patent, provided that the conditions laid down in the Implementing Regulations are fulfilled.

(2) If the Examining Division is of the opinion that the European patent application or the invention to which it relates does not meet the requirements of this Convention, it shall refuse the application unless this Convention provides for a different legal consequence.

(3) The decision to grant a European patent shall take effect on the date on which the mention of the grant is published in the European Patent Bulletin.

Article 98   Publication of the specification of the European patent

The European Patent Office shall publish the specification of the European patent as soon as possible after the mention of the grant of the European patent has been published in the European Patent Bulletin.

Article 109   Interlocutory revision

(1) If the department whose decision is contested considers the appeal to be admissible and well founded, it shall rectify its decision. This shall not apply where the appellant is opposed by another party to the proceedings.

(2) If the appeal is not allowed within three months of receipt of the statement of grounds, it shall be remitted to the Board of Appeal without delay, and without comment as to its merit.

第97条　特許の付与又は出願の拒絶

(1) 審査部は、欧州特許出願及びその出願に係る発明が、本条約の要件を満たしていると認める場合には、欧州特許を付与する旨の決定をする。ただし、施行規則に定める要件を満たしている場合に限る。

(2) 審査部は、欧州特許出願又はその出願に係る発明が本条約の要件を満たしていないと認める場合には、別段の法的帰結が本条約により定められている場合を除き、出願を拒絶する。

(3) 欧州特許を付与する決定は、その旨が欧州特許公報に掲載された日に効力を生じる。

第98条　欧州特許明細書の発行

欧州特許庁は、欧州特許を付与する旨が欧州特許公報に掲載された後、速やかに欧州特許明細書を発行する。

第109条　中間修正

(1) その決定が争われている部課は、審判の請求が受理されるべきものであり、かつ、十分な根拠があると認める場合には、その決定を修正する。この規定は、審判請求人が審判手続において他の当事者と対立している場合には適用されない。

(2) 請求の理由を記載した書面の受領後3月以内に審判の請求が許可されない場合には、その請求は、遅滞なく、かつ、実体についての意見を付することなく、審判部に送付される。

Article 121 Further processing of the European patent application

(1) If an applicant fails to observe a time limit vis-à-vis the European Patent Office, he may request further processing of the European patent application.

(2) The European Patent Office shall grant the request, provided that the requirements laid down in the Implementing Regulations are met. Otherwise, it shall reject the request.

(3) If the request is granted, the legal consequences of the failure to observe the time limit shall be deemed not to have ensued.

(4) Further processing shall be ruled out in respect of the time limits in Article 87, paragraph 1, Article 108 and Article 112a, paragraph 4, as well as the time limits for requesting further processing or re-establishment of rights. The Implementing Regulations may rule out further processing for other time limits.

Article 122 Re-establishment of rights

(1) An applicant for or proprietor of a European patent who, in spite of all due care required by the circumstances having been taken, was unable to observe a time limit vis-à-vis the European Patent Office shall have his rights re-established upon request if the non-observance of this time limit has the direct consequence of causing the refusal of the European patent application or of a request, or the deeming of the application to have been withdrawn, or the revocation of the European patent, or the loss of any other right or means of redress.

(2) The European Patent Office shall grant the request, provided that the conditions of paragraph 1 and any other requirements laid down in the Im-

第121条　欧州特許出願についての手続の続行

(1)　出願人は、欧州特許庁に対して期限を遵守できないときは、欧州特許出願について手続の続行を請求することができる。

(2)　欧州特許庁は、当該請求が施行規則に定める要件を満たしていると認める場合には、その請求を許可する。さもなければ、欧州特許庁は、その請求を却下する。

(3)　請求が許可されたときは、期限を遵守しなかったことによる法的効果は生じなかったものとみなす。

(4)　第87条(1)、第108条及び第112a条(4)の期限については、手続の続行は認められず、手続の続行又は権利の回復の請求期限についても同様に手続の続行は認められない。施行規則は、その他の期限についても手続の続行を認めないとすることができる。

第122条　権利の回復

(1)　状況によって必要とされる相当の注意を払ったにもかかわらず、欧州特許庁に対し期限を遵守することができなかった欧州特許出願人又は欧州特許権者は、その期限の不遵守による直接の結果として、欧州特許出願若しくは請求が拒絶され、その出願が取り下げられたものとみなされ、欧州特許が取り消され、又はその他の権利若しくは救済手段が喪失した場合には、請求により、自らの権利を回復させることができる。

(2)　欧州特許庁は、当該請求が(1)及び施行規則に定める要件を満たしていると認める場合には、当該請求を許可する。さもなければ、欧州特許庁は、

plementing Regulations are met. Otherwise, it shall reject the request.

(3) If the request is granted, the legal consequences of the failure to observe the time limit shall be deemed not to have ensued.

(4) Re-establishment of rights shall be ruled out in respect of the time limit for requesting re-establishment of rights. The Implementing Regulations may rule out re-establishment for other time limits.

(5) —

(6) —

Article 123   Amendments

(1) The European patent application or European patent may be amended in proceedings before the European Patent Office, in accordance with the Implementing Regulations. In any event, the applicant shall be given at least one opportunity to amend the application of his own volition.

(2) The European patent application or European patent may not be amended in such a way that it contains subject-matter which extends beyond the content of the application as filed.

(3) The European patent may not be amended in such a way as to extend the protection it confers.

Article 153   The European Patent Office as designated Office or elected Office

(1) The European Patent Office shall be

その請求を却下する。

(3) 請求が許可されたときは、期限を遵守しなかったことによる法的効果は生じなかったものとみなす。

(4) 権利の回復を請求するための期限については、権利の回復は認められない。施行規則は、その他の期限についても権利の回復を認めないとすることができる。

(5) 省略

(6) 省略

第123条　補正

(1) 欧州特許庁における手続において、欧州特許出願又は欧州特許について、施行規則に従って、補正をすることができる。いかなる場合においても、出願について自発的に補正をする機会が少なくとも1回は出願人に与えられる。

(2) 欧州特許出願又は欧州特許について、その出願の出願時の内容を超える対象を含むように補正をしてはならない。

(3) 欧州特許について、それによる保護を拡張するように補正をしてはならない。

第153条　指定官庁及び選択官庁としての欧州特許庁

(1) 欧州特許庁は、

(a) a designated Office for any State party to this Convention in respect of which the PCT is in force, which is designated in the international application and for which the applicant wishes to obtain a European patent, and

(b) an elected Office, if the applicant has elected a State designated pursuant to letter (a).

(2) An international application for which the European Patent Office is a designated or elected Office, and which has been accorded an international date of filing, shall be equivalent to a regular European application (Euro-PCT application).

(3) The international publication of a Euro-PCT application in an official language of the European Patent Office shall take the place of the publication of the European patent application and shall be mentioned in the European Patent Bulletin.

(4) If the Euro-PCT application is published in another language, a translation into one of the official languages shall be filed with the European Patent Office, which shall publish it. Subject to Article 67, paragraph 3, the provisional protection under Article 67, paragraphs 1 and 2, shall be effective from the date of that publication.

(5) The Euro-PCT application shall be treated as a European patent application and shall be considered as comprised in the state of the art under Article 54, paragraph 3, if the conditions laid down in paragraph 3 or 4 and in the Implementing Regulations are fulfilled.

(6) The international search report drawn up in respect of a Euro-PCT application or the declaration replacing it, and their international publication, shall take the place of the European search report and the mention of its

(a) 特許協力条約の効力が発生している本条約の締約国であって、国際出願において指定され、かつ、出願人がその国際出願においてその締約国について欧州特許を取得することを望むすべての締約国に対して指定官庁となり、

(b) 出願人が(a)により指定された国を選択した場合には、選択官庁となる。

(2) 欧州特許庁が指定官庁又は選択官庁であり、かつ、国際出願日が与えられた国際出願は、通常の欧州出願と同等である（Euro-PCT 出願）。

(3) 欧州特許庁の公用語でされた Euro-PCT 出願の国際公開は、欧州特許出願の公開に代わり、その旨が欧州特許公報に掲載される。

(4) Euro-PCT 出願が他の言語で公開された場合には、出願人は、公用語による翻訳文を欧州特許庁へ提出するものとし、欧州特許庁は、その翻訳文を公開する。第67条(3)の規定に従うことを条件として、第67条(1)及び(2)の仮保護は、その公開日より効力を生じる。

(5) Euro-PCT 出願は、(3)又は(4)及び施行規則に定める要件が満たされている場合には、欧州特許出願として扱われ、第54条(3)に定義する技術水準を構成するものとみなす。

(6) Euro-PCT 出願について作成された国際調査報告又はそれに代わる宣言及びその国際公開は、欧州調査報告及びその公開の旨の欧州特許公報への掲載に代わる。

publication in the European Patent Bulletin.

(7) A supplementary European search report shall be drawn up in respect of any Euro-PCT application under paragraph 5. The Administrative Council may decide that the supplementary search report is to be dispensed with or that the search fee is to be reduced.

(7) 補充欧州調査報告は、(5)にいうすべての Euro-PCT 出願について作成される。理事会は、補充欧州調査報告の免除又は調査手数料の減額について決定をすることができる。

Chapter 7

Filing of EP Applications

欧州特許出願

Leonard L. Werner-Jones

MEMO

▶ 欧州特許庁に直接出願する場合に、出願書類にクレームが含まれていなくても出願日が確定され、その後、欧州特許庁から補正命令がきます（§1）。日本の実務では、願書にクレームが添付されていなければ、不適法な手続であって、その補正をすることができないとして出願が却下されます（特許法第18条の2）。

▶ 日本の外国語書面出願に相当する規定が欧州特許条約にもあります。欧州特許庁に直接出願する場合に日本語で出願することができ、出願日から2月内に翻訳文の提出が求められます（§1）。

▶ PCTルートで欧州段階に移行する場合、移行期限は優先日から31月と設定されています。調査手数料（補充欧州調査が作成される場合）、更新手数料、及び締約国の指定手数料の支払いがあります（§2）。書類提出及び支払期限を過ぎてしまった場合は、救済を受けることができます（第13章参照）。

▶ 分割出願ができるのは、出願が特許庁に係属している場合に限られます（§3）。特許査定後でも分割出願ができるという日本の実務（第44条第1項）と異なります。日本語で欧州出願をした場合は、日本語で分割出願をすることができます。この点、日本の実務と同じです。

Introduction

When filing at the EPO, there are two major categories of applications for applicants to consider: 1) direct EP applications, or 2) Euro-PCT applications. While several of the requirements are the same, there are also distinct differences which separate these applications and how they should be handled. A third general category, that applies to both direct EP applications and Euro-PCT applications, is the possibility of filing a EP divisional application based on either the direct EP application or the Euro-PCT application as the parent application. The EP divisional application is in turn issued a distinct EP application number and is considered a separate and individual application.

The path required for properly filing an application at the EPO can be complicated and difficult to follow, as issues concerning formal requirements, fees and terms must all be considered. The EPO has issued two guides to assist interested parties in maneuvering through the criteria for successful filing at the EPO. For direct EP applications, the EPO has prepared *"How to get a European patent"*; for Euro-PCT applications the EPO has prepared *""Euro-PCT Guide": PCT Procedure at the EPO"*, which are both available as free PDFs on the EPO homepage. While these guides, in general, outline the prosecution at the EPO, they are particularly helpful in navigating the requirements for filing at the EPO.

Without intending to address all issues that may arise with filing at the EPO, the most important filing requirements are considered below for direct EP applications, Euro-PCT applications, and follow-up divisional filings.

1 Filing of Direct EP Applications

A direct EP application is an application which has not been accorded a European filing date and is filed directly with the EPO as an application for examina-

はじめに

　欧州特許庁に出願するに際して、出願人には、1)直接的な欧州特許出願をするか、2)Euro-PCT出願をするという2つの主要な出願カテゴリーがある。これらの出願間では出願要件のいくつかが同じである一方、明らかな違いもみられ、それにより2つの出願カテゴリーは区別され、どのように扱うべきかについても異なる。第三のカテゴリーは、直接的な欧州特許出願とEuro-PCT出願の双方に適用され、直接的な欧州特許出願又はEuro-PCT出願を親出願とする分割出願である。分割出願にも独自の欧州特許出願番号が発行され、別個独立の出願とみなされる。

　欧州特許庁に適切に出願するために必要な経路は複雑で、かつ、追従困難なことがある。方式的要件、料金、期間に関する問題のすべてを考慮する必要があるためである。欧州特許庁は2種類のガイドブックを発行し、出願の基準をクリアして欧州特許庁への出願がうまくいくよう出願人を支援している。欧州特許庁は、直接的な欧州出願については「欧州特許を取得する方法」を作成し、Euro-PCT出願については「Euro-PCTガイド：EPOにおけるPCT手続」を作成している。どちらも欧州特許庁ホームページから無料のPDFファイルとして入手可能である。これらのガイドブックには、欧州特許庁における出願手続の概要が記載されており、欧州特許庁に対する出願要件を考慮して手続を進めるのに特に役立つ。

　欧州特許庁への出願について生じ得るすべての問題に取り組むつもりはないが、直接的な欧州特許出願、Euro-PCT出願、その後に行われる分割出願について、最も重要な出願要件を以下で検討する。

1　直接的な欧州特許出願

　直接的な欧州特許出願とは、いまだ欧州出願日が与えられていない出願であり、かつ、欧州特許庁による審査を求める出願として欧州特許庁に直接提出さ

tion at the EPO. In general, the requirements of a direct EP application are laid down in Art. 78 EPC. Art. 78(1) EPC requires the application to contain:

- a request for the grant of a European patent;

- a description of the invention;

- one or more claims;

- any drawings referred to in the description or the claims; and

- an abstract.

Further, the application must satisfy the requirements laid down in the Implementing Regulations.

Art. 78(2) EPC requires the timely payment of the filing fee and the search fee.

While the maze of requirements laid down in the Implementing Regulations can appear to be endless, important is Rule 40(1) EPC (in combination with Art. 80 EPC), which defines the date of filing of a European patent application as the date on which the documents filed by the applicant contain:

- an indication that a European patent is sought;

- information identifying the applicant or allowing the applicant to be contacted; and

- a description or reference to a previously filed application.

An interesting and newly introduced option with the EPC2000 for acquiring a

れた出願である。直接的な欧州特許出願の要件は、第78条に規定されている。第78条(1)は、出願に以下が含まれることを要求する。

・　欧州特許の付与を求める願書

・　発明の記載（明細書）

・　１つ以上のクレーム

・　明細書又はクレームにおいて言及されている図面

・　要約書

さらに、当該出願は、施行規則に規定された要件を満たさなければならない。

第78条(2)は、出願手数料及び調査手数料を適切な時期に支払うことを要求する。

施行規則に定められた要件は複雑で終わりがないように見える一方、重要なのは、第80条の関連規定である規則40(1)である。そこでは、以下の事項を含む書類を出願人が提出した日を欧州特許出願の出願日と定めている。

・　欧州特許を求めるという表示

・　出願人を特定する情報又は出願人と連絡をとることが可能な情報

・　明細書又は先に提出された出願の参照

出願日を取得するためにEPC2000とともに新たに導入されたオプションが

filing date is the possibility of merely referring to a previously filed application. As explained in Rule 40(2) EPC, the filing date and number of that application and the office with which it was filed must be stated. Such reference shall also indicate that it replaces the description and any drawings. While this option provides a new basis for applicants to file with the EPO, additional requirements including timely filing of certified copies and translations create a complicated mix of constellations that must be considered but which go beyond the scope of this summary.

Once the application has been assigned a filing date, Rule 57 EPC, entitled *"Examination as to formal requirements"*, applies. The general points of examination of Rule 57 EPC are as follows:

- the application is in an EPO language (e.g. where an application is filed in Japanese a translation must be provided within 2 month of filing);

- a proper request for grant of a European patent is provided;

- the application contains one or more claims;

- the application contains an abstract;

- the filing fee and the search fee have been paid;

- a proper designation of the inventor is provided;

- where appropriate, one or more claims to priority are provided;

- where appropriate, proper representation is provided (e.g. an applicant who does not have residence or place of business in a contracting state can file the application itself but needs (duly appointed) representation for all subsequent acts);

ある。それは、先にされた出願を単に参照することで出願日を確保することができるものであり興味深い。規則40(2)に規定されているように、当該先の出願の出願日及び番号、並びに当該先の出願の提出先である官庁を記載する必要がある。かかる参照には、それが明細書及び図面に取って代わるものであることを表示する。この新たなオプションは、出願人らが欧州特許庁に出願をすることに新たな根拠をもたらす一方で、認証謄本及び翻訳文を適時に提出すること等の追加的な要件が課され、考慮すべき複雑多様な事項を生み出す。これについては本概要の範囲ではない。

出願日が付与された出願には、規則57にいう「方式要件に関する審査」が適用される。規則57の審査の概略点は次のとおりである。

- 出願が欧州特許庁の公用語である言語でされていること（例えば、出願が日本語でされた場合、翻訳文を出願から２月以内に提出する必要がある）

- 欧州特許の付与を求める適切な請求がなされていること

- 出願には１つ以上のクレームが含まれていること

- 出願には要約が含まれていること

- 出願手数料及び調査手数料が支払われていること

- 発明者の適切な特定がなされていること

- 該当する場合は、１つ以上の優先権が主張されていること

- 該当する場合は、適切な代理がされていること（例えば、締約国内に住所又は営業所を有しない出願人は、自身で出願をすることができるが、その後のすべての行為につき、（適法に選任された）代理人が必要である）

- the application meets the physical requirements (e.g. text / format requirements); and

- where appropriate, a sequence listing is provided.

An interesting outcome of the revisions made in the EPC2000 is the possibility of filing and/or paying for one or more claims either on entry into the European regional phase or after filing the application.

For example, if the claims are filed subsequent to the filing of the application but prior to the formal examination pursuant to Rule 57 EPC, the EPO will not send out an invitation to file claims (i.e. Rule 58 EPC). On the other hand, if claims have not been provided by the time of formal examination, the EPO will issue a Rule 58 EPC invitation to file claims, which specifies a two month term. In the event that this term is not met, the application will be refused (i.e. Art. 78(1)(c) EPC with Art. 90(5) EPC). Here, it is important to realize that further processing is ruled out, and thus not available for failure to respond to the two month term set in Rule 58 EPC (i.e. Art. 121 EPC with Rule 136(4) EPC), albeit re-establishment is available.

Similarly, claim fees may also be paid at a later date after filing of the application. For example, when the claims are filed with the application, or shortly thereafter, the claim fees due for claims exceeding 15 (i.e. the EPO only charges claim fees for the 16th and each subsequent claim; Rule 45(1) EPC) may be paid within one month of filing the claims (i.e. Rule 45(2) EPC). In the event that this term is not met, the EPO will issue a communication requesting payment of the claim fees due and will set a second one month term. In the event that this second term is not met, the claim(s) concerned shall be deemed to be abandoned. The applicant, however, still has the opportunity to request further processing within a two month term to allow for the claims to be reinstated and thus considered for prosecution. A similar scenario is possible in regard to a reference to an earlier application, as well as after a Rule 58 EPC invitation to file claims.

- 出願が物理的要件（例えば、テキスト／フォーマットの要件）を満たすこと

- 該当する場合は、配列表が提出されていること

EPC2000の改正点で特に関心をひくのは、1つ以上のクレームの提出と、それについての料金の支払いとが出願後にできるようになったことである。

例えば、出願後であるが規則57に基づく方式審査より前にクレームが提出されると、欧州特許庁はクレームを提出するよう求める指令を発送しない（規則58）。一方、クレームが方式審査の時点までに提出されなかった場合は、欧州特許庁は、規則58の指令を発行し、2月の期間を指定してクレームを提出するよう求める。この期間にクレームが提出されなければ、出願は拒絶される（第90条(5)並びに第78条(1)(c)）。ここで、規則58で指定された2月の期間に応答しない不履行については手続の続行が認められない。よって手続の続行が利用できないことを理解されたい（第121条、規則136(4)）。ただし、権利回復措置を利用することはできる。

同様に、出願がされた日の後にクレーム料を支払ってもよい。例えば、出願とともにクレームが提出された場合、又は出願後まもなくしてクレームが提出された場合は、15を超えるクレームについて支払うことになっているクレーム費用（欧州特許庁は、第16クレーム及びその後の各クレームについてのみ、クレーム料を請求する。規則45(1)）は、クレーム提出後、1月以内に支払ってもよい（規則45(2)）。この期間が遵守されない場合は、欧州特許庁はクレーム料の支払いを求める通知を発行し、第二の1月の期間を設定する。この第二の期間が遵守できない場合は、クレーム料金不払いのクレームは放棄されたものとみなされる。一方、出願人は、2月の期間内に手続の続行を請求する機会を依然として有しており、クレームが回復されれば審査において考慮される。先の出願の参照についても同様のシナリオが可能であり、クレームを提出するよう求める規則58の指令後についても同様である。

250   Chapter 7: Filing of EP Applications

Another example of extending the time requirements of Rule 57 EPC concerns the language of the application. As explained in Art. 14(2) EPC, the application can be filed in any language including Japanese; a translation of this application into one of the EPO official languages (i.e. English, German or French) must however be filed within a two month term. If this two month term is not met, the application shall be deemed to be withdrawn. Here too, the possibility of further processing is ruled out (i.e. not available), but re-establishment is available.

While there are several requirements to be observed, the EPC provides considerable leeway for applicants to correct possible deficiencies. For example, for the request for grant of a patent, the use of an appropriate form is mandatory (Form 1001, Rule 41 EPC). A deficiency in this respect can be remedied within two months of invitation (Rule 58 EPC). Again, further processing is not available, but re-establishment is available. This also applies for deficiencies in case of compulsory representation. Deficiencies regarding the physical requirements of the application documents, e.g. paper, layout, tables, margins, numbering reference signs etc. (Rule 57(i) EPC) may also be remedied within two months of invitation (Rule 58, further processing excluded, re-establishment available). With respect to a sequence listing (Rule 57(j) EPC), if required or if it contains deficiencies, the applicant has two months to correct it and pay a late furnishing fee (Rule 30(3) EPC, here further processing is available). The filing and search fees (Art. 78(2) EPC) are due within one month of filing (Rule 38 EPC / Rule 45 EPC). The page fee is due within one month of filing the application / first set of claims / copy of previous application (Rule 38 EPC). Failure to observe those time limits triggers a loss of rights (Rule 112 EPC), however, further processing is available on request. The designation/extension fee is due within six months of the mention of the publication of the search report (time i.e. limit to request examination).

規則57の時期的要件を延長する他の例は、出願の言語に関するものである。第14条(2)に規定されているように、日本語を含むすべての言語で出願をすることができる。ただし、欧州特許庁の公用語（英語、ドイツ語、フランス語）の1つを用いた翻訳文を、2月の期間内に提出する必要がある。この2月の期間を遵守できないときは、出願は取り下げられたものとみなされる。ここでも、手続の続行の可能性はない（すなわち利用できない）が、権利回復措置は利用できる。

　遵守すべきいくつかの要件がある一方で、欧州特許条約は、起こり得る不備を是正するために十分な余地を出願人に与えている。例えば、特許付与を求める願書については、特定の様式を使用することが必須である（規則41、様式1001）。この点の不備は、指令から2月以内に是正することができる（規則58）。ここでもまた、手続の続行は利用できないが、権利回復措置が利用可能である。これは強制代理の場合における不備にも当てはまる。用紙、レイアウト、表、余白、引用符号の番号付け等、出願書類の物理的要件に関する不備（規則57(i)）も、指令から2月以内に是正することができる（規則58、手続の続行は除外され、権利回復措置が利用可能である）。配列表（規則57(j)）に関しては、要求された場合、又は不備を含んでいる場合は、出願人は2月以内にこれを是正し、かつ、遅延提出手数料を支払う（規則30(3)）。このとき手続の続行が利用できる。出願手数料と調査手数料（第78条(2)）は、出願から1月以内に支払う必要がある（規則38）／（規則45）。ページ費用は、出願から1月以内／最初のクレーム一式の提出から1月以内／先の出願の謄本の提出から1月以内に支払う必要がある（規則38）。これらの期限を守らなかった場合は、権利の喪失を招く（規則112）が、手続の続行が請求により利用できる。締約国／拡張国の指定手数料は、調査報告が公開された日から6月以内（審査請求の期限）に支払う必要がある。

2 Filing of Euro-PCT Application

A Euro-PCT application is an international application which has been accorded an international filing date and designates Europe as a designated region. A Euro-PCT application is equivalent to a regular direct EP application.

Prosecution of a Euro-PCT application starts only after the 31-month period, however, it may be accelerated on request both in the international phase (i.e. early entry on request) as well as in the European regional phase (i.e. PACE program).

Similar to a direct EP application and Rule 57 EPC, the EPC lays down the requirements that are to be fulfilled on entry into European regional phase in Art. 153 EPC, combined with Rule 159 EPC. As an aid to assist applicants in fulfilling these requirements, applicants are encouraged to use Form 1200 for entry into the European phase, however, this is not a requirement.

Briefly, Rule 159 EPC requires:

- supply, where applicable, the translation of the international application;

- specify the application documents, as originally filed or as amended, on which the European grant procedure is to be based;

- pay the filing fee;

- pay the designation fee if necessary;

- pay the search fee, where a supplementary European search report has to be drawn up;

- file the request for examination if necessary;

2　Euro-PCT 出願

　Euro-PCT 出願は、国際出願日が付与された国際出願であって、指定領域として欧州を指定したものである。Euro-PCT 出願は通常の直接的な欧州特許出願と同等である。

　Euro-PCT 出願の手続は、国際出願から31月の期間が経過してから開始されるが、国際段階と欧州領域段階とにおいて、請求により迅速化させることができる。すなわち、請求による早期の移行化と PACE プログラムによる迅速化である。

　直接的な欧州特許出願及び規則57と同様に、欧州特許条約は、第153条及びその関連規定である規則159において、欧州領域段階移行に必要な要件を規定している。これらの要件を満たすための支援として、出願人は欧州段階に移行する際に様式1200を使用するよう奨励されている。しかし、これは要件ではない。

　簡単に述べると、規則159は以下を要求している。

- 該当する場合は、国際出願の翻訳文を提出する。

- 欧州特許付与手続の基礎となる出願当初又は補正後の出願書類を特定する。

- 出願手数料を支払う。

- 必要な場合は、締約国の指定手数料を支払う。

- 補充欧州調査報告書が作成されるべき場合は、調査手数料を支払う。

- 必要な場合は、審査請求をする。

- pay the renewal fee in respect of the third year if the fee has fallen due earlier; and

- file, where applicable, the certificate of exhibition

As outlined above for Rule 159 EPC, the applicant is required to specify the application documents, as originally filed or as amended, on which prosecution is to be based. While this provision allows applicants to file amendments of the application on entry of the European regional phase, including, for example, entire replacement pages or even a complete set of amended claims, the strict criteria followed by the EPO as to whether inadmissible subject matter has been added (i.e. Art. 123(2) EPC) of course still apply.

In the event that the applicant, however, is not in a position to provide such amendments, particularly in the form of newly drafted claims, the EPC provides an additional opportunity to file such in response to the Rule 161 EPC invitation, which is issued shortly after filing with a six month term. In the event that the claims are more than 15, additional claim fees are due and which are to be paid, at the latest, by the Rule 161 EPC term (i.e. Rule 162 EPC). Here, further processing is available, albeit two requests for further processing would be necessary if a new set of claims exceeding 15 claims forms the basis for the request for further processing.

Depending on which designated office the applicant has elected for the ISA in the international phase, amendments / comments may be required in response to the EPO's Rule 161 EPC invitation. For example, in the event that the applicant has elected the EPO as the ISA in the international phase, the applicant would be required to provide amendments / comments to a negative written opinion provided in the international phase in response to the Rule 161 EPC invitation. On the other hand, if claim amendments are provided on entry into the European regional phase, no comments to the negative written opinion are necessary in response to the Rule 161 EPC invitation. By following this strategy, detailed com-

- 第３年度に関する更新手数料の支払期限が到来している場合は、当該更新手数料を支払う。

- 該当する場合は、博覧会の証明書を提出する。

　規則159に関して上記に概要を述べたように、出願人は、出願手続の基礎となる出願当初又は補正後の出願書類を特定する必要がある。この規定により、出願人は、欧州領域段階移行の際に、すべての差替ページ又は一式の補正されたクレームを提出すること等により、出願の補正をすることができるが、新規事項の追加について欧州特許庁が遵守する厳格な基準（第123条(2)）が依然として適用される。

　その一方、出願人が（とりわけ、新たなクレームの形式で）上記補正をしようとしない場合に備えて、欧州特許条約は、規則161の指令に応答して補正書を提出する追加の機会を出願人に与えている。当該指令は、出願をした直後に発行され、６月の応答期間を指定する。クレームの数が15を超える場合は、追加のクレーム費用を支払わなければならず、規則161の期限までに遅くとも支払う必要がある（すなわち、規則162）。ここで、クレーム数が15を超える新たなクレームが手続の続行の請求の基礎となる場合、手続の続行が利用できるが、手続の続行のためには２つの請求が必要である。

　国際段階でどの国際調査機関が出願人により選択されたかにより、欧州特許庁による規則161の指令に応答して補正／意見書が求められる場合がある。例えば、国際段階で欧州特許庁が出願人により選択された場合は、出願人は、規則161の指令に応答して、国際段階で出された書面による否定的な見解に対して補正書／意見書を提出することを求められる。他方で、欧州領域段階に移行する際にクレームの補正が提出される場合は、書面による否定的な見解に対応するために、規則161の指令に応じる必要はない。この戦略に従うことにより、当該書面による見解に対する応答を、出願手続のより遅い段階まで遅らせることができる。

ments in regard to the written opinion may be postponed for a later stage of prosecution.

Where an application is not filed in one of the official EPO languages, the translation of the international application required under Art. 153(4) EPC must be filed (Rule 159(1)(a) EPC). The language of the translation becomes the language of the proceedings before the EPO. Further processing and re-establishment are available (PCT overrules Rule 136(3) EPC).

As with the direct EP applications, the applicant is provided opportunities to remedy deficiencies, if necessary. For example, the filing fee provided for in Art. 78(2) EPC, including a page fee for any page above 35 (not including the sequence listing), must be paid within 31 months (Rule 159(1)(c) EPC), otherwise the application is deemed withdrawn and no longer has any prior right effect. Here, both further processing and re-establishment are available. Further, the applicant must pay the designation fee if the period under Rule 39 EPC (i.e. within six months of the date on which the European Patent Bulletin mentions the publication of the European search report) has expired earlier (Rule 159(1)(d) EPC). Designation of one or more contracting states may be withdrawn at any time up to the grant of the patent. If the designation fee is not paid in due time, the application is deemed withdrawn, further processing is available (fee 50% of designation fee). The extension fees must also be paid within the same period as the designation fee. Where a supplementary European search report is to be drawn up, the search fee additionally needs to be paid (Rule 159(1)(e) EPC).

According to Rule 159(1)(f) EPC, the applicant is required to file the request for examination provided for in Art. 94 (written request and payment of examination fee). If the examination fee is not paid in due time, the application is deemed withdrawn, further processing is available and the further processing fee is 50% of the examination fee. Additionally, the applicant is required to pay the renewal fee (Rule 159(1)(g) EPC) in respect of the third year provided for in Art. 86(1) EPC, if the fee has fallen due earlier under Rule 51(1) EPC (i.e. the last day of the

欧州特許庁の公用語の1つで国際出願がされていない場合は、第153条(4)の規定に従い国際出願の翻訳文を提出する必要がある（規則159(1)(a)）。翻訳文の言語が欧州特許庁に対する手続の言語となる。手続の続行及び権利回復請求が利用できる（PCTは、規則136(3)を除外している）。

直接的な欧州出願と同様に、必要に応じて不備を是正する機会が出願人に与えられる。例えば、第78条(2)に規定された出願費用（35ページを超えるページについてのページ費用が含まれるが、配列表はカウントされない）は、31月以内に支払う必要があり（規則159(1)(c)）、支払われなかった場合は、出願は取り下げたものとみなされ、先願としての権利の効果を有しない。ここでは、手続の続行請求と権利回復請求の双方とも利用できる。また、出願人は、規則39による期間（すなわち、欧州調査報告が欧州特許公報にて公開された日から6月）が、先に満了している場合は、指定手数料を支払う必要がある（規則159(1)(d)）。締約国の指定は、特許付与に至るまで、いつでも取り下げることができる。指定手数料が適切な時期に支払われない場合は、出願は取り下げたものとみなされ、手続の続行が利用できる（指定手数料の50％の費用）。拡張費用も指定手数料と同一期間内に支払う必要がある。補充欧州調査報告が作成される場合は、さらに調査費用を支払う必要がある（規則159(1)(e)）。

規則159(1)(f)の規定により、出願人は、第94条に規定された審査請求（書面による請求及び審査手数料の支払い）をする必要がある。審査手数料が適切な時期に支払われない場合は、出願は取り下げたものとみなされる。この場合は手続の続行が利用でき、手続の続行の費用は審査手数料の50％である。さらに、出願人は、規則51(1)に規定された納付期限（欧州特許出願の出願日に対応する日を含む月の末日）が先に到来している場合は、第86条(1)に規定された第3年度分の更新手数料を支払う必要がある（規則159(1)(g)）。当該期間の満了後であっ

month containing the anniversary of the date of filing of the European patent application). After expiry of the relevant period, the renewal fee can still be paid with 50% surcharge within a 6 month period from the due date (no further processing is available, re-establishment is also possible).

Additionally, it may be required to provide data concerning the inventor (Rule 163(1) EPC), number / copy of priority application (Rule 163(2) EPC), and / or the applicant's address, nationality and state of residence / principle place of business (Rule 163(4) EPC), file a sequence listing (Rule 163(3) EPC), appoint a representative (Rule 163(5) EPC), limit the application to one invention after a non-unity finding, file a certificate of exhibition or provide any search results for a priority application (all of theese may be carried out on invitation by the EPO with respective terms).

3 Filing of Divisional Application

A direct European application, a Euro-PCT application, or a divisional application derived from either a direct European application or a Euro-PCT application may be divided by filing one or more divisional applications. The divisional application, however, must be filed while the parent application is still pending. An application is considered to be pending up to, but not including, the date that the European Patent Bulletin mentions the grant of the patent.

While it is not possible to validly file a divisional application when the parent application has been refused, withdrawn or deemed to be withdrawn, it is possible to file a new divisional application after refusal of an application in examination proceedings if the time limit for filing a notice of appeal has not expired (i.e. two months of notification of the decision to refuse the application; Enlarged Board of Appeal decision G 1/09).

In general, the procedure concerning the divisional application is independent

ても、更新手数料は納付締め切り期日から6月の期間内であれば50％の追加手数料とともに支払うことができる（手続の続行は利用できず、権利回復請求は可能である）。

さらに、発明者に関する情報を提出すること（規則163(1)）、基礎出願の番号／写し（規則163(2)）を提出すること、配列表を提出すること（規則163(3)）、出願人の住所、国籍、居住国／主な営業所のある国についての情報を提出すること（規則163(4)）、代理人を選任すること（規則163(5)）、単一性なしと認定された出願を単一の発明に限定すること、博覧会の証明書を提出すること、基礎出願に関する調査結果を提出すること等が出願人に求められる場合がある（これらすべては、欧州特許庁から各期間を指定した通知が発行された後に行うことができる）。

3　分割出願

　直接的な欧州出願、Euro-PCT出願、又は直接的な欧州出願若しくはEuro-PCT出願に基づく分割出願に基づき、1つ以上の分割出願をすることができる。分割出願は、親出願が欧州特許庁に係属している間にしなければならない。出願は、欧州特許公報に特許が付与された旨が掲載された日（当日を含まない）に至るまで係属中であるとみなされる。

　特許出願が拒絶され、取り下げられ、又は取り下げたとみなされた場合は、分割出願を有効にすることができないが、審判請求書を提出する期限が終了していなければ、審査過程において出願が拒絶された後（拒絶査定の通知から2月）に、新たな分割出願をすることができる（拡大審判部の審決G 1/09）。

　一般に、分割出願に関する手続は親出願に関する手続からは独立しており、

from the procedure concerning the parent application, and the divisional application is treated as a new application, with the exception that the effective date remains the filing date or the priority date, as appropriate, of the parent application. Also, the right to file a divisional application in respect of an earlier application is only available to the registered applicants for the earlier applications jointly and not to one of them individually.

Similar to a direct EP application, claims may be filed after filing the divisional application, even if the parent application is no longer pending. In such a case, the EPO will issue a Rule 58 EPC communication, inviting the applicant to provide claims on which prosecution may be based with a two month term. In the event that this term is not met, there is no possibility of further processing and the application will be refused.

Also, a divisional application may be filed by reference to the parent application. On the other hand, routine to European patent practice is for the applicant to file the divisional application again, in its entirety, with the exception that the original claims of the parent are included as embodiments in the body of the specification and no longer as claims. This ensures that all of the subject matter of the original application is provided for in the divisional application, in particular for purposes of Art. 123(2) EPC (i.e. added matter), while at the same time allowing for a different set of claims to be filed with the divisional.

Such a new set of claims need not be limited to subject-matter in the claims of the parent application, however, they may not be extended beyond the content of the parent application as originally filed, i.e. such that the skilled person is presented with information not directly and unambiguously derivable from parent (Art. 76(1) EPC). On the other hand, double-patenting may be an issue if the divisional application claims the exact same subject-matter as granted in the parent application (i.e. G 1/05 and G 1/06).

The divisional application is to be filed in the language of the proceedings

分割出願は新たな出願として扱われるが、例外として有効出願日は、親出願の出願日、又は該当する場合には優先日である。また、先の共同出願に基づき分割をする権利は、先の出願について登録された出願人が共同でのみ利用することができ、これらの者が個別に利用することはできない。

直接的な欧州出願の場合と同様に、分割出願についても出願をした後にクレームを提出することができ、クレーム提出時には、その親出願が係属していなくてもよい。この場合、欧州特許庁は、規則58の通知を発行し、出願手続の基礎となるクレームを2月の期間内に提出する機会を出願人に与える。この期間にクレームが提出されなければ、手続の続行の可能性はなく、出願は拒絶される。

また、親出願を参照することにより分割出願をすることができる。他方で、親出願をそっくりそのまま使って分割出願をすることが欧州特許実務では通常である。この実務では、親出願の原クレームを、クレームとしてではなく、分割出願の明細書の本文中に実施形態として含め、異なる一組のクレームを分割出願とともに提出することができる。こうすることにより、原出願で開示されたすべての対象が分割出願に確実に含まれる。この実務は、第123条(2)（すなわち、新規事項の追加の禁止）要件に対応する目的からである。

このような新たなクレームは、親出願のクレームの対象に限定される必要はないが、当初に提出された親出願の内容を超えて拡張されたものであってはならない。すなわち、親出願から直接的かつ一義的に導き出されない情報を当業者に提示してはならない（第76条(1)）。他方、分割出願のクレームの対象が親出願の特許付与された対象とまったく同一である場合はダブルパテントの問題が出てくる（G 1/05及びG 1/06）。

分割出願は、親出願の手続言語（規則36(2)）、又は（親出願が欧州特許庁の公

(Rule 36(2) EPC) of the parent or the language in which the parent was filed (if the parent is not in an official EPO language). In the latter case, a translation is to be provided within two months of filing (Rule 36(2) EPC) or on invitation to rectify failure to observe the time limit (Rule 58 EPC). This period of two months is excluded from further processing, but re-establishment is available.

A divisional application is deemed to have been filed on the date of filing of the parent application and enjoys any right of priority (Art. 76(1) EPC). The priority documents need not be filed again. Filing and search fee must be paid within one month of filing (Rule 36(3) EPC) and the designation fee must be paid within 6 month of the mention of the publication of the search report for the divisional (Rule 36(4) EPC). All contracting states are designated states, which, at the time of filing the divisional, are designated for the parent (Art. 76(2) EPC).

用語でされていない場合）親出願の出願の言語でされなければならない。後者の場合、出願から又は期限不遵守を是正すべきとの指令から２月以内に翻訳文を提出しなければならない（規則36(2)、規則58）。この２月の期間は手続の続行規定から除外されているが、権利回復請求は利用できる。

　分割出願は親出願の出願日にされたものとみなされ、優先権の効果があればそれを享受する（第76条(1)）。優先権書類を再び提出する必要はない。出願手数料及び調査手数料は、出願から１月以内に支払う必要があり（規則36(3)）、締約国の指定手数料は、分割出願についての調査報告が特許公報にて公開された日から６月以内に支払う必要がある（規則36(4)）。分割出願時に親出願について指定されているすべての締約国が分割出願で指定される（第76条(2)）。

Chapter **8**

Claims

クレーム

Matthias Wolf

MEMO

▶ 第84条は、クレームの記載要件について規定しており、日本特許法第36条第5項及び第6項に相当します（§1）。

▶ サポートという用語は第123条第2項との関連で使われることもありますので、本書ではあえて「裏付け」という訳語を第84条との関連で使っています。欧州特許庁は、第84条のこの「裏付け」の要件を形式的及び実体的要件の双方であるとして解釈しています（§1.4）。

▶ 出願時の技術常識に照らしても、クレームに記載の発明の範囲まで明細書に開示された内容を拡張ないし一般化できるとはいえない場合に、第84条違反になります。発明の効果がクレームの範囲全体にわたって達成される程度を考慮することは進歩性の判断にも関連します。クレームされた範囲全体にわたって当業者が発明を実施するには開示が不十分である場合は、第83条違反になります。第84条違反は特許異議の申立ての理由ではないため、条文の選択は異議申立手続において重要です。

▶ 欧州実務では、クレームのカテゴリーが3つあり、原則、カテゴリーごとに1つの独立クレームが認められます（§2）。

▶ 欧州特許庁により行われる具体的なクレーム解釈については、§3を参照してください。

Introduction

The claims of European patents and patent applications are of the utmost importance. They are the basis for the assessment of patentability before the EPO in examination as well as in opposition and appeal proceedings, and also in national invalidation proceedings. Also, they determine the extent of protection conferred by a European patent or patent application when it comes to infringement litigation before national courts. Compared therewith, the description and drawings may be used only for interpreting the claims (Article 69(1) EPC and the Protocol on the Interpretation of Article 69 EPC).

Herein, we will set out the key requirements for claims under European practice.

1 Requirements of EPC

In view of the fundamental function of the claims, the proper drafting of claims is very important. Also, it is not surprising that requirements with respect to contents and form exist which are taken quite seriously by the EPO. A well drafted set of claims should

- comply with the formal requirements of the EPC;
- provide a broad scope of protection;
- allow for enough freedom for possible later amendment and limitation, and
- where possible, even foresee and include future developments.

A core provision of the EPC relating to the claims is Article 84 EPC, which

はじめに

欧州特許及び欧州特許出願において、クレームはとても重要である。欧州特許庁の審査だけでなく、特許異議申立て及び審判手続、並びに、国内無効手続において、クレームは特許要件を判断する基礎となる。また、国内裁判所に対して侵害訴訟が提起されたとき、クレームは、欧州特許又は特許出願により与えられた保護の範囲を画定する。これに対して、明細書及び図面は、クレームを解釈する目的でのみ用いられる（第69条(1)及び第69条の解釈に関する指令）。

本章では、欧州特許実務におけるクレームの重要な要件について述べる。

1　欧州特許条約の要件

クレームの基本的な機能に鑑みると、クレームを適切に起案することは非常に重要である。また、欧州特許庁がクレームの内容及び形式に関しての要件を重視していることは驚くべきことではない。適切に起案されたクレームは、以下のとおりである。

・　欧州特許条約の形式的要件に適合している。

・　広汎な範囲の保護を与える。

・　後の補正及び限定に対する十分な余地を与える。

・　可能であれば、その後の展開を予測し、これを含む。

クレームについて中核を成す法規は第84条にあり、以下のように規定されて

reads:

> *The claims shall define the matter for which protection is sought. They shall be clear and concise and be supported by the description.*

Thus, when selecting the claim language to define an invention, Article 84 includes four requirements which must be taken into account, i.e. that the claims:

- define the matter for which protection is sought,

- are clear,

- are concise, and

- are supported by the description.

In the following sub-sections, we will discuss these requirements in more detail.

1.1 The Claims shall Define the Matter for Which Protection is Sought

This requirement set out in Article 84 EPC is supplemented by Rule 43(1) EPC the first sentence of which states that the claims *shall define the matter for which protection is sought in terms of the technical features of the invention*. This means that statements relating to non-technical features such as commercial advantages should be avoided. Several types of technical features may be used to define an invention:

- structural features, such as the description of an arrangement of parts in a mechanical device, apparatuses, or chemical formulae,

いる。

　クレームには、保護が求められている事項を特定する。クレームは、明確かつ簡潔に記載されていなければならず、明細書により十分な裏付けがされていなければならない。

発明を特定するクレームの文言を選択するに際し、考慮されるべき要件として、第84条は以下の４つを包含する。

・　保護が求められている事項が特定されていること。

・　明確に記載されていること。

・　簡潔に記載されていること。

・　明細書により十分な裏付けがされていること。

以下、上記要件を詳細に考察する。

1.1　クレームは保護が求められている事項を特定する

第84条に規定されるこの要件は、規則43(1)第一文により補足され、クレームは発明の技術的特徴の観点から保護が求められている事項を特定すると規定されている。これは商業上の利益等の非技術的特徴に関する記載を避けるべきであることを意味している。発明を特定するためには、以下に示すように複数のタイプの技術的特徴を使用することができる。

・　構造的特徴（機械的デバイスにおける部品の配置、装置又は化学式）

- <u>compositions</u> defined in terms of the nature and/or amounts of the ingredients, such as alloys or pharmaceutical composition,

- <u>functional</u> features identifying specific functions or effects of individual elements, such as a *"means for supply power"* or a *"foaming agent"* (if the function relates to the claimed teaching in its entirety it is more a purpose of use feature; see below),

- <u>process</u> features defining a technical activity,

- intended <u>use</u> features, defining the claimed teaching in terms of specific purposes of use for which it must be suitable, such as a *"mold for molten steel"*.

- <u>parameter</u> features, such as the definition of a substance by its melting point.

However, the applicant cannot entirely freely choose which kind of features to use to define the invention. In particular, the Guidelines for Examination in the EPO state that functional features can only be used if a skilled person would have no difficulty in providing some means of performing the claimed function without exercising inventive skill. Parameter features can only be used where the invention cannot be adequately defined in any other way. Products can only be defined using process features (so called product-by-process claims) where there is no other information available in the application to define the product satisfactorily using structural, composition, or parameter features.

1.2 The Claims shall be Clear

The meaning of a claim should be clear to the person skilled in the art from the wording of the claim alone. The case law of the EPO has developed numerous guidelines on the meaning of *"clear"* in Article 84 EPC. Therefore, it is worth-

- 合金又は医薬組成物等の、成分の性質及び／又は分量の観点から特定される<u>組成物</u>

- 個々の構成要件に特有の機能又は効果を特定する<u>機能的特徴</u>（例えば「電力を供給する手段」又は「発泡剤」）（ここで、その機能がクレームの教示全体に関連する場合は、用途が特徴となる。以下参照）

- 技術的動作を特定する<u>方法</u>の特徴

- 意図する<u>用途</u>の特徴であって、適切であるべき用途について特定の目的の観点からクレームの教示を特定するもの（例えば「溶鋼用金型」）

- <u>パラメータ</u>の特徴（例えば、融点による物質の特定）

　ただし、出願人は、どの種類の特徴で発明を特定するかについて、必ずしも自由に選択することはできない。特に、欧州特許庁の審査基準によれば、機能的特徴は、クレームされた機能を実行する手段を当業者が創作能力を発揮することなく提供することが困難ではない場合にのみ使用できる。パラメータの特徴は、他のいかなる手段によっても発明を適切に特定できない場合にのみ使用できる。構造、組成物又はパラメータの特徴を使用して物を十分に特定するために利用可能な情報が出願書類にはない場合にのみ、方法の特徴を使用して物を特定できる（いわゆるプロダクト・バイ・プロセスクレーム）。

1.2　クレームが明確であること

　クレームの意味が当該クレームの文言のみから当業者にとって明確であることが必要である。欧州特許庁のケースローは、第84条における「明確」の意味に関する多くの基準を構築してきた。よって、欧州特許出願のためにクレーム

while to bear in mind the following points when drafting and prosecuting claims for European patent applications:

Good practice:

- Include all features which are essential for the invention, i.e. all of the features which are necessary for achieving the technical effect of the invention. This is especially important if the description states that such features are essential.

- Include detailed definitions of the measurement methods allowing the unambiguous definition of any parameters used in the claims.

- Make sure that the features are defined in term of proper units and, where needed, the basis for units used (such as "%" can be wt.-%, vol.%, mol.-%, ..., and molecular weights can be based on a weight average, number average, ...).

Bad practice:

- Using relative terms such as *"thin"*, *"wide"* or *"strong"*. If unavoidable, make sure that these terms are defined either in the claims themselves or in the application.

- Using features which define the result to be achieved by the claimed invention. For example, using a parameter which defines the high stability of chemical composition as a claim feature, when the technical effect achieved by the invention is improved stability.

- Using vague terms such as *"about"* or *"approximately"* in the claims. If such terms are used, it is preferable that they be defined in the description.

を起案して出願手続を行う際には、以下の点を念頭に置く必要がある。

良い実務：

- 発明に不可欠なすべての特徴（すなわち、発明の技術的効果を達成するために必要なすべての特徴）を含める。これは当該特徴が不可欠であることを明細書が記載している場合は特に重要である。

- クレームで使用されるあらゆるパラメータを一義的に特定するための測定方法について詳細な定義を含める。

- 適切な単位（必要に応じて、使用される単位の基準）を使って特徴を特定する（「％」は、重量％、容量％、モル％、であり得るし、分子量は、重量平均、数平均に基づくこともある）。

悪い実務：

- 「細い」、「広い」、「強い」等の相対的な用語を使用する。相対的用語の使用が避けられない場合は、クレーム自体又は出願書類のいずれかでこれらの用語を定義する。

- クレームに記載された発明により達成される結果を使って特徴を特定する。例えば、発明により達成される技術的効果が改良された安定性である場合に、クレームの特徴として化学組成物の高い安定性を定義するパラメータを使用する。

- クレーム中に「約」や「おおよそ」等の曖昧な用語を使用する。かかる用語が使用される場合は、明細書中でこれらの用語を定義することが好ましい。

- Using trademarks. Objections are generally raised to the use of such terms in the claims. Therefore, if these terms are used in the claims or description, they should ideally be accompanied by a generic description.

- Referring to the drawings or description in the claims.

1.3 The Claims shall be Concise

This requirement relates both to the claims in their entirety, and to each individual claim.

There is a financial motivation for applicants to file not more than 15 claims in a European patent application, as significant claims fees are due for the 16th and subsequent claims (September 2016: € 235 per claim up the 50th claim, and € 580 for each further claim). Therefore, applicants tend to restrict the number of claims filed, with the result that it is rare for the EPO to object that the claims are not concise in their entirety for containing too many claims.

Objections to the conciseness of individual claims may be raised where wording is repeated due either to typographical errors or the incorrect use of dependent claims. While the use of alternatives in claims is permissible, an objection may also be raised to claims containing such a large number of alternatives that it is difficult to determine the scope of the claim.

1.4 The Claims shall be Supported by the Description

The EPO interprets this requirement of Article 84 EPC as being both a formal and substantive requirement.

In order to fulfil the formal requirement, there must be literal basis in the description for each of the claims. This can normally be achieved by including a

- 商標を使用する。クレーム中にかかる用語を使用することは一般的に認められない。よって、これらの用語をクレーム又は明細書で使用する場合は、一般的な記載を伴うことが好ましい。

- クレームで図面又は明細書に言及する。

1.3　クレームの記載が簡潔であること

この要件は、全体としてのクレーム一式及び個々のクレームの双方に関連する。

16番目以降のクレームについては高額なクレーム料金の支払いが課されるため、欧州特許出願においては、15以下のクレームを提出することが出願人にとって経済的である（2016年9月現在：50番目のクレームまで1クレームにつき、235ユーロ、それ以降の各クレームにつき、580ユーロ）。よって、出願人は、提出するクレームの数を制限する傾向にあり、結果的に、過度に多くのクレームを含んでいるためにクレームの記載が全体として簡潔でないという趣旨の拒絶理由が欧州特許庁から提起されることは稀である。

個々のクレームの記載が簡潔でないという趣旨の拒絶理由は、誤記又は従属クレームの誤った使用のいずれかにより文言が繰り返された場合に提起される可能性がある。クレーム中で選択肢の使用は認められるが、クレームの範囲を決定することが困難なほどの多数の選択肢を含むクレームに対しては、拒絶理由が提起される可能性がある。

1.4　クレームが明細書により十分に裏付けされていること

欧州特許庁は、第84条のこの要件を形式的及び実体的要件の双方であるとして解釈している。

形式的要件に適合するためには、各クレームについて明細書に文言上の根拠が必要である。通常は、明細書に1つセクションを設けて各クレームの対象を

section of the description in which the subject matter of each claim is reproduced.

The substantive requirement is based on the fundamental principle of European patent law that that the scope of protection should be consistent with the technical teaching of the patent. As a result, the claims should not be broader than is justified by the invention disclosed in the description and drawings of the application. Claims are typically generalizations of the invention disclosed in the description, and the EPO position is that the claim may cover all obvious modifications of, equivalents to, and uses of the invention described. In particular, it is permitted that the claims be broad enough to cover all embodiments which can *reasonably be predicted* by the person skilled in the art to exhibit the technical effect of the invention.

The onus is on the Examiner to provide well-founded reasons that the skilled person could not extend the teaching of the description to the whole of claimed subject matter, using routine methods of experimentation or analysis. According to the Guidelines for Examination in the EPO, the Examiner should support such objections with published documents. It is only once such reasoned arguments have been set out that the burden of demonstrating that the claim is fully supported switches to the applicant. To illustrate this point, we refer to the following example:

Claim:

A process of treating plant seeds, comprising the step of subjecting the seed to a temperature of 1–2°C for 1 day.

Description:

A general section repeating the wording of the claim and explaining that the claimed seeds deliver plants with improved resistance to low temperatures.

再現することにより、当該形式的要件を満たすことができる。

実体的要件は、特許の技術的教示とその保護の範囲とが一致しているべきであるという欧州特許法の根本原理に基づいている。その結果として、クレームは、出願の明細書及び図面において開示された発明により十分な根拠が示されるよりも広いものであってはならない。クレームは、通常、明細書で開示された発明の一般化であり、欧州特許庁は、明細書に記載された発明の自明な変更、均等物及び用途のすべてをクレームが包含することができるという立場をとっている。特に、クレームは、発明の技術的効果を明らかにするために当業者が合理的に予測できるすべての実施形態を包含する程度に十分広いことが認められる。

実験又は分析のありふれた手法を用いて当業者が明細書の教示をクレームされたすべての対象に拡張できないことについては、十分な理由を提示する責任が審査官にある。欧州特許庁の審査基準によると、審査官はかかる理由を公開された文献で裏付ける必要がある。この理由付けがなされると、クレームが十分に裏付けられているという立証責任は出願人に転換される。この点を例証するために、以下の例に言及する。

クレーム：

植物の種子を処理する方法であって、種子を1日間、1～2℃の温度にさらすステップを備えた方法。

明細書：

明細書中の発明の概要には、クレームの文言が繰り返され、クレームに記載された種子により、低温に対する改良された耐性を有する植物が生じることが

An example relates to one type of plant seeds only, showing that the plants resulting from the treated seeds have improved resistance to low temperatures.

Objection:

The Examiner objects that the claim is not supported by the description, and provides evidence that certain types of seeds rapidly irreversibly decompose at temperatures below 5°C.

In this situation, unless the applicant can provide convincing evidence or arguments that the process is generally applicable, the claim must be restricted to the types of plant seeds which can reasonably be predicted to exhibit the technical effect of the invention. It would not be enough to assert that the process is applicable to all plant seedlings.

Although such an objection can be raised under Article 84 EPC, it can also be raised under Article 83 EPC on the basis that the disclosure is insufficient to enable the skilled person to carry out the invention over the whole of the claimed scope. This requirement is discussed in more detail elsewhere in the present book, see the Chapter on the Disclosure Requirement. Although the choice of Article under which this objection is raised is unimportant in Examination Proceedings, it is critical in Opposition Proceedings as Article 84 EPC is not a valid ground of opposition.

A consideration of the extent to which the effect of an invention is achieved across the scope of the claims is also relevant to the assessment of inventive step, as discussed in the Chapter on Inventive Step.

Special requirements for support by the description apply where the technical

記載されている。

実施例には、植物の種子の1タイプのみに関し、処理された種子から生じる植物が低温に対する改良された耐性を備えていることが示されている。

拒絶の理由：

審査官は、クレームが明細書により裏付けされていないと指摘し、特定のタイプの種子が5℃未満の温度で急速に回復不可能に分解するという証拠を提示している。

この状況では、当該方法が一般的に適用可能であることを出願人が説得力のある証拠を提出するか、説得力のある議論をしなければ、発明の技術的効果を示すことが合理的に予測できる植物の種子の種類にクレームの範囲を減縮する必要がある。当該方法がすべての植物苗に適用できることを主張するのは十分でないと思われる。

第84条に基づく拒絶理由が提起され得るが、クレームに記載された範囲全体にわたって当業者が発明を実施するには開示が不十分であることに基づき第83条に基づく拒絶理由も提起され得る。第83条の要件についての詳しい説明は「開示要件」の章を参照されたい。この拒絶理由が提起される際の根拠条文の選択は審査手続においては重要でないが、第84条は特許異議の申立ての理由として有効ではないため、条文の選択は異議申立手続においては重要な意味を持つ。

「進歩性」の章で考察するように、発明の効果がクレームの範囲全体にわたって達成される程度を考慮することは進歩性の判断にも関連する。

クレームの技術的特徴がその機能により特定される場合には、明細書による

features of the claims are defined by their function. If only one way of achieving this function is exemplified in the application, the Examiner may object that the claim is not supported by the description unless it can be argued that the skilled person would appreciate that other means could be used for the same function.

For example, if a claim feature relates to a *"means for supplying power"*, and the description discloses an embodiment wherein the *"means for supplying power"* is a battery, no clarity objection would arise if the skilled person would understand that a solar panel or mains supply could be used in place of the battery. If however, no means beyond the concrete example given in the description are known for carrying out the claimed function, then a clarity objection may be raised.

1.5   Procedural Matters

Clarity is first assessed by the Search Division before drawing up the European search report. If the Examiner considers that the European patent application is so unclear that it is impossible to carry out a meaningful search, the applicant will be requested to file a statement indicating which subject-matter should be searched. This procedure is discussed in greater detail in the chapter specifically addressing the aspect of the EPO search proceedings below.

Clarity is also assessed by the Examiner during prosecution. If the Examiner considers the claims to be unclear and this deficiency is not remedied or overcome by argument, the application will be refused.

Article 84 EPC is neither a ground of opposition, nor a ground for revocation in national courts. As a result, clarity is only discussed in opposition proceedings to the extent that an amendment of the granted claims introduces a lack of clarity (so decided by the Enlarged Board of Appeal of the EPO in the decision **G 3/14**).

裏付けについて特別の要件が適用される。この機能を達成する方法が1つだけ出願書類に例示されている場合は、審査官は、当該クレームが明細書により裏付けされていないという拒絶理由を提起し得る。ただし、他の手段を用いても同じ機能が達成できることを当業者であれば認識できると主張できる場合はこの限りでない。

例えば、クレームの特徴が「電力を供給する手段」に関するものであり、明細書には実施形態が開示され「電力を供給する手段」が電池である場合、電池の代わりに太陽電池パネル又は主電源を使用できることを当業者が理解できるのであれば、上記の拒絶理由は生じない。しかし明細書に与えられた具体例以外の手段が、クレームされた機能を実施するものとして知られていなければ、上記の拒絶理由が提起され得る。

1.5 手続的事項

クレームの明確性は、欧州調査報告を作成する前に、調査部により最初に判断される。審査官は、欧州特許出願があまり明確でなく、意味のある調査ができないと考える場合は、どの対象が調査されるべきかを示す記載を提出するよう出願人に求める。この手続については、欧州特許庁の調査手続を扱っている後の章でより詳細に考察する。

明確性は審査過程でも審査官によって考慮される。審査官がクレームは不明確であり、この不備は意見書によっても是正されず、克服できないと考える場合は、出願は拒絶される。

第84条違反は特許異議の申立ての理由ではなく、各締約国の裁判所における取消理由でもない。結果として、明確性は、特許されたクレームの補正をすることにより明確性の欠如が導入される範囲で特許異議申立手続において検討されるに過ぎない（拡大審判部の審決 G 3/14における決定）。

2 Kinds of Claims

2.1 Categories

There are two basic kinds of claim: those to physical entities (products, apparatus, system), or those to activities (method, process, use). In addition to these groups, claims on pharmaceuticals can also be drafted in a *"medical use"* format, directed to a compound for use in a method of treating a certain disease. Such claims are interpreted by the EPO as purpose-limited product claims.

2.2 One Independent Claim per Category

According to Rule 43(2) EPC, a European patent application may contain more than one independent claim in the same category only if the subject-matter of the application involves one of the following:

(a) a plurality of interrelated products,

(b) different uses of a product or apparatus,

(c) alternative solutions to a particular problem, where it is inappropriate to cover these alternatives by a single claim.

The EPO interprets the term *"interrelated"* in Rule 43(2)(a) to mean different objects that complement each other or work together. Examples of such objects are: a plug and socket; a transmitter and receiver; an intermediate and final chemical product; and a gene, a gene construct, a host, a protein, and a medicament.

"Different uses of a product or apparatus" as defined in Rule 43(2)(b) include claims directed to further medical uses when a first medical use is known, and claims directed to the use of the same compound for multiple purposes, such as

2　クレームの種類

2.1　カテゴリー

クレームには基本的に２種類がある。物理的実体（製品、装置、システム）についてのクレームと、行為（方法、プロセス、用途）についてのクレームである。これらのグループに加え、医薬に関するクレームは、特定の病気を治療する方法で使用される化合物を対象とする「医薬用途」の形式で起案することもできる。かかるクレームは、目的が限定された物のクレームとして、欧州特許庁により解釈される。

2.2　各カテゴリーごとに１つの独立クレーム

規則43(2)によると、欧州特許出願は、出願の対象が以下の１つに該当する場合にのみ、同一のカテゴリーに２つ以上の独立クレームを含んでいてもよい。

(a)　相互に関連する複数の物

(b)　物又は装置の異なる用途

(c)　特定の課題に対する別の解決手段で、これらの別の解決手段が単一のクレームにより包含されることが不適切な場合

欧州特許庁は、規則43(2)(a)の「相互に関連する」という文言を、互いに補完する又は協働する異なる客体を意味するものと解釈する（当該客体の例：プラグとソケット；送信機と受信機；化学物質の中間体及び最終製品；並びに遺伝子、遺伝子構築物、宿主、タンパク質及び薬剤）。

規則43(2)(b)で規定される「物又は装置の異なる用途」には、第一医薬用途が知られている場合のさらなる医薬用途を対象とするクレームや、同一の化合物の多用途（例えば、髪の毛を強化する用途と髪の毛の成長を促進する用途）を対象

for fortifying hair and promoting hair growth.

Examples of *"alternative solutions to a particular problem, where it is inappropriate to cover these alternatives by a single claim"* according to Rule 43(2)(c) are groups of chemical compounds, or two or more processes for the manufacture of such compounds.

At the search stage, if the Examiner is of the opinion that the claims to be searched contain more than one independent claim per claim category, the applicant will be invited to indicate the claims on which the search is to be carried out. If the applicant fails to provide such an indication in due time, the EPO will carry out the search on the basis of the first claim in each category (Rule 62a(1) EPC). If the applicant does not agree with the Examiner that the claims contain more than one independent claim per claim category, the burden of proof is on the applicant to provide convincing arguments that one of the three exceptions set out in Rule 43(2) EPC applies. For details we refer to the section on EPO search proceedings below.

Even if no objection is raised during the search, an objection may still be raised during Examination.

2.3 Dependent Claims

Rule 43(4) EPC defines a dependent claim as any claim which includes all the features of any other claim. Under European practice, dependent claims may refer back to one or more independent or dependent claims, or to both independent and dependent claims. In addition, dependent claims may also refer to independent claims in two categories as alternatives.

The introduction of such multiple dependencies is a most valuable tool under EPC practice. Different from other jurisdictions multiple dependencies are not considered as multiple claims, and thus there is no requirement for paying addi-

とするクレームが含まれる。

規則43(2)(c)による「特定の課題に対する別の解決手段で、これらの別の解決手段が単一のクレームにより包含されることが不適切な場合」の例は、化合物の複数のグループや、当該化合物の製造のための２つ以上の方法である。

調査段階で、調査対象クレームに、クレームのカテゴリーにつき２つ以上の独立クレームが含まれているという見解を示す場合は、審査官は、調査が行われるクレームを特定するよう出願人に求める。審査官の求めに出願人が応答しない場合、欧州特許庁は、各カテゴリーの最初のクレームに基づき調査を行う（規則62a(1)）。この点について審査官に同意できない場合、出願人は、規則43(2)に規定された３つの例外の１つが適用されることについて出願人は立証責任を負い、説得力のある議論をする必要がある。詳細については、欧州調査の章（第10章）で言及する。

調査の過程で拒絶理由がなんら提起されなかった場合でも、審査過程で拒絶理由が提起され得る。

2.3 従属クレーム

規則43(4)は、他のクレームのすべての特徴を含むクレームとして従属クレームを定義する。欧州実務では、従属クレームは１つ以上の独立又は従属クレーム、あるいは独立及び従属クレームの双方を参照することができる。従属クレームは、２つのカテゴリーの独立クレームを選択肢として参照することもできる。

かかる複数の従属クレームを用いることは、欧州特許実務において最も貴重な手段である。他の法域と異なり、複数の従属があっても多数のクレームとはみなされないため、複数の従属が用いられても、追加のクレーム料金を支払う

tional claim fees when multiple dependencies are introduced.

As multiple dependencies are not permitted in some jurisdictions outside of Europe, applicants form outside Europe sometimes submit claim sets in which dependent claims have only single dependencies. However, due to the strict approach to added matter adopted by the EPO (see the Chapter on Amendments below), this can later cause problems when amending the claims to combine the subject matter of two or more dependent claims.

From the perspective of European law, a simple way in which the risk of such added matter objections can be reduced (at the time of filing outside of Europe, such as in the case of an International (PCT) patent application) is to include the subject matter of the claims as a series of *"embodiments"* in the description, in which the embodiments corresponding to the dependent claims include back-references to multiple embodiments. Support for amendments combining the subject matter of two or more dependent claims can then be found in the corresponding embodiments.

2.4 Alternatives and Options

As noted above, claims fees are due in respect of the 16th and each subsequent claim. Therefore, there is a strong financial motivation to reduce the number of claims in European patent applications. One way in which this can be achieved is to combine the subject matter of dependent claims as alternatives or options in a single claim. Such claims are allowable before the EPO as long as they do not introduce a lack of clarity.

3   Claim Interpretation by EPO

The EPO is principally concerned with assessing the patentability of claims. To do so, the Boards of Appeal of the EPO have developed a number of guide-

必要はない。

　欧州以外の一部の法域では複数の従属が認められないため、欧州以外の地域からの出願人は、従属クレームが1つのクレームにのみ従属するクレーム一式を提出することがある。しかし、新規事項の追加に対する欧州特許庁の厳格なアプローチ（「補正」の章参照）により、クレームを補正して2つ以上の従属クレームの対象を組み合わせる場合、後に問題が生じることがある。

　欧州特許実務の観点から、かかる新規事項追加のリスクを低減させる簡単な方法は、欧州以外での出願時（例えば、国際特許出願の場合）に、一連の「実施形態」としてクレームの対象を明細書に含めることである。ここで、従属クレームに対応する実施形態には複数の実施形態の参照が含まれる。こうすることにより、2つ以上の従属クレームの対象を組み合わせる補正の根拠を、対応する実施形態に見出すことができる。

2.4　選択肢及び任意な特徴

　すでに述べたように、第16番目のクレームとその後の各クレームに関しては、クレーム料金の支払いが課される。よって、欧州特許出願ではクレームの数を減らすことに大きな経済的動機付けがある。これが達成できる1つの方法は、1つのクレームに選択肢又は任意な特徴として、従属クレームの対象を組み合わせることである。かかるクレームは、明確性の欠如を導入しない限り、欧州特許庁において認められる。

3　欧州特許庁によるクレーム解釈

　欧州特許庁は、主に、クレームの特許要件を判断することに関与している。欧州特許庁の拡大審判部は、クレーム解釈を行うための多くの基準を構築して

lines for claim construction.

- Each claim should be read giving the words the meaning and scope which they normally have in the technical field of the invention, unless the description gives the words a special meaning. As a result, if the description gives a term a special meaning, it is generally desirable to include this definition within the claims themselves, in order to fulfill the clarity requirements of the EPC, and also to ensure that the special meanings are taken into account during the search and examination.

- The claim should also be read in an attempt to make technical sense out of it: such a reading may depart from the literal meaning of the claims.

- A claim to an *"Apparatus/product B for carrying out the process C"* is construed by the EPO as covering any apparatus suitable for carrying out the process. As a result, a claim to *"A mold for molten steel"* would lack novelty over any mold which was suitable for holding molten steel. Meanwhile, because a plastic mold has a melting point *lower* than that of molten steel, it would clearly not be suitable for carrying out the claimed process, and therefore would not be novelty destroying.

- On the other hand, the claim *"Process D for doing activity E"* is not interpreted as covering any process suitable for doing activity E. Instead, the technical effect is interpreted as a functional feature of the method. A method which was suitable for doing activity E but was not put to that use in the prior art would therefore not take away the novelty of this type of claim.

- Meanwhile, a claim *"Process F of making product G for achieving technical effect H"* is construed by the EPO to mean that the method or process has to be merely suitable for that use. Consequently, a prior disclosure of a method F for making the same product G without an indication of the par-

きた。

- 明細書がクレームの用語に特別の意味を与えない限りは、各クレームを解釈する際には、発明の技術分野で通常有する意味及び範囲がその用語に与えられる。その結果、明細書が特別の意味をその用語に与える場合は、定義をクレームそのものに含めることが一般的に好ましく、これにより欧州特許条約の明確性の要件が満たされ、特別の意味が調査及び審査手続で考慮されることにもなる。

- クレームは、それ自体で技術的意味を成すように解釈すべきである。かかる解釈により、クレームの文言上の意味から離れる場合もある。

- 「プロセスCを実行するための装置／物B」というクレームは、プロセスを実行するために適したすべての装置を包含するものとして、欧州特許庁により解釈される。結果として、「溶鋼用型」についてのクレームは、型であって溶鋼を保持するために適しているものに対して新規でない。一方で、プラスチック型は、溶鋼の融点より低い融点を有するため、クレームされたプロセスを実行するのには適していないことが明らかであり、新規性を喪失させることとはならない。

- 一方、「行為Eを行うためのプロセスD」というクレームは、行為Eを行うために適したすべてのプロセスを包含するものとは解釈されない。技術的効果は当該方法の機能的特徴として解釈されるからである。よって、行為Eを行うために適しているが、先行技術では当該使用のために使われていない方法は、このタイプのクレームの新規性を喪失させないであろう。

- 一方、「技術的効果Hを達成するために、物Gを製造するプロセスF」というクレームは、欧州特許庁により、当該方法又はプロセスは当該使用に適している必要があることを意味するに過ぎないと解釈される。結果として、同一の物Gを製造する方法Fの先行開示は、技術的効果Hを達成す

ticular purpose of achieving a technical effect H would anticipate this claim.

- A claim to *"The use of product J for achieving effect K"* is regarded by the EPO as being equivalent to *"A process for achieving effect K using substance J"*. Thus the claim is interpreted as relating to a process and not to a product J recognizable (e.g. by labelling or additives) as intended for use for achieving effect K.

- In contrast, a claim directed to *"the use of a process L for achieving the technical effect M"* is interpreted as being equivalent to a claim directed simply to the process L.

- For applications having filing or priority dates before 29.01.2011, claims in the Swiss-type format *"The use of a substance or composition for the manufacture of a medicament for a specified therapeutic application"* are interpreted by the EPO as being novel if the substance, the method of manufacture, or therapeutic application was not disclosed in the prior art. This interpretation is only applied to substances or compositions for medical uses.

- For applications granted on or after 13.12.2007, claims in the first medical use format *"Substance for use as a medicament"* or the second medical use format *"Substance for use in the treatment of disease"* will be interpreted as purpose-limited product claims. As a result, first medical use claims are interpreted as novel if the substance has not previously been used as a medicament, while second medical use claims are interpreted as novel if the substance has not previously been used for that specific medical indication.

- Product-by-process claims are interpreted by the EPO as being novel only if the product itself is novel. Therefore, it is normally necessary to provide evidence or convincing arguments that the process defined in the

るという特別の目的を示していなくてもこのクレームの新規性を喪失させる。

- 「効果Kを達成するための物Jの使用」というクレームは、欧州特許庁により、「物Jを使用して効果Kを達成するためのプロセス」と均等であるとみなされる。よって当該クレームは、プロセスに関するものであり、効果Kを達成するための用途として（例えば、標識することにより又は添加物により）認識される物Jに関するものではないと解釈される。

- これとは対照的に、「技術的効果Mを達成するためのプロセスLの使用」というクレームは、単にプロセスLを対象とするクレームと均等であると解釈される。

- 2011年1月29日よりも前に出願日又は優先日を有する特許出願については、「特定の治療に適用する医薬物を製造するための物質又は組成物の使用」というスイスタイプのクレームは、欧州特許庁により、物質、製造方法又は治療用途が先行技術で開示されていない場合は新規であると解釈される。この解釈は、医薬用途のための物質又は組成物のみに適用される。

- 2007年12月13日以降に特許が付与された出願については、第一医薬用途形式のクレームである「医薬として使用される物質」又は第二医薬用途形式のクレームである「病気の治療のために使用される物質」は、目的の限定された物のクレームとして解釈される。結果として、第一医薬用途クレームは、物質が医薬として過去に使用されていなかった場合は、新規であると解釈され、一方で第二医薬用途クレームは、物質が当該特定の医療適用に過去に使用されていなかった場合は、新規であると解釈される。

- プロダクト・バイ・プロセスクレームは、欧州特許庁により、製造された物自体が新規である場合にのみ、新規と解釈される。よって、通常は、クレームで特定されるプロセスにより明確な特性を有する物が生じるとい

claim leads to a product with distinct properties.

- Product-by-process claims in the format "*Product M obtained by the process N*" and "*A product M obtainable by the process N*" will be interpreted by the EPO as having equivalent scope. As a result, both claim formats would lack novelty over a prior art product which has the same properties as the product made by the process in the claim, even if that prior art product is made by a different process. As the scope of both claim formats is interpreted differently in some EPC contracting states, it is desirable to use the broader "*obtainable*" language in European patent applications.

- Optional features do not limit the scope of the claim. However, as discussed above, the introduction of such features into claims may be useful when reducing the number of claims.

4 Summary

The present section outlines some general and fundamental aspects of how claims should be drafted, what formal requirements have to be observed, and what types of claims and features for defining the teaching of an invention are available. Due to the central relevance of the claims in patents and patent applications there are many other aspects of patent practice which are in the one or the other way connected to/relative for the claims. These aspects, as far as not addressed here, are discussed in greater detail elsewhere in the present book, and questions not answered here might find an answer in these more specific chapters.

う証拠又は説得力ある議論を展開することが必要となる。

- 「プロセスNにより得られた物M」及び「プロセスNにより得ることのできる物M」という形式のプロダクト・バイ・プロセスクレームは、欧州特許庁により、均等の範囲を有するとして解釈される。結果として、双方の形式のクレームは、先行技術に係る物が異なるプロセスにより製造される場合であっても、クレームの当該プロセスにより製造される物と同一の特性を有する先行技術に係る物からみて新規性がない。双方のクレーム形式の範囲は、欧州特許条約の一部の締約国では異なって解釈されるため、欧州特許出願では、より広い「得ることのできる」という文言を使用することが好ましい。

- 任意の特徴は、クレームの範囲を限定しない。しかし、上記で考察したように、かかる特徴をクレームに取り込むことは、クレームの数を減少させる際に有用となる場合がある。

4　まとめ

　本章では、どのようにクレームを起案すべきか、どのような形式的要件を満たすべきか、発明の教示を特定するにはどのようなタイプのクレーム及び特徴を利用することができるかに関する一般的及び基本的な側面を取り上げた。クレームは、欧州特許及び欧州特許出願との関連で中心的な役割を果たすため、クレームに関係した／関連する多くの側面がほかにもある。本章で扱われていない側面は、本書の他の章で詳細に考察されている。また、本章で未解決の問題については、他の章にその答えを見出すことができるだろう。

Chapter **9**

Priority

優先権

James M. Ogle

MEMO

- ▶ 第87条に基づく優先権主張出願は、パリ条約第4条及び日本特許法第41条に相当します。国外優先権主張のみを定めるパリ条約と異なり、欧州出願に基づく「国内」優先権主張も認めています（§1.1）。

- ▶ 第87条に従えば、優先権主張出願時において先の出願について査定又は審決が確定している場合でも、優先権を有効に主張することができます（§1.1参照）。この点、日本の国内優先権主張出願と異なります（特許法第41条第1項第4号）。欧州では、優先権の基礎出願がみなし取下げとなることはありません。この点、日本の実務（特許法第42条第1項）と異なり、優先権主張出願に対して、基礎出願それ自体が引例となることもあり得ます（§3.1参照）。

- ▶ 出願をする権利と優先権とは別個のものとして扱われます（§1.2）。

- ▶ 第87条にいう「同一の発明」と「最初の出願」については、拡大審判部の審決によりその意味が明らかにされています（§1.3及び§1.4）。

- ▶ 第88条(2)は、複合優先権について規定しており、第88条(3)と併せて「部分優先」について概念的に規定しています（§3.1）。「部分優先」の解釈については、2つの流れが欧州特許庁のケースローにあり、拡大審判部の審決が待たれています（§3.1）。

▶ 日本の実務における複合優先権については、日本特許庁審査基準をご参照ください。

Introduction

This chapter provides an overview of the main aspects of claiming priority which are of practical importance for patent applicants in Europe, covering both well-settled, essential requirements and issues which are currently not yet resolved under European practice and therefore expose applicants to risks. The unsettled questions include the requirements for the valid transfer of priority rights and being able to rely upon "partial priority" in the case of generic terms in claims that have been broadened beyond the disclosure of the priority document. The latter issue is also highly relevant for the risks of "toxic" self-collision with a European application from the same patent family (e.g., a "toxic divisional application").

1 Basic Requirements for Claiming Priority under the EPC

The main principles of priority under the EPC are set out by Art. 87(1) EPC which reads:

> *Any person who has **duly filed, in or for** (a) any State party to the **Paris Convention** for the Protection of Industrial Property or (b) any Member of the **World Trade Organization**, an application for a patent, a utility model or a utility certificate, **or his successor in title**, shall enjoy, for the purpose of filing a European patent application in respect of **the same invention**, a right of priority during a **period of twelve months** from the date of filing of the **first application**.*

The terms shown in boldface above highlight six basic requirements for successfully claiming priority, namely that priority under the EPC can only be claimed 1) from an application that was duly filed in an **eligible territory**; 2) from an **eligible type** of application; 3) if the application claiming priority was

はじめに

本章では、解決済みの基本的な要件や現時点では未解決の問題を含め、欧州特許出願人にとって実務的に重要な優先権主張に関する主な状況を概説する。未解決の問題としては、(1)優先権を有効に移転するための要件や、(2)優先権書類の開示内容を超えて拡張された包括的用語がクレームにある場合の「部分優先」の享受に関する問題が挙げられる。後者の問題は、同じ特許ファミリーの欧州出願（例えば、「toxic な分割出願」）と自己衝突するリスクにも関係する。

1　欧州特許条約による優先権主張の基本的な要件

欧州特許条約による優先権の主な原則は、第87条(1)に以下のように規定されている。

> 次のいずれかの国において又はいずれかの国について、特許、実用新案登録又は実用新案証の**出願を正規にした者又はその承継人**は、**最初の出願の日から12月の期間**、**同一の発明**について欧州特許出願をすることに関し優先権を有する。
> (a)　工業所有権の保護に関する**パリ条約**の締約国、又は
> (b)　**世界貿易機関**の加盟国

太字で示されている用語は、優先権主張の６つの基本的な要件である。すなわち、以下の場合にのみ、欧州特許条約による優先権を主張することができる。１）基礎出願が、**適格な領域**内で正規にされた出願であること、２）基礎出願が、**適格な種類**の出願であること、３）優先権主張出願が、最先の優先日

filed within **twelve months** of the earliest claimed priority date; 4) by the **same applicant** who filed the priority application or by his **successor in title**; 5) in respect of the **same invention**; and 6) from the **first application** by the applicant (or by his predecessor in title) for the subject matter in question.

1.1 Basic Formal Requirements

Priority under the EPC may be claimed from applications filed *"in or for"* any of the currently 176 contracting states of the Paris Convention or the currently 161 member states of the World Trade Organization. Unlike Art. 4A(1) of the Paris Convention, which only provides for priority claims from applications filed in other countries than the country of the first application (external priority), the EPC also recognises internal priority, i.e. from previous European applications. Priority may also be claimed from PCT applications.

Priority may be claimed from no other types of intellectual property rights than the applications for patents or utility models/certificates as expressly recited in Art. 87(1) EPC. However, for these types of filing, the establishment of the valid filing date is sufficient to give rise to a right to claim priority. The subsequent fate of the priority filing is irrelevant. Priority may also validly be claimed, for example, from filings from which a patent has already been granted at the time the application claiming priority is filed.

If the application claiming priority is filed later than the 12-month maximum priority interval of Art. 87(1), the EPC provides that the application may be filed and re-establishment of rights requested within the following two months (Art. 122 and Rule 136 EPC).

However, such requests are successful only in exceptional circumstances, i.e. when the applicant satisfies the onerous requirement that the 12-month time limit was missed in spite of all due care required by the circumstances having been taken.

から12月以内に出願されること、4）優先権主張出願の出願人が、基礎出願の**出願人と同一又はその承継人**であること、5）優先権主張出願に係る発明が、基礎出願に係る発明と**同一の発明**であること、及び、6）その対象が出願人（又はその承継人）による**最初の出願**に基づくこと。

1.1　基本的な方式要件

現在のところ、176カ国のパリ条約締約国又は161カ国の世界貿易機関の加盟国のいずれかの国において又はいずれかの国について出願された出願に基づいて、欧州特許条約による優先権を主張することができる。最初の出願の国以外の国で出願された出願に基づく優先権主張（国外優先権）のみを定めるパリ条約第4A条(1)とは異なり、欧州特許条約では、先の欧州特許出願に基づく国内優先権も認められている。PCT出願に基づいて優先権を主張することもできる。

第87条(1)に明記されているように、優先権は、特許出願又は実用新案登録／実用新案証の出願という知的所有権に基づいて主張することができる。これらの出願については、有効な出願日を確保すれば優先権が発生する。基礎出願のその後の経過は問題でない。例えば、優先権主張出願時においてすでに許可されている特許に係る出願に基づいて、優先権を有効に主張することもできる。

第87条(1)の優先期間（12月）よりも後に優先権主張出願をする場合は、欧州特許条約の下では、その出願の後2月以内に権利回復請求をすることができると規定されている（第122条、規則136）。

しかしながら、権利回復請求が認められるのは、例外的な場合（すなわち、状況によって必要とされる相当の注意を払ったにもかかわらず、12月の期限を徒過したという厳格な要件を満たす場合）のみである。

1.2 Applicant Identity and the Transfer of Priority Rights

Under Art. 87(1) EPC, if the applicant of the priority application is not the same as the applicant of a subsequent application claiming the priority, a claim to priority will be invalid if a valid succession in title to the right to claim priority cannot be established.

If one or more applicants are added at the time of filing the subsequent application, the joint filing and priority claim implies the consent of all parties that the priority right is to be transferred to the larger group of co-applicants. No further proof of transfer is then required. In all other cases of "applicant mismatch", a valid transfer must be demonstrated. The EPC is, however, silent on the formal requirements for a valid transfer of a priority right, and the national requirements across Europe vary. This leads to legal uncertainty and non-uniform case law and practice both within the EPO and under the national practices across Europe.

Generally, it may be taken to be settled practice under the EPC that right to claim priority must be validly transferred before the subsequent application claiming priority has been filed. Deficiencies in the transfer cannot be remedied retroactively. This view has been confirmed, e.g., by recent English High Court decisions. In decision T 62/05, an EPO Board of Appeal applied very strict formal requirements to the transfer of priority rights, requiring that, just as for the assignment of a European patent application as such (Art. 72 EPC), the assignment of priority rights must be in writing and signed by both parties. As long as this approach is not expressly abandoned by the EPO, the best-practice recommendation can only be that the strict, formal requirements prescribed by T 62/05 should be adhered to for the assignment of any priority right which may in future become relevant under the EPC.

However, the approach that currently appears to be preferred by many EPO tribunals is that the transfer of a priority right – which under European practice is generally and in principle considered to be separate and independent from the

1.2 出願人の同一性及び優先権の移転

第87条(1)によれば、基礎出願の出願人が優先権主張出願の出願人と同一ではなく、優先権の有効な承継が認められない場合には、優先権主張は無効である。

優先権主張出願時に一又は複数の出願人を追加する場合、優先権を主張して共同出願をすることは、当該共同出願の出願人に優先権が移転されるべきことに当事者全員が同意をしていることの暗示である。その後に追加の移転証明書を提出することは必要とされない。その他の「出願人不一致」の場合には、移転が有効であることを立証しなければならない。一方、有効な優先権移転に関する方式要件は欧州特許条約に規定されておらず、締約国の国内要件は様々である。このため、欧州特許庁内においても、欧州全域における国内実務においても、法的に不安定であり、ケースローは一様ではない。

欧州特許条約の下では、優先権を主張して出願をする前に、優先権を有効に移転しなければならないというのが一般的な実務である。移転の不備を遡及的に救済することはできない。このような考えは、例えば、最近のイギリス高等裁判所の判決によって支持されている。審決T 62/05では、欧州特許庁の審判部は、非常に厳格な方式要件を優先権の移転に適用した。この方式要件では、欧州特許出願の譲渡（第72条）と同様に、優先権の譲渡も、両当事者の署名入りの書面によってなされなければならない。欧州特許庁がこのアプローチを明確に破棄しない限り、欧州特許条約が将来的に関係する可能性がある優先権の譲渡については、T 62/05に示された厳格な方式要件を遵守することが最良の実務であろう。

しかしながら、欧州特許庁の多くの審判部によって現時点で好まれているアプローチは、優先権の移転（欧州実務では、特許出願の移転とは分離及び独立していると一般には考えられている）が「関連」国内規定に基づいて有効であるこ

transfer of a patent application as such –needs to be shown to be valid under the "relevant" national provisions. Such an approach is consistent with the absence of express provisions in the EPC and goes back to earlier EPO Appeal Board decision J 19/87. It will generally depend on (1) the determination of the country of the "relevant" national law, and (2) the provision of legal expert opinion evidence in order to establish how that national law applies to the case in question.

Under this approach it currently remains unsettled by which principle the applicable national law is to be chosen in international constellations, e.g., if the parties to the transfer agreement are based in different countries and the priority application has been filed in yet another country. In principle, the relevant law under this approach may be (1) the law of the country/territory in which the priority application was filed, or (2) the law with which the contract governing the transfer of the priority right has the closest connection (which may vary depending on the particular circumstances of each case).

Generally, the third possible approach applies the law of the territory in which the later application claiming priority is filed. T 62/05 applied a form of this third approach, and this is also the approach taken under the national law of many countries. It leads to the problem that any agreement document governing the transfer of priority right must comply with the formal requirements for the transfer of priority in any territory in which protection might eventually be desired, even before any subsequent application claiming priority has been filed, i.e. in practice often long before any final decision is typically made on the territorial coverage that is required for a given invention (see e.g., Bremi, EPI Information 1/10:17-24 for discussion).

Thus, in practice, applicants worldwide who eventually wish to obtain patent protection in EPC territory should, when transferring priority rights, adhere to the strict standard of T 62/05 and moreover to any requirements in individual countries in which protection may be desired or which are associated with either the priority application or the transfer agreement.

とを示さなければならないというものである。このアプローチは、欧州特許条約に明文が存在しないことと矛盾せず、欧州特許庁の審判部による先の審決Ｊ 19/87に立ち返るものである。このアプローチは、一般に、(1)「関連」国内法の国による判断や、(2)その国内法を当該事案にいかに適用するべきかを確立するための法律専門家の意見証拠の提供に依存する。

このアプローチの下では、集団が国際的である場合（例えば、移転契約の当事者の住所又は居所が様々な国にあり、それらの国とは別の国で基礎出願がされた場合）に、適用可能な国内法をどの原則によって選択すべきかという問題が現時点では未解決である。原則として、このアプローチの関連法としては、(1)基礎出願がされた国／領域の法律、又は、(2)優先権の移転を管理する契約と密接に関係する法律（各事案の特定の状況に極めて依存する）を挙げることができる。

考えられ得る第三のアプローチは、一般に、後の出願が出願された領域の法律を適用するものである。Ｔ 62/05では、この第三のアプローチの形式を適用した。また、この第三のアプローチは、多くの国々の国内法で採用されているアプローチである。このため、優先権を主張して出願をする前であっても（すなわち、実務上は、所与の発明についてその保護が必要とされる領域についての最終決定を行うかなり前から）、優先権の移転を決定する同意書は、保護を望む領域における優先権の移転に関する方式要件を満たさなければならないという問題が生じる（例えば、Bremi, EPI Information 1/10：17-24を参照のこと）。

よって、実務上は、欧州特許条約の領域内で特許保護を求める出願人は、優先権を移転する場合には、Ｔ 62/05の厳格な基準を遵守することに加えて、保護を求める各国（あるいは、基礎出願又は移転同意に関係する各国）の要件を遵守するとよい。

1.3 Same Invention

The EPO Enlarged Board of Appeal in decision G 2/98 interpreted the *"same invention"* requirement as requiring the same strict, formalistic "subject matter" or "disclosure" test which the EPO also applies to the questions of added subject matter in the case of claim amendments or divisional applications, and also when assessing novelty. Priority was thus only to be acknowledged for subject matter of a claim which the skilled person can derive directly and unambiguously, using common general knowledge, from the priority application as a whole.

More flexible standards that had sometimes been applied prior to decision G 2/98 were thus rejected. In a later decision (G 2/10), the Enlarged Board of Appeal has confirmed the uniform applicability of this "uniform concept of disclosure" (also referred to interchangeably as a "disclosure test" or a "subject matter test") in the various above-mentioned areas of the law under the EPC.

1.4 First Application

This sixth basic requirement mentioned above is derivable, in particular, from Art. 87(1) in conjunction with Art. 87(4) EPC, which reads:

> A subsequent application in respect of the **same subject-matter** as a previous first application and filed in or for the same State shall be **considered as the first application** for the purposes of determining priority, provided that, at the date of filing the subsequent application, the previous application has been withdrawn, abandoned or refused, without being open to public inspection and without leaving any rights outstanding, and has not served as a basis for claiming a right of priority. The previous application may not thereafter serve as a basis for claiming a right of priority.

Thus, a subsequent application containing subject matter that was previously filed in a *"previous first application"* can nevertheless be considered as the eligi-

1.3 同一の発明

審決G 2/98では、欧州特許庁の拡大審判部は、「同一の発明」の要件として、クレームの補正又は分割出願の場合における新規事項追加の問題に適用され、また新規性の判断においても適用されるテストである厳格な「対象テスト」又は「開示テスト」を要求すると解釈した。よって、関連技術分野の技術常識を用いて、基礎出願全体から当業者が直接的かつ一義的に導き出すことができるクレームの対象についてのみ、優先権が認められるとされた。

よって、審決G 2/98よりも前に適用されていた柔軟な基準は認められなかった。後の審決（G 2/10）において、拡大審判部は、この「開示についての統一された概念（「開示テスト」又は「対象テスト」とも称される）を欧州特許条約の下での上述した様々な法領域で一様に適用することを確認した。

1.4 最初の出願

上述した６つ目の基本的な要件は、特に、以下の第87条(4)と併せて第87条(1)を解釈することで導き出せる。

> 先の最初の出願と**同一の対象**について同一の国において又は同一の国についてされた後の出願は、当該後の出願の出願日において、先の出願が公衆の閲覧に付されないで、かつ、いかなる権利をも存続させないで、取り下げられ、放棄され又は拒絶の処分を受けたこと、及びその先の出願がまだ優先権の主張の基礎とされていないことを条件として、優先権の決定をするに際して**最初の出願**とみなされる。当該先の出願は、その後、優先権の基礎とすることができない。

よって、「先の最初の出願」で出願された対象を含む後の出願は、さらなる要件（「先の最初の出願」が、最初から存在しなかったのと同じように、そのすべて

ble *"first application"* for the purpose of validly claiming priority, if a number of further requirements are met, which essentially amount to the timely elimination of the *"previous first application"* including all of its legal effects, just as though it had never existed.

The Enlarged Board in G 2/98 also expressly equated the meaning of the expression *"the same invention"* in Art. 87(1) EPC with the concept of *"the same subject-matter"* to which Art. 87(4) EPC refers in the context of determining which filing is the relevant *"first application"* for the purposes of assessing entitlement to priority. The *"first application"* for particular subject matter is therefore also determined according to the above-mentioned disclosure test.

2 Procedural Formalities

According to Rule 52 EPC, the declaration of priority may in principle still be made within and corrected 16 months from the earliest priority date claimed. However, any such correction must be submitted within four months of the date of filing of the European application claiming priority, and a declaration of priority may not be made or corrected after a request for early publication of the application claiming priority has been filed.

By the same 16-month deadline, European patent applicants must file a copy of any priority application, certified by the authority with which the priority application was filed. The EPO waives that requirement in certain cases, i.e., currently, if the priority application is a Japanese, Korean or Chinese patent or utility model application; a US application; or an EP application; a PCT application filed with the EPO as receiving office.

Where the priority application is not in English, French or German and during any proceedings at the EPO the EPO considers that the validity of the priority claim may be relevant to patentability, the EPO requires a translation of that

の法的効果を含めて適切な時期までに消滅していること）が満たされる場合には、優先権主張に関して適格な「最初の出願」とみなされる。

審決G 2/98では、拡大審判部は、優先権の享受の判断においてどの出願が「最初の出願」であるかを決定する際に、第87条(1)の「同一の発明」という表現の意味を、第87条(4)の「同一の対象」という概念と同等であるとみなした。よって、特定の対象に関する「最初の出願」は、上述した開示テストに従って決定される。

2　手続的要件

規則52によれば、原則として、最先の優先日から16月以内に、優先権主張の申立て及びその訂正をすることができる。一方、こうした訂正は、優先権を主張する欧州特許出願の出願日から4月以内にしなければならない。優先権主張出願の早期公開請求をした後では、優先権の申立てをすること又はその訂正をすることはできない。

同じ16月の期限までに、欧州特許出願の出願人は、基礎出願の写しを提出しなければならない。この写しは、基礎出願をした当局によって証明されたものでなければならない。特定の場合（すなわち、基礎出願が、日本、韓国又は中国の特許出願若しくは実用新案登録出願、米国出願、又は欧州出願、又は欧州特許庁を受理官庁として出願されたPCT出願である場合）には、この要件は免除される。

基礎出願が英語、フランス語又はドイツ語によるものでなく、かつ、優先権主張の有効性が特許性に関連すると欧州特許庁が考える場合には、欧州特許庁は、公用語の1つによるその出願の翻訳文を義務付ける。代わりとして、当該

application into one of the official languages to be filed. Alternatively, a declaration may be submitted that the European patent application is a complete translation of the previous application. In the case of noncompliance with such an invitation, the right to priority in question is lost.

3 Partial Priority

3.1 Legal Basis, Currently Unresolved Issues, and the Problem of "Toxic" Priority Entitlement

The claiming of multiple priorities and the concept of "partial priority" in the context of a single patent claim are provided for by Art. 88(2) EPC, second sentence, which reads:

> *Where appropriate, multiple priorities may be claimed **for any one claim**.*

Although this provision only refers to *"multiple priorities"*, it is well recognized that it also applies to *"partial priority"* in a narrow meaning (Schricker GRUR Int 1967, 3), i.e., also if only a single priority is claimed. The priority date may then apply to one part of the subject matter of a claim, and the filing date to the remainder of the claim.

Regarding European patent applications claiming subject matter that was added after the date of at least one priority application, Art. 88(3) EPC also provides:

> *If one or more priorities are claimed in respect of a European patent application, the right of priority shall cover only those elements of the European patent application which are included in the application or applications whose priority is claimed.*

欧州特許出願が先の出願の完全な翻訳文である旨の宣誓書を提出することができる。欧州特許庁の求めに応じない場合には、優先権は喪失する。

3 部分優先

3.1 法的根拠、現時点で未解決の問題、及び「toxic な」優先権の問題

第88条(2)第二文では、単一のクレームとの関連において、複合優先権の主張及び「部分優先」の概念が以下のように規定されている。

> 適切な場合には、いずれか1つのクレームについて複合優先権を主張することができる。

この規定は、「複合優先権」について言及するのみであるが、これは、狭義の意味において「部分優先」にも適用されると認識されている（Schricker GRUR Int 1967, 3）。すなわち、単一の優先権のみが主張される場合である。この場合、クレームの対象の一部に対して優先日が適用され、当該クレームの残余部に対しては出願日が適用されると考えられる。

少なくとも1つの基礎出願をした日後に、新たな対象をクレームに追加して欧州特許出願をする場合に関して、第88条(3)では、以下のように規定されている。

> ある欧州特許出願について一又は二以上の優先権が主張される場合には、当該欧州特許出願の構成部分のうちその優先権が主張されている一又は二以上の出願に含まれる部分についてのみ優先権が及ぶ。

This further confirms that a claim of a European patent application may cover subject matter going beyond what was disclosed in a priority application, and may then only be partially entitled to priority, namely only for subject matter which was disclosed in the priority application. A claim may thus in principle be split into "partial priority domains" of subject matter having different effective dates, depending on whether the subject matter in question is entitled to a particular priority claim.

Under current EPO practice such "splitting" of the claim scope will generally not pose particular problems when the different domains are expressly individualized as alternatives by the wording of the claim and these alternatives also correspond exactly to "elements" that either are or are not disclosed in a priority application. However, it is currently not decided whether such subject matter "splitting" is allowable when the possible "alternative subject matters" forming partial priority domains are not made explicit in the claim but are merely encompassed within a generic term that has been broadened in comparison to any term disclosed in the priority application. This is the principal question that currently stands to be decided in case G 1/15 of the EPO Enlarged Board of Appeal. Typical examples are the broadening of a chemical formula or of a numerical range, but the question may affect any aspect of a claim that has been broadened in a generic manner in comparison to the priority document.

One line of EPO case law will in such circumstances not acknowledge partial priority for narrower subject matter that has basis only in the priority application and is not individualised as such in the claim (e.g., T 1127/00, T 184/06, T 1443/05, T 1877/08 and T 476/09). This restrictive approach requires that different subject matter domains corresponding to different effective dates must be expressly identified as distinct alternatives by the wording of the claim. The word "or" must be used in the claim in order to distinguish the alternative subject matter domains. This approach is based on a restrictive interpretation of a statement found in previous decision G 2/98 of the Enlarged Board of Appeal according to which *"The use of a generic term or formula in a claim for which multiple priorities*

第88条(3)は、欧州特許出願のクレームが、基礎出願に開示された内容を超える対象を含む場合があること、そしてこの場合には、優先権を部分的にしか享受することができない（すなわち、優先権を享受することができるのは、基礎出願に開示された対象についてのみである）ことを認めている。よって、原則として、その対象が特定の優先権を享受するか否かに応じて、異なる基準日を有する「部分優先ドメイン」にクレームを分割することができる。

　異なるドメインがクレームの文言によって選択肢として明示的に個別化されており、かつ、それら選択肢が基礎出願に開示されている「構成部分」又は開示されていない「構成部分」に正確に対応している場合は、現行の欧州特許実務では、クレームの範囲をこのように「分割」しても特に問題はない。一方、「部分優先ドメイン」を構成することができる「選択的対象」がクレームで明示されておらず、基礎出願に開示された用語と比較して拡張された包括的用語に含まれている場合に、このような対象の「分割」が可能であるか否かについては、現時点では判断されていない。これは、欧州特許庁の拡大審判部による事件G 1/15で判断されるべき重要な問題である。典型的な例は、化学式の拡張又は数値範囲の拡張であるが、この問題は、優先権書類と比較して包括的に拡張されたクレームに対して影響を及ぼす可能性がある。

　欧州特許庁ケースローの１つの流れによれば、こうした状況の場合、基礎出願にのみ根拠を有する狭い範囲の対象で、基礎出願で個別化されてクレームされていないものについては、部分優先が認められない（例えば、T 1127/00、T 184/06、T 1443/05、T 1877/08及びT 476/09）。この限定的なアプローチでは、異なる基準日に対応する異なる対象は、クレームの文言によって別々のものとして明確に特定されていなければならない。クレームにおいて、「又は」という文言を、選択的対象を区別するために使用しなければならない。このアプローチは、拡大審判部による先の審決G 2/98の限定的な解釈に基づくものである。審決G 2/98には次のように記載されている：「第88条(2)第二文に基づき主張する複数優先に係るクレームにおいて包括的用語又は一般式を使用すること

are claimed in accordance with Article 88(2) EPC, second sentence, is perfectly acceptable under Articles 87(1) and 88(3) EPC, <u>provided that it gives rise to the claiming of a limited number of clearly defined alternative subject-matters</u>" (point 6.7 of the reasons).

However, a different line of case law represented by cases T 1222/11 and T 571/10 has argued that the above restrictive approach fails to recognize that the Enlarged Board in G 2/98 took a teleological and historical approach to the interpretation of Art. 88(2) EPC, second sentence, and held that the legislative intent underlying this provision was expressed by a particular "Memorandum" drawn up by FICPI for the Munich Diplomatic Conference prior to the adoption of the EPC, on the issue of multiple and partial priorities in the case of a single claim. T 1222/11 and T 571/10 therefore follow the approach to this issue that is explained in the Memorandum, and interpret the "proviso" of G 2/98, point 6.7 of the reasons (underlined above) entirely differently.

According to this much more lenient approach, when the terms in a claim have been broadened compared to the corresponding disclosure in the priority document, a partial priority entitlement is simply to be acknowledged to the extent that the claim scope corresponds to the disclosure of the priority document. The broadened, generic claim scope in question is thus "conceptually" divided into subject matter domains having different effective dates purely on the basis of the narrower disclosure in the priority document. This purely "conceptual" subdivision of the claim is independent of both the wording of the claim as such and the content of the later application as a whole.

Under the restrictive approach, when a generic term such as a chemical formula or numerical range is broadened with respect to the priority application, priority is lost entirely. Any intervening disclosure corresponding to the content of the priority application during the priority interval will thus destroy the novelty of the claim. In contrast, under the lenient "Memorandum approach" the priority entitlement is automatically maintained to the extent that subject matter is dis-

は、第87条(1)及び第88条(3)に基づきまったく問題ない。ただし、限られた数の明確に定義された選択的な対象をクレームするものに限る」(理由のpoint 6.7)。

　その一方、審決T 1222/11及びT 571/10に代表される別の流れのケースローによれば、上記限定的なアプローチは、第88条(2)第二文の解釈につきG 2/98において拡大審判部がとったアプローチを認識していない。G 2/98において、拡大審判部は、第88条(2)第二文の解釈に対して目的論的、かつ、歴史的なアプローチを採用し、単一クレームの複合優先及び部分優先の問題について、欧州特許条約の採択前にミュンヘン外交会議のためにFICPIが作成した「メモランダム」によってこの規定の立法趣旨が表現されていると判断した。よって、T 1222/11及びT 571/10は、この問題に対してメモランダムで説明されているアプローチに従うものであり、G 2/98の「ただし書き」(理由のpoint 6.7) をまったく違うように解釈している。

　この寛大なアプローチによれば、クレームの用語が、優先権書類の対応する開示内容と比較して拡張されている場合には、クレームの範囲が優先権書類の開示内容に対応する範囲内で部分優先が認められる。よって、拡張された包括クレームの範囲は、優先権書類の狭い開示に単に基づき、異なる基準日を有する対象に「概念的に」分割される。こうしてクレームを「概念的に」分割することは、クレームの文言それ自体や、後の出願の全体の内容とは無関係である。

　限定的なアプローチの下では、包括的用語（例えば、化学式又は数値範囲）が基礎出願に対して拡張されている場合、優先権は完全に喪失する。よって、基礎出願の内容に対応する引例が優先期間中に存在する場合には、クレームの新規性が否定される。対照的に、寛大な「メモランダムアプローチ」の下では、その対象が基礎出願に開示されている範囲で優先権が自動的に維持されるため、基礎出願の内容に対応する引例からクレームは保護される。

closed in the priority application, which will protect the claim from any intervening disclosure corresponding to the content of the priority application.

Therefore, the above-mentioned difference in approach to the acknowledgement of partial priority in the case of generic claim broadening compared to the priority application evidently also profoundly affects the extent to which "toxic divisional applications" and "toxic published EP priority applications" affect patent applicants in Europe. Under the EPC, the above-mentioned intervening disclosure may be, e.g., content of a divisional, co-divisional or a parent application that is entitled to priority. It may also be priority application itself, if that was also a European application and was prosecuted further at least to publication. Once published, any such related application is, in principle, considered to be an independent European patent application, such that any of its content that is entitled to the priority date is considered to be earlier-filed/later-published prior art under Art. 54(3) EPC and thus relevant for the novelty of a broadened claim that has lost its entitlement to that priority date.

Under the lenient "Memorandum approach", if a claim is generically broadened beyond the priority application, the priority-entitled disclosure of such related applications would (at least in all but very exceptional cases) not become prior art at all, due to the automatic protection that is afforded by the lenient concept of partial priority. However, under the restrictive approach, priority applications (if European and published), and in any case any priority-entitled content of published divisional, co-divisional and parent applications will generally become "toxic" and destroy the novelty of claims which have been generically broadened beyond the priority application (cf., e.g., EPO Board of Appeal decisions T 1443/05, T 1496/11 and the discussion in T 557/13, the referring decision in G 1/15).

Considering at least that it is common practice (1) to improve inventions in the course of the priority interval and broaden the scope of the protection that is sought in a later application claiming priority and (2) to file divisional applications, at least the problem of "toxic divisional/co-divisional/parent" applications

よって、基礎出願と比較して拡張している包括クレームの場合には、部分優先の認定に対する上記アプローチの違いは、「toxicな分割出願」及び「公開されたtoxicなEP基礎出願」が特許出願人に影響を与える程度にも深刻な影響を出願人に与える。欧州特許条約の下では、上述した優先期間中の引例としては、例えば、優先権を享受する分割出願、同時係属分割出願又は親出願の内容が考えられる。基礎出願が欧州出願であり、少なくとも公開されている場合には、基礎出願それ自体が引例になることもあり得る。原則として、このような関連出願は公開されると独立した欧州特許出願とみなされるため、優先日を享受するその内容は、第54条(3)の先行技術と考えられ、当該優先日の享受を喪失した拡張クレームの新規性に影響を与える。

寛大な「メモランダムアプローチ」の下では、クレームが基礎出願の範囲を超えて包括的に拡張されている場合であっても、部分優先が寛大に解釈されて自動的な保護が提供されるため、このような関連出願における優先権を享受する開示内容は（例外的な事案を除くすべての事案において）先行技術にはならない。一方、限定的なアプローチの下では、公開された欧州出願である基礎出願や、公開された分割出願、同時係属分割出願及び親出願の優先権を享受する内容は、一般に「toxic」であり、基礎出願の範囲を超えて包括的に拡張されたクレームの新規性を否定する（例えば、欧州特許庁の審判部による審決T 1443/05、T 1496/11や、T 557/13、G 1/15を参照のこと）。

(1)優先期間内に発明を改良して後の出願で優先権を主張して求める保護範囲を拡張することや、(2)分割出願をすることが一般的な実務であることを考慮すると、「メモランダムアプローチ」を適用することをG 1/15の拡大審判部が明確にしなければ、「toxicな分割出願／併存分割出願／親出願」の問題は、広範

will be quite widespread and serious under the EPC, if the Enlarged Board of Appeal in G 1/15 does not clarify that the "Memorandum approach" applies. All of these issues in principle also affect the national practices of EPC contracting states, which take into account the practice of the EPO, also regarding partial priority and "toxicity" of applications from the same patent family.

3.2 Best-Practice Measures to Safeguard Substantive Priority Rights

Various best-practice principles follow from the above, in particular from the concepts of "same invention", "first application" and the current lack of certainty over the acknowledgement of partial priority in the case of generic terms.

From the very beginning of the filing process, i.e., when the first, priority-founding patent application is drafted for a new invention, care should be taken that all wordings in the application meet, as far as possible, a standard of clarity, in the sense that it is conceivable that they could, if necessary, serve to define the limits of a claim. Also under the lenient "Memorandum approach" to partial priority, such a standard of clarity may be of critical importance, because any future partial priority domain encompassed by a later-broadened generic claim is defined exclusively by wordings found in the priority application. It is quite possible that the EPO Enlarged Board may in future explain that the "proviso" of G 2/98 (*"provided that it gives rise to the claiming of a limited number of clearly defined alternative subject-matters"*) in fact primarily imposes a standard of clarity under the "Memorandum approach" (see also Lawrence, EPI Information 1/15:23-25). Thus, there is a risk that content of a priority application could be held in sufficiently clear to define a partial priority domain within a later, broadened generic claim but could nevertheless (e.g. via a divisional application which retains the content) destroy the novelty of that claim. In such situations, the problem of "toxic divisionals" (or other related applications) would arise even under the "Memorandum approach" to partial priority.

When drafting applications that claim priority, if the invention has been devel-

囲に及ぶ重大な問題になる。部分優先や、同一特許ファミリーの出願の「toxicity」に関しても、欧州特許条約の締約国は欧州特許実務を考慮に入れているため、これらの問題は、欧州特許条約の締約国の国内実務にも影響を与える。

3.2 優先権を実質的に確保するための最良の実務

「同一の発明」、「最初の出願」といった概念や、包括的用語について部分優先が認められるか否かが不確かであるといったことから、優先権を確保するための最良の実務が異なる。

出願段階の当初から（すなわち、新たな発明に関する最初の基礎出願を起案する際に）、その出願の文言を用いてクレームの境界を定義しなければならないことをふまえて、その出願の文言が明確性の基準を可能な限り満たすように注意すべきである。後の出願の包括クレームに含まれる部分優先に係る範囲は、基礎出願の文言によってのみ規定されるため、部分優先に対する寛大な「メモランダムアプローチ」の下では、このような明確性の基準が重要であり得る。将来的には、欧州特許庁の拡大審判部は、G 2/98の「ただし書き」（「限られた数の明確に定義された選択的対象をクレームするものであれば」）が、実際は「メモランダムアプローチ」の下での明確性の基準を課すものであると説明することになろう（Lawrence, EPI Information 1/15：23-25も参照のこと）。よって、基礎出願の内容を十分明確に記載して後の出願の包括クレームにおける部分優先に係る範囲を定義することはできるが、それでもやはり、後の出願の包括クレームの新規性が否定されるリスクがある。例えば、基礎出願の内容が記載された分割出願によってである。このように、部分優先に対する「メモランダムアプローチ」の下であっても、「toxic な分割出願」（又は他の関連出願）の問題が起きる。

優先権主張出願を起案する際、その発明が基礎出願後に改良されたものであ

oped further after the first filing, never remove or change the definitions (or wordings in general) used in the first filing, only add to them. This should be done in an individualised manner, which will even allow the formulation of entirely separate claims directed only to the later-added subject matter, should that become necessary due to the establishment of the restrictive approach to partial priority in the future (entirely separate claims are in fact the equivalent of separating alternatives by the conjunction "or" as is required by the restrictive approach to partial priority).

Additionally, appropriate expanded generic definitions may and indeed should be included in such cases, so that the flexibility of the Memorandum approach may be exploited, if it is confirmed by the Enlarged Board. However, the original, narrower subgenus or embodiment was used in the priority application(s) should also be retained in the description of the later application. Moreover for potentially important subject matter, the "difference" in subject matter represented by the desired, broadened generic term minus the original narrower subgenus of the priority application should also be expressly spelled out as an express fall-back position, in case it is eventually after all necessary to amend generic claims by formulating equivalent claims in which partial priority domains are individualized using the word "or" according to the current restrictive approach to partial priority. That is because according to EPO Enlarged Board decision G 2/10 it is not always possible to assume that such subject matter that remains as a "difference" (or "logical complement") after a narrower subgenus or embodiment has been carved out of a broader generic definition will be acknowledged as being originally disclosed in an implicit manner. Whether that is possible will depend on the specific circumstances of each case.

The possibility that the Memorandum approach will become established appears to makes it more important to observe the twelve-month period after the earliest filing of the narrowest embodiment of an invention. This is the "flipside" of the principle that partial priority domains may be identified "conceptually" within a generic claim scope by comparison with narrower disclosures in the pri-

るならば、最初の出願で用いた定義（又は一般的な文言）を削除又は変更せずに、その定義への追加のみ行うべきである。部分優先に対する限定的なアプローチが将来的に採用された場合に備えて、後の出願で追加された対象のみに係る完全に別個のクレームを作ることができるようにそれぞれの様式で対処すべきである（部分優先に対する限定的なアプローチが要求するように、完全に別個のクレームは、「又は」という接続詞によって分離される選択肢と同等である）。

さらに、拡大審判部がメモランダムアプローチを採用した場合に備えて、メモランダムアプローチの柔軟性を利用することができるように、適切に拡張された包括的な定義を含めるべきである。一方、後の出願の明細書では、基礎出願で用いた元の下位概念又は実施形態も記載すべきである。また、部分優先に対する現行の限定的なアプローチに対応するために、「又は」という文言を用いて部分優先に係る範囲を区別したクレームに包括クレームを補正しなければならない事態に備えて、重要になる可能性のある対象については、優先権主張出願の上位概念の対象から基礎出願の下位概念の対象を除いたものに相当する「相違点」を選択肢として明確に記載すべきである。なぜなら、欧州特許庁の拡大審判部による審決 G 2/10によれば、広い包括的定義から下位概念又は実施形態が削られた後に「相違点」（又は「論理的補足」）として残る対象が、出願時において暗黙的に開示されたものであるとは必ずしも認められないためである。それが可能であるか否かは、各事案の具体的な状況による。

メモランダムアプローチが確立される可能性により、最も狭い下位概念の発明について最初に出願をした後の12月の期間の遵守が重要と思われる。これは、基礎出願の狭い開示内容と比較することによって、部分優先のドメインが包括クレームの範囲内で「概念的に」特定され得る原則の「フリップサイド」である。審決 T 1222/11に係る不服審判事件でこのことが示された。この事件

ority application. It was revealed in practice by the case underlying decision T 1222/11. For coherence on all aspects of priority, the Board in that case applied the same approach to assessing, by comparison with yet earlier applications, whether the priority application was in fact the first application for all "conceptually" identifiable priority domains its disclosure encompassed. A yet earlier-filed application by the same applicant that was published in the priority interval and disclosed a narrow embodiment encompassed by the definition used in both the priority application and the claim in question therefore ultimately destroyed the novelty of the claim. Priority could not be claimed in the scope of the narrow embodiment because at least in the "partial subject matter domain" of that narrow embodiment, the priority application was not the "first application".

If a priority application is filed outside EPC territory, then its publication after the priority interval cannot lead to "toxicity" in Europe. If a priority application is filed within EPC territory (either as an EP application or a national application), best practice rules dictate that its publication should be prevented if at all possible, in order to avoid all risks from "toxic priority" arising from the priority application as such, in the jurisdiction of the priority application.

In any event, however, neither the jurisdiction in which the priority application as filed is nor prevention of its publication avoids the risk of "toxicity" between European members of a patent family that may arise if a divisional application is filed within EPC territory and the claims of either the parent or a divisional case are not (or not fully) entitled to priority. Thus, before any divisional application is filed, it is recommendable to assess the priority entitlement of both the current parent claims and the intended claims for the divisional case. If it is foreseeable that content of a divisional application may potentially become "toxic" to the claims of its parent (or of another divisional application) which have lost priority entitlement, it may in some cases be helpful to remove the potentially novelty-destroying content from the specification of the divisional before it is filed. If a problem with priority and potential "toxicity" is recognised only after a divisional application has been filed, then – only in the time period between filing and publi-

で審判部は、基礎出願に開示された「概念的に」区別可能な優先ドメインのすべてについて、その基礎出願が実際のところ最初の出願であったか否かを、さらに先の出願と比較することによって判断するにあたり、優先権全般における均一性の観点から、同一のアプローチを適用した。同一出願人による別の先の出願が優先期間中に公開され、そこには、基礎出願及び当該クレームの両方で用いられた定義による下位概念が開示されていたため、当該クレームの新規性は、先の出願によって否定された。少なくとも下位概念の「一部の対象」については、基礎出願は「最初の出願」ではなかったため、その下位概念の範囲内で優先権を主張することができなかった。

基礎出願が欧州特許条約の領域外でされる場合は、基礎出願が優先期間後に公開されたとしても、欧州においては問題にならない。基礎出願を欧州特許条約の領域内で（EP出願又は国内出願として）出願するならば、基礎出願それ自体から生じる「toxicな優先権」のリスクを避けるために、可能であれば、基礎出願の公開を防ぐべきである。

しかし、基礎出願を欧州特許条約の領域外で出願することや、基礎出願の公開を防ぐことによっては、分割出願を欧州特許条約の領域内で出願する場合で、親出願又は分割出願のクレームが優先権を（完全には）享受することができないときに生じる特許ファミリー間の「toxicity」リスクを避けることはできない。よって、分割出願をする前に、親出願のクレーム及び分割出願のクレームの両方について、優先権を享受することができるか否かを検討することを推奨する。分割出願の内容が、優先権を享受することができない親出願（又は別の分割出願）のクレームに対して「toxic」になる可能性があれば、分割出願をする前に、新規性を否定する内容を分割出願の明細書から削除することができる。分割出願をした後（分割出願をしてから公開までの間）に、優先権や潜在的「toxicity」の問題を認識した場合には、分割出願やその優先権主張の取下げを検討することができる。

cation of a divisional application – it may be relevant to consider withdrawing the divisional application or, in rare cases, its priority claim.

When drafting the claims of a divisional application or claim amendments during the prosecution of an application, if possible, formulate any claims that may partially lack priority in a way which expressly individualises the subject matters having different effective dates, using the conjunction "or" – or entirely separate claims – so as to comply with the restrictive approach to partial priority. However, under the strict disclosure test that applies to the assessment of the basis of divisional claims in the original disclosure of the parent and to claim amendments during prosecution, this of course requires suitable, correspondingly individualised textual basis in the relevant original disclosure as filed. As noted above, this requires a drafting practice that is adapted as far as possible to EPO practice as an upstream measure at the earliest stages of any filing strategy that is intended to cover Europe.

In principle, if earlier-filed/later-published prior art under Art. 54(3) EPC is citeable against a claim, one solution can in some cases be to formulate an "undisclosed" disclaimer that has textual basis in the relevant disclosure of that prior art, rather than in the application itself, in order to avoid the disclosure (Enlarged Board of Appeal decisions G 1/03 and G 2/03). This may, in principle, of course also be considered if a divisional application or a published priority document has become "toxic" and partial priority, for whatever reason, cannot provide a solution. However, the use of such disclaimers is associated with its own particular risks, due to the strict conditions such disclaimers must satisfy according to G 1/03 and G 2/03. In particular there exists the risk that such a disclaimer, introduced during prosecution, is held unallowable in post-grant opposition proceedings because it removes more than is necessary to restore novelty over the earlier-filed/later-published prior art. This may lead to an "inescapable" added-matter trap, because the disclaimer cannot be appropriately narrowed or removed without contravening the prohibition of post-grant claim broadening. For this reason alone, in particular if a filing from the same patent family has become "toxic", or

ある出願の審査中にクレームを補正する際、又は分割出願のクレームを起案する際に、可能であれば、部分優先についての限定的なアプローチに対応できるように、「又は」という接続詞を用いて、異なる基準日を有する対象を明確に個別化し、優先権を部分的に欠くクレームを作る。一方、親出願の当初の開示内容に基づいて分割出願のクレームの根拠を検討する際、又は出願手続中にクレームを補正する際に適用される厳格な「開示テスト」の下では、適切に相当する個別化された文言上の根拠が出願当初の開示内容にあることが求められる。このため、上記のように、欧州での保護を求める出願の初期段階において、可能な限り欧州特許実務に合わせて起案をする必要がある。

原則として、先に出願され／後に公開された第54条(3)の先行技術がクレームに対して引用され得る場合には、その先行技術の関連する開示内容を回避するために、テキストベースで「開示されていない」ディスクレーマを作成することも1つの解決策である（拡大審判部による審決G 1/03及びG 2/03）。分割出願又は公開された優先権書類が「toxic」になった場合であって、なんらかの理由により部分優先によって解決することができない場合にも、ディスクレーマを検討することができる。一方、G 1/03及びG 2/03によれば、ディスクレーマが満たさなければならない条件は厳格であるため、ディスクレーマの使用はリスクを伴う。特に、審査中に追加されたディスクレーマは、特許異議申立手続において認められないと判断されるリスクがある。第54条(3)の先行技術に基づく新規性欠如を回避するのに必要なものよりも多くをクレームから除外してしまうためである。特許後にはクレームの範囲を拡張できないため、ディスクレーマを適切に減縮又は削除することはできず、ディスクレーマの追加は、「回避不可能な」新規事項追加になる可能性がある。この理由1つにおいても、同一特許ファミリーの出願が「toxic」になった場合は特にであるが、第54条(3)の先行技術に開示された新規性を欠如させ得る事項が優先権書類の開示

in any other circumstances in which the potentially novelty-destroying disclosure in an earlier-filed/later-published citation is covered by disclosure the priority document, a solution to restore novelty arising out of partial priority would, in principle, be preferable.

に包含される他の状況においても、原則として、部分優先によって新規性を回復する解決策が好ましい。

Chapter *10*

European Search

欧州調査

Georg Siegert

MEMO

▶ 欧州特許庁においても、日本特許庁と同じく、クレームに記載された発明のうち、発明の単一性の要件に照らして審査対象となる範囲を調査対象とし、補正によりクレームに繰り入れられる蓋然性が高いと判断される開示事項も調査対象とすることができます（§1）。

▶ 欧州調査対象から除外される事項は、日本特許庁の実務とおおよそ同じです（§1.1）。ただし、欧州実務では、1つのカテゴリーにつき独立クレームを1つしか含むことができないという基本原則がありますので、調査の開始段階から形式的違反の通知を受けることがあります（§1.1 i))。また、出願の単一性が満たされていないと審査官が考える場合（調査で発見された引例との関係で事後的に発明の単一性を満たさない場合を含む）、クレームに最初に記載されている発明について部分的な調査報告が作成されます。調査対象でないクレームに記載された発明について出願手続を進めたい場合は、追加の手数料を支払う必要があります。実体審査に入らないと反論する機会がありません（§1.1 ii))。

▶ 欧州特許実務では、一部の例外を除き、出願及びそれに係る発明が欧州特許条約の要件を満たすか否かについての見解書が調査段階において発行されます（§1.2）。見解書の内容を見てから審査請求をすることができます。審査請求がすでにされている場合は、見解書を受けてから出願の続行を希望するか否かの意思表示をすることができます。

▶　欧州特許出願がPCTルートから欧州段階に移行されたものである場合は、欧州特許庁が国際調査機関等でない限り、欧州補充調査が行われ、規則164の改正により、発明の単一性欠如の問題については、直接的な欧州特許出願の場合と同様に扱われるようになりました（§2）。

▶　拡張欧州調査報告には、欧州（補充）調査報告と見解書が含まれます。出願人は、見解書の内容が否定的なものである場合、拡張欧州調査報告に応答しなければなりません（§3）。

Introduction

The unit within the EPO that is responsible for carrying out the search and drawing up the search report for an application is the Search Division. The task of the Search Division is primarily to carry out searches and to draw up the European Search Reports in relation to European patent applications. The Search Division also carries the search and draws up the search report for Euro-PCT applications for which the EPO acts as designated or elected Office and which has been accorded an international date of filing, the so called supplementary European searches. In this chapter we will summarize the procedural matters concerning the European Search Report and the supplementary European Search Report.

1 The Extended European Search Report

1.1 The European Search Report

According to Art. 92 the EPO shall draw up and publish a European search report in respect of the European patent application on the basis of the claims, with due regard to the description and any drawings. Hence, the search is not restricted by the literal wording of the claims but the examiner is considering the content of the claims in light of the description and drawings. Further, where technical features which are not present in the claims are indicated in the description as essential for the solution of the stated problem, these features are included in the search. Insofar as possible the search also covers subject-matter to which the claims might reasonably be expected to be directed after they have been amended.

Before receiving the European search report, where the European application does not derive from an earlier international application (the so called direct European patent application) the applicant may not amend the description, claims or

はじめに

欧州特許庁において出願の調査及び調査報告の作成を担当する部門は調査部である。欧州特許出願に関して調査を行って欧州調査報告を作成することが調査部の主な任務である。調査部は、欧州特許庁が指定官庁又は選択官庁となるEuro-PCT出願であって、国際出願日が認められたEuro-PCT出願についても調査（いわゆる補充欧州調査）を行って調査報告を作成する。本章では、欧州調査報告及び補充欧州調査報告に関する手続事項を概説する。

1 拡張欧州調査報告

1.1 欧州調査報告

第92条によれば、欧州特許庁は、明細書及び図面に適切な考慮を払ったうえでクレームに基づいて欧州特許出願についての欧州調査報告を作成及び公開する。よって、審査官は、クレームに記載された文言によって制限されることなく、明細書及び図面を考慮してクレームの内容を検討する。さらに、クレームに存在しない技術的特徴が課題の解決に不可欠であると明細書に記載されている場合、これらの特徴は調査に含まれる。調査では、可能な限り、補正により合理的に予想され得るクレームの対象もカバーされる。

欧州調査報告を受け取る前は、欧州特許出願が国際出願に由来しない出願（直接的な欧州特許出願）である場合、出願人は、その出願の明細書、クレーム又は図面を補正することができない。したがって、調査は、出願当初に提出さ

drawings of the European patent application. Accordingly, the search is directed to the claims as originally filed or the claims as filed under Rule 57(c) or 58.

The EPC does not provide for a time limit for issuing the European search report. However, the applicant may request an accelerated search under the program for accelerated prosecution of the European patent applications (PACE). In this case the EPO makes an effort to issue the search report as soon as possible. For European patent applications claiming no priority (first filings) the EPO carries out an accelerated search within six months of the date of filing without the need for a separate request. In such cases the applicant must indicate his intention not to file a declaration of priority.

Before starting with the search the examiner analyzes the claims of the European patent application in view of the requirements for technical character of the claimed subject-matter (Art. 52(2), (3)), non-exclusion from patentability under Art. 53, susceptibility of industrial application (Art. 57), conciseness and clarity of the claims (Art. 84, Rule 43(2)) as well as unity of the invention (Art. 82, Rule 44). Based on such analysis the examiner may exclude certain subject-matter from the search.

In the following we will discuss the procedural matters in case of non-compliance with these requirements.

i) If the patent application contains a plurality of independent claims in the same category and the examiner considers that the exceptional situations of Rule 43(2)(a)-(c) are not applicable (i.e. the examiner believes that the claims **lack conciseness**), the examiner will issue a **communication under Rule 62a(1)**. This communication is an invitation for the applicant to indicate, within two months, the claims complying with Rule 43(2), on the basis of which the search is to be carried out.

In response to this communication the applicant may react in four dif-

れたクレーム、又は規則57(c)若しくは58に基づいて提出されたクレームを対象とする。

　欧州特許条約は、欧州調査報告の発行について期限を定めていない。一方で、出願人は、早期審査プログラム（PACE）を利用することにより、欧州特許出願について早期調査を請求することができる。この場合、欧州特許庁は、調査報告を可能な限り早く発行するように努める。優先権を主張しない欧州特許出願（第一国出願）については、別個に請求がなくとも、欧州特許庁は、出願日から6月以内に早期調査を行う。このような場合、出願人は、優先権宣言書を提出しない意思表示をしなければならない。

　調査を開始する前に、審査官は、以下の要件を考慮して欧州特許出願のクレームを分析する：クレームの対象が技術的性質を有すること（第52条(2)、(3)）、特許性の例外に該当しないこと（第53条）、産業上利用できること（第57条）、クレームの記載が簡潔、かつ、明確であること（第84条、規則43(2)）、及び、発明の単一性を満たすこと（第82条、規則44）。このような分析に基づき、審査官は、調査から特定の対象を除外することができる。

　以下、これらの要件を満たさない場合の手続事項について説明する。

i)　特許出願に同じカテゴリーの独立クレームが複数含まれており、規則43(2)(a)～(c)の例外規定が適用されないと審査官が考える（すなわち、クレームが**簡潔性を欠く**と審査官が思う）場合、審査官は、**規則62a(1)の通知**を発行する。この通知は出願人に対し、2月の期間を指定して規則43(2)の要件を満たすクレームでそれに基づいて調査が行われるべきものを表示するよう求める指令である。

　　この通知に対し、出願人には4つの異なる応答の仕方がある。

ferent ways:

- If the applicant does not wish to dispute the examiner's opinion, the applicant may indicate the independent claims that fulfill the requirements of Rule 43(2) and that he wishes to have searched.

- If the applicant finds the objection not justified, the applicant may contest the examiner's opinion. The burden of proof to show that the claims indeed fulfill the requirements of Rule 43(2) lies with the applicant. Hence, in this situation the applicant must provide reasons why the requirements of Rule 43(2) are fulfilled. If the examiner is not convinced by the applicant's argumentation, the examiner will search on the basis of the first independent claim per category. As an alternative, the applicant may as a main request, request that the claims as filed be completely searched by providing reasons why the requirements of Rule 43(2) are fulfilled, and as an auxiliary request, in the case the examiner is not convinced by the applicant's arguments, indicate the subject-matter to be searched.

- The applicant may find the objection only partly not justified and wishes that part of the plurality of independent claims in the same category be searched. Similar to the above situation, the burden of proof lies with the applicant to show that that part of the plurality of independent claims satisfies the requirements of Rule 43(2). If the examiner finds the indicated claims not to comply with Rule 43(2), the examiner will search the independent claim with the lowest number indicated by the applicant.

- The applicant may also decide not to reply to the invitation. In this case the examiner carries the search on the basis of the first independent claim in each category.

The final responsibility whether the communication under Rule 62a(1) was justified lies with the Examining Division. During substantive exam-

- 出願人は、審査官の見解に反論しない場合、規則43(2)の要件を満たす独立クレームであって、出願人が調査を望む独立クレームを示すことができる。

- 出願人は、当該通知で提起された拒絶理由が正当でないと考える場合、審査官の見解について争うことができる。クレームが規則43(2)の要件を満たすことを示す立証責任は出願人にある。それゆえに、この状況では、出願人は、規則43(2)の要件が満たされている理由を示さなければならない。審査官は、出願人の反論に納得しない場合には、カテゴリーごとの最初の独立クレームに基づいて調査する。出願人は、別の対応案として、メインリクエストとして、規則43(2)の要件が満たされている理由を示すことによって、提出してあるクレームが完全に調査されるよう請求することができ、補助リクエストとして、審査官が出願人の反論に納得しない場合に備えて調査を望む対象を示すことができる。

- 出願人は、当該通知で提起された拒絶理由の一部が正当でないと考える場合、同じカテゴリーの複数の独立クレームの一部を調査するように請求することができる。上記状況と同様に、複数の独立クレームの一部が規則43(2)の要件を満たすことを示す立証責任は出願人にある。審査官は、当該クレームが規則43(2)の要件を満たさないと判断した場合には、出願人が示した独立クレームのうち、クレームの番号が最も小さいものを調査する。

- 出願人は、この指令に応答しないこともできる。この場合、審査官は、各カテゴリーの最初の独立クレームに基づいて調査を行う。

規則62a(1)の通知が正当であったか否かの最終責任は審査部にある。審査部は、規則62a(1)の通知が正当であると実体審査において判断した場

ination, if the Examining Division finds the communication under Rule 62a(1) justified, it shall invite the applicant to restrict the claims to the searched ones (Rule 62a(2)). If in response the applicant contests the restricted search and the Examining Division is convinced by the applicant's arguments, an additional search will be carried out at the examination stage.

ii) In some cases the examiner may consider that the application **does not comply with** the requirements for **unity** of the invention (Art. 82). In such cases the examiner will initially only draw up a partial search report for the invention first mentioned in the claims (Rule 64(1) first sentence). The examiner will send the partial search report to the applicant together with an **invitation under Rule 64(1)** to pay a further search fee for each further invention to be searched. The partial search report will indicate how many different inventions the examiner considers to be present in the application, and which of the claims belong to each of the identified inventions.

The opinion that the application does not comply with the requirements for unity cannot be contested in the search stage. Hence, in reply to the invitation under Rule 64(1) the applicant may either choose to pay additional search fee(s) or choose not to pay any additional search fee.

The applicant may choose all identified inventions for a further search, but may also make a sub-selection. In other words, if the partial search report identifies the presence of n inventions, each corresponding to certain claims, the applicant may choose to pay between 0 and n-1 search fees, depending on which of the claims not searched in the partial search report he selects to have searched.

The applicant may contest the finding of the search division during the substantive examination of the application. If the examiner considers the opinion not justified, the paid additional search fee(s) will be refunded. If

合、調査が行われたものにクレームを限定するよう出願人に求める（規則62a(2)）。これに対して、出願人が限定的な調査について争い、審査部が出願人の反論に納得した場合、審査段階で追加の調査が行われる。

ii) 出願が発明の**単一性**の要件を**満たさない**と審査官が判断する場合もある（第82条）。このような場合、審査官は、クレームに最初に記載されている発明について部分的な調査報告を作成する（規則64(1)第一文）。審査官は、部分的な調査報告を出願人に送付すると同時に、**規則64(1)の指令**を発し、出願人に対して、調査を望む各発明について追加の調査手数料を支払うよう求める。部分的な調査報告には、出願に存在すると審査官が考える異なる発明の数と、どのクレームが特定された各発明に属するのかが示される。

調査段階では、出願が単一性の要件を満たさないという見解について争うことはできない。それゆえに、規則64(1)の指令に対して、出願人は、追加の調査手数料を支払うか、追加の調査手数料を支払わないかのいずれかを選択する。

追加の調査について、出願人は、特定されたすべての発明を選択することができるが、そのいくつかを選択することもできる。換言すれば、部分的な調査報告でn個の発明が特定された場合で、その各々が特定のクレームに対応するとき、出願人は、部分的な調査報告で調査されなかったクレームのうち、どのクレームについて調査を望むかに応じて、0からn-1個分の調査手数料を支払うことを選択することができる。

出願の実体審査において、出願人は、調査部の判断について争うことができる。調査部の見解が正当ではないと審査官が考える場合、支払った追加の調査手数料は返還される。当該見解が正当であると審査官が考える場

the examiner considers the opinion justified the examination will proceed on the basis of the searched invention, or where several inventions have been searched, on the basis of the searched invention(s) and corresponding claims selected by the applicant.

The non-payment of further search fee(s) deprives the applicant of the right to choose with which invention to continue in the application, as he is bound to the searched invention (G 2/92).

iii) In some situations the examiner may consider that the patent application fails to such an extent to comply with the requirements of the EPC that it is **impossible to carry out a meaningful search** regarding the state of the art on basis of all or some of the subject-matter claimed (**Rule 63(1)**). Important requirements include the technical character of the claimed subject-matter (Art. 52(2), (3)), the non-exclusion from patentability (Art. 53), the susceptibility of industrial application (Art. 57), the sufficiency of disclosure (Art. 83), clarity and conciseness of the claims and support of the claims by the description (Art. 84). Here we will present several non-limiting examples where Rule 63 may find application for subject-matter not complying with Art. 83 and 84.

- One example is a broad claim supported by only a limited disclosure covering a small part of the scope of the claim. Here, the requirement underlying the application of Rule 63 would be Art. 83 and 84.

- Another example involves claims lacking conciseness. This may involve for instance a large number of claims or many possibilities within a claim (e.g. by use of many 'and/or' clauses) that make burdensome to determine the subject-matter for which protection is sought.

- A further example relates to claims lacking clarity. For instance, the

合、調査された発明に基づいて審査が進行するか、又は複数の発明が調査された場合には、調査がされた発明と、それに対応するクレームで出願人により選択されたものとに基づいて審査が進行する。

追加の調査手数料を支払わない場合、調査が行われた発明に限定されるので（G 2/92）、出願人は、その出願においてどの発明を継続させるかを選択する権利を有しない。

ⅲ）　審査官は、クレームの範囲全体又は一部につき欧州特許出願が欧州特許条約の要件を満たしていない程度において、技術水準に照らして**有意義な調査を行うことができない**と判断する場合もある（**規則63(1)**）。重要な要件として以下が挙げられる：クレームの対象が技術的性質を有すること（第52条(2)、(3)）、特許性の例外に該当しないこと（第53条）、産業上利用できること（第57条）、開示が十分であること（第83条）、クレームの記載が明確かつ簡潔であること、及び、明細書によりクレームが裏付けされていること（第84条）。以下、出願が第83条及び第84条の要件を満たしていないと規則63により通知され得るいくつかの非限定的な例を示す。

- 一例として、クレームの範囲が広いにもかかわらず、そのごく一部をカバーする限定的な開示によってしか裏付けられていないクレームが挙げられる。この場合、規則63の適用の根拠は、第83条及び第84条の要件である。

- 別の例は、簡潔性を欠くクレームである。例えば、クレームの数が多いか、又は（例えば、「及び／又は」の多用により）多くの可能性が１つのクレームに含まれているため、保護を求める対象を決定するのに手間がかかる場合である。

- さらに別の例は、明確性を欠くクレームである。例えば、クレームの対

subject-matter is defined using parameter(s) that cannot be compared with the prior-art, because the prior-art does not employ the same parameter or employs no parameter at all.

- Still further examples involve claims in divisional applications extending beyond the content of the earlier application as filed.

In reply to the invitation under Rule 63 the applicant may react in three different ways:

- The applicant may simply indicate the subject-matter to be searched and explain why a meaningful search is possible for that subject-matter;

- The applicant may dispute the findings of the examiner. In this case the applicant must provide arguments why a meaningful search is possible. If the examiner is convinced by the applicant's arguments, the examiner will issue a full search report. If the examiner is not convinced or only partly convinced, the examiner will determine which subject-matter can be searched and will issue a partial search report for that subject-matter. In exceptional situations the examiner may issue a declaration that no meaningful search is possible. The applicant may, as a main request, file arguments against the findings of the examiner, and as an auxiliary request, indicate subject-matter to be searched.

- If the applicant decides not to reply to the invitation, the examiner will determine what to search.

As indicated above, based on the applicant's reply the examiner may issue a full search report, a partial search report or in exceptional situations a declaration that no search could be carried out.

Where the examiner has drawn up a partial search report, during the

象がパラメータで特定される場合であって、先行技術が同じパラメータを使用していないか、又はパラメータをまったく使用していないため先行技術との比較が不可能なときである。

− さらに別の例は、先の出願の出願当初の内容を超えた分割出願のクレームである。

規則63の指令に対し、出願人には3つの異なる応答の仕方がある。

− 出願人は調査を望む対象を示し、その対象について有意義な調査が可能である理由を説明することができる。

− 出願人は、審査官の判断に反論することができる。この場合、出願人は、有意義な調査が可能である理由を述べなければならない。審査官は、出願人の反論に納得した場合には、完全な調査報告を発行する。審査官は、出願人の反論に納得しないか又は部分的に納得した場合には、調査可能な対象を決定し、その対象について部分的な調査報告を発行する。例外的な状況では、審査官は、有意義な調査が不可能である旨の宣言書を発行することができる。出願人は、メインリクエストとして、審査官の判断に対する反論を提出することができ、補助リクエストとして、調査を望む対象を示すことができる。

− 出願人がこの指令に応答しない場合、審査官は調査すべき対象を決定する。

上記のように、出願人の応答に基づいて、審査官は、完全な調査報告、部分的な調査報告、又は例外的な状況では調査を行うことができない旨の宣言書を発行することができる。

調査部の審査官が部分的な調査報告を作成した場合、実体審査におい

substantive examination the Examining Division will invite the applicant to restrict the claims to the subject-matter searched, unless it finds that the invitation was not justified (Rule 63(3)). If in response the applicant contests the restricted search and the Examining Division is convinced by the applicant's arguments, an additional search will be carried out at the examination stage.

In the exceptional cases where the examiner has issued a declaration that no meaningful search is possible, the application will not contain searched subject-matter. Following the text of Rule 63(3) *"invite the applicant to restrict the claims to the subject-matter searched"* the applicant cannot maintain any claim, as no subject-matter has been searched, leading to a refusal of the application. A possibility to continue with the invention is to file a divisional application in which claims have been formulated that the search division will deem searchable.

iv) In some situations the examiner may issue a communication under Rule 62a(1) and Rule 63. In response the applicant may indicate the claims that fulfill the requirements of Rule 43(2) and the subject-matter to be searched and explain why a meaningful search is possible. The subject-matter of both indications must correspond to each other. The applicant may also challenge the findings of the examiner by submitting a reasoned reply to both invitations. Further, the applicant may reply to only one of the invitations or to none. In this case the examiner decides what to search.

v) If in addition to an invitation under Rule 62a(1) and/or Rule 63 a non-unity objection is raised the applicant's reply may deal only with the first invention identified by the examiner. Similar to the case in ii) above, the applicant may pay additional search fee(s).

vi) Another reason for excluding a subject-matter from the search is non-payment of claims fees. The search does not include claims above the

て、審査部は、この指令が正当ではないと判断しない限り、調査が行われた対象にクレームを限定する機会を出願人に与える（規則63(3)）。これに対して、出願人が限定的な調査について争い、審査部が出願人の反論に納得した場合、審査段階で追加の調査が行われる。

　有意義な調査が不可能である旨の宣言書を審査官が発行した例外的な場合は、調査が行われた対象が出願に存在しない。規則63(3)の本文「調査が行われた対象にクレームを限定する機会を出願人に与える」の文言に従うと、調査が行われた対象が存在しないので、出願人はいかなるクレームも維持することができず、出願が拒絶される。当該発明については、調査部により調査が可能となるようにクレームを作成して分割出願をすることができる。

iv)　審査官は、規則62a(1)及び規則63の通知を発行する場合もある。これに対して、出願人は、規則43(2)の要件を満たすクレームと調査を望む対象とをともに提示し、有意義な調査が可能である理由を説明することができる。両提示の対象は互いに対応していなければならない。出願人は、両指令に対する応答書を提出することによって、審査官の判断に反論することもできる。さらに、出願人は、指令の一方にのみ応答することもできるし、又はまったく応答しないこともできる。この場合、審査官が調査対象を決定する。

v)　規則62a(1)及び／又は規則63の通知による指令に加えて単一性欠如の拒絶理由が提起された場合、出願人は、審査官が特定した最初の発明についてのみ対応することができる。上記ii)の場合と同様に、出願人は追加の調査手数料を支払うことができる。

vi)　調査からある対象を除外する別の理由は、クレーム手数料の不払いである。15個を超えるクレームで追加の手数料が支払われなかったはものは

number of fifteen for which no additional fee has been paid (Rule 45(1) and (3), Rule 162(1) and (4)).

Hence, based on the above considerations the examiner will issue a full search report, a partial search report, or in exceptional cases a declaration that no meaningful search is possible.

According to Rule 61(1) the search report mentions those documents, available to the EPO at the time of drawing up the report, which may be taken into consideration in deciding whether the invention to which the patent application relates is new and involves an inventive step. The search report classifies the documents according to the following categories: X: particularly relevant document when taken alone; Y: particularly relevant document when taken into combination with another document classified as Y; A: document defining the general state of the art, O: non-written disclosure; P: intermediate document published in the priority interval or on the date of priority, T: document published after the filing or priority date and cited for the principle or theory underlying the invention, E: potentially conflicting patent document (prior right), D: document cited in the application and L: document throwing doubt on a priority claim, establishing the publication date of another citation or relevant for double patenting.

Apart from these documents the search report could also mention claims or group of claims that were not included in the search for the reasons discussed above.

When the search is conducted less than 18 months after the filing date it will not be possible at the time of the search to completely search for potentially conflicting European and international patent applications within the meaning of Art. 54(3), i.e. patent applications that were not published before the priority/filing date of the application under search, but which themselves have an earlier priority/filing date and could be relevant for

調査に含まれない（規則45(1)及び(3)、規則162(1)及び(4)）。

　そのため、上記検討事項に基づけば、審査官は、完全な調査報告、部分的な調査報告、又は例外的な場合には有意義な調査が不可能である旨の宣言書を発行する。

　規則61(1)によれば、調査報告は、当該報告作成時に欧州特許庁が利用可能な文献であって、特許出願に係る発明が新規性及び進歩性を有するかを決定するうえで考慮に入れることができる文献に言及する。調査報告は、次のカテゴリーに従って文献を分類する。X：単独で利用する場合でも特に関連のある文献、Y：別の文献（Yと分類されるもの）と組み合わせて利用する場合に特に関連のある文献、A：一般的な技術水準を特定する文献、O：書面によらない開示、P：優先期間内又は優先日に公開された中間的な文献、T：出願日又は優先日よりも後に公開された文献であって発明の基礎となる原理又は理論について引用されたもの、E：潜在的に抵触する特許文献（先願としての権利）、D：出願で引用された文献、L：優先権主張に疑義を生じさせる文献、別の引用文献の公開日を立証する文献又は二重特許に関連する文献。

　これらの文献以外に、調査報告は、上述した理由により調査に含まれなかったクレーム又は一群のクレームに言及することもできる。

　出願日後18月以内に調査が行われる場合、第54条(3)の意味における潜在的に抵触する欧州特許出願及び国際特許出願（すなわち、調査に係る出願の優先日／出願日よりも前に公開されなかった特許出願であって、より早い優先日／出願日を有し、新規性に関連し得る特許出願）について完全な調査を行うことは、調査時において不可能である。当該調査は、審査部による実体審査中に完了することがある。

novelty. If applicable, this search will be finished during substantive examination by the Examining Division.

1.2 Search Opinion

According to Rule 62(1) the search report is accompanied by an opinion on whether or not the application and the invention to which it relates meet the requirements of the EPC. In other words, the opinion will list specific objections that the search examiner has, or it will indicate that all requirements of the EPC appear to be met and that a communication under Rule 71(1) or (3) can be expected once the examination stage is entered.

The search report and the search opinion together constitute the **Extended European Search Report (EESR)**.

The search opinion is a mandatory non-binding opinion. The applicant has the possibility to avoid the issuance of the search opinion in cases when the examination fee was paid before the search report is transmitted to the applicant and the applicant waived the right to the communication pursuant to Rule 70(2). In this case, the examination starts immediately after completion of the search report.

The search opinion is not published together with the search report (Rule 62(2)), but is available to the public by way of file inspection after publication of the patent application.

The search opinion may contain reasoned objections to the patent application. This is the so called negative search opinion. These objections may relate to substantive matters, for example objections that the subject-matter is not patentable, and/or relate to formal matters, for example that some claims are not clear.

1.2　調査見解書

規則62(1)によれば、出願及びそれに係る発明が欧州特許条約の要件を満たすか否かについての見解書が調査報告に添付される。換言すれば、見解書には、調査審査官が有する具体的な拒絶理由が列挙されるか、さもなければ（現段階では）欧州特許条約のすべての要件が満たされていると思われ、審査段階に入れば規則71(1)又は(3)の通知が予想される旨が示される。

調査見解書は調査報告とともに**拡張された欧州調査報告（EESR）**を構成する。

調査見解書は、拘束力のない見解を提供する。出願人は、調査見解書の発行を回避できる場合がある。それは、調査報告が出願人に送付される前に審査手数料が支払われており、かつ、規則70(2)の通知を受ける権利を出願人が放棄した場合である。この場合は、調査報告の完了後すぐに審査が開始される。

調査見解書は調査報告とともには公開されないが（規則62(2)）、特許出願の公開後に、書類の閲覧により一般公衆に利用可能となる。

調査見解書には、出願及びそれに係る発明が欧州特許条約の要件を満たさない理由が含まれる。これは、いわゆる否定的な調査見解書である。当該理由は、実体的な事項（例えば、クレームの対象が特許を受けることができないというもの）及び／又は形式的な事項（例えば、一部のクレームが明確ではないというもの）に関する。

In the situations discussed above in which the examiner has excluded subject-matter from the search, the search opinion also invites the applicant to limit the claimed subject-matter on the searched subject-matter.

If the examiner is at the opinion that the application and the invention to which it relates satisfy the requirements of the EPC the examiner will issue a positive search opinion that simply contains a statement giving a positive general opinion. However, if it was not possible to carry out a complete search on potentially conflicting European and international patent applications falling under Art. 54(3), a top-up search will be carried by the Examining Division as discussed above. This will be indicated in the search opinion.

The examiner may issue a positive search opinion even for cases where minor amendments of the application documents may be needed in order for the application to proceed toward a grant of a European patent. In such situations the Examining Division may carry out the necessary amendments in the text proposed for grant appended to the communication under Rule 71(3).

2 Supplementary European Searches

According to Art. 153(7) a supplementary European search report is drawn up in respect of Euro-PCT applications as indicated in the Introduction above. However, for international applications entering the European phase, no supplementary European Search Report is drawn for the cases where the EPO was the International Searching Authority of the Supplementary International Searching Authority.

Application documents on which the search is based are the documents as specified by the applicant when the application enters the European phase. Alternatively, if the applicant amended the application documents within the non-extendible time period of six-months from notification of communication pursuant

上述のように調査から除外された対象がある場合は、調査見解書においてもまた、審査官はクレームの対象を調査が行われた対象に限定する機会を出願人に与える。

審査官の見解が、出願及びそれに係る発明が欧州特許条約の要件を満たしているというものである場合、審査官は肯定的な調査見解書を発行し、肯定的な一般的見解を示す。しかしながら、第54条(3)の潜在的に抵触する欧州特許出願及び国際特許出願について完全な調査を行うことができなかった場合、上述したように、審査部は追加の調査を行う。このことは、調査見解書において示される。

出願書類に補正が必要な場合、それが軽微であれば審査官は、欧州特許の付与に向けて肯定的な調査見解書を発行することができる。このような状況では、審査部は、規則71(3)の通知に添付される補正案において、必要な補正をすることができる。

2 補充欧州調査

第153条(7)によれば、本章の「はじめに」で触れた Euro-PCT 出願について補充欧州調査報告が作成される。一方、欧州特許庁が国際調査機関又は補充国際調査機関であった場合には、欧州段階に移行した国際出願について補充欧州調査報告は作成されない。

補充欧州調査は、欧州段階に出願が移行する際に出願人が特定した書類に基づいて行われる。あるいは、規則161(1)の通知から（延長できない）6月の期間内に出願人が出願書類を補正した場合は、補正後の出願書類に基づいて補充欧州調査が行われる。

to Rule 161(1), the amended application documents serve as basis for the supplementary European search.

The supplementary European Search Report is accompanied by the search opinion. In general the supplementary European Search Report has the same form as the Extended European Search Report. However, in the case of a supplementary European Search Report it is also permissible to have no documents cited in the supplementary European Search Report. In such case the expression "No further relevant documents disclosed" appears in the search report. In such cases, the search opinion gives an opinion on patentability of the invention in view of the state of the art cited in the International Search Report.

As from 01.11.2014 when the amended Rule 164 entered into the force, when a problem of lack of unity of the invention arises, the supplementary European Search Report is drawn up on the invention or group of inventions first mentioned in the claims. Together with the partial search report the applicant receives an invitation to pay further search fees for every invention other than the one first mentioned in the claims (Rule 164(1)). In response to this invitation the applicant follows the same procedure as described above in case of direct European applications. Other EPC provisions, for example Rule 62a and Rule 63 discussed above are also applicable in the procedure under the amended Rule 164(1).

The amended Rule 164 applies to all Euro-PCT application for which the supplementary European search report has not been drawn up by 01.11.2014.

3 Response to the Extended European Search Report

According to Rule 70a(1), in the opinion accompanying the European search report, the EPO shall give the applicant the opportunity to comment on the ex-

補充欧州調査報告には、調査見解書が添付される。一般的に、補充欧州調査報告は、拡張欧州調査報告と同じ形式である。一方、補充欧州調査報告の場合、文献が引用されないことがある。このような場合、当該調査報告には「開示された関連文献の追加なし」と記載される。このような場合、調査見解書には、国際調査報告で引用された技術水準を考慮した発明の特許性についての見解が示される。

改正された規則164が発効された2014年11月1日以後、発明の単一性欠如の問題が生じた場合は、クレームに最初に記載された発明又は一群の発明についてのみ、補充欧州調査報告が作成される。部分的な調査報告とともに、出願人は、クレームに最初に記載された発明以外の発明について、追加調査手数料の支払いを求める規則164(1)の指令を受ける。この指令に対し、出願人は、直接的な欧州出願について上述した手続と同じ手続に従う。欧州特許条約の他の規定（例えば、上記規則62a及び規則63）についても、改正された規則164(1)に定められた手続に適用される。

改正された規則164は、2014年11月1日までに補充欧州調査報告が作成されなかったすべてのEuro-PCT出願に適用される。

3 拡張欧州調査報告に対する応答

規則70a(1)によれば、欧州特許庁は、拡張欧州調査報告について意見を述べる機会を、欧州調査報告に添付された見解書において出願人に与え、適切な場

tended European search report and, where appropriate, invite him to correct any deficiencies noted in the opinion accompanying the European search report and to amend the description, claims and drawings within the period referred to in Rule 70, paragraph 1 i.e. within six months from publication of the search report. Within the same period the applicant must file the request for examination.

According to the text of Rule 70a(1) *"where appropriate"* the EPO invites the applicant to correct any deficiencies noted in the opinion. This applies to cases where the opinion is negative and there are deficiencies that the applicant must correct. In this case the response to the invitation under Rule 70a(1) is mandatory. In response the applicant may contest the negative findings of the examiner by providing an explanation for the reasons why the applicant does not agree with the examiner's objections. The applicant may also respond by submitting amended claims and/or amended description in view of the raised objections. In this case the applicant should indicate what has been changed and indicate the basis for the changes in the original application documents. In addition, the applicant may also submit voluntary amendments in accordance with Rule 137(2).

When, as discussed above, the opinion is positive because there are no deficiencies that should be corrected, or there are only minor deficiencies that the Examining Division will correct in a communication under Rule 71(3), the EPO does not issue an invitation. The applicant may still file amendments on his own volition under Rule 137(2) and correct errors under Rule 139.

However, if the applicant filed the request for examination before the search report and the search opinion were communicated to him, the period to respond to the opinion and/or to file any voluntary amendments is equal to the period within which the applicant must indicate that he wishes to proceed further with the application. This period is communicated to the applicant in a communication under Rule 70a(2).

For Euro-PCT applications subject to a preparation of the supplementary Eu-

合は、規則70(1)にいう期間内（すなわち、調査報告の公開から6月以内）に、欧州調査報告に添付された見解書に記載された欠陥を是正し、明細書、クレーム及び図面について補正をする機会を出願人に与える。出願人は、上記の期間内に出願審査の請求をしなければならない。

規則70a(1)の本文によれば、「適切な場合は」、欧州特許庁は、見解書で指摘された欠陥を是正する機会を出願人に与える。これは、見解書が否定的であり、出願人によって是正されるべき欠陥が存在する場合に適用される。この場合、規則70a(1)の指令に対して応答する必要がある。当該応答では、出願人は、審査官により提起された拒絶理由に同意しない理由を説明することによって、審査官の否定的な見解について争うことができる。また、出願人は、提起された拒絶理由を考慮して、補正されたクレーム及び／又は明細書を提出することもできる。この場合、出願人は、変更箇所を示し、その変更の根拠を当初の出願書類に基づき示さなければならない。さらに、出願人は、規則137(2)に従い自発的に補正書を提出することもできる。

是正すべき欠陥が存在しないため見解書が肯定的である場合や、軽微な欠陥しか存在せず規則71(3)の通知において審査部により是正されるであろう場合は、上述したように、欧州特許庁は、当該指令を発行しない。出願人はそれでもなお、規則137(2)に基づいて自発的に補正書を提出し、規則139に基づいて誤記の訂正をすることができる。

一方で、調査報告及び調査見解書が出願人に通知される前に、出願人が審査請求をしている場合は、見解書に対して応答する期間及び／又は自発的に補正書を提出する期間は、当該出願を続行させる意思を示すために指定された期間に等しい。この期間は、規則70a(2)の通知において出願人に伝えられる。

補充欧州調査報告が作成されるEuro-PCT出願（上記参照）については、欧

ropean Search Report as discussed above, the EPO will also invite the applicant to respond to the search opinion within the period for confirming to continue with the prosecution.

If the applicant does not respond to the invitation pursuant to Rule 70a(1) or 70a(2) within the communicated time period, the application is deemed to be withdrawn. These periods are in general non-extendible. An extension of the time limit (beyond the six months) is allowed only in exceptional cases.

州特許庁は、出願手続の継続（出願の続行）を確認するための期間内に調査見解書に対して応答するように出願人に求める。

　規則70a(1)又は70a(2)の指令に対して、通知された期間内に出願人が応答しない場合は、出願は取り下げられたものとみなされる。一般的に、これらの期間は延長不可である。（6月を超える）期間の延長は、例外的な場合にのみ認められる。

Chapter 11

Substantive Examination

実体審査

Christiane Stein-Dräger

MEMO

- ▶ 審査請求ができる期間については、欧州特許公報にて欧州調査報告が公開された日後6月が終了するまでと規則70で規定されています（§1）。

- ▶ 欧州特許条約には、実体審査における「拒絶理由」という特別の項目は設けられておらず、欧州特許条約に定める要件を満たしていない場合に出願が拒絶されると規定されています（主な要件については§2）。

- ▶ 審査段階では、出願を拒絶する前に、少なくとも1回は審査部から第94条(3)の規定に従う通知が発行されます。第94条(3)の規定によれば、審査官は、必要な場合は何度でも、期間を指定して、出願人に対して、意見書を提出し、かつ、第123条(1)に従って出願の補正をする機会を与えます（§3）。日本の実務では、拒絶理由通知の種類に応じてクレームの補正ができる範囲に制限が課されますが（特許法第17条の2第5項）、欧州実務ではそのような制限はありません。

- ▶ また、欧州特許が各国の権利の束である点で、異なる複数セットのクレームが許可されることもあります（§4）。

- ▶ 審査の最終段階では、特許付与を意図する正文書を添付した規則71(3)の通知が発行されます。この通知に添付された正文書は権利書の原本としてたいへん重要ですので、出願人に確認の機会が与えられます（§5）。

▶ 欧州審査官は、出願人との意思疎通を確保するためにインタビューを活用することに消極的です（§6）。

▶ 欧州実務では、補助リクエストとして口頭審理の請求をすることが頻繁です。こうすることにより、口頭審理の機会なくして拒絶査定を受けることはありません（§7）。

▶ 拒絶査定がされた場合（§8）、出願人は拒絶査定不服審判を請求することができ、審判請求理由記載書を追って提出することができます（§9）。審判請求時に補正がされない場合でも、まず審査部により審判請求の審査が行われ、審査部が特許をすることができないと判断した場合は、特許庁長官を経由せず、審判部にケースが送られます（§9）。この点、日本の実務（特許法第162条）と形式的に異なります。

▶ 早期審査手段を活用する場合は、§10の注意事項を参照してください。欧州特許実務は日本とアメリカの特許実務と異なりますから、PPHプログラムは必ずしも有効ではありません。

Introduction

This part relates to the examination proceedings which are performed after the filing of an application at the EPO and after the issuance of the search opinion. It may be that, at the beginning of the examination proceedings, amendments made by the applicant himself have already been filed, for example in response to the search opinion.

A European Examiner is entrusted with the substantive examination proceedings wherein the Examiner is selected depending on the technical field to which the application relates. The Examiner is a member of the Examining Division, usually consisting of three members.

The purpose of the examination proceedings is to ensure that the application meets the requirements of the European Patent Convention (EPC). The prime task of the Examiner is to deal with the substantive requirements. At the end of the examination procedure the Examining Division will either issue a decision to grant a patent or will refuse the application. The presentation of important aspects of the examination proceedings takes into account the "Guidelines for Examination in the EPO", November 2015, especially Parts C and H thereof.

1 Procedural Requirements

Some formal requirements have to be fulfilled before the Examining Division can start the examination of a European patent application. The applicant has to file a request for examination and he has to pay the official examination fee. According to Rule 70 EPC the request for examination may be filed from the date on which the application is filed up to the end of six months after the date on which the the European search report is published in the European Patent Bulletin. Within the same time frame also the designation fees have to be paid.

はじめに

本章では、欧州特許庁へ出願がされ、かつ、調査見解書が発行された後に行われる審査手続について述べる。審査手続の開始時には、例えば調査見解書への応答として、出願人によりすでに補正書が提出されている場合もある。

実体審査手続は審査官に任され、出願に関連する技術分野に応じて審査官が選ばれる。当該審査官は、通常3名からなる審査部の構成員である。

審査手続の目的は、欧州特許条約の要件を出願が満たすよう確実にすることである。審査官の主要な職務は、実体要件の取扱いである。審査部は審査手続の最終段階で特許付与又は出願拒絶の決定を行う。「2015年11月付欧州特許庁審査基準（特にC部及びH部）」を考慮しながら審査手続の重要な側面について説明する。

1　手続的要件

審査部が欧州特許出願の審査を開始する前に、いくつかの方式要件が満たされている必要がある。出願人は、審査請求をするとともに審査請求手数料を支払わなければならない。規則70によれば、当該出願の出願日から、欧州特許公報にて欧州調査報告が公開された日後6月が終了するまでの間に審査請求をすることができる。この期間中に指定手数料も支払う必要がある。

If the examination request is not filed, the application is deemed to be withdrawn (Art. 94(2) EPC). Then the applicant has a possibility to file a request for further processing in accordance with Art. 121(1) EPC wherein an official fee has to be paid and the omitted act must be completed within a time limit of two months.

2 Substantive Requirements

According to Art. 52 EPC there are four basic requirements for patentability: (a) there must be an invention belonging to any field of technology, (b) the invention must be susceptible of industrial application, (c) the invention must be new, and (d) the invention must be based on an inventive step. The invention must be described in a manner that it can be carried out by a person skilled in the art (Art. 83 EPC). Furthermore, the invention must be defined by means of technical features and must relate to a technical problem and thus define the technical features in order to define the subject-matter for which protection is sought, in the claims.

Art. 52(2) EPC contains a non-exhaustive list of things which are not regarded as inventions. This list includes discoveries, scientific theories, mathematical methods, aesthetic creations, schemes, rules and methods for performing mental acts, playing games or doing business, and programs for computers or presentation of information. Art. 53 EPC defines some exceptions to patentability, namely matter which would be contrary to the "ordre public" or morality. European patents are neither granted in respect of methods for treatment of the European or animal body by surgery or therapy and diagnostic method practiced on the human or animal body wherein this provision does not apply to products, in particular substances or compositions, for use in any of these methods (Art. 53(c) EPC).

出願審査の請求がされないときは、当該出願は取り下げられたものとみなされる（第94条(2)）。その場合、出願人は、第121条(1)の規定により、手続の続行を請求することができるが、2月以内に所定の手数料を支払い、かつ、遺漏した手続を完了させなければならない。

2 実体的要件

第52条の規定によれば、特許性の基本的な要件には以下の4つがある。すなわち、(a)技術分野に属する発明であること、(b)その発明が産業上利用できること、(c)その発明が新規性を有すること、及び、(d)その発明が進歩性を有することである。発明は、当該技術分野における専門家が実施することができるように記載されていなければならない（第83条）。さらに、発明は、技術的特徴によって特定されていなければならず、技術的課題に関連していなければならない。よって、保護を求める対象を特定するためには、発明の技術的特徴をクレームで特定する必要がある。

第52条(2)には、発明とみなされない事項が非限定的に列挙されている。これには、発見、科学の理論、数学的方法、美的創造物、精神的行為、ゲーム又は事業を行うための計画、ルール及び方法、コンピュータプログラム、並びに、情報の提示が含まれる。第53条は、特許性の例外に当たる事項を特定している。「公の秩序」又は善良の風俗に反するおそれのある事項がその1つである。また、人間又は動物の体を手術又は治療により処置する方法及び人間又は動物の体を診断する方法についても欧州特許は付与されない。ただし、この規定は、これらの方法のいずれかで使用するための物（特に物質又は組成物）には適用されない（第53条(c)）。

3 Official Action: Reply of the Applicant

As has been pointed out in the previous chapters, an applicant may perform claim amendments in response to the search opinion. At the beginning of the examination procedure, the Examiner must check whether those subsequently filed claims satisfy the requirements of Art. 123(2) EPC, i.e. that they do not contain added subject-matter. If the basis for the amendments is not evident for the Examiner, he may send a communication pursuant to Rule 137(4) EPC to the applicant. It is then applicant's duty to submit the corresponding information to the Examiner.

At the beginning of the examination proceedings the Examiner studies the application documents. Usually the Examiner has already started studying the application documents because he was responsible for carrying out the search and for submitting to the applicant the search opinion. In such a case he merely concentrates on any reply to the search report and on the amendments that have possibly been filed by the applicant in response to the search opinion.

If the Examiner has further objection, for example because there are some deficiencies in view of the amendments, or objections as to lack of patentability, unity or sufficiency of disclosure, then he has to issue the communication in accordance with Art. 94(3) EPC. According to Art. 94(3) EPC the Examiner shall invite the applicant, as often as necessary, to file his observations and, subject to Art. 123(1) EPC, to amend the application.

For preparing the communication the Examiner will consider those prior art documents which have been cited in the previous search report, together with any possible amendments as filed by the applicant. Thus, the Examiner will consider the claims which are currently pending so that in case of amendments he will not consider the original claims. According to Rule 71(2) EPC the communication should contain a reasoned statement which requirements of the EPC are not met. In general all objections should be raised in the first official action. Un-

3 庁通知：出願人の応答

先の章で述べられているように、出願人は、調査見解書に応答してクレームの補正をすることができる。審査官は、審査手続の開始時に、出願後に提出された（補正された）クレームが第123条(2)の要件を満たしているか（出願時における出願内容を超える対象を含んでいないこと）を確認する。補正の根拠が明らかでない場合には、審査官は、規則137(4)の規定に従い出願人に通知する。出願人は、該当する情報を審査官に提出する義務を負う。

審査官は、審査手続の開始時に、出願書類を検討する。審査官は調査を実施し調査見解書を作成する任務を負っていたため、この段階では、通常の場合、出願書類の検討がすでに開始されている。そのような場合、審査官は、調査報告書に対する応答や、調査見解書に対応して提出されている補正書の検討に取り組む。

審査官は、補正に関して欠陥があるとの拒絶理由や、特許性、単一性又は開示の十分性の欠如の拒絶理由を提起する場合は、第94条(3)に従う通知を発する。第94条(3)によれば、審査官は、必要な場合は何度でも、出願人に対して、意見書を提出し、かつ、第123条(1)に従って出願の補正をする機会を与えなければならない。

審査官は、庁通知の作成にあたり、出願人により提出された補正書とともに先の調査報告に引用された先行技術文献を検討する。審査官は、補正がされた場合には当初のクレームを考慮せずに審査に係属するクレームを検討する。規則71(2)によれば、庁通知書には、欧州特許条約の要件が満たされないと考える理由を含めなければならない。一般に、当該理由のすべてを最初の庁通知で述べなければならない。残念ながら、最初の庁通知にすべての理由が含まれていない場合もある。審査官は、審査手続の後の時点でさらなる先行技術文献を認

fortunately, it sometimes happens that the first communication does not contain all the objections. It may for example happen that the Examiner becomes aware of further prior art documents at a later time during the examination proceedings so that in view of this he may issue a further communication at a later state of the proceedings. It may also happen that in a first communication objections only in regard to e.g. the admissibility of amendments or the scope of the claims are made and that in a further official action objections in regard to lack of patentability are raised.

The communication contains an invitation to the applicant to file his observations and to correct any deficiencies or to file any amendments. Concerning the amendments the applicant has a possibility to perform amendments to the descriptions and/or the claims and/or the drawings.

When performing amendments, the applicant should be aware of the requirements of Rule 137 EPC. According to Rule 137(2) EPC the applicant may amend the description, claims and drawings of his own volition in response to communications by the European Patent Office under Rule 70a(1) or (2) EPC or Rules 161/162 EPC. According to Rule 137(3) EPC no further amendment may be made without the consent of the Examining Division. Even though this rule seems to contain a rather strict requirement in regard to the possibility to perform amendments to the application documents, the claims of a European patent application are oftentimes amended several times after the filing date and prior to the grant of a European patent. This is due to the general rule that the Examiner should always balance the interests of the applicant and the procedural efficiency. In view of this it is quite common that an applicant performs amendments to the claims after receipt of the European search report and, if necessary, also after receipt of the first communication pursuant to Art. 94(3) EPC.

The communication not only contains the above-mentioned invitation to the applicant to file the observations and to correct any deficiencies or to perform amendments, but it must also contain a time period for filing the reply. According

識し、それに鑑みて審査手続の後の段階で庁通知をさらに発行することもある。また、例えば、補正要件又はクレームの範囲に関する否定的な見解のみが最初の庁通知に含まれ、特許性要件についての否定的な見解はさらなる庁通知で指摘される場合もある。

審査官は、庁通知にて、出願人に対して、意見書を提出して不備を是正するか又は補正書を提出する機会を与える。補正についていえば、出願人は明細書及び／又はクレーム及び／又は図面について補正をすることができる。

出願人は、補正をする際に、規則137の要件を認識しておくべきである。規則137(2)によれば、出願人は、規則70a(1)若しくは(2)又は規則161/162に基づく欧州特許庁からの通知に応答して、自らの意思により、明細書、クレーム及び図面について補正をすることができる。規則137(3)によれば、その後の補正は審査部の同意を得ない限り行えない。出願書類について行う補正についてかなり厳しい要件が定められているようにみえるだろうが、出願日の後、かつ、欧州特許が付与される前に欧州特許出願のクレームに複数回の補正が行われることが頻繁にある。審査官は常に出願人の利益と手続的な効率のバランスを取るべきであるという欧州特許庁の一般原則によるものである。このような事情により、出願人は、欧州調査報告の受領後に、必要であれば審査官から第94条(3)の最初の通知を受けた後にも、クレームの補正を行うことが多い。

当該庁通知は、意見書を提出して不備を是正し、補正書を提出する機会を出願人に与えるだけでなく、出願人が応答するための期間も指定する。規則132(2)によれば、指定期間は、2月以上4月以下とされている。一定の事情の下で

to Rule 132(2) EPC the time limit is not less than two months and not more than four months. Under certain circumstances it may be up to six months. In general the Examiner sets a four months' deadline for filing a reply to the objections raised therein. If necessary, the applicant may file a request for extension of said time limit for further two months so that in such a case the total time limit is six months for the issuance of the communication.

Sometimes it will become necessary for the applicant to ask the Examiner for a further extension of the time limit. This will be granted only very exceptionally and in view of a reasoned statement. Such a reasoned statement may be e.g. that additional experiments are necessary for showing the inventive step.

The failure to reply in due time will cause the application to be deemed withdrawn. Then the applicant has the possibility to file a request for further processing in accordance with Art. 121 EPC.

In its reply, the applicant should deal with each and every objection raised in the communication. Where necessary the claims and/or the description should be amended. If the claims have already been amended, the description should be adapted to the amended claims. The adaption of the description may also be filed at a later time, for example at the time where the Examiner has acknowledged that amended claims fulfil the requirements of the EPC.

In case the communication contained novelty and/or inventive step objections, the applicant should explain the differences between each of the prior art documents cited by the Examiner and the subject-matter of the (possibly amended) claims. Thus, the novelty and the inventive step should be discussed. The discussion of the inventive step should be based on the problem-solution-approach as adopted by the EPO. Thus, it is necessary to discuss the technical effects resulting from the difference with respect to the closest prior art. Quite often the applicant performs additional experiments, especially on the field of chemistry, in order to show the technical effects with respect to a specified prior

は、最長6月までとすることができる。一般に、審査官は庁通知で提起する拒絶理由に応答するための期間として4月を指定する。必要に応じて、出願人は指定された応答期間をさらに2月延長する請求をすることができる。その場合、応答期間は庁通知の発行から合計で最長6月までとなる。

時には、出願人は、審査官に対しさらに延長を求めることが必要な場合もある。これは、極めて異例な場合にのみ、理由の陳述を考慮して許可される。理由の陳述とは、例えば、「進歩性を示すために追加実験が必要とされること」等である。

指定された期間内に応答がない場合には、出願が取り下げられたものとみなされる。その場合でも、出願人は第121条の規定に基づき手続の続行を請求することができる。

出願人は、自らの応答において、庁通知で提起された各拒絶理由に対応しなければならない。必要な場合には、クレーム及び／又は明細書の補正をしなければならない。クレームがすでに補正されている場合には、クレームの補正に対応するべく明細書を補正しなければならない。例えば、補正後のクレームが欧州特許条約の要件を満たしていると審査官が認めた場合に、補正後のクレームに対応させた明細書を後から提出することもできる。

出願人は、補正されたクレームの提出とともに、審査官が引用した先行技術文献についても検討し、各先行技術文献とクレームの対象（又は補正されたクレームの対象）との相違点を示さなければならない。そして、新規性と進歩性について議論する必要がある。進歩性の議論は、欧州特許庁の採用する課題解決アプローチに基づく。よって、最も近い先行技術との違いに起因する技術的効果について述べる必要がある。出願人は、特に化学の分野では、特定先行技術文献との関連で技術的効果を示すために追加実験を行うことが多い。欧州特許庁は、実体審査手続中に追加の実験データを提出することを出願人に認めている。一方、新たな実験データは、特許出願にすでに記載又は暗示されている

art document. The filing of additional experimental data during the substantive examination proceedings is admissible before the EPO. However, new experimental data must be based on those technical effects which are already described in the patent application or which are implied by or at least related to the technical problem initially suggested by the original application text.

Concerning any amendments the applicant has to indicate where basis for the amendments can be found in the original application text. Even combinations of amended features should be based on the application documents as filed. Currently, no handwritten amendments are allowable.

The reply of the applicant should also contain a request to the Examiner to submit a further official action or to have a telephone discussion with the applicant's representative or even to summon for oral proceedings before the members of the Examining Division. These additional requests serve to avoid any rejection merely on the basis of the written arguments.

The Examiner has to check the letter of reply and the amended documents, if any. It may happen that on the basis of the reply filed by the applicant the Examiner is convinced that a patent should be granted. The Examiner may call the applicant's European representative if there are only some minor objections to be dealt with. If the Examiner maintains substantive objections he will issue a second communication pursuant to Art. 94(3) EPC which contains a reasoned statement why he still maintains some or all of the objections previously raised. Sometimes the Examiner raises new objections or refers to new prior art documents.

4 Several Sets of Claims

It may happen that during the examination procedure the applicant files more than one set of amended claims. For example he may file an amended set of claims in accordance with a Main Request and one or more sets of claims in ac-

技術的効果に基づいているか、当初出願書類に最初に提示された技術的課題に少なくとも関連している必要がある。

　出願人は、すべての補正について、当初出願書類のどこに各補正の根拠が見出せるかを提示しなければならない。補正された特徴の組合せも当初出願書類に基づいている必要がある。現在、手書きの補正書は認められない。

　出願人は、応答書において、審査官に対して、庁通知をさらに発行すること、出願人の代理人と電話で議論すること、又は、審査部の構成員の面前で口頭審理を行うための召喚状を発行する請求をさらに含めるべきである。これらの追加的請求は、書面による主張だけを基に出願が拒絶されてしまうことを回避するために有用である。

　審査官は、応答書（及び存在する場合には補正書）を検討する。出願人の応答に基づいて、特許を付与すべきであると審査官が確信する場合がある。解決すべきことが些細な拒絶理由のみである場合には、審査官は出願人の代理人に電話をかけることもできる。実質的な拒絶理由を維持する場合は第94条(3)に従い２回目の庁通知を発行する。この通知にはすでに提起した拒絶理由のいくつか又はすべてを維持する理由の陳述を含める。審査官が新たな拒絶理由を提起する場合又は新たな先行技術文献に言及する場合もある。

4　複数セットのクレーム

　出願人は、審査手続中に、補正されたクレームを複数セット提出することもできる。例えば、出願人は、メインリクエストとして補正されたクレームを１セット提出することができ、補助リクエストとしてさらに１セット又は複数セ

cordance with the one or more Auxiliary Requests. Together with these various sets of claims he should submit the arguments why according to his position each of these sets of claims fulfils the requirements of the EPC.

It may even happen that the applicant files more than one set of claims in view of Art. 139(2) EPC. According to this Article national rights of earlier date can be invoked, after the grant of the European patent, in national proceedings. Where these national rights exist, the applicant has a legitimate interest in submitting separate claims wherein one set of claims is filed in regard to such a national right. The filing of two sets of claims should then be allowed. However, it is the responsibility of the applicant to make the necessary limitation of the scope of the application with respect to the national right. If a separate set of claims is filed during the substantive examination proceedings in view of a national right having an earlier filing date, the Examiner will usually not examine as to whether this second set of claims contains the correct and necessary limitation with respect to this national right. He will only check the admissibility of the amendments in the light of the original disclosure.

5   Final Stage of Examination Proceedings

If the Examiner considers that the claims are allowable and meet the requirements of the EPC, then he should check whether the description should be amended. The Examiner himself may perform some amendments to the description to adapt it to the claims. He may even insert a brief reference to the prior art documents cited by him. Alternatively, he may also call the applicant's European representative by telephone in order to discuss as to which further amendments should be performed. Typical examples of the amendments which may be made by the Examiner himself include the conversion of units into the correct SI units, the correction of some linguistic errors or even the deletions of some vague statements such as "and the like". He may even insert into the claims some reference numerals.

ットのクレームを提出することができる。出願人はこれらの複数セットのクレームと一緒に、各セットのクレームが欧州特許条約の要件を満たす理由を述べるべきである。

　出願人は、第139条(2)を考慮してクレームを複数セット提出することもある。この条項によれば、欧州特許が付与された後に、それよりも先の出願日を有する国内の権利を国内手続において行使することができる。こうした国内の権利が複数存在する場合、各権利に関して別々のセットのクレームを提出することについて出願人は正当な利益を有する。そのような場合、2セットのクレームの提出も許容されるべきである。一方、国内の権利との関係で出願の範囲に必要な制限を設けることは出願人の責任である。先の出願日を有する国内の権利を考慮して実体審査手続中に別のセットのクレームが提出される場合、審査官はこの2番目のセットのクレームについては、当該国内の権利との関係で正確、かつ、必要な制限が含まれているか否かを通常は審査しない。審査官は、当初の開示をふまえて補正が許可されるかを検討するのみである。

5　審査手続の最終段階

　審査官は、クレームが欧州特許条約の要件を満たしており許可可能であると判断した場合には、明細書に補正が必要か否かを検討しなければならない。クレームの補正に対応するために、審査官自身が明細書の補正をすることもある。また、審査官は、自らが引用した先行技術文献への簡単な言及を明細書に挿入することもある。これに代えて、審査官は、出願人の欧州代理人に電話連絡し、追加補正を行うべきかについて協議することもある。審査官自身が補正をする典型的な例としては、正しいSI単位への単位換算の挿入、言語の誤りの訂正、「……等」のような曖昧な表現の削除がある。クレームに参照番号を挿入することもある。

If the Examiner is convinced that a patent should be granted, the Examining Division must inform the applicant of the text on the basis of which it intends to grant a patent (Rule 71(3) EPC). If amendments are proposed, these must be identified in this text. The communication under Rule 71(3) EPC also includes the invitation to pay the fee for grant and publishing and to file the translations of the claims in the two languages of the EPO other than the language of the proceedings. Thus, if the application was filed in the English language, the claims have to be translated into German and French.

The communication under Rule 71(3) EPC sets a time limit of four months which is not extendable. If the applicant pays the fees and files the translations, this act will be considered as an approval to the text intended for grant (Rule 71(5) EPC). The quality of the translation of the claims will not be checked by the EPO. This is the duty of the applicant.

The communication under Rule 71(3) EPC additionally contains the title of the invention in the three languages of the EPO. The communication also contains the name of the applicant and the international patent classification. Concerning the renewal fee it contains the information that if the fee is due between the issuance of the communication under Rule 71(3) EPC and the proposed date of the publication of the mentioning of the grant, the publication will be performed only after the renewal fee has been paid.

Whenever the EPO submits the communication under Rule 71(3) EPC it is the responsibility of the applicant to check whether the application documents are complete and whether any amendments as proposed by the Examiner are acceptable to him. The four months' time limit for paying the grant and publishing fee and for filing the translations of the claims will be the last possibility for the applicant to check the whole application documents.

Accordingly, the communication under Rule 71(3) EPC contains important information and explicitly specifies the text on the basis of which a patent should

特許を付与するべきであると審査官が納得した場合、審査部は出願人に対して特許の付与において使用する予定の正文書を通知しなければならない（規則71(3)）。補正が提案されている場合、それらはこの正文書中で特定される。また、規則71(3)の通知は、特許付与及び特許掲載公報を発行するための手数料の納付、及び、出願の手続言語以外の2つの欧州特許庁公用語によるクレームの翻訳文の提出を求める。したがって、英語による出願の場合、クレームをドイツ語とフランス語に翻訳する必要がある。

規則71(3)の通知は、上記納付・提出の期限を4月と定めており、これを延長することはできない。出願人が手数料を納付し、翻訳文を提出した場合、出願人は、特許の付与において使用される予定の正文書を承認したものとみなされる（規則71(5)）。欧州特許庁はクレームの翻訳文の品質を確認しない。かかる確認を行う義務は出願人にある。

さらに、規則71(3)の通知には、発明の名称（欧州特許庁の3つの公用語で表記されたもの）についての情報も含まれる。また、同通知には、出願人の名称及び国際特許分類も記載される。また、規則71(3)の通知には更新手数料に関する情報も含まれ、同通知の発行日と欧州特許を付与する旨が掲載された特許公報の発行予定日との間に更新手数料の納付期限が到来する場合、更新手数料が納付されるまでは当該特許公報を発行しないと記されている。

欧州特許庁により規則71(3)の通知が発行された場合、出願人は出願書類が完全であるか否か及び審査官の提案する補正を受け入れることができるか否かを検討する責任を常に負っている。付与・特許掲載公報の発行手数料の納付及びクレームの翻訳文提出のための4月の期間は、出願人が出願書類全体を確認することができる最後の機会である。

したがって、規則71(3)の通知は、重要な情報を記載し、かつ、特許の付与において使用される正文書を明記するものである。

be granted.

6 Interacting with the Examiner

The examination of a European application does not involve a mere negotiation with the Examiner regarding patentability. It is necessary to engage proactively with the Examiner. Each objection raised in the official actions, must be addressed in a reasonable manner. It is, of course, legitimate to argue that objections are not justified. However, success is unlikely if it is attempted to overcome objections using superficial arguments or inappropriate claim amendments. Amendments must respond to the specific objections that have been raised, and arguments should be explained in full either why it is considered that the objections are not justified or why it is felt that the objections have been overcome by amendment or, for instance, by the filing of supplementary experimental evidence.

Examiners often require supplementary experimental evidence in order to prove that claims involve an inventive step over their entire scope. The experimental evidence must be appropriate in that it must represent a fair comparison with the closest prior art and enable generalization of the demonstrated advantage over the entire scope of the claims.

EPO prosecution is primarily a written procedure. It is not common to have a face-to-face interview with an Examiner, unless the Examiner agrees that an interview may be useful in order to resolve confusion regarding the Examiner's or applicant's arguments. Rather than a face-to-face interview, a telephone conversation may be sufficient for this purpose. A telephone conversation can also be helpful in order to resolve minor issues such as when the Examiner considers that the claims are allowable and all that is required is adaption of the description.

Interviews and telephone conversations are not formal procedures since any

6 審査官とのやりとり

　欧州特許出願の審査においては、特許性に関する単なる交渉を審査官とするだけではない。審査官とは積極的に関わっていく必要がある。庁通知で提起された各拒絶理由について合理的な方法で対処する必要がある。当然、かかる拒絶理由に根拠がないと主張することもできる。しかし、表面的な議論をしたり、不適切にクレームの補正をすることで当該拒絶理由を解消しようと試みても成功する可能性は低い。特定の拒絶理由に対しては補正をして応答しなければならない。審査官により提起された拒絶理由に根拠がないとか、補正若しくは補足的な実験的証拠等によりその拒絶理由が解消されると考える理由について十分に説明しなければならない。

　審査官は、クレームの範囲全体にわたって進歩性があると立証する補足的な実験的証拠を求めることがある。実験的証拠は、最も近い先行技術に対して公正な比較を提示し、かつ、実証された有利な効果がクレームの全範囲にわたることを証明する観点で適切なものでなければならない。

　欧州特許庁の審査は主として書面審査である。審査官又は出願人の主張の曖昧さを解決するためにインタビューが有用であると審査官が認めない限り、審査官と対面でインタビューが行われることはあまりない。この目的では、対面のインタビューでなく電話での協議で十分であろう。クレームを認めることができると審査官が考えており、明細書の補正のみが必要とされる場合等の細かい事項を解決するために電話協議が有用となることがある。

　審査官と交わされたすべての合意は審査部の他の2名の審査官の見解に左右

agreement reached with the Examiner is subject to the views of the other two members of the Examining Division. For this reason, Examiners are often reluctant to discuss substantive issues by telephone. Submitting written arguments regarding substantive issues is in any case typically the best way to ensure that the Examiners understand applicant's arguments. Thus, in general, EPO prosecution differs from the prosecution before other patent offices in that there is a limited scope for interaction with the Examiner other than in writing.

7   Ex Parte Oral Proceedings

If deficiencies persist in an application after the applicant has responded to an official action, it is open to the Examiner to consult with the other members of the Examining Division. If there is agreement, he may issue a decision of refusal, or, if previously requested by the applicant, issue a summons to oral proceedings. If the applicant has requested oral proceedings as an auxiliary measure, the application cannot be refused until oral proceedings have been held. Failure to appoint oral proceedings following a request is a fundamental procedural violation and any decision taken becomes null and void.

It is difficult to predict when a summons to oral proceedings will be issued in place of a further examination report. This is heavily dependent on the preferences of the Examiner. Certain Examiners are content to keep issuing official actions until all objections are deemed to have been overcome. At the other extreme, if oral proceedings have been requested, some Examiners are all too happy to issue a summons following the applicant's response to the first official action. From the EPO's perspective, this practice is in line with the overriding principle that the final decision, i.e. grant or refusal, should be taken after as few steps as possible. The issuance of a summons forces the applicant to carefully consider its position in the face of a notification of intended refusal. Some practitioners have reported an increased tendency of Examiners to issue a summons rather than a second examination report. This is particularly so when oral proceedings have been re-

されるため、審査官とのインタビュー及び電話協議は正式な手続ではない。この理由により、審査官は重要な事項を電話で協議することに関しては往々にして消極的である。いかなる場合も、出願人の主張が審査官に理解されるよう確実にする目的上、重要事項については出願人の主張を書面により提出することが通常は最善の方法である。このように、欧州特許庁における出願手続は、審査官との書面以外でのやりとりの範囲が限られているという点で、一般的に、他の特許当局における出願手続とは異なる。

7 査定系口頭審理

出願人が庁通知に対して応答した後も出願に不備が残っている場合、審査官は審査部の他の審査官と協議することができる。合意があれば、審査官は、拒絶の決定を下すことができ、あるいは事前に出願人から請求があれば、口頭審理召喚状を発行することもできる。出願人が予備的措置として口頭審理を請求している場合、口頭審理が行われるまで出願を拒絶することはできない。口頭審理の請求を受けてその予定を定めないことは、基本的な手続上の違反に当たり、そのような場合の決定はそのすべてが無効となる。

審査報告書（第94条(3)に従う庁通知）をさらに発行することに代えてどのような場合に口頭審理召喚状が発行されるのかを予測することは難しい。このことは、審査官の好みに大きく左右される。審査官のなかには、すべての拒絶理由が解消されたとみなされるまで庁通知を発行し続けることで良しとする者もいる。それとは正反対に、口頭審理の請求がされた場合、最初の庁通知に出願人が応答すると快諾して召喚状を発行する審査官もいる。欧州特許庁の視点からすると、できるだけ少ない手続で最終決定（すなわち、特許の付与又は出願の拒絶）を行うべきであるとの大原則に沿っているのは後者である。召喚状の発行は、拒絶の通知が意図されている状況に面して自らの立場を注意深く考慮することを出願人に強いるものである。2回目の審査報告書を発行するよりも口頭審理召喚状を審査官が発行する傾向にあると報告する実務家もいる。このことは、口頭審理が予備的措置として請求された場合に特に当てはまる。

quested as an auxiliary measure.

If a serious attempt has been made to overcome the objections raised in the first examination report but a summons has been issued nonetheless, it may be difficult to succeed at oral proceedings without amending the claims or submitting new arguments or evidence. Sometimes it is possible to convince the Examining Division to change its mind when presenting arguments orally in a face-to-face manner. The two members of the Examining Division other than the primary Examiner will likely have had little contact with the case prior to the oral proceedings, so it may be possible to convince these members of the merits of the application by engaging with them in person.

In response to the summons and prior to the oral proceedings, it is possible to file amendments and written arguments. At this stage, it is advisable to file one or more auxiliary claim sets in case that the Examining Division maintains its objections against the main claim set. If the Examining Division takes the view that an auxiliary claim set is allowable, it will communicate this to the applicant before the oral proceedings and give the applicant the opportunity to withdraw higher ranking claims sets so that the oral proceedings can be cancelled.

8   Refusal of European Patent Applications

If, despite the applicant's arguments or amendments of the claims or the filing of evidence, the Examining Division maintains the objections, the application will be refused. A refusal may even be made at the end of the oral proceedings before the Examining Division. Then the Examining Division issues a written decision which must be based on the grounds on which the application is refused. It may only be based on the grounds or evidence on which the applicant has had an opportunity to comment (right to be heard) (Art. 113(1) EPC). The written decision must contain the substantiation why the patent cannot be granted.

第1回目の審査報告書で提起された拒絶理由を解消するために真剣な取り組みがなされたにもかかわらず口頭審理召喚状が発行された場合、クレームの補正又は新たな議論若しくは証拠の提出をともなわずに口頭審理で成功を収めることは難しい。直接口頭で議論をすることで、審査部を説得して考えを改めさせることが可能な場合もある。主担当審査官以外の審査部の2名の審査官は口頭審理の前には対象の出願にほとんど関係していない可能性が高いため、これらの審査官と直接に話をすることで、出願の利点について他の審査官を説得することができることもある。

召喚状に応答して、口頭審理の前に、補正書及び意見書を提出することができる。この段階では、審査部がメインのクレーム（メインリクエスト）に対する拒絶理由を維持する場合に備え、1セット以上の補助クレーム（補助リクエスト）を提出することが望ましい。審査部が、いずれかの補助リクエストであれば認めることができるとの見解を持っている際には、審査部は口頭審理の前にその旨を出願人に通知し、口頭審理が中止されるよう上位クレームを取り下げる機会を出願人に与える。

8　欧州特許出願の拒絶

拒絶理由に対して出願人が議論し、クレームの補正をし、又は証拠を提出したにもかかわらず、審査部がその拒絶理由を維持した場合、出願は拒絶される。審査部の面前での口頭審理の終了時に拒絶の判断が下されることもある。その後、審査部は文書により決定を発行するが、この決定は拒絶理由に基づくものでなければならない。かかる決定は、出願人が自らの意見を表明する機会を与えられた理由又は証拠に基づくものでなければならない（聴聞を受ける権利）（第113条(1)）。当該決定には、特許が付与できない理由が詳細に記載される。

9 Appeal Procedure: Interlocutory Revision

The applicant who is adversely affected by the decision to refuse the application has a right to appeal (Art. 107 EPC). The appeal has a suspensive effect. The notice of appeal has to be filed within two months of notification of the written decision. Together with the notice of appeal an official fee for the appeal has to be paid (Art. 108 EPC). Within four months of notification of the written decision, the statement setting out the grounds for the appeal has to be filed (Art. 108 EPC).

If the Examining Division considers the appeal to be admissible and well-founded, it shall rectify its decision (Art. 109(1) EPC). If the appeal is not allowed within three months of receipt of the statement of grounds, it shall be remitted to the Board of Appeal without delay, and without comment as to its merit (Art. 109(2) EPC).

Thus, the Examiner has to consider the reasons for the appeal. It is therefore recommendable to file any further amended sets of claims (Main Request and optionally one or more Auxiliary Requests) in order to convince the Examining Division that the claims of one of these sets of claims are allowable. Together with the grounds for the appeal the applicant may even file any additional experimental data in favor of the inventive step and in view of the closest prior art.

If the Examining Division takes the stand that on the basis of either one of the above-mentioned sets of claims a patent should be granted, the reasons for the appeal will not be remitted to the Board of Appeal. Then the Examining Division will send a further communication to the applicant. If, together with the reasons for the appeal the applicant filed amended claims and an amended description, and if the Examining Division rectifies its decision, the next communication will be the communication under Rule 71(3) EPC.

If the Examining Division does not rectify its decision, the appeal procedure

9　審判手続：中間修正

　出願拒絶の決定により不利な影響を受けた出願人は、審判を請求する権利を有する（第107条）。審判請求は未決定の効果を有する。審判請求書は、文書により決定が通知された日から2月以内に提出しなければならない。審判請求書とともに所定の審判請求手数料を納付しなければならない（第108条）。当該通知の日から4月以内に審判請求の理由を記載した書面（以下、理由記載書）を提出する必要がある（第108条）。

　審査部は、審判請求が許可されるべきものであり、かつ、確かな根拠に基づくものであると認める場合は、拒絶の決定を修正する（第109条(1)）。理由記載書の受理から3月以内に審判請求が認められない場合は、審判請求は、遅滞なく、かつ、実体についての意見を付すことなく審査部から審判部に送られる（第109条(2)）。

　このように、審査官は審判請求の理由を検討しなければならない。よって、補正されたクレームを複数セット（メインリクエスト及び任意で1つ以上の補助リクエスト）提出し、それらのうち1つは認められるべきものであると審査部を説得することが望ましい。理由記載書とともに、出願人は、最も近い先行技術を考慮したうえで当該出願の進歩性の主張に有利な追加の実験データを提出することもできる。

　審査部が、前述のクレームセットの1つに基づき特許を付与するべきであるとの立場をとる場合、審判請求書は審判部には送られない。その場合、審査部は出願人に対してさらに通知を行う。出願人が審判請求書とともに補正されたクレーム及び補正された明細書を提出し、かつ、審査部が自らの決定を修正する場合、規則71(3)の通知が次に発行される。

　審査部が自らの決定を修正しない場合には、審判部における審判手続が開始

before the Board of Appeal will start. Concerning this procedure reference is made to the chapter "Appeal procedure" in this book.

10 Accelerated Prosecution

The backlog of unexamined European applications has increased in recent years. It is not uncommon for applicants to wait several years for the examiner's reaction to a submission filed in response to objections. The EPO is aware of the growing backlog. There are several cost-free measures available for accelerating the prosecution of an application should there be a desire to obtain a patent quickly.

10.1 PACE

Applicants may request accelerated search and examination under the PACE programme. A request for accelerated search is not necessary for European applications having no claim to priority; in such cases, the EPO issues the extended search report within six months of the filing date. For applications which do claim priority, the EPO only promises that it will make every effort to issue the extended search report "as soon as possible". In the case of a request for accelerated examination, the EPO aims to issue a first examination communication within three months of receipt of the applicant's response to the search opinion or, in the case of Euro-PCT applications for which the EPO was the International Searching Authority, within three months of the response to the Rule 161 Communication, provided that the PACE request is filed with the response. The three month period also applies to subsequent examination communications. It is, however, important for applicants to cooperate by responding within the initial term set by the examining division. Requests for term extensions will likely cause a loss of PACE status.

される。この手続については、本書の「審判」の章で述べる。

10 早期審査

近年、未審査の欧州特許出願の処理待ち件数が増加している。出願人が、拒絶理由通知に応答した後、審査官からの反応を得るまでに数年待たされることは稀ではない。欧州特許庁は、処理待ち件数の増加を認識している。特許の迅速な取得を望む場合には、出願手続を早めるためにいくつかの無料の手続が利用できる。

10.1 PACE

出願人は、PACEプログラムの下で調査及び審査を早めるよう請求することができる。優先権を主張していない欧州特許出願については、早期調査の請求を必要としない。そのような場合、欧州特許庁は拡張欧州調査報告を出願日から6月以内に発行する。優先権を主張している欧州特許出願の場合、欧州特許庁は「できるだけ早く」拡張欧州調査報告を発行するよう最大限の努力を尽くすと約束するのみである。早期審査請求について、欧州特許庁は、調査見解書への応答書を出願人から受領した後3月以内、又は欧州特許庁が国際調査機関となっているEuro-PCT出願の場合には規則161通知に対する応答書を受領した後3月以内に最初の審査報告書を発行することを目指している。ただし、PACE請求が応答書とともに提出されることを条件としている。この3月の期間の設定は、その後の審査報告書にも適用される。一方、出願人は、審査部により最初に指定された期間内に応答することが重要である。指定期間を延長する請求をすると、PACE資格を失う可能性が高い。

10.2 Patent Prosecution Highway (PPH)

The PPH consists of a number of bilateral and trilateral agreements between the world's major patent offices, including the EPO, USPTO, JPO, UKIPO and KIPO. The aim of the PPH is to reduce the burden on examiners by allowing them to make use of work done by other patent offices in respect of equivalent applications. It is certainly possible to use PPH in order to accelerate the prosecution of a European application. However, this is not a given. The differences between the practices of the various patent offices inevitably mean that the conclusions of foreign examiners may not be accepted by EPO examiners.

The EPO has signed PPH agreements with the USPTO and the JPO. Under these agreements, it is possible to have a European application processed under the PPH programme by amending the claims so that they correspond to claims which have been deemed allowable by the USPTO/JPO for a corresponding application. This applies not only to European applications claiming priority from, or serving as a priority application for, US/JP applications, but also to European applications derived from, or claiming priority from, international applications for which the USPTO/JPO acted as the ISA and, if applicable, the IPEA. Overall, it is necessary for the European and reference applications to be linked by a common application.

In order to be eligible for participation in the PPH, examination of the European application must not have commenced. Moreover, it is necessary for all of the claims of the European application to have the same scope or a narrower scope than the allowed claims of the reference application. The European application must not contain additional independent claims beyond those contained in the reference application. A declaration to this effect must be filed with the PPH request. Additional requirements are the filing of copies of all of the office actions issued in respect of the reference application, copies of the non-patent documents cited in these office actions, a copy of the claims of the reference application that have been deemed allowable and, in the case of a Japanese reference application,

10.2 特許審査ハイウェイ（PPH）

PPHは、欧州特許庁、米国特許商標庁、日本特許庁、イギリス知的財産権庁及び韓国特許庁を含む世界の主要特許当局間における二者間及び三者間の協定により構成されている。PPHは、ある（先行）特許庁で行われた特許出願の審査結果を別の特許庁が利用できるようにすることで審査官の負担軽減を目指している。欧州特許の出願手続を早めるためにPPHを利用することはたしかに可能ではあるが、これは既定の事実ではない。特許当局の実務は様々に異なるため、外国審査官の結論が欧州特許庁の審査官には受け入れられない可能性も必然的に存在する。

欧州特許庁は、米国特許商標庁及び日本特許庁の各々とPPH協定を交わしている。これらの協定に基づき、米国特許商標庁／日本特許庁がすでに認めたクレームに相当するべく、対応する出願のクレームを補正することにより、PPHプログラムの下で欧州特許出願が処理されるよう請求することができる。これは、アメリカ／日本での出願に基づき優先権を主張している欧州特許出願（又はアメリカ／日本での出願についての優先権主張の基礎をなす欧州出願）だけでなく、米国特許商標庁／日本特許庁が国際調査機関及び（該当する場合）国際予備審査機関として行動する国際出願から派生する（又はこれに基づいて優先権を主張する）欧州出願にも適用される。概して、欧州出願と参照対象出願とが関連付けられていることが必要である。

PPHの利用資格を得るには、欧州特許出願の審査がすでに開始されていてはならない。さらに、欧州特許出願のクレームの範囲は、参照対象出願においてすでに認められているクレームと同等又はそれより狭いものでなければならない。欧州特許出願には、参照対象出願に含まれるクレームの範囲を超える追加的な独立クレームが含まれていてはならない。それについての宣言をPPHリクエストとともに提出する必要がある。追加的な要件は、参照対象出願について当該特許当局から発行されたすべての通知の写し、これらの特許当局通知で引用された非特許文献の写し、参照対象出願ですでに認められたクレームの写し、及び（日本での特許出願を参照する場合には）庁通知及びクレームの翻訳文を提出することである。

translations of the office actions and claims.

It is not necessary for all of the claims of the reference application to have been deemed allowable. A PPH request can be filed on the basis of a reference application for which a positive opinion has been issued in respect of only some of the claims.

The PPH may be an effective way to accelerate the prosecution of a European application. However, as a note of caution, it should be remembered that the EPO has unique requirements as regards patentability. An amended claim accepted by a US or JP examiner may be found by the EPO examiner to add subject-matter extending beyond the content of the application as originally filed. It is also possible that the claims of a European application are prejudiced by a post-published European application which is not citable against the reference application. Conversely, the limitations of the claims in the reference application may not be necessary in order to overcome objections raised by the EPO examiner. The pros and cons of a request for PPH should therefore be weighed up on a case-by-case basis. A request for PPH may do nothing more than unnecessarily limit the scope of the claims of a European application without dealing with the EPO examiner's objections.

11 Further Remarks: Reduction of Costs

Obtaining a European patent is not a cheap exercise. Aside from representative's fees, there are a number of official fees, some of which are variable. Being aware of these fees can help to reduce the overall costs of prosecution. Official fees can be minimized in the following ways:

- File the application with a maximum of 15 claims in order to avoid excess claim fees (currently EUR 225 for the 16th to the 50th claims and EUR 555 for the 51st and each subsequent claims.

参照対象出願のクレームがすべてにおいて認められている必要はない。参照対象出願のクレームのうちいくつかについて肯定的見解がすでに出されていれば、それに基づいてPPHの請求をすることができる。

PPHは、欧州特許出願の出願手続を早めるために効果的な方法であろう。しかし、注意点として、欧州特許庁が特許性について独自の要件を持つことを覚えておく必要がある。アメリカ又は日本の審査官が認めた補正されたクレームについて、出願時における出願内容を超える対象を含むように補正されていると欧州特許庁の審査官は判断することがある。また、対象の欧州特許出願のクレームがその出願後に公開された欧州特許出願（参照対象出願に対しては引用されない）によって不利益を被ることもある。逆に、欧州特許庁の審査官により提起された拒絶理由を解消する目的において、参照対象出願におけるクレームの限定が必要とされないこともある。よって、PPHの請求をすることのメリットとデメリットは個別的に比較検討する必要がある。PPHの請求が、欧州特許庁審査官からの拒絶理由に対処することなく、欧州出願のクレームの範囲を不必要に限定するだけに終わることもある。

11　追記：経費削減

欧州特許の取得は安価な手続ではない。代理人手数料のほかに、所定の手数料がいくつかあり、金額が変動するものもある。これらの手数料について認識しておくことは、手続全体の経費削減に役立つだろう。所定の手数料は以下の方法で最小限に抑えることができる。

- 超過クレーム手数料（現在、第16番目から50番目までの各クレームについては225ユーロ、第51番目のクレーム及びそれに続く各クレームについては555ユーロ）を避けるため、提出する出願に含めるクレーム数は最大15までと

- Reduce the number of pages of the specification so as to reduce or avoid the excess page fees.

- File applications online - this provides a saving of costs versus other forms of filing.

- Avoid unnecessary penalty fees such as the 50% surcharge for late payment of a renewal fee and the fee for further processing.

12 Summary

Patent prosecution before the EPO is constantly developing. The developments are driven by the EPO's desire to improve the efficiency of prosecution as well as an increased cooperation with other patent offices. Despite the best intentions of the EPO, certain changes have created pitfalls for the unwary. It is therefore essential to have an understanding of the impact of the changes as and when they are made in order to make the best use of the European prosecution procedure. Clear communication between applicants and their representatives is also important for providing a backdrop to the prosecution process and obtaining optimal protection.

する。

- ページ数についての追加手数料を避けるため、明細書のページ数を抑える。

- オンラインで出願する（他の形式の出願に比べ経費が削減できる）。

- 更新手数料の遅延納付に伴う50％の追加手数料及び手続の続行にかかる手数料などの罰則的手数料を回避する。

12　まとめ

　欧州特許庁における出願手続は絶えず進展し続けている。この進展は、欧州特許庁の効率向上への熱意と他の特許当局からの協力の拡大によって起きている。最善を求める欧州特許庁の意図にもかかわらず、一部の実務変更が思わぬ落とし穴となっている。よって、欧州特許出願手続を最大限に活用するためには、実務変更が行われるごとに、その影響を理解することが非常に重要である。また、出願人とその代理人との間での確実なコミュニケーションも、出願経過の背景を把握し、かつ、最大の保護を得るために重要である。

Chapter 12

Amendments

補 正

Morten Garberg

MEMO

▶ 第123条(2)には、補正のできる範囲が規定されています。当該条文は、出願手続の段階であるか、特許付与後の手続であるかにかかわらず、どの時点でなされた補正についても適用されます。よって、本書では、特許付与前後の手続について「補正」という用語を使っています。

▶ 日本特許法の第17条の2第5項によると、日本の特許実務では、補正をする時期によって、その基準となる範囲が異なりますが、欧州特許実務では、最初の拒絶理由通知及び最後の拒絶理由通知という概念がなく、「当初の出願書類に記載した事項」を補正ができる範囲の基準としています（§1）。

▶ 欧州実務では、補正が第123条(2)の要件を満たしているか否かの判断には、「直接的かつ一義的に導き出せること」の原則が採用されます（§2.2）。この点、日本特許庁審査基準によれば、当初明細書等に明示的に記載された事項だけではなく、明示的な記載がなくても、当初明細書等の記載から自明な事項に補正することは、新たな技術的事項を導入するものではないから許される、と説明されています（第Ⅳ部第2章参照）。一般的に、欧州特許実務では補正要件が厳しいといえます（§2）。

▶ 特許されたクレームが第123条(2)の要件違反を含んでいると特許後に判断されることが多々あります。この場合、第123条(3)との関係で補正違反を解消することができなくなる場合があります（§3）。

▶ 第123条(2)の要件がどのように判断されるかについては、§4～§7を参照してください。

▶ 「数値範囲」については、開示された広い数値範囲に、好ましい範囲の一方の端点を組み合わせることができます（§4）。

▶ 第1章で紹介した「2リストの原則」に従えば、2つ以上のリストから個々の選択肢を選んで「特徴の組合せ」を作る補正は、基本的に、第123条(2)の要件を満たさないとされます（§5）。

▶ 欧州実務では、中間概念化が認められることもありますが、そのためには非常に厳しい条件が課されています（§6）。この点、現行の日本特許庁審査基準には、「また、［明細書に］24℃と25℃の実施例が記載されている場合は、……当初明細書等の記載全体からみて24～25℃の特定の範囲についての言及があったものと認められる場合もある。……このような場合は、実施例のない場合と異なり、数値限定の記載が当初からなされていたものと評価でき、新たな技術的事項を導入するものではない」と記載されています（第Ⅳ部第2章参照）。

▶ 誤記の訂正については、「明らかな誤記」と「明らかな訂正」であることの解釈が必要とされます（§8）。誤記の訂正は確認的な意味を持つものに過ぎないことと、実質的な訂正になると許可される可能性は低いことから、出願人にとって誤記の訂正を行う価値は少ないように思われます。

Introduction

In all of the major patent systems of the world, an applicant may amend his patent application (and in particular the claims) after the patent application has been filed. This can be done e.g. to take into account objections which have been raised by the responsible patent office. It is also universally true that a patent applicant is restricted to some extent in the amendments he can make. This is also true for proceedings at the EPO.

Generally, it is considered that there is a public policy reason for restricting an applicant's possibility to amend. Firstly, because the state of the art is defined based on the filing date of the application in question, it makes sense that only inventions which were actually disclosed by the applicant on the filing date can be protected in that application. Secondly, it is considered that any third party should be able to obtain a copy of a published patent application belonging to their competitors, and reasonably be able to predict which claims may be granted. This is only possible if amendment options are restricted.

Compared to other jurisdictions, the EPO is quite restrictive in terms of allowability of amendments, and in particular in the context of assessing whether a given amended claim finds adequate support in the original application text. When an applicant at the EPO asks to make an amendment, it is the applicant that has the burden of proof in showing that the amended claim finds a proper basis in the original application text. Furthermore, the standard of proof needed is a high one; although the EPO typically only requires proof on the basis of the "balance of probability", there are some specific cases where a point has to be proven "beyond reasonable doubt". This much higher standard of proof is applied by the EPO in the context of basis for amendments, as is clear from a long line of Case Law stretching back to the 1980s.

When comparing three major jurisdictions such as the EPO, the JPO and the USPTO, it is generally considered that the EPO takes the toughest view on allow-

はじめに

　世界の主要な特許制度のすべてにおいて、特許出願の出願人は、その出願（特にクレーム）について補正をすることができる。例えば、管轄特許庁により提起された拒絶理由を考慮したうえで補正をすることが可能である。どの国の特許制度においても、補正にはある程度の制限が設けられているのが事実である。欧州特許庁の手続においても例外ではない。

　補正ができる範囲を制限することに関しては、一般的な見方として、公益に基づく理由が存在する。第一に、その出願の出願日に基づいて技術水準が認定されるので、出願日において実際に開示された発明だけがその出願において保護され得るというのは理に適っている。第二に、第三者の立場からすると、競争相手が行った特許出願の公開内容の写しが取得可能であるべきであり、そしてどのクレームが特許になり得るのか当然予測可能でなければならない。これは、補正可能な範囲に制限が課されてはじめて可能になる。

　欧州特許庁は、他の管轄特許庁と比べて、補正の認容についてはかなり制限的であり、特に、補正されたクレームが当初出願書類に適切な根拠を有するかについて厳しく判断する。欧州特許庁において補正をしようとする際、補正されたクレームについて当初出願書類に適切な根拠があることを証明する責任は出願人側にある。さらに、出願人には高い立証基準が要求される。欧州特許庁は、通常は「蓋然性の均衡」に基づく証明を求めるが、一部の事案においては、ある点について「合理的な疑いを超える」程度の証明が必要になる。1980年代から続くケースローで示されるように、欧州特許庁は補正の根拠に関しては、こちらのかなり高い立証基準を適用している。

　欧州、日本、米国の三極特許庁で比較してみると、一般的な見方として補正の認容の観点でいちばん厳しい立場をとっているのは欧州特許庁であり、その

ability of amendments followed by Japan. The USPTO generally takes a much more liberal approach so that claim amendment there is significantly easier from a formal perspective.

1 Art. 123(2) EPC: Prohibition of Added Matter

The most important article of the EPC from the perspective of allowability of amendments is Art. 123(2) EPC, which prohibits amendments which add new matter. This EPC article applies to amendments made at any time, i.e. both during prosecution and in post-grant proceedings such as opposition cases. Art 123(2) EPC is not immediately concerned with the scope of the claims, but rather with their information content. This means that both a narrowing amendment and a broadening amendment can cause non-compliance with Art. 123(2) EPC; in practice, it is often narrowing amendments which result in added matter problems.

In order to test whether a given amendment adds matter or not, it is necessary to compare the information content of the amended claim with the information content of the application as filed. If the amended claim includes no new information, then it complies with Art. 123(2) EPC.

For the purposes of this comparison, it is of course necessary to know what the application as filed is. It has been established through Case Law that the application as filed includes the description, claims and drawings (see G 3/89). If the European patent application is a normal European patent application, it is the documents which are filed the EPO which are the relevant ones. If priority is claimed from an earlier application, e.g. an earlier Japanese application, then the priority document cannot be taken into account (see T 260/85). If the application is a PCT application, e.g. filed in Japanese and later entered into the EP Regional Phase with the filing of a translation, the application as filed would be the original

次が日本特許庁である。米国特許商標庁では概してかなり寛大なアプローチが採用されているため、同庁におけるクレームの補正は形式的な観点からいえばかなり容易なものとなっている。

1 　第123条(2)： 新規事項追加の禁止

補正の認容という点から見て欧州特許条約で最も重要な条文は、新規事項を追加する補正を禁止する第123条(2)である。欧州特許条約における当該条文は、出願手続であるか、特許付与後の手続（例えば、特許異議申立事件等）であるかにかかわらず、どの時点でなされた補正についても適用される。第123条(2)は、クレームの範囲に直接関わるものではなく、どちらかといえばそこに含まれる情報量に関するものである。つまり、クレームの範囲を縮小する補正も拡大する補正も第123条(2)違反につながる可能性がある。実務においては、範囲を縮小する補正で新規事項追加の問題が生じることが多い。

補正が新規事項の追加にあたるか否かをテストするためには、補正されたクレームの情報量と当初の出願書類の情報量とを比較する必要がある。補正されたクレームに新たな情報が含まれていなければ、その補正は第123条(2)の要件を満たしていることになる。

このような比較を行うためには、当然のことながら、当初の出願書類とは何かを把握する必要がある。ケースローで認められているところによれば、当初の出願書類とは、明細書、クレーム及び図面を含むものである（G 3/89参照）。その出願が通常の欧州特許出願である場合、該当するのは欧州特許庁に提出された書類である。先の出願（例えば先に出願した日本出願）に基づき優先権を主張している場合でも、優先権書類を考慮に入れることはできない（T 260/85参照）。PCT出願の場合、（例えば日本語で出願したPCT出願を、翻訳文を提出して欧州段階に移行した場合）日本語で最初に出願したPCT出願書類が当初の出願書類となる（第70条(2)参照）。具体的にいえば、このケースでは、欧州段階移行

Japanese-language PCT application (see Art. 70(2) EPC). Specifically, the translation filed on entry into the EP Regional Phase does not count as the application as filed in such a situation. Also, the abstract is never part of the application as filed for the purposes of assessing added matter (see T 246/86).

2 How to Compare Information Content?

Unfortunately, there is no simple test which can be applied to give a conclusive answer as to whether or not a given amendment complies with Art. 123(2) EPC. Instead, this must be assessed on a case-by-case basis bearing in mind the prevailing Case Law.

2.1 The Novelty Test

There has been one attempt at developing a model which allows an easy prediction of whether or not an amendment is allowable. This is called the "novelty test". Unfortunately, the novelty test is of limited use. When applied, it can give a positive or negative result. A negative result means that it can be said, with certainty, that the amendment in question is not allowable. However, a positive result is not so clear; this only means that the amendment could be allowable, but it could also be unallowable. Thus, this test can be used to prove that a given amendment is not acceptable, but it can never be used to prove that an amendment is in accordance with the law.

The novelty test is relatively simple to apply. One simply takes the amended claim and compares it with the application as filed, pretending that the entire application as filed is a prior art document. One then examines whether the amended claim is novel over the "pretend prior art document". If the result of the analysis is that the claim is novel, then this is a clear indication that the amendment in question is not allowable. If the claim is not novel, no clear conclusion is possible.

時に提出する翻訳文は「当初の出願書類」には含まれない。また、要約書は、新規事項追加の判断においては当初の出願書類には決して含まれない（T 246/86参照）。

2　情報量の比較方法

所与の補正が第123条(2)の規定に適合しているか否かという点については、残念ながら、明確に答えを出せるような簡易なテストはない。よって、有力なケースローをふまえつつ、ケース・バイ・ケースで判断するよりほかはない。

2.1　新規性テスト

補正が認められるか否かについて容易に予測するモデルを作ろうとする試みがなされてきた。これは「新規性テスト」と呼ばれるものだが、残念ながらこの新規性テストの有用性は限られている。このテストを適用すると、補正が「可」か「不可」のいずれかの結果が出る。結果が「不可」であれば、その補正は認められないと確実にいうことができる。しかし、結果が「可」の場合はそれほど明確ではなく、単に、その補正が認められる場合と認められない場合とがあることを意味する。よって、このテストにより、当該補正は認められないものだと証明することはできるが、当該補正が法律に従っていると証明することはできない。

新規性テストの使い方は比較的簡単である。まず、補正されたクレームを当初の出願書類と単純に比較するのだが、このとき当初の書類全体を先行技術文献とみなして比較を行う。そして、当該補正されたクレームがその「みなし先行技術文献」と比べて新規なものであるかを検討する。検討の結果、補正されたクレームに新規性があるということになれば、当該補正は認められないことが明らかである。当該補正されたクレームに新規性がない場合、明確な結論は得られない。

2.2 The Principle of Direct and Unambiguous Derivability

Because the novelty test does not provide a conclusive answer, there are situations where further analysis is necessary in order to conclusively find out whether a given amendment is acceptable or not. The admissibility of an amendment is to be decided solely on the basis of an examination of whether the amendment is directly and unambiguously derivable from the application as filed (see T 288/92).

The standard of "direct and unambiguous derivability" is therefore the currently applied standard. There is a significant body of Case Law which explains how this is to be assessed in certain specific situations: sections 4-6 of this chapter analyze some of this Case Law.

Generally speaking, the EPO does not have a strict requirement that any wording used in an amended claim must be found in the application as filed. However, experience shows that EPO Examiners are extremely skeptical if any new words (i.e. words not present anywhere in the application as filed) are used in an amended claim; this will invite high levels of scrutiny and it is almost certain that an explanation will be required why this has been done. It is therefore generally safer to only use wording which is found in the application as filed. Even when relying only on the original wording, there is no guarantee that an amendment will be allowed because the EPO is very interested in examining whether a change of context of the original wording has been made, which change of context might add new information. Therefore, although this is in itself not enough to be safe from the strict added matter assessment, it is a good start.

2.2　直接的かつ一義的に導き出せることの原則

新規性テストでは決定的な答えを出すことができないため、場合によっては、ある補正が認められるか否かを確実に判断するにはさらなる検討が必要になる。補正の認容性の判断は、当該補正が当初の出願書類から直接的かつ一義的に導き出せるものか否かという審査に基づいて専ら行われる（T 288/92参照）。

この「直接的かつ一義的に導き出せること」の基準が、現在用いられている適用基準である。欧州特許庁のケースローでは、この基準が個別の具体的事例においてどのように判断されるべきかが説明されている。本章のセクション4～6でケースローの事例のいくつかを分析する。

欧州特許庁は、原則として、補正されたクレームに用いられるすべての文言が当初の出願書類に見出されるべきとする厳格な要件は課していない。ただし経験からいえば、欧州特許庁の審査官は、補正されたクレームに新しい文言（すなわち、当初の出願書類にまったく記載されていない文言）が用いられているかどうかを非常に懐疑的な目で見ながら審査を行うようである。よって、入念に精査する必要があるうえに、新しい文言が用いられている場合は説明を求められる可能性が高い。よって、原則としては当初の出願書類に記載されている文言のみを用いるほうが安全である。ただし、出願当初の文言のみに基づく場合であっても、補正が認められるという保証はない。なぜなら欧州特許庁は、出願当初の文言が用いられている文脈に変更がないか、その文脈の変更によって新たな情報の追加が生じていないかという点につき、非常に注意深く審査を行うためである。よって、上記安全策は、新規事項追加についての厳しい判断に対して十分に安全とはいえないが、よい手始めにはなる。

3 Art. 123(3) EPC and Its Interplay with Art. 123(2) EPC

Art. 123(3) EPC applies only to post-grant amendments, e.g. amendments during opposition proceedings. While Art. 123(2) EPC is about the information content of claims, Art. 123(3) EPC deals with something else, namely the scope of the claims. Art. 123(3) EPC basically says that, after grant, a claim may not be amended so as to extend the scope of protection relative to the granted claims. This is assessed in a rather simple way; if there is an embodiment which falls within the amended claim, but which is not covered by any granted claim, then the scope of protection has been extended.

One important characteristic of European Patent Law results from the interplay between the two parts of Art. 123 EPC, when taken in conjunction with the fact that non-compliance with Art. 123(2) EPC is a ground of opposition. The issue is best explained by way of a simple example:

Imagine that a European patent application is filed with a relatively broad claim. The Examiner raises an objection of lack of patentability, to which the applicant responds by amending the claim to introduce several restricting features. The Examiner accepts the amendment and grants a patent based on the amended claims which were filed. If the patent is now opposed, an opponent can argue that the patent is invalid because of the amendment made. Although it was accepted by the Examiner, if an opponent can convincingly argue that the amendment in fact does not comply with the requirements of Art. 123(2) EPC, then the patent will be revoked unless the patentee can further amend the claims in order to fix the problem by further amendment. This is where the interplay with Art. 123(3) EPC arises; as explained above, it is not possible to extend the scope of protection after grant, for which reason it would not be possible during opposition to remove a limiting feature which had been introduced into the claim before grant. Therefore, if an amendment made during prosecution is in fact not allowable (despite the examiner believing it is acceptable), this will render the granted patent

3　第123条(3)と第123条(2)との相互関係

　第123条(3)は、特許付与後の補正（例えば、特許異議申立手続における補正）にのみ適用される規定である。第123条(2)がクレームの情報量に関する規定であるのに対し、第123条(3)は別の側面、すなわちクレームの範囲に関する規定である。第123条(3)によれば、特許が付与された後は、特許されたクレームと比較してその保護範囲を拡張するように当該クレームを補正してはならない。その判断は、ある程度簡単に行うことができる。つまり、補正されたクレームの範囲に入る実施形態が特許されたクレームでカバーされない場合は、保護範囲が拡張されているということになる。

　ここで、第123条(2)違反は特許異議の申立理由になることを考えると、第123条に存在する2つの規定の関係から、欧州特許法のある重要な特徴が浮かび上がる。以下に示す簡単な例とともに、この問題を説明する。

　例えば、欧州特許出願が比較的広いクレームで出願されたとする。審査官から特許性欠如の拒絶理由が提起され、これに対し出願人は、限定的特徴をいくつか導入することによりクレームを補正して応答する。審査官がこの補正を認め、当該補正されたクレームに基づいて特許を付与する。その後、特許異議の申立てがされた場合、異議申立人は、この補正を理由に当該特許が無効であると主張することができる場合がある。審査官により補正が認められたとしても、その補正がじつは第123条(2)の要件を満たしていないという異議申立人の主張が通ったならば当該特許は取り消される。それを避けるために特許権者はクレームをさらに補正することで問題を解決し得る。ここで、第123条(3)との関係が問題となる。すでに述べたとおり、特許が付与された後では、その保護範囲を拡張することができない。このため、特許付与前にクレームに導入された限定的部分を特許異議申立手続で取り除くことはできない。よって、出願手続で行った補正がじつは認められないものであった場合（たとえ審査官がその補正を認める立場をとっていたとしても）、保護範囲をさらに狭める代替策であって当初の出願書類に十分な根拠がある策がなければ、当該補正が原因で特許

vulnerable to revocation unless there are narrower fallback positions available which have an adequate basis in the application as filed.

It is because of this interplay between the two parts of Art. 123 EPC, and because added matter is a ground of revocation in Europe, that European patent attorneys are often very careful about restricting amendments made during prosecution. Because experience has shown that valuable patents can be revoked for added matter, even when an examiner has approved the amendment in question, European patent attorneys often prefer to advise cautiously on amendment matters in order to provide the best advice for their clients and in order to ensure that the granted patents are not vulnerable to formal attacks.

4 Numerical Ranges

One type of amendment which often comes up in all technical fields is the restriction of a broad numerical range to a narrower one. Generally speaking, when an originally filed claim indicates a broad range, the applicant is not free to narrow this as he sees fit; narrowing of the range is only possible if the application as filed provides an adequate basis for the desired narrowing. The ideal situation is that the narrower range which the applicant wants to amend to is expressly disclosed in the application as filed; then the amendment to that disclosed range will be possible. It may also be possible to rely on only one endpoint of a preferred sub-range, and use this in conjunction with the endpoint of the original broader range; for example, if the original claim discloses a range of 2-8% and a preferred range of 4-6% is disclosed, it should be possible to amend the claim to refer to either e.g. 2-6% or e.g. 2-4% (see T 2/81 and T 1170/02). Generally speaking, it is not possible to generate new endpoints for a numerical range from isolated values disclosed, e.g. from individual data points disclosed in a table or graph but not mentioned as being interesting as endpoints of a range.

が取り消されるおそれがある。

　第123条の前記2つの規定間にこのような関係があることや、欧州特許実務においては新規事項の追加が特許の取消事由となることから、欧州弁理士は出願手続中に減縮補正をすることについて非常に慎重な姿勢を示す場合が多い。クライアントに最良の助言を提供するため、かつ、特許が付与された後での形式的な攻撃を避けるために、欧州弁理士は補正事項については慎重な助言を行うことを好む。それは、新規事項の追加を理由に（審査官が当該補正を認めていたとしても）重要な特許が取り消される可能性があるという経験に基づくものである。

4　数値範囲

　どの技術分野でもよくある補正の1つが、広い数値範囲を狭い範囲に限定するというものである。一般的に、出願当初のクレームに広い数値範囲が記載されている場合でも、出願人は思うまま自由にその範囲を縮小することはできない。数値範囲の縮小が可能なのは、希望する縮小範囲について当初の出願書類に十分な根拠がある場合のみである。出願人が補正をしようとする縮小範囲が当初の出願書類に明示的に開示されているのが理想の状態であり、この場合は当該開示された数値範囲に補正することができる。「好ましい」部分範囲の一方の端点値のみを用い、これを元の広い範囲の端点値と組み合わせることも可能である。一例として、元のクレームに2〜8％という範囲が開示されており、好ましい範囲として4〜6％という範囲が開示されている場合、例えば2〜6％、あるいは2〜4％とクレームの補正をすることができる（T 2/81、T 1170/02参照）。ただし、原則として、独立に開示された数値（例えば、表やグラフ中に個別のデータ数値として開示されてはいるが、ある数値範囲の端点値として特に取り上げられているわけではない数値）を用いて、新たに数値範囲の端点値とすることはできない。

5 Feature Combinations

As mentioned above, the EPO generally considers that the wording found in an amended claim should ideally be found also in the application as filed in order for the amendment to be allowable. However, there are also many situations where the amended claim only includes originally disclosed words, but the amendment still is not allowable. This can happen e.g. because the EPO believes although the claim includes only originally disclosed features, the original disclosure did not specifically foresee the combination of features recited in the amended claim, so that a new information is generated by the way the features have been combined.

In this context, there is a strong line of Case Law at the EPO relating to the generation of new information by the carrying out of selections from multiple lists. According to this line of Case Law, where the information in the claim can only be arrived at by singling out items from two or more lists in the original disclosure, which items were not specifically highlighted in the application as filed as being preferred, will result in the generation of new matter.

As an example, one could consider the original, general disclosure of the reaction of two compound, namely a compound of type A and a compound of type B. The original disclosure might mention that the compound of type A could be A1, A2, A3, A4 or A5 and that the compound of type B could be B1, B2, B3, B4 or B5. If, based on this disclosure, the applicant were to write an amended claim directed to the reaction of A3 with B4, the EPO would very likely consider that Art. 123(2) EPC has not been complied with because two selections would need to be made from two lists in the original disclosure to arrive at the amended claim.

Conversely, it would likely be acceptable to write a claim to the reaction of compound A3 with a compound of type B; this is because this claim could be arrived at only by selecting from one list, whereas the EPO only sees the problem

5　特徴の組合せ

　前述のとおり、欧州特許庁は、補正が認められるものであるためには、補正されたクレームに記載された文言が当初の出願書類にも記載されていることが理想的であるという原則をとっている。しかし、補正されたクレームが当初に開示された文言のみを含むにもかかわらず、その補正がなお認められないケースも多々ある。このようなケースは、例えば、補正されたクレームに特徴の組合せが記載されている場合、それらの特徴が当初に開示されたものであっても、当該組合せとして当初の開示から明確に予見可能なものではなく、複数の特徴を組み合わせることで新規な情報が生み出されると欧州特許庁が考える場合に生じる。

　この点について、欧州特許庁には、複数リストからの選択により新たな情報を作り出すことに関する主流のケースローがある。この流れのケースローによると、当初開示された2つ以上のリストからそこにある各項目を選び出すことによってのみクレームの情報量に到達する場合に、当初の出願書類で当該選び出された各項目が特に好ましいものとして強調されていなければ、新規事項となる。

　例えば、当初の開示が一般的で、A種の化合物とB種の化合物という2つの化合物の反応について記載されている場合を想定する。当初の開示において、「A種の化合物がA1、A2、A3、A4又はA5であってもよい」と記載され、また「B種の化合物は、B1、B2、B3、B4又はB5であってもよい」と記載されているとする。出願人がこの開示を根拠に、A3とB4の反応というかたちにクレームを補正しようとすると、当該補正されたクレームに到達するためには当初に開示された2つのリストから2つの選択をしなければならないという理由によって、欧州特許庁の判断により第123条(2)違反とされる可能性が非常に高い。

　逆に、クレームの記載を「化合物A3と化合物B種との反応」というかたちにすれば認められる可能性が高くなる。なぜなら欧州特許庁が問題視するのは2つ以上のリストからそれぞれ選択が行われる場合のみであって、このケース

when selections are made from two or more lists.

Also potentially acceptable would be a claim where individual options are not picked, but only a shortening of the original list is carried out; thus, it is possible that it would be allowable to write a claim directed to the reaction between a compound which is any of A1, A2 or A3 with any of compounds B2, B3 or B4. However, an amendment of this type would have to be looked at quite carefully also from the general context to see whether it would be allowable, as this is a borderline area.

Reverting to the singling out of individual members from lists, it must be mentioned that although this is generally not allowed when two or more lists are involved, it can be allowable if the application as filed highlights the members of the lists which are the ones selected in the amendment. Such "preselection" or "highlighting" could e.g. arise from these being the only ones used in the examples, these being used in at least one example together, or these members being specifically said to be the single, most preferred members of each list. Thus, depending on the circumstances, it may be possible to make multiple selections from multiple groups.

Although this line of Case Law was developed on the basis of literal lists of items, e.g. lists of substituents or lists of reagents, its application has been broadened significantly and it can fairly be said to apply whenever multiple options are given for any feature. Thus, the concept of "selection from multiple lists" comes up quite often in practice.

6   Intermediate Generalizations

Another area where the EPO takes a strict approach is when mixing parts of the original disclosure which were originally disclosed at different levels of generality. This commonly comes up when features are taken from an example and

では1つのリストからの選択だけで得られるクレームとなっているためである。

　また、個別のオプションを選択するのではなく、当初のリストの範囲を縮小しただけのクレームも認められる可能性がある。つまりクレームの記載を「A1、A2又はA3のいずれかの化合物とB2、B3又はB4のいずれかの化合物との反応」というかたちにすれば、認められる可能性がある。ただしこのタイプの補正については、認められるか否かの境界線上にあるので、全体を通して極めて慎重に検討する必要がある。

　複数リストから個々の選択肢を選び出す場合に話を戻すと、2つ以上のリストが関与している補正は、原則として認められないが、当初の出願書類中でそれらの選択肢が強調されていた場合はその補正が認められる可能性があるということを述べておきたい。例えば、それらの選択肢のみが複数の実施例で用いられている場合、又はそれらの選択肢が一緒に少なくとも1つの実施例で用いられている場合、あるいはそれらの選択肢が各々のリストの唯一最も好ましいものであると具体的に記載されている場合等には、このような「事前選択」又は「強調」があるということができよう。したがって、状況によっては複数の群から複数の選択を行うことも可能といえるであろう。

　このケースローの流れは、文言による項目のリスト、例えば置換基のリストや試薬のリスト等に関して構築されてきたものだが、その適用範囲は多岐にわたっており、どのような特徴であっても複数の選択肢が存在する場合には常に適用可能といってよいであろう。よって、実務においてはこの「複数のリストからの選択」という概念に出会うことが非常に多い。

6　中間概念化

　欧州特許庁が厳しいアプローチをとっているもうひとつの領域は、当初の開示では異なる概念レベルで記載されている各部分を混合させるという事案である。このようなことが起こるのは通常、ある実施例からいくつかの特徴を取り

used to amend an originally filed claim. This typically would attract an objection from the EPO examiner, as the EPO generally considers that the skilled person, when confronted with the disclosure of a specific example, would assume that the example discloses a "package" of features from which it is not normally allowed to extract individual features and so separate them from the other specific features.

Therefore, it is generally very difficult to amend a pre-existing claim based only on an example without accidentally contravening Art. 123(2) EPC, for which reason this is generally not advisable. If, in a specific situation, this is strictly necessary, it is possible to extract a feature from an example if it can be successfully argued that the features from the example which were not used as limitations in the claim would not be understood by the skilled reader as being essential and are not described as such in the original disclosure, the feature left behind are not indispensable to the function of the claimed item, and the features which are taken and those which are left behind are not strongly linked to one another.

The problem of intermediate generalizations is not only seen when Examples are relied on for amendments; this can apply to any situation where some information from two parts of the disclosure is blended together, especially when some information contained in those parts is left unused.

7 Disclaimers

Claims most often use positive features to define the invention and limit it from the prior art, it is also possible sometimes for an invention to be defined in part by negative features. These are called disclaimers, and rather than define the features which characterize the invention, they define specifically what the invention is not.

As a trivial example, one could consider defining a car by a positive feature

出し、その特徴を用いて出願当初のクレームを補正する場合である。欧州特許庁の審査官は、この種の補正を認めない。というのも、欧州特許庁の一般的な考え方として、ある特定の実施例の開示に直面した当業者は、当該実施例に開示されているのは複数の特徴の「パッケージ」と推測し、そこから個々の特徴を抜き出すことにより、それらを他の具体的特徴から切り離すことは通常はできないというものである。

　よって、ある実施例のみを根拠として既存のクレームを補正しようとすると、意図せず第123条(2)違反に陥ることになる。そのため、このような補正は原則として推奨しない。特定の状況下で、このような補正が絶対に必要という場合には、ある実施例からある特徴を抽出することも可能であろうが、その実施例の特徴のうち当該クレームの限定に用いない特徴については、当業者が必須のものとは考えないであろうし、当初の開示においてもそのようには記載されておらず、また、その残りの特徴はクレームに記載された事項の作用に必要不可欠なものではなく、さらに、抽出された特徴とそれ以外の特徴は互いに強く関連しないという議論をして認められなければならない。

　中間概念化の問題は、補正の根拠が実施例である場合に限られず、開示に係る2カ所の情報が互いに混合されており、特にこれらの箇所に含まれる情報のうち一部が利用されていないという事案にも適用される。

7　ディスクレーマ

　クレームにおいては、肯定的特徴を使って発明を特定して先行技術との差別化を図ることがほとんどであるが、場合によっては、否定的特徴によって発明をある程度は特定することも可能である。これは「ディスクレーマ」と呼ばれるもので、発明の特性を示す特徴を特定するのではなく、当該発明に該当しないものを具体的に特定する手法である。

　単純な例でいうと、肯定的特徴（例：自動車は日本製である）と否定的特徴

(e.g. the car has been made in Japan) and a negative feature (e.g. the car is not red). The claim would then read "*A Japanese car, with the proviso that the car is not red*", and the text "*… with the proviso that the car is not red*" is the disclaimer.

As will be understood, a disclaimer can of course be included in an originally filed claim; for the purpose of this chapter, we will look only at how and when a disclaimer can be introduced into a claim as an amendment.

When considering whether an amendment to introduce a disclaimer is allowable, there are three separate scenarios to consider.

7.1 Scenario 1: The Application as Filed Discloses the Preferred Absence of a Certain Feature

If the application as filed expressly discloses that a certain feature is preferably absent, then it is typically allowed to introduce a disclaimer which specifically says that the feature in question is not included. For this type of disclaimer, the amendment is treated like any other amendment and so it must simply be examined whether or not the claim including the disclaimer is "directly and unambiguously derivable" from the application as filed.

7.2 Scenario 2: The Application as Filed does not at All Mention the Feature to be Disclaimed

On the face of it one might think that it is not possible to disclaim a feature if that feature was not at all disclosed in the application as filed. However, the introduction of such disclaimers is possible under a very limited set of circumstances (see G 1/03).

According to the Enlarged Board of Appeal, a so-called undisclosed disclaimer can be used to restore novelty over a prior art document, but only if that prior

(例:自動車は赤色ではない)によって自動車を特定することができる。この場合、クレームの記載としては「日本製の自動車であって、該自動車は赤色ではない」ということになり、この「該自動車は赤色ではない」という部分がディスクレーマである。

出願当初のクレームにディスクレーマを含めることも当然に可能であるが、本章の目的上、クレームにディスクレーマを補正として導入する方法及びその時期に関してのみ検討を進めることにする。

ディスクレーマを導入する補正が認められるか否かを検討するにあたっては、想定すべきケースが3つある。

7.1　ケース1:当初の出願書類に、ある特徴の不在が好ましいものとして開示されている場合

当初の出願書類において、ある特徴が存在しないことが好ましい旨が明示的に記載されている場合、当該特徴が含まれない旨を明確に示すディスクレーマを追加することは大抵可能である。このタイプのディスクレーマの場合、当該補正は他の種類の補正と同様に扱われる。つまり単純に、当該ディスクレーマを含むクレームが当初の出願書類から「直接的かつ一義的に導き出せる」ものであるか否かについて審査される。

7.2　ケース2:当初の出願書類にディスクレーマの対象とする特徴がまったく記載されていない場合

一見したところ、当初の出願書類にまったく開示されていない特徴ならば、その特徴をディスクレーマの対象とすることは不可能だと思われるだろう。しかし、ごく一定の限られた状況においては、このようなディスクレーマを伴う補正が可能である（G 1/03参照)。

拡大審判部によると、いわゆる第54条(3)の先行技術カテゴリーに該当する先行技術文献に対して新規性を回復しようとするときには、いわゆる未開示のデ

art document falls into the so called Art. 54(3) EPC prior art category. As is explained elsewhere in this book, prior art documents in this category are other European patent applications which have an earlier filing date but a later publication date relative to the claim in question. This particular use of undisclosed disclaimers is perhaps the most frequent one. Nevertheless, disclaimers of this type should be used with caution; if a disclaimer is used incorrectly or worded wrongly, it could add matter and lead to serious validity problems. Accordingly, disclaimers of this type should only be used with caution.

A second situation where an undisclosed disclaimer could be used is to restore novelty over a pre-published prior art document, but only where the anticipation caused by the prior art is a so called "accidental anticipation". Subsequent Case Law has defined what is meant by an "accidental anticipation", and it is clear now that the EPO considers this to be extremely limited. In particular, a prior art document which would be considered by the skilled person (even if it would be considered and immediately rejected, or immediately dismissed as being unhelpful) by definition cannot contain an accidental anticipation. An accidental anticipation can only take place in a document which would not at all have been considered by the skilled person; this is of course very rare in practice, as it would require the prior art document to be in a completely different field.

A third situation where an undisclosed disclaimer could be used is to remove subject-matter which is non-patentable for non-technical reasons; for example, if a claim encompasses both, excluded (methods of treatment) and non-excluded (cosmetic methods), it would be possible to use a disclaimer to make it clear that the claim covers only the cosmetic uses.

When an undisclosed disclaimer is used, there are various conditions that must be complied with. The disclaimer cannot remove more than necessary, which means that if it is used for novelty purposes it must only exclude embodiments which are actually novelty-destroying. The disclaimer cannot be relevant

ィスクレーマを利用することができる。本書の第3章でも説明されているように、当該カテゴリーの先行技術文献とは、対象となるクレームに関してその出願日よりも前に出願され、かつ、該出願日以後に公開された他の欧州特許出願である。この未開示のディスクレーマは、最も頻繁に利用されているものであろう。ただし、この種のディスクレーマを利用する際には注意が必要である。ディスクレーマの文言の使い方が正しくなかったり語句の誤用があったりすると、新規事項の追加とされ、権利の有効性に深刻な問題が生じ得るからである。したがって、この種のディスクレーマは必ず慎重に用いなければならない。

未開示のディスクレーマが利用可能な2つ目の状況は、公開済の先行技術文献に対して新規性を回復しようとする場合であるが、当該先行技術が原因となる新規性喪失がいわゆる「偶発的な新規性喪失」であるときに限られる。「偶発的な新規性喪失」の意義については後続のケースローにより定義がなされているが、現在明らかなのは、欧州特許庁がこれを極めて限定的に捉えているということである。具体的には、当業者が当然考慮に入れるであろう先行技術文献（考慮されても直ちに拒絶されるか、あるいは有用でないとして直ちに却下されるようなものを含む）は、偶発的な新規性喪失を生じさせない。偶発的な新規性喪失は、当業者ならば決して考慮に入れなかったであろう文献のみにより起こる。すなわち、当該先行技術文献が完全に異なる分野に属する文献であることを要するので、当然実務上このようなケースは非常に稀である。

未開示のディスクレーマが利用可能な3つ目の状況は、非技術的な理由により特許を受けることができない対象を取り除く場合である。例えば、あるクレームに除外対象（治療方法）と非除外対象（美容方法）の両方が含まれる場合、ディスクレーマを用いることで当該クレームの範囲が美容用途に限定されるように明確にすることが可能であろう。

未開示のディスクレーマを利用するときは、様々な条件を満たす必要がある。ディスクレーマは必要以上のものを排除するものであってはならない。すなわち、もし新規性確保の目的でディスクレーマを使うのであれば、実際に新規性を否定する態様のみを除外すべきである。また、ディスクレーマは進歩性

to inventive step, and the resulting claim (including the disclaimer) must be clear.

7.3 Scenario 3: The Feature to be Disclaimed is Disclosed in the Application as Filed, but Only Positively

It is generally speaking possible to use a positive original disclosure as a basis for a negative disclaimer (see G 2/10). Thus, going back to the original disclaimer example, if the application as filed disclosed that it is preferable that the car is red, then it may be possible to expressly disclaim red cars by amendment. The Enlarged Board of Appeal did however say in their decision that a "reality check" is to be performed, and that a disclaimer of this type cannot be used if the subject-matter of the claim, once the disclaimer has been taken into account, is not directly and unambiguously derivable from the original application text. The Case Law is still currently being developed here so that amendments of this type are still controversial.

8 Rule 139 EPC and Correction of Errors

Rule 139 EPC allows for the correction of errors, e.g. linguistic errors, typing errors, and other such mistakes. Such errors may be corrected on request of the applicant, at any time while proceedings are going on at the EPO. If the request for correction relates to the application text, then the correction must be obvious to the skilled reader. This means that the EPO has to be convinced that (i) the skilled person would immediately see that there is a mistake; and (ii) the skilled person would immediately understand that nothing other than the offered correction is what was intended.

This strict test means that corrections are often difficult to carry out at the EPO.

の判断において考慮されるべきではない。さらに、当該クレーム（ディスクレーマを含むクレーム）は明確でなければならない。

7.3　ケース3：ディスクレーマによる除外の対象となる特徴が当初の出願書類に開示されているが、肯定的な開示のみである場合

原則として、出願当初の肯定的な開示をもって、否定的なディスクレーマの根拠とすることが可能である（G 2/10参照）。最初のディスクレーマの例に戻るが、もし当初の出願書類に「該自動車は赤色であることが好ましい」と記載されていた場合、ディスクレーマを用いた補正により赤色の自動車を明示的に除外できる可能性がある。ただし拡大審判部はその審決において、「現実性の確認」がなされるべきであると述べており、さらに、もしそのディスクレーマを考慮に入れたならば当該クレームの対象を当初の出願書類から直接的かつ一義的に導き出すことができないという状況下においては、この種のディスクレーマを用いることはできないと述べている。このケースローは今なお発展段階にあり、この種の補正についてはまだ議論の余地がある。

8　規則139と誤りの訂正

規則139は、誤記（例えば、言語上の誤り、タイプの誤り、その他の錯誤）の訂正を認める規定である。欧州特許庁に出願が係属中であれば、出願人の請求によりいつでもこれらの誤記を訂正することができる。誤記の訂正の請求が出願書類の記載事項に関するものである場合、その訂正は当業者から見て明白なものでなければならない。つまり、以下の点で欧州特許庁を説得しなければならない。(i)当業者であればそれが誤記であると直ちにわかること、及び、(ii)当業者であれば提示された訂正が意図していた対象以外のものに当たらないと直ちに理解できること。

このような厳格な判断基準により、欧州特許庁における誤記の訂正は容易でない場合が多い。

The European Patent Office takes the view that a correction of an error is merely declaratory in nature; in other words, it simply makes it clear to everyone what was originally meant, and as such the correction does not change the meaning of the original erroneous text.

Because corrections are generally difficult to carry out and only have a declaratory nature, there is often not a particularly high value for applicants associated with the correction of these errors, although it can only be assessed on a case-by-case basis whether it is possible and meaningful to correct a given mistake.

In practice, it is rather cumbersome to correct an error after grant unless post-grant opposition proceedings are going on at the EPO. This is because the EPO no longer considers itself to be responsible, so that the correction has to be arranged at each individual national patent office. Therefore, if an applicant notices errors in the application text and would like to correct these, it is advisable to do so before grant.

9 Conclusion

The EPO's strict approach to the assessment of added matter is a defining characteristic of European Patent Law and is a real difference with respect to e.g. Japanese practice. Because added matter is a ground of opposition, it is an issue which should be taken very seriously by applicants; in particular, it is important for applicants to understand that it is ultimately his responsibility to ensure that any amended claim presented to the EPO does not contain added matter. Even if the EPO examiner is prepared to allow a claim, this does not constitute a final decision that the claim does not contain added matter; the amended claim is still open to a legal challenge after grant by an adverse third party. For these reasons, it is extremely important for applicants to obtain careful advice from their European representatives when amending their claims.

欧州特許庁は、誤記の訂正は単なる確認的な性質を持つものだという立場をとっている。言い換えれば、誤記の訂正はもともと何を意味していたか誰が見ても明らかにするためのものであり、訂正は元の誤った記載の意味を変更するものではない。

ある誤りの訂正に関してそれが可能で有意義であるか否かは個々の事案に応じて判断するしかないが、訂正は行うのが概して容易ではなく、確認的な性質を有するものでしかないため、多くの場合、誤記の訂正は出願人にとってあまり価値がない。

特許付与後の誤記の訂正は、特許異議申立手続が欧州特許庁に係属している場合でない限り、実務上かなり面倒な手続となる。これは、特許後の訂正に関して、欧州特許庁はすでに管轄外であるという立場をとっており、当該訂正は各国の国内特許庁にて行われるべきだからである。よって、出願書類の記載上の誤りに気づいてその訂正を希望する場合は、特許付与前に訂正を行うようアドバイスする。

9　結論

新規事項追加の判断に関する欧州特許庁の厳格なアプローチは欧州特許法を特色付けるものであり、日本等における特許実務から実質的に異なる。新規事項の追加は特許異議の申立ての理由になるため、これについて出願人は極めて慎重に対処しなければならない。特に、補正されたクレームを欧州特許庁に提出する場合、それが新規事項の追加とならないよう確かめるのは最終的には出願人の責任だということを、出願人自身が理解しておくことが重要である。欧州特許庁の審査官が、補正されたクレームを許可する意向を示したとしても、それが新規事項の追加でないとする最終的な決定となるわけではない。その補正されたクレームは、特許付与後に敵対する第三者から法的なチャレンジを受ける危険がある。このため、クレームを補正する際には欧州代理人に慎重なアドバイスを求めることが極めて重要になる。

To the extent that Japanese applicants file PCT applications with the intention of entering the European Regional Phase, it also makes sense to draft these applications bearing in mind some of the amendment difficulties which are often encountered in Europe. In particular, it makes sense to foreshadow strong fallback positions especially by disclosing preferred features in preferred combinations. It also makes sense to look carefully at the examples in the application text, and to consider adding some further description text highlighting key elements or key features of the examples to allow these to be used more conveniently for amendment.

日本の出願人が PCT 出願をする場合であって、それを欧州段階に移行する意図があるときは、欧州において頻繁に直面する補正の制限を念頭に置いて出願書類を起案したほうがよい。具体的には補正の根拠となる代替案となるものを記載しておいたほうがよく、そのためには、好ましい特徴を好ましい組合せで記載しておくとよい。また、出願書類のなかでも実施例の記載を慎重に検討し、実施例中の重要な構成要件や重要な特徴を強調する記載を明細書中にさらに加えることで、それらを補正に利用しやすいよう配慮しておくことが賢明である。

Chapter 13

Remedies

救済

Matthias Kindler

▶ 欧州特許条約には、手続の続行（第121条）と権利の回復（第122条）という2種類の救済措置があります（§1）。

▶ 手続の続行（第121条）は、出願手続について設定又は指定された期間を遵守することができなかった場合、理由のいかんにかかわらず、利用できる救済手段です（§2）。ほとんどの出願手続について「手続の続行」を請求することができますが、この規定により救済を受けることができないものは第121条(4)に限定列挙されています（§2.2）。手続の続行が請求できるものの具体例を§2.3で挙げています。PCT 出願の欧州段階移行期限、調査段階で発行された見解書への応答期間、審査部から発行された庁通知への応答期間を遵守できなかったときにも「手続の続行」を請求することができます。「手続の続行」の請求は、規則135の要件を満たせば、理由のいかんにかかわらず認められますので、救済手段であるだけでなく、費用を伴う期間延長の手段とも考えられます。

▶ 権利の回復（第122条）は、非常に限られた場合にその請求が認められます。この点は、日本で最近導入された実務に似ています。

▶ 欧州特許庁に日本語で直接に出願をする場合や、日本語で PCT を出願をして欧州段階へ移行する際に必要とされる翻訳文が期間内に提出されないときは、手続の続行は認められておらず、規則58の通知により翻訳文提出期限が設定されるという独自の救済規定が設けられています（§2.2及び§2.3）。

1 Area of Application

In case the applicant or proprietor has failed to observe a time limit vis-à-vis the European Patent Office (EPO), the European Patent Convention (EPC) offers the remedies of

- **Further Processing** under Article 121 in connection with Rule 135, and of

- **Re-establishment of Rights** under Article 122 in connection with Rule 136.

The requirements and procedures in connection with these remedies will be summarized and discussed in the following. Further information may be found in the EPO Examination Guidelines (Guidelines E-VII 2).

As a remark, the pendency of an application does not constitute a time limit in the sense of Article 121 or 122 EPC. This means that for the late filing of a divisional application, with the parent application no longer pending, these remedies are not available.

Furthermore, the fixed date of oral proceedings does not represent a time limit, either. Thus, the remedies are not applicable in case the applicant or proprietor failed to attend the oral proceedings.

2 Further Processing

2.1 General Outline

According to Article 121(1), an applicant who fails to observe a time limit vis-à-vis the EPO may request further processing of the European patent application.

1　救済の適用対象

出願人又は特許権者が欧州特許庁に対して手続期間を遵守することができなかった場合、欧州特許条約の定めにより以下の救済を受けることができる。

- **手続の続行**：第121条及び関連規定である規則135

- **権利の回復**：第122条及び関連規定である規則136

以下、これら救済規定の要件やその手続について簡単にまとめながら議論していく。なお、詳細な情報については欧州特許庁審査基準（審査基準 E-VII 2）を参照されたい。

まず注意事項として、出願の「係属」は、第121条又は第122条にいう「期間」には該当しない。つまり、親出願がもはや係属しておらず、分割出願の提出が遅れた場合には、これらの規定による救済を利用することができない。

また、口頭審理の指定期日もこの「期間」には当たらない。よって、これらの規定による救済は、出願人又は特許権者が口頭審理に出席できなかった場合には適用されない。

2　手続の続行

2.1　概要

第121条(1)の規定により、出願人は、欧州特許庁に対して手続期間を遵守することができなかった場合、欧州特許出願について手続の続行を請求すること

This implies that the procedure of further processing is only available in examination proceedings.

The general outline of the procedure can be summarized as follows. If the applicant has failed to observe a time limit, the EPO issues a Communication under Rule 112 EPC, notifying the applicant of the loss of rights and the respective legal consequences. The loss of rights is not limited to a lapse (deemed withdrawal) or refusal of the application as a whole, but may also be a merely partial loss of rights (e.g., loss of claims for which no claim fees have been paid).

In reply to this Communication, the applicant may request further processing. The requirements for the request are stipulated in Rule 135 EPC:

- The request has to be filed within a time limit of two months of the Communication.

- A respective fee for further processing has to be paid.

- The omitted act (e.g., filing of a response, payment of fees) has to be completed within the time limit for making the request.

In case the omitted act is the filing of a response to an Official Action, then the completion of the omitted act requires the filing of a substantive response. Merely filing e.g., a request for term extension or a request for oral proceedings does not satisfy the requirements of Rule 135 EPC (see J 16/92).

The fee for further processing is stipulated in Art. 2(12) of the Rules relating to Fees. In case of a late payment of fees, the fee for further processing corresponds to a surcharge of 50% of the relevant fee; otherwise it is a fixed amount of presently 250 EUR.

If the requirements are met, then the EPO grants the request for further pro-

ができる。出願手続においてのみ手続の続行が可能だということである。

当該手続は、以下のとおり概略される。出願人が手続期間を遵守することができなかった場合、欧州特許庁は規則112の通知を発行し、権利の喪失及びそれに伴う法的効力について出願人に知らせる。権利の喪失には、出願全体の失効（みなし取下げ）や拒絶に限られず、権利の一部喪失（例えば、クレーム料の不足により一部のクレームが失われた場合）も含まれる。

この通知に対する応答として、出願人は手続の続行を請求することができる。請求の要件については、規則135において以下のように定められている。

- 庁通知から2月以内に当該請求をしなければならない。

- 手続の続行に係る所定の手数料を納付しなければならない。

- 遺漏した手続（例えば、応答書の提出や料金の納付）を、当該請求期間内に完了させなければならない。

例えば、「遺漏した手続」が「庁通知に対する応答書の提出」である場合、遺漏した手続の完了のためには、実体的内容の応答書を提出する必要がある。期間延長請求や口頭審理の請求を単にするだけでは、規則135に規定される要件を満たすことにはならない（J 16/92参照）。

手続の続行に係る手数料は、手数料に関する規則の第2条(12)に定められている。料金の遅延支払いの場合、手続の続行のための手数料は、規定手数料の50％増の額となる。それ以外の場合は、現時点では一律250ユーロとなっている。

各要件が満たされれば、欧州特許庁は、手続の続行についての請求を許可す

cessing. The legal effect of the granted request is that the legal consequences of the failure to observe the time limit are deemed not to have ensued (Art. 121(3)).

In practice, the option of further processing may not only be used as a remedy for accidentally missed time limits in examination proceedings, but also as a two-month term extension with costs.

2.2 Exceptions for Which No Further Processing is Available

Generally, the procedure of further processing is applicable to most time limits in connection with the patent application, except those laid down in Article 121(4) and Rule 135(2).

The exceptions in Article 121(4) are those which are particularly relevant in view of legal certainty, and include the 12 month priority term (Art. 87(1)), the appeal term (Art. 108) and the time limit for the petition for review (Art. 112a), and, of course, the time limits for requesting further processing itself and for requesting a re-establishment of rights. Re-establishment of rights may be possible for these time limits under certain conditions (except, of course, the time limit for re-establishment of rights itself).

Most exceptions of Rule 135(2) refer to time limits, for which the EPC already provides a separate remedy on its own, so that further processing is not required:

- Rule 6(1) and Rule 36(2): Term for filing the translation of the European patent application or the divisional application, if the application has not been filed in an Official Language (English, French or German); If these time limits are not met, then the EPO will issue an invitation under Rule 58 EPC to file the missing translation within a period of two months.

- Rule 40(3): Term for filing a certified copy of the application documents

る。請求が許可された場合の法的効力は、手続期間の不遵守により発生した法的結論が生じなかったものとみなされることである（第121条(3)）。

手続の続行の規定は、実務においては、出願段階の手続期間を意図せずに徒過してしまった場合の救済手段としてだけではなく、費用の支払いと引き換えに2月の追加期間を得る手段としても利用することができる。

2.2 手続の続行が適用されないもの

手続の続行は、原則的には、特許出願に関する期間のほとんどに適用されるが、例外として、第121条(4)及び規則135(2)に列挙されるものに関しては適用除外となっている。

第121条(4)で適用除外として定められているものは、特に法の確実性の観点から妥当と思われるものであり、具体的には、12月の優先期間（第87条(1)）、審判請求期間（第108条）、再審理の申請期間（第112a条）、そして当然ながら、手続の続行それ自体の請求期間や権利回復の請求期間等である。なお、これらの期間については、一定の条件を満たせば権利の回復の適用を受けることができる（ただし当然のことながら、権利の回復それ自体の請求期間は除かれる）。

規則135(2)の規定で除外されているもののほとんどは、以下に示すとおり各々対応する救済規定がすでに欧州特許条約に設けられており、手続の続行を請求する必要がないものである。

- 規則6(1)及び規則36(2)：欧州特許出願又は分割出願の際に公式言語（英語、フランス語、又はドイツ語）以外の言語で出願した場合の翻訳文提出期間。この期間を徒過した場合、2月以内に当該未提出の翻訳文を提出するよう求める規則58に基づく通知が欧州特許庁より発行される。

- 規則40(3)：欧州特許出願の際に規則40(2)に基づく先の出願についての参

if the European patent application has been filed by reference to an earlier application according to Rule 40(2). If this limit is not met, then the EPO will issue an invitation under Rule 55 EPC to file the missing translation within a period of two months.

- Rule 51(2)-(5): Terms in connection with renewal fees (as this rule provides own regulations for late paying of renewal fees).

The above-mentioned Rules 55 and 58, as well as Rules 56 and 59 relate to terms for the applicant to correct defects in the application documents and the priority terms upon invitation of the EPO, and thus already represent a remedy by themselves. Therefore, further processing is excluded.

For the time limits of Rules 62a (independent claims of the same category), 63 (incomplete search) 64 (search report in case of non-unity) and 164 (unity issues in connection with PCT applications), further processing is not available, either. Instead of seeking remedy, the applicant may either try to challenge the respective objections (e.g., of non-unity) in examination proceedings or file a divisional application.

Other exceptions, for which no further processing is available, include the time limit of Rules 16(a) (relating to entitlement issues), 31(2) (deposit of biological material) and 112(2) (requesting an appealable decision on a loss of rights).

2.3 Examples

Further processing is available for most time limits in examination proceedings, except for those relating to the formal requirements, which have their own remedies.

In case the applicant files the application, e.g, in Japanese language and fails to observe the term for submitting the translation into an Official language of the

照を含めて出願した場合の（先の）出願書類の認証謄本の提出期間。この期間を徒過した場合、2月以内に当該未提出書類を提出するよう求める規則55に基づく通知が欧州特許庁より発行される。

- 規則51(2)〜(5)：更新手数料に関する期間（この規定自体に更新手数料の期間後納付に関する取り決めが設けられている）。

上記の規則55及び58、並びに、規則56及び59は、欧州特許庁からの求めに応じて出願書類に関する不備を是正できる期間及び優先期間に関連し、これら自体がすでに救済規定となっている。よって、手続の続行が適用されない。

規則62a（同一カテゴリーに属する複数の独立クレーム）、規則63（不完全調査）、規則64（単一性欠如の場合の調査報告）、規則164（PCT出願に関する単一性欠如）に基づく期間についても、手続の続行は適用されない。これらの場合、出願人は救済を求めずとも、出願手続において各欠陥（例えば単一性欠如等）を解消するよう努めるか、あるいは分割出願をすればよい。

その他、手続の続行が適用されないものとしては、規則16(a)（権利資格の問題に関する規定）、規則31(2)（生物学的材料の寄託）及び規則112(2)（権利喪失に関し審判請求をすることができる決定の請求）の期間が挙げられる。

2.3 具体例

手続の続行は、出願段階の手続に係るほぼすべての期間に適用されるが、独自の救済規定が設けられている方式要件に関する手続については除外されている。

出願人が、例えば日本語で欧州特許出願をした場合に欧州特許庁の公式言語（英語等）による翻訳文を提出する期間を遵守できなかったときは、欧州特許

EPO (e.g. English), the EPO will issue an Invitation under Rule 58 EPC to file the translation within 2 months from the notification of said Invitation. For a failure to comply with this additional 2-month term of Rule 58, however, further processing is not available.

As regards the entry of the EP regional phase (time limit of 31 months from the priority date, according to Rule 159 EPC), further processing is available.

Turning to the initiation of the examination proceedings, the EPO sets a time limit of 6 months in the Communication under Rules 70 and 70a EPC. If the applicant fails to meet these time limits, further processing is available. However, it has to be noted that two separate time limits may be involved: The time limit of Rule 70 for requesting examination or confirming the maintenance of the application, and the time limit of Rule 70a for addressing the objections raised in the search opinion. If both are missed, two requests for further processing would be necessary, and for both, a respective fee has to be paid. This means that in case the applicant intends to maintain the application in accordance with Rule 70, but more time is required for elaborating a response to the search report in accordance with Rule 70a, it is advisable to file the confirmation to maintain the application within the term of Rule 70, and request further processing only with respect to the term of Rule 70a.

As apparent from this example, the procedure of further processing may be used not only as a remedy, but also as a kind of response term extension with costs. For instance, in examination proceedings, the EPO may refuse a request for term extension beyond 6 months, so that the application will be deemed to be withdrawn in case no response has been filed. The procedure for further processing thus offers a further two-month term for the response.

庁より規則58に基づく通知が発行され、その通知から2月以内に翻訳文を提出するよう求められる。ここで、当該規則58にいうさらなる2月の期間を徒過すると手続の続行が利用できない。

欧州領域段階への移行期間（規則159の規定による優先日から31月の期間）について、手続の続行が利用できる。

次に審査手続の開始について述べると、欧州特許庁により規則70及び70aに基づく通知にて6月の期間が設定され、出願人がこの期間を徒過した場合は、手続の続行を請求することができる。ただし、2つの別の期間が関わっているのでこの場合は注意を要する。すなわち、出願審査の請求又は出願の維持（続行）の確認に係る規則70の期間と、調査報告の否定的見解に対する応答に係る規則70aの期間である。もし両方の期間を徒過した場合、それら2つについてそれぞれ手続の続行を請求する必要があり、請求に係る手数料もそれぞれ納付しなければならない。よって、例えば規則70に対しては、出願を維持（続行）する意思を表示して応答する予定だが、規則70aに対しては、調査報告に応答するために検討する時間をさらに要するという場合には、規則70の期間内に出願を維持する意思がある旨を表示し、規則70aの期間については手続の続行を請求することが望ましい。

この例からもわかるとおり、手続の続行は救済手段であるだけでなく、費用は伴うものの、一種の応答期間延長の手段にもなり得る。例えば、審査手続において6月を超える期間延長の請求は欧州特許庁により却下される可能性があるうえ、これに対しなんら応答手続を行わなかった場合にはその出願は取り下げられたものとみなされるが、このとき手続の続行請求を行うことで、その応答について2月の期間をさらに得ることができる。

3 Re-Establishment of Rights

3.1 General Outline

The second, more complex remedy offered by the EPC is the re-establishment of rights pursuant to Article 122 and Rule 136 EPC.

According to Article 122(1) EPC, the remedy is available to both <u>applicants and proprietors</u>, who <u>in spite of all due care</u> required by the circumstances having been taken, were <u>unable to observe a time limit</u> vis-à-vis the European Patent Office, if the non-observance of this time limit has the <u>direct consequence</u> of causing the refusal of the European patent application or of a request, or the deeming of the application to have been withdrawn, or the revocation of the European patent, or the loss of any other right or means of redress.

The time limits set by the Opposition Division, e.g., for filing a response to a notice of opposition, do not have these direct consequences, so that a re-establishment of rights is not possible for these time limits.

As regards the applicable time limits, a re-establishment of rights is only available for those time limits for which no further processing is available (Rule 136(3)). Furthermore, re-establishment of rights is not applicable in case the missed time limit is the time limit for requesting re-establishment of rights itself (Art. 122(4)). As a corollary, this means that if the above-discussed time limit for requesting further processing has been missed, re-establishment of rights is available.

The time limit and the requirements for requesting a re-establishment of rights are stipulated in Rule 136:

- The time limit for the request for re-establishment of rights generally is two months of the removal of the cause of non-compliance with the period,

3 　権利の回復

3.1 　概要

　欧州特許条約における２つ目の救済手段は第122条及び規則136に基づく権利の回復であるが、これはさらに複雑である。

　第122条(1)の規定によると、当該救済は出願人及び特許権者の両者に利用可能であり、状況によって必要とされる相当の注意を払ったにもかかわらず、欧州特許庁に対し手続期間を遵守することができなかった場合に、その期間の不遵守による直接の結果として、欧州特許出願若しくは請求が拒絶され、その出願は取り下げたものとみなされ、欧州特許が取り消され、又はその他の権利若しくは救済手段が喪失したときに利用される。

　なお、異議部により設定される期間（例えば、特許異議申立書に対する答弁書提出の期間）は、上記の直接の結果を有しないので、権利の回復は適用されない。

　適用可能な期間について述べると、手続の続行を利用できない期間のみが権利の回復の対象となり得る（規則136(3)）。権利の回復の請求期間そのものを徒過した場合には、その期間について権利回復の適用を受けることはできない（第122条(4)）。当然の結果として、先に挙げた手続の続行を請求するための期間を徒過した場合には、権利の回復が利用できる。

　権利の回復を請求するための期間及びその要件は規則136に定められているが、以下にこれをまとめる。

－　権利の回復を請求するための期間は、原則として、期間不遵守の理由の除去から２月以内で不遵守期間の経過から遅くとも１年以内である。

but at the latest within one year of expiry of the unobserved time limit.

- In case the request for re-establishment of rights concerns the priority term (Art. 87(1)) or the time limit for the petition for review (Art. 112a), then the request has to be filed within 2 months of the expiry of the period.

- An official fee has to be paid (Rules relating to Fees, Art. 2(13), presently 635 EUR).

- The omitted act has to be completed; and

- The request has to include the grounds on which it is based and the facts on which it is based. This means, in particular, that it has to be substantiated that the failure to observe the time limit occurred in spite of all due care.

If these requirements are met and the EPO is satisfied that the failure occurred in spite of all due care, the request will be granted, which again has the legal effect that the legal consequences of the failure to observe the time limit are deemed not to have ensued (Art. 122(3)).

3.2 Deposition of Biological Material

Rule 31(2) is exempted from further processing, and is not explicitly mentioned among the exempted time limits for re-establishment of rights. Still, a re-establishment of rights is not possible for Rule 31(2) in view of the requirement of sufficiency of the disclosure.

In summary, Rule 31 requires that a sample of the biological material has been duly deposited no later than the filing date, and the respective time limits of Rule 31(2) are intended for ensuring that the relevant deposit information has been communicated to the EPO before the publication of the application (or earli-

- 優先期間（第87条(1)）又は再審理の申請期間（第112a条）に関して権利の回復を請求する場合は、その期間の終了から2月以内に請求書を提出しなければならない。

- 庁手数料を納付しなければならない（手数料に関する規則の第2条(13)、現時点では635ユーロ）。

- 遺漏が生じた手続を完了させなければならない。

- 請求書には、その根拠となる理由及びそれが依拠する事実を記載しなければならない。具体的には、あらゆる相当の注意をしたにもかかわらず期間を遵守できなかったことを立証しなければならない。

上記の要件が満たされており、かつ、相当の注意をしたにもかかわらず期間を遵守できなかったものと欧州特許庁により認められた場合は、当該請求が許可される。その法的効力は、手続続行の場合と同様、期間の不遵守により発生した法的結論が生じなかったものとみなされることである（第122条(3)）。

3.2 生物学的材料の寄託

規則31(2)は手続続行の規定においては除外されており、権利回復の規定においては除外する期間として明記されていない。しかし、規則31(2)は実施可能要件に関するものであるという観点から、権利の回復は適用されない。

手短にいえば、規則31は生物学的材料のサンプルを出願日以前に寄託することを求めるものであり、規則31(2)における各期限は、該当する寄託情報を出願の公開前に（あるいは書類閲覧権が存在する場合はより早い段階で）欧州特許庁に知らせることを目的として定められたものである。

er in case there exists a right for file inspection).

As explained in the reasons explained in the Notice of the EPO in published in the Official Journal 10/2010, page 498, compliance with Rule 31 is crucial in connection with sufficiency of the disclosure, which must be established at the filing date and cannot be remedied at a later stage. Section 3.10 of said notice states:

> *"Consequence of the failure to comply with the requirements of Rule 31 EPC, on the contrary, is that the biological material cannot be considered as having been disclosed pursuant to Article 83 EPC by way of reference to the deposit (see Guidelines C-II 6.3). The information provided for in Rule 31(1) (c) and, where applicable, (d) EPC may not be submitted after expiry of the time limit set out in Rule 31(2) EPC since the time limit under Rule 31(2) EPC is excluded from further processing by Rule 135(2) EPC and because <u>a lack of disclosure cannot be remedied by way of re-establishment under Article 122</u> EPC (see G 2/93, op. cit.)."*

As a result, despite the fact that it is not mentioned in Article 122 or Rule 136, re-establishment of rights for the time limit of 31(2) EPC is not possible in view of the fact that the sufficiency of the disclosure must be established at the filing date.

3.3 Opposition Proceedings

The wording of Article 122 only applies to applicants and proprietors, not to opponents. Thus, for the opponent, no remedy is available in case the opponent failed to observe the opposition term or the opposition appeal term.

However, the Enlarged Board of Appeal has created an exception for the filing of the Grounds for Appeal (G 1/86). This was justified, inter alia, by the principle

欧州特許庁の公報（2010年10月号、498頁）では、規則31の遵守は実施可能要件との関連で重要なものであって、この要件は出願日の時点で満たされているべきものであり、後からその不備について救済を受けることはできないと理由が述べられている。官報のセクション3.10の記述を以下に示す。

「一方、規則31の要件を満たしていない場合は、当該生物学的材料について、寄託の参照をもって第83条の規定に基づく開示がなされたものとはみなされない（審査基準 C-II 6.3参照）。ここで、規則31(2)の期間は規則135(2)の規定により手続続行の適用対象から除外されており、また<u>実施可能要件に関しては第122条に基づく権利の回復による救済の対象とならない</u>ため、規則31(1)(c)、及び該当する場合は規則31(1)(d)に規定する情報については、規則31(2)に定める期間の満了後に提出することはできない（G 2/93, op. cit. 参照）。」

よって、第122条又は規則136のいずれにも明記されていないが、実施可能要件は出願日の時点で満たされているべきという観点から、規則31(2)に係る期間については権利回復の適用を受けることができない。

3.3　特許異議申立手続

第122条に規定する文言は出願人及び特許権者にのみ適用されるものであり、特許異議申立人には適用されない。よって、申立人は、特許異議申立期間や特許異議申立てに係る審判を請求するための期間を遵守できなかった場合は、救済を受けることができない。

ただし、拡大審判部の決定により、審判請求の理由書の提出に関しては例外とされている（G 1/86）。これは、裁判の手続を行うすべての者に、手続上同

that all parties to proceedings before a court must be accorded the same procedural rights.

3.4 Substantiation of the Request

The substantiation of the request pursuant to Rule 136(2) must conclusively set out all grounds and facts on which the case relies. The factual basis cannot be altered after expiry of the time limit. A request for re-establishment of rights which relies on general statements only and contains no specific facts does not satisfy the requirement for a duly substantiated request (J 15/10).

Specifically, J 15/10 states that the request for re-establishment of rights must set forth the precise cause of non-compliance with the time limit concerned (i.e. a fact or obstacle preventing the required action within the time limit), specify at what time and under which circumstances the cause occurred and was removed, and present the core facts making it possible to consider whether all due care required by the circumstances had been taken to comply with the time limit concerned.

It is not sufficient to file merely general statements without concrete facts identifying the reasons and the chronological sequence of events which lead to the non-compliance (J 19/05). Filing an insufficiently substantiated request and a second submission with further substantiation is only acceptable if the second submission is still within the time limit (T 287/84). While all facts have to be brought forward within the time limit, it may be possible to file evidence for the facts at a later stage (T 324/90).

3.5 Time Limit for the Request

The time limit of Rule 136(1) is generally within two months of the removal of the cause of non-compliance with the period, but at the latest within one year of expiry of the unobserved time limit.

等の権利が与えられなければならないという原則に則ったものである。

3.4 請求の理由

規則136(2)によるところの請求の理由においては、当該事件が依拠する理由及び事実のすべてを明確に記載しなければならない。根拠事実は、請求期間の経過後は変更することができない。権利回復請求の根拠として一般的事項のみが記載されており、具体的事実が記載されていない場合、その請求は十分に立証されているとはいえず、当該規則の要件を満たさない（J 15/10）。

具体的には、J 15/10によれば、権利回復請求書には該当する期間を遵守できなかった原因（すなわち、請求期間内に必要な手続を行うことを妨げた事実又は障害）を詳細に記載し、いつどのような状況でその原因が発生し、またそれが除去されたのかを明確にし、さらに、その期間を遵守するために状況により必要とされる相当の注意が払われていたか否かの判断を可能にするような核心的事実を示す必要がある。

不遵守に至った理由の時系列的な事象を特定する具体的事実を記載することなく、一般的事項のみを記載して提出するだけでは不十分である（J 19/05）。理由が不十分に記載された請求書を提出した後に、追って理由を補充する書面を提出する場合、これが認められるのは後者の提出も請求期間内に行われる場合のみである（T 287/84）。すべての事実を請求期間内に提出する必要があるが、その事実に関する証拠については後日提出することができることもある（T 324/90）。

3.5 請求期間

規則136(1)に基づく期間は、原則として、手続期間を遵守しなかった理由がなくなった日から2月以内で不遵守となった期間が経過した後1年以内に限られる。

The cause of non-compliance and the removal thereof is a matter of fact which has to be determined in consideration of the merits of the individual case (J 27/90).

Often, the cause of non-compliance involves some error in the carrying out of the party's intention to comply with the time limit. The party does not then realize that the error has occurred, and that the time limit has not been complied with, until this fact has been brought to his attention (J 29/86). In these cases, the relevant date of removal of the cause of non-compliance is the day, on which said fact is brought to the party's attention, e.g., by the receipt of a respective Official Communication, so that the person responsible for the application or the patent should have discovered the error.

The date of actual receipt of the communication is of relevance, not the date of the deemed notification, e.g., pursuant to Rule 126(2) EPC (i.e., date of the communication plus 10 days) (J 7/82).

The relevant date is usually the date on which the communication is received by the responsible person, who generally is either the applicant himself or the authorized representative. If the applicant instructs the authorized representative not to pass on any further communication from the EPO (here: to a computerized service firm for renewal fee payment), then the applicant cannot rely on the fact that information notified to the authorized representative and necessary for continuing the proceedings was lacking (J 27/90).

Under exceptional circumstances, the cause for non-compliance with a time limit may be constituted by financial difficulties (J 22/88).

3.6 Due Care

The condition of "all due care required by the circumstances" has been subject to numerous decisions of the Boards of Appeal of the EPO. Generally, it is

不遵守の理由及びその除去は、個々の事件の具体的事情を勘案して認定されるべき事項である（J 27/90）。

不遵守の理由は当事者が期間を遵守しようとしてその意図することを実行する過程で起こるなんらかの過失を伴うものが多い。そうすると、当事者は、過失が発生したことにも、期間を徒過したということにも気づかず、指摘されてはじめてその事実を知ることになる（J 29/86）。このようなケースでは、「不遵守の理由が除去された日」に該当するのは、例えばその件に関して特許庁から通知を受けて当事者がその事実に気づき、それにより当該出願又は特許の責任者がその過失を認識すべき状態になった日である。

重要になるのは通知を実際に受けた日であって、例えば、規則126(2)の通知のみなし配達日（すなわち郵送日から10日目）はこれに該当しない（J 7/82）。

該当日となるのは、通常、責任者である者、原則として出願人本人又は授権代理人が通知を受けた日である。出願人が授権代理人に対し今後特許庁からの通知は転送不要と指示していた場合（この件の代理人は更新手数料納付を請け負う電子処理型の業者である）、情報の通知が授権代理人に対してなされたために手続を進めるのに必要な情報を欠いていたということを根拠とする出願人の主張は認められない（J 27/90）。

特別な事情の下では、経済的困窮が「期間不遵守の理由」を構成する場合もある（J 22/88）。

3.6 相当の注意

「状況によって必要とされる相当の注意」という条件に関しては、欧州特許庁審判部による多くの審決がこれを論点としている。原則として、各事案にお

necessary to consider the specific circumstances and the merits of each case (T 287/84). Pursuant to T 30/90, "all due care" means the standard of care that the notional reasonably competent patentee, applicant or representative would employ in the relevant circumstances. According to T 1289/10, this also takes into account the known problems associated with the procedure and known solutions how to avoid them.

For the normal case where the cause of non-compliance with a time limit involves some error in the carrying out of the party's intention to comply with the time limit, due care is considered to have been taken if non-compliance with the time limit results either from exceptional circumstances or from an isolated mistake within a normally satisfactory monitoring system (J 2/86, J 3/86).

Exceptional circumstances may include force majeure, unforeseeable errors in the course of organizational upheaval or restructuring, sudden illness, and others. Generally, the exceptional circumstances need to be explained, and it has to be substantiated why these circumstances lead to an accidental failure to comply with the time limit.

For substantiating that there was an isolated mistake in an normally satisfactory monitoring system, it firstly is required to plausibly show that the system for monitoring time limits existed at the relevant time, normally operated reliably, and included appropriate safety measures, cross-checks, etc., in order to comply with the requirements.

The criterion of due care has to be met by the responsible person, which is the applicant or the appointed representative. If the responsible person entrusts tasks to an assistant (e.g., an employee), and the error was caused by the assistant, the responsible person has to establish that the assistant was reasonably selected, instructed and supervised.

ける個別の状況や具体的事情を勘案する必要がある（T 287/84）。T 30/90によると、「相当の注意」とは、該当する状況において概念上の一般的能力を有する特許権者、出願人又は代理人に期待される注意水準をいう。また、T 1289/10によると、該手続に関する既知の問題やそれを回避するための既知の解決手段も考慮するものとしている。

　期間不遵守の理由がなんらかの過失を伴うものであり、当事者が期間を遵守しようとしていてこの過失が発生したという通常のケースにおいては、当該期間不遵守が特別な事情により生じたものであるか、あるいは通常であれば十分に機能する管理システムの下で起こった異例のミスにより生じたものである場合には、相当の注意が払われていたものとみなされる（J 2/86、J 3/86）。

　特別な事情に当たるものとしては、不可抗力、組織の変動や再編に伴う予見不可能なエラー、急病などが挙げられる。原則として、特別な事情がある場合はこれを説明する必要があり、その事情が意図せぬ期限徒過につながってしまったという理由を十分に説明しなければならない。

　通常であれば十分に機能する管理システム下において異例のミスが生じたことを立証するには、まずその期限管理システムが該当する時点で存在しており、通常は確実に運用されていたこと、必要事項を遵守するために適切な安全対策やダブルチェック等が実施されていたこと等を説得できるように示す必要がある。

　「相当の注意」の基準を満たすべき者は、責任者であり、それは出願人又は指定代理人である。責任者が業務を補助者（従業員等）に行わせている場合であって、生じた過失が補助者によるものであったときは、当該補助者が適切に選任され、指示され、かつ、監督されていたことを責任者が立証しなければならない。

Part *III*

Procedures after Grant

特許付与後の手続

Legal Text

Article 68 Effect of revocation or limitation of the European patent

The European patent application and the resulting European patent shall be deemed not to have had, from the outset, the effects specified in Articles 64 and 67, to the extent that the patent has been revoked or limited in opposition, limitation or revocation proceedings.

Article 99 Opposition

(1) Within nine months of the publication of the mention of the grant of the European patent in the European Patent Bulletin, any person may give notice to the European Patent Office of opposition to that patent, in accordance with the Implementing Regulations. Notice of opposition shall not be deemed to have been filed until the opposition fee has been paid.

(2) The opposition shall apply to the European patent in all the Contracting States in which that patent has effect.

(3) Opponents shall be parties to the opposition proceedings as well as the proprietor of the patent.

(4) Where a person provides evidence that in a Contracting State, following a final decision, he has been entered in the patent register of such State instead of the previous proprietor, such person shall, at his request, replace the previous proprietor in respect of such State. Notwithstanding Article 118, the previous proprietor and the person making the request shall not be regarded as joint proprietors unless both so request.

法規

第68条　欧州特許の取消し又は限定の効果

　　欧州特許出願及びその結果として生ずる欧州特許は、第64条及び第67条に定められる効果については、特許異議の申立て、限定又は取消しの手続において特許が取り消され又は限定された範囲においてはじめから存在しなかったものとみなす。

第99条　特許異議の申立て

(1)　何人も、欧州特許を付与する旨が欧州特許公報に掲載された後9月以内に限り、欧州特許庁に、施行規則に従って、その特許に対する異議を申し立てることができる。特許異議の申立ては、特許異議申立手数料が納付されるまでは、されたものとみなされない。

(2)　特許異議の申立ては、欧州特許が効力を有するすべての締約国における欧州特許に及ぶ。

(3)　特許異議申立人は、特許権者とともに特許異議申立手続の当事者となる。

(4)　ある締約国において、いずれかの者が最終決定に従い、前特許権者に代わり当該締約国の特許原簿に記録されたときは、その者は、請求により、当該締約国に関し、前特許権者に代わる。第118条の規定にかかわらず、前特許権者及び当該請求をする者は、双方の請求がない限り、特許権の共有者とはみなされない。

Article 100 Grounds for opposition

Opposition may only be filed on the grounds that:

(a) the subject-matter of the European patent is not patentable under Articles 52 to 57;

(b) the European patent does not disclose the invention in a manner sufficiently clear and complete for it to be carried out by a person skilled in the art;

(c) the subject-matter of the European patent extends beyond the content of the application as filed, or, if the patent was granted on a divisional application or on a new application filed under Article 61, beyond the content of the earlier application as filed.

Article 101 Examination of the opposition
– Revocation or maintenance of the European patent

(1) If the opposition is admissible, the Opposition Division shall examine, in accordance with the Implementing Regulations, whether at least one ground for opposition under Article 100 prejudices the maintenance of the European patent. During this examination, the Opposition Division shall invite the parties, as often as necessary, to file observations on communications from another party or issued by itself.

(2) If the Opposition Division is of the opinion that at least one ground for opposition prejudices the maintenance of the European patent, it shall revoke the patent. Otherwise, it shall reject the opposition.

(3) If the Opposition Division is of the opinion that, taking into consider-

第100条　特許異議の申立ての理由

特許異議の申立ては、次のいずれかの理由に基づいてすることができる。

(a)　欧州特許の対象が第52条から第57条の規定により特許を受けることができないとき

(b)　欧州特許が、その技術分野の専門家が実施することができる程度に明確かつ十分に、その発明を開示していないとき

(c)　欧州特許の対象がその出願の出願時の内容を超えているとき、又は、欧州特許が分割出願について若しくは第61条に規定する新たな出願について付与された場合において先の出願の出願時の内容を超えているとき

第101条　特許異議の申立ての審査
　　　　　—欧州特許の取消し又は維持

(1)　特許異議の申立てが受理された場合には、異議部は、施行規則に従って、第100条に定める特許異議の申立ての理由の少なくとも1つが欧州特許の維持を妨げるか否かを審査する。審査の過程で、異議部は、当事者らに対し、必要に応じて何度でも、他の当事者からの又は異議部が発した通知について意見書を提出するよう求める。

(2)　異議部は、特許異議の申立ての理由の少なくとも1つによって、欧州特許を維持することができないと認める場合には、特許を取り消す。その他の場合には、特許異議の申立てを棄却する。

(3)　異議部は、特許異議申立手続において特許権者がした補正を考慮したう

ation the amendments made by the proprietor of the European patent during the opposition proceedings, the patent and the invention to which it relates

(a) meet the requirements of this Convention, it shall decide to maintain the patent as amended, provided that the conditions laid down in the Implementing Regulations are fulfilled;

(b) do not meet the requirements of this Convention, it shall revoke the patent.

Article 103 Publication of a new specification of the European patent

If the European patent is maintained as amended under Article 101, paragraph 3(a), the European Patent Office shall publish a new specification of the European patent as soon as possible after the mention of the opposition decision has been published in the European Patent Bulletin.

Article 105 Intervention of the assumed infringer

(1) Any third party may, in accordance with the Implementing Regulations, intervene in opposition proceedings after the opposition period has expired, if the third party proves that

(a) proceedings for infringement of the same patent have been instituted against him, or

(b) following a request of the proprietor of the patent to cease alleged infringement, the third party has instituted proceedings for a ruling that he is not infringing the patent.

(2) An admissible intervention shall be treated as an opposition.

えで、以下の決定をする。

(a) 特許及びそれに係る発明が本条約の要件を満たしていると認める場合には、施行規則に定める要件が満たされていることを条件として、その特許を補正された形式で維持する。

(b) 特許及びそれに係る発明が本条約の要件を満たしていないと認める場合には、その特許を取り消す。

第103条　新たな欧州特許明細書の発行

欧州特許庁は、第101条(3)(a)の規定により欧州特許が補正された形式で維持されたときは、特許異議の申立てに関する決定の旨が欧州特許公報に掲載された後、速やかに新たな欧州特許明細書を発行する。

第105条　侵害者とされた者の参加

(1) いかなる第三者も、次のことを証明する場合には、特許異議申立期間が経過した後、施行規則に従って、特許異議申立手続に参加することができる。

(a) 同一の特許についての侵害訴訟がその者に対して提起されたこと、又は

(b) 特許権者が被疑侵害行為を停止するよう請求した後に、当該第三者が当該特許を侵害していないとの判決を求める訴訟を提起したこと

(2) 参加の申請が受理されると、当該参加は、特許異議の申立てとして取り

Article 105a Request for limitation or revocation

(1) At the request of the proprietor, the European patent may be revoked or be limited by an amendment of the claims. The request shall be filed with the European Patent Office in accordance with the Implementing Regulations. It shall not be deemed to have been filed until the limitation or revocation fee has been paid.

(2) The request may not be filed while opposition proceedings in respect of the European patent are pending.

Article 105b Limitation or revocation of the European patent

(1) The European Patent Office shall examine whether the requirements laid down in the Implementing Regulations for limiting or revoking the European patent have been met.

(2) If the European Patent Office considers that the request for limitation or revocation of the European patent meets these requirements, it shall decide to limit or revoke the European patent in accordance with the Implementing Regulations. Otherwise, it shall reject the request.

(3) The decision to limit or revoke the European patent shall apply to the European patent in all the Contracting States in respect of which it has been granted. It shall take effect on the date on which the mention of the decision is published in the European Patent Bulletin.

扱われる。

第105a 条　限定又は取消しの請求

(1) 特許権者は、請求により、欧州特許を取り消すことができ又はクレームの補正をして欧州特許を限定することができる。その請求は、施行規則に従って、欧州特許庁にする。限定又は取消しの請求は、限定又は取消しのための手数料が納付されるまでは、されたものとみなされない。

(2) この請求は、特許異議申立手続が欧州特許庁に係属している間はすることができない。

第105b 条　欧州特許の限定又は取消し

(1) 欧州特許庁は、欧州特許の限定又は取消しについて、施行規則に定める要件が満たされているか否かを審査する。

(2) 欧州特許庁は、限定又は取消しの請求が上記の要件を満たしていると認める場合は、施行規則に従って、その欧州特許を限定し又は取り消す決定をする。その他の場合には、当該請求を棄却する。

(3) 欧州特許を限定し又は取り消す決定は、その付与の対象となっているすべての締約国における欧州特許に適用される。当該決定は、欧州特許公報にその旨が掲載された日に効力を生じる。

Article 105c Publication of the amended specification of the European patent

If the European patent is limited under Article 105b, paragraph 2, the European Patent Office shall publish the amended specification of the European patent as soon as possible after the mention of the limitation has been published in the European Patent Bulletin.

Article 106 Decisions subject to appeal

(1) An appeal shall lie from decisions of the Receiving Section, Examining Divisions, Opposition Divisions and the Legal Division. It shall have suspensive effect.

(2) A decision which does not terminate proceedings as regards one of the parties can only be appealed together with the final decision, unless the decision allows a separate appeal.

(3) The right to file an appeal against decisions relating to the apportionment or fixing of costs in opposition proceedings may be restricted in the Implementing Regulations.

Article 107 Persons entitled to appeal and to be parties to appeal proceedings

Any party to proceedings adversely affected by a decision may appeal. Any other parties to the proceedings shall be parties to the appeal proceedings as of right.

Article 108 Time limit and form

Notice of appeal shall be filed, in accordance with the Implementing

第105c条　補正された欧州特許明細書の発行

　欧州特許庁は、第105b条(2)の規定により欧州特許が限定された場合には、その旨が欧州特許公報に掲載された後、速やかに、補正された欧州特許明細書を発行する。

第106条　審判に服する決定

(1)　受理課、審査部、異議部及び法律部の決定に対しては審判を請求することができる。審判の請求は、執行停止の効力を有する。

(2)　当事者の一方について手続を終了させない決定に対しては、その決定により別個に審判の請求ができる場合を除き、最終決定に対する請求とともにのみ審判を請求することができる。

(3)　特許異議申立手続の費用の分担又は確定に関する決定に対して審判を請求する権利は、施行規則によって制限される。

第107条　審判を請求することができる者及び審判手続の
　　　　　当事者となれる者

　手続に関与した者であって決定によって不利な影響を受けた者は、審判を請求することができる。当該手続の他の当事者は、当然に審判手続の当事者となる。

第108条　期限と方式

　審判を請求するときは、審判の請求に係る決定の通知の日から2月以内

Regulations, at the European Patent Office within two months of notification of the decision. Notice of appeal shall not be deemed to have been filed until the fee for appeal has been paid. Within four months of notification of the decision, a statement setting out the grounds of appeal shall be filed in accordance with the Implementing Regulations.

Article 110   Examination of appeals

If the appeal is admissible, the Board of Appeal shall examine whether the appeal is allowable. The examination of the appeal shall be conducted in accordance with the Implementing Regulations.

Article 111   Decision in respect of appeals

(1)   Following the examination as to the allowability of the appeal, the Board of Appeal shall decide on the appeal. The Board of Appeal may either exercise any power within the competence of the department which was responsible for the decision appealed or remit the case to that department for further prosecution.

(2)   If the Board of Appeal remits the case for further prosecution to the department whose decision was appealed, that department shall be bound by the ratio decidendi of the Board of Appeal, in so far as the facts are the same. If the decision under appeal was taken by the Receiving Section, the Examining Division shall also be bound by the ratio decidendi of the Board of Appeal.

Article 112   Decision or opinion of the Enlarged Board of Appeal

(1)   In order to ensure uniform application of the law, or if a point of law of fundamental importance arises:

に、施行規則に従って、審判請求書を欧州特許庁に提出する。審判請求手数料が納付されるまでは審判の請求はされたものとみなされない。当該決定の通知の日から4月以内に、施行規則に従って、請求の理由を記載した書面を提出するものとする。

第110条　審判の請求についての審理

　　審判部は、審判の請求が適法になされたときは、審判の請求が認められるべきか否かを審理する。審判の請求についての審理は、施行規則に従って行う。

第111条　審決

(1)　審判部は、審判の請求が認められるべきか否かを審理した後に、審決する。審判部は、審判の請求に係る決定をした部課の権限範囲内における権限を行使することができ、又はさらに審理させるために事件を当該部課に差し戻すことができる。

(2)　さらに審理させるために事件が差し戻された場合において、事実関係が同一であるときは、当該部課は、審判部の審決理由に拘束される。審判の請求に係る決定が受理課によってなされた場合には、審査部も、審判部の審決理由に拘束される。

第112条　拡大審判部の審決又は意見

(1)　法律の均一な適用を確保するために、又は重要な法律問題が生じた場合において、以下の措置がある。

(a) the Board of Appeal shall, during proceedings on a case and either of its own motion or following a request from a party to the appeal, refer any question to the Enlarged Board of Appeal if it considers that a decision is required for the above purposes. If the Board of Appeal rejects the request, it shall give the reasons in its final decision;

(b) the President of the European Patent Office may refer a point of law to the Enlarged Board of Appeal where two Boards of Appeal have given different decisions on that question.

(2) In the cases referred to in paragraph 1(a) the parties to the appeal proceedings shall be parties to the proceedings before the Enlarged Board of Appeal.

(3) The decision of the Enlarged Board of Appeal referred to in paragraph 1(a) shall be binding on the Board of Appeal in respect of the appeal in question.

Article 112a Petition for review by the Enlarged Board of Appeal

(1) Any party to appeal proceedings adversely affected by the decision of the Board of Appeal may file a petition for review of the decision by the Enlarged Board of Appeal.

(2) The petition may only be filed on the grounds that:

(a) a member of the Board of Appeal took part in the decision in breach of Article 24, paragraph 1, or despite being excluded pursuant to a decision under Article 24, paragraph 4;

(b) the Board of Appeal included a person not appointed as a member of the Boards of Appeal;

(a) 審判部は、上記目的のために審決が必要であると認めるときは、事件についての手続が係属中に、自ら又は審判手続の当事者の請求により、問題を拡大審判部に付託する。審判部は、当該請求を却下した場合には、最終審決においてその理由を示す。

(b) 特許庁長官は、2つの審判部が法律問題について異なる決定をしたときは、拡大審判部にその問題を付託することができる。

(2) (1)(a)に該当するときは、審判手続の当事者は、拡大審判部の手続の当事者となる。

(3) (1)(a)にいう拡大審判部の審決は、問題となった審判事件について審判部を拘束する。

第112a 条 拡大審判部による再審理の申請

(1) 審判手続の当事者であって審判部の審決によって不利な影響を受けたものは、拡大審判部による再審理の申請をすることができる。

(2) 申請は、次に掲げる理由のいずれかに基づいてのみすることができる。

(a) 審判部の構成員が、第24条(1)の規定に違反して、又は第24条(4)の規定に基づく決定により除斥されているにもかかわらず、その決定に関与したこと

(b) 審判部の構成員として任命されていない者が審判に加わっていたこと

(c) a fundamental violation of Article 113 occurred;

(d) any other fundamental procedural defect defined in the Implementing Regulations occurred in the appeal proceedings; or

(e) a criminal act established under the conditions laid down in the Implementing Regulations may have had an impact on the decision.

(3) The petition for review shall not have suspensive effect.

(4) The petition for review shall be filed in a reasoned statement, in accordance with the Implementing Regulations. If based on paragraph 2(a) to (d), the petition shall be filed within two months of notification of the decision of the Board of Appeal. If based on paragraph 2(e), the petition shall be filed within two months of the date on which the criminal act has been established and in any event no later than five years from notification of the decision of the Board of Appeal. The petition shall not be deemed to have been filed until after the prescribed fee has been paid.

(5) The Enlarged Board of Appeal shall examine the petition for review in accordance with the Implementing Regulations. If the petition is allowable, the Enlarged Board of Appeal shall set aside the decision and shall re-open proceedings before the Boards of Appeal in accordance with the Implementing Regulations.

(6) —

Article 113 Right to be heard and basis of decisions

(1) The decisions of the European Patent Office may only be based on grounds or evidence on which the parties concerned have had an opportunity to present their comments.

(c) 第113条に規定する基本的違反が生じていたこと

(d) 審判手続において、施行規則に定める他の基本的な手続的瑕疵があったこと

(e) 施行規則に定める要件の下に定められた犯罪行為がその決定に重大な影響を与えたこと

(3) 再審理の申請は、執行停止の効力を有さない。

(4) 再審理の申請は、施行規則に従って、理由を付した書面の形式である。(2)(a)から(d)までに基づく申請は、審判部による決定の通知から２月以内にするものとする。(2)(e)に基づく申請は、犯罪行為が確定した日から２月以内であって、いかなる場合でも審判部による決定の通知から５年を超えないうちにするものとする。申請は、指定された手数料が納付されるまでは、されたものとみなさない。

(5) 拡大審判部は、施行規則に従って、当該申請について審理する。拡大審判部は、申請を許可するときは決定を破棄し、施行規則に従って、審判部における手続を再開させる。

(6) 省略

第113条　聴聞を受ける権利及び決定の根拠

(1) 欧州特許庁の決定は、関係当事者が自己の意見を述べる機会が与えられた理由又は証拠に基づいてのみ行われる。

(2) The European Patent Office shall examine, and decide upon, the European patent application or the European patent only in the text submitted to it, or agreed, by the applicant or the proprietor of the patent.

Article 114 Examination by the European Patent Office of its own motion

(1) In proceedings before it, the European Patent Office shall examine the facts of its own motion; it shall not be restricted in this examination to the facts, evidence and arguments provided by the parties and the relief sought.

(2) The European Patent Office may disregard facts or evidence which are not submitted in due time by the parties concerned.

Article 115 Observations by third parties

In proceedings before the European Patent Office, following the publication of the European patent application, any third party may, in accordance with the Implementing Regulations, present observations concerning the patentability of the invention to which the application or patent relates. That person shall not be a party to the proceedings.

Article 116 Oral proceedings

(1) Oral proceedings shall take place either at the instance of the European Patent Office if it considers this to be expedient or at the request of any party to the proceedings. However, the European Patent Office may reject a request for further oral proceedings before the same department where the parties and the subject of the proceedings are the same.

(2) Nevertheless, oral proceedings shall take place before the Receiving

(2) 欧州特許庁は、出願人又は特許権者により提出され若しくは同意された書類にのみ基づき欧州特許出願又は欧州特許について審理し、決定をする。

第114条　職権による審理

(1) 手続において、欧州特許庁は、職権で事実を審理し、当該審理においては、当事者らが提出した事実、証拠及び議論並びに求められた救済に制限されない。

(2) 欧州特許庁は、関係当事者らが適時に提出しなかった事実又は証拠を無視することができる。

第115条　第三者による意見

欧州特許庁の手続において、欧州特許出願の公開後に、いかなる第三者も、施行規則に従って、出願に係る発明の特許性に関して意見を述べることができる。ただし、その者が欧州特許庁における手続の当事者となることはできない。

第116条　口頭審理

(1) 口頭審理は、欧州特許庁がそれを適切であると認める場合には欧州特許庁の要請により、又は手続のいずれかの当事者の請求により生じる。ただし、欧州特許庁は、手続の当事者及び対象が同一である場合には、同部課におけるさらなる口頭審理の請求を却下することができる。

(2) もっとも、受理課が口頭審理を適切であると認めるか、又は受理課が欧

Section at the request of the applicant only where the Receiving Section considers this to be expedient or where it intends to refuse the European patent application.

(3) Oral proceedings before the Receiving Section, the Examining Divisions and the Legal Division shall not be public.

(4) Oral proceedings, including delivery of the decision, shall be public, as regards the Boards of Appeal and the Enlarged Board of Appeal, after publication of the European patent application, and also before the Opposition Divisions, in so far as the department before which the proceedings are taking place does not decide otherwise in cases where admission of the public could have serious and unjustified disadvantages, in particular for a party to the proceedings.

州特許出願を拒絶することを意図する場合に限り、出願人の請求により、受理課において口頭審理が行われる。

(3) 受理課、審査部及び法律部における口頭審理は、公開されないものとする。

(4) 欧州特許出願が公開された後の審判部及び拡大審判部における口頭審理並びに異議部における口頭審理は、公開することが手続の当事者の一方に重大で、かつ、不当な不利益を与えるおそれがある場合には、口頭審理を行う部門が公開に反対しない限りにおいて、決定の言渡しを含み公開して行われる。

Chapter 14

Opposition Procedure

特許異議申立手続

Veit-Peter Frank

MEMO

▶ 欧州特許庁における異議申立手続は、異議部による第一審と審判部による第二審（控訴審）に分かれています。異議部の決定に対して裁判所に訴訟を提起するという日本の制度と異なり、第二審である控訴審も欧州特許庁内の機関で扱われます。

▶ 欧州特許に対する異議の申立てができるのは、特許掲載公報の発行日から9月で、「何人」には特許権者は含まれません（§1）。

▶ 欧州特許条約では特許異議申立ての理由が第100条に限定列挙されており、日本特許法第113条に類似しますが、クレームの記載が明確でないこと、簡潔でないこと、明細書により裏付けされていないこと（第84条違反）は、特許異議申立ての理由になっていません（§2）。

▶ 異議申立書は方式審査を経た後に3人の審査官から構成される異議部に送られます。このうちの1人は、通常、審査手続を主担当した担当審査官です（§3）。日本の特許異議申立ての制度では審判官の合議体により異議申立ての審理がされますから（日本特許法第114条第1項）、この点、欧州実務は大きく異なります。

▶ 異議申立ての審理は、基本的には書面審理ですが、日本の異議の申立制度と異なり、特許権者及び申立人の双方が口頭審理を請求することができます（§4）。口頭審理が行われることが頻繁です。

▶ 特許異議申立手続において、特許権者はクレームの補正をするこ

とができますが、特許異議申立理由に応答する補正でなければなりません。欧州特許条約に定める要件をすべて満たしている場合に、その補正は認められます（§5）。

▶ 異議申立期間が経過した後でも、第105条の要件を満たす場合には、第三者は、特許異議申立手続へ参加することができます（§6）。特許異議申立事件の第二審手続への参加も、特定の要件が満たされれば可能です（§6）。

▶ 異議部による異議申立手続は、異議申立てを却下する、特許を取り消す、又は特許を補正された形式で維持するのいずれかの決定で終了します（§7）。異議部の決定に対して不服のある者は、特許権者であるか申立人であるかを問わず、その決定に対して審判を請求することができます（第15章参照）。日本の特許制度のように無効審判制度が併設されていませんので、審判請求をせずに異議部の決定が確定した場合は、不服のある申立人は、各国の裁判所で特許取消裁判（又は無効裁判）を請求することになります（§7）。

Introduction

The European Patent Convention (EPC) provides for a possibility for a third party to **challenge a European patent after grant** by means of **filing an opposition**. The proceedings take place before certain institutions within the EPO - the **Opposition Division** for the first instance, and the **Board of Appeal** for the (final) second or appeal instance.

In this chapter, an attempt is made to cast some light on the basic concept underlying the EP Opposition and its legal framework, in terms of the procedural aspects as well as the grounds on which an opposition can be based.

1 Formal Requirements

The basic provision governing the Opposition procedure under the EPC is Art. 99. According to Art. 99(1) EPC within nine months from the publication of the mention of the grant of the European patent in the European Patent Bulletin, any person may give notice to the European Patent Office of opposition to that patent, in accordance with the Implementing Regulations. Notice of opposition shall not be deemed to have been filed until the opposition fee has been paid.

Oppositions can therefore only be filed for a limited period of time, namely, for a period of **nine months** from the mention of the grant of the patent. Oppositions filed earlier will enter into the EPO's respective file, but they will not be treated as an opposition. They are considered to constitute third party observations under Article 115 EPC (Guidelines for the Examination in the EPO D-IV 1.1). Oppositions which are filed later will be rejected as being inadmissible under Rule 77(1) EPC. There is no way to extend the opposition period, and there is also no possibility of *re-establishment of rights*. The same is true for the payment of the opposition fee.

はじめに

欧州特許条約は、**特許異議申立書を提出する**ことによって、**特許付与後に欧州特許に対して異議を申し立てる機会を第三者に与えている**。特許異議申立手続は、欧州特許庁内の特定の組織（第一審は**異議部**、（最終）第二審／控訴審は**審判部**）で行われる。

本章では、手続面だけではなく、特許異議の申立ての理由の観点から、特許異議の申立ての根底にある基本概念及びその法的枠組みについて考える。

1　方式要件

特許異議申立手続に関する基本的な規定は第99条である。第99条(1)によれば、何人も、欧州特許を付与する旨が欧州特許公報に掲載された後9月以内に限り、欧州特許庁に、施行規則に従って、その特許に対する異議を申し立てることができる。特許異議申立手数料が納付されるまでは、異議の申立てはされたものとはみなされない。

よって、限られた期間（すなわち、特許が付与された旨の掲載から9月）にのみ、特許異議申立書を提出することができる。それよりも前に提出された特許異議申立書は欧州特許庁の各包袋に入るが、特許異議の申立てとしては扱われない。このような申立ては、第115条に基づいて、第三者の意見を構成するものとみなされる（審査基準 D-IV 1.1）。当該期間を過ぎて提出された特許異議申立書は、規則77(1)に従い、受理することができないものとして却下される。特許異議申立期間を延長する方法はなく、権利の回復の機会もない。特許異議申立手数料の納付についても同様である。

One aspect of Article 99 EPC is the fact that "any person" may file an Opposition. While in the early days of the EPC this was construed to also include the patentee, G 9/93 stipulated that the patentee is not "any person" and, thus, may not oppose his own patent. Patentees can request voluntary limitations or revocations using the new centralized European limitation procedure according to Art 105a, which was introduced with the revision of the EPC ('EPC2000'). Alternatively, voluntary limitations can be requested separately before the national patent offices of each and every designated state. A notice of opposition may also be filed jointly by more than one person. In such case the opposition is admissible on the payment of only one opposition fee (G 3/99). Oppositions can also be inherited or succeeded to as a part of an overall succession in law.

The formulation "any person", however, has also been the focus of much debate for another reason. Many times opponents do not want to unveil their identity to patentee for business reasons. For many years in the past, this has been virtually impossible as the EPO considered oppositions filed by a "man of straw", i.e. someone who has no interest in the Opposition and merely acts to conceal the identity of an interested party, to be inadmissible. In a later decision (G 4/97) however, the EPO moved away from this practice. Following this decision, oppositions filed by a "man of straw" are no longer generally inadmissible unless they constitute an abusive circumvention of the law (e.g., when the man of straw acts on behalf of the patentee).

Rule 76 EPC sets forth a number of requirements which are of further importance. This rule requires inter alia that the notice of opposition comprises a statement of the extent to which the European patent is opposed and of the grounds on which the opposition is based, as well as an indication of the facts and evidence presented in support of these grounds. These requirements define the framework within which the opposition will be examined. If the opponent limits the extent to which the European patent is opposed, the Opposition Division has no power to decide on subject matter not opposed (G 9/91 and G 10/91). According to Rule 81, the Opposition Division shall examine those grounds for opposi-

第99条には、「何人」も異議を申し立てることができるとある。欧州特許条約が設立された初期の頃は、「何人」には特許権者も含まれると解釈されていたが、審決G 9/93において、特許権者は「何人」ではないため、自らの特許に対して異議を申し立てることはできないと明記された。特許権者は、第105a条に新設された一元的限定又は取消手続（「EPC2000」で導入されたものである）を用いて、自発的な限定又は取消しを請求することができる。あるいは、各指定国の特許庁において、自発的な限定を個別に請求することができる。また、複数の者が共同して特許異議申立書を提出することができる。このような場合、特許異議の申立ては、1件分の特許異議申立手数料を納付すれば受理される（G 3/99）。法律による承継の一環として、特許異議の申立てを相続又は継承することもできる。

　一方、「何人」という語句は、別の理由により多くの議論の焦点となっている。申立人は、ビジネス上の理由により、自らの身元を特許権者に明かしたくない場合が多い。申立人が身元を明かさないことは、過去何年にもわたって事実上不可能であった。「ストローマン」（すなわち、その特許異議の申立てに利害関係がなく、利害関係人の身元を隠すために行動するに過ぎない者）が提出した異議申立書は却下されると欧州特許庁により考えられていたためである。しかしながら、その後の審決（G 4/97）において、欧州特許庁はこの実務を変えた。この審決の後、「ストローマン」が提出した特許異議申立書は、不正な脱法行為（例えば、ストローマンが特許権者のために行動する場合）を構成しない限り、もはや却下されない。

　規則76には、重要ないくつかの要件がさらに規定されている。特に、この規則では、欧州特許に対する異議の申立ての範囲及び根拠理由についての陳述、並びにその理由の裏付けとして提出する事実及び証拠の表示が特許異議申立書に含まれることが要求されている。これらの要件は、特許異議申立ての審理の枠組みを規定している。欧州特許に対する異議の申立ての範囲を申立人が限定する場合、異議部は、異議が申し立てられていない対象については職権により決定をすることができない（G 9/91及びG 10/91）。規則81の規定によれば、異議部は、特許異議申立書における申立人の陳述において提起された理由を審理しなければならない。申立人が提起していない理由については、異議部は、職

tion which are invoked in the opponent's statement of grounds in the notice of opposition. Grounds for opposition not invoked by the opponent may be examined by the Opposition Division of its own motion if they would *prima facie* seem to prejudice the maintenance of the patent (G 10/91).

2 Grounds for Opposition

The grounds on which an Opposition under the EPC may be based are set forth in Article 100 EPC, which reads:

This list of grounds for opposition under the EPC is **exhaustive**. Other grounds, such as an alleged *lack of clarity* (T 23/86, T 792/95) (Art. 84), or *lack of unity* (G 1/91) (Art. 82) are not valid grounds for filing an opposition under the EPC, even though clarity of the claims and unity of the inventions are mandatory requirements for the grant of a patent. However, amendments filed during opposition proceedings must comply with the clarity requirement (but not with the requirement of unity of invention). In a recent decision (G 03/14) the Enlarged Board of Appeal concluded that in considering whether for the purposes of Art. 101(3), a patent as amended meets the requirements of the EPC, the claims of the patent may be examined for compliance with the requirements of Art. 84 only when, and then only to the extent that the amendment introduces non-compliance with Art. 84.

Also, *unlawful usurpation* is not a valid ground in proceedings before the EPO, but it is, e.g. in national German proceedings.

The ground of Opposition under Art. 100(a) includes the "classic" requirements for patent rights as laid down in Articles 52 to 57 EPC.

While the grounds of Articles 52, 53 and 57 EPC are not frequently used, even though they are highly important in certain technological areas, the gist of the

権により、それを審理することができるが、当該理由がその特許の維持を妨げることが明らかと思われるときに限られる（G 10/91）。

2 特許異議の申立ての理由

特許異議の申立ての理由（以下、特許異議申立理由）は、第100条に規定されている。

特許異議申立理由は第100条に掲げられたものに限られる。「明確性欠如」（T 23/86、T 792/95）（第84条）、「単一性欠如」（G 1/91）（第82条）等の他の理由は、クレームの明確性及び発明の単一性が特許付与の必須要件であっても、欧州特許条約に基づく特許異議申立理由ではない。一方、特許異議申立手続中に補正がされた場合、その補正は、明確性の要件（発明の単一性の要件はない）を満たさなければならない。最近の審決（G 03/14）において、拡大審判部は、第101条(3)の趣旨において、補正後の特許が欧州特許条約の要件を満たすか否かを検討する際に、その補正が第84条に違反する事項を導入した場合に当該違反事項を導入した範囲についてのみ、第84条の要件の遵守について特許のクレームを審理することができると結論した。

また、「冒認出願」は、欧州特許庁の特許異議申立手続では有効な申立理由ではないが、例えば、ドイツの国内訴訟では有効である。

第100条(a)の特許異議申立理由には、第52条～第57条に示されている特許権に関する「典型的な」要件が含まれている。

特許異議申立理由としては、第52条、第53条及び第57条に基づくものは、特定の技術分野で非常に重要であっても、それほど用いられることはなく、「新

EP oppositions is based on an alleged *lack of novelty* and/or a *lack of inventive step*. Although looking at Art. 100(a) it seems that there is only one ground of opposition, in G 7/95 the Enlarged Board of Appeal came to the opinion that Art. 100(a) embraces many grounds of opposition and that lack of novelty is indeed a different ground from lack of inventive step. Specifically, the Enlarged Board of Appeal in its decision defined a ground as an individual legal basis for objection to the maintenance of the patent. This issue is important since in appeal stage fresh grounds of oppositions may in principle not be introduced, unless the patent proprietor agrees.

The ground of opposition under Art. 100(b) - *lack of sufficient disclosure* - is quite frequently brought up in EP Opposition procedures, although it is often misconstrued. Many times this ground is forwarded because an opponent is of the opinion that the claims do not allow the skilled person to practice the invention. However, for an attack based on this ground it is not sufficient to only consider the claims. Rather, this ground can only lead to a revocation of the patent, if the patent as a whole does not sufficiently disclose the invention. A typical case where Art. 100(b) can lead to the revocation of a patent is the situation where the claims recite a parameter which is not properly defined in the specification.

Art. 100(c) - *added subject matter* - provides for a very delicate ground of opposition, both for the EPO examiner and the person who has prosecuted the case. While simple additions can most often easily be removed and thus a total revocation can be avoided, there is also the less favorable situation of the *"inescapable trap"*. This situation arises if the main claim contains non-disclosed matter, i.e. added matter, which limits the protective scope of the patent. Such matter cannot remain in the claim in view of Art. 100(c), but it also cannot be removed from the claim, as this would lead to a broadening of the protective scope. Such a broadening of the protective scope after grant is not allowable under Article 123(3) EPC. This clearly leads to a no-win situation for the patentee and it will invariably lead to the revocation of the patent.

規性欠如」及び／又は「進歩性欠如」に基づくものが中心である。第100条(a)からすると、特許異議申立理由は１つしかないと思われるが、拡大審判部は、G 7/95において、第100条(a)は複数の特許異議申立理由を包含し、新規性欠如と進歩性欠如とは実際は異なる理由であるとの見解を示した。具体的には、拡大審判部は、その審決において、個々の理由が特許の維持に対する異議の法的根拠になることを明確にした。控訴審では、原則として、特許権者が同意しない限り、特許異議申立理由を新たに追加することができないため、この問題は重要である。

第100条(b)の特許異議申立理由である「開示十分性の欠如」は、特許異議申立手続において極めて頻繁に用いられるが、誤解されることが多い。多くの場合、申立人は、当業者による発明の実施をクレームが可能にしないという意見でこの理由を提出する。しかしながら、この理由に基づく攻撃の場合、クレームを検討するだけでは足りない。正しくは、特許が全体として発明を十分に開示していない場合にのみ、この理由は特許の取消しにつながり得る。第100条(b)が特許の取消しにつながり得る典型的な事例は、明細書で適切に定義されていないパラメータがクレームに記載されている場合である。

第100条(c)「新規事項の追加」は、欧州特許庁の審査官と出願手続をした者との双方にとって非常にデリケートな特許異議申立理由である。単なる追加は、ほとんどの場合において、容易に削除することができるため、全体の取消しを回避することができるが、「不可避のトラップ」という好ましくない状況もある。開示されていない事項（すなわち、追加された事項）であって特許の保護範囲を限定するものをメインクレームが含む場合にこの状況が起こる。第100条(c)を鑑みれば、このような事項をクレームに残すことはできないが、クレームから削除すると保護範囲が拡張するため、クレームから削除することもできない。特許付与後におけるこのような保護範囲の拡張は、第123条(3)に基づいて認められないからだ。これは明らかに、特許権者にとって勝ち目のない状況になり、特許の取消しが避けられなくなる。

3 Written Proceedings

Once the opposition has been filed, upon examination of the formalities it will be brought to the attention of an *Opposition Division*. The Opposition Division is composed of three EPO examiners, at least two of whom have not taken part in the Grant Proceedings of the patent to which the Opposition relates (Art. 19(2)). A first member of the Opposition Division, who is usually the most experienced and *never* the examiner who was in charge of the case prior to grant, will be the chairman. As the examiner who examined the case is, of course, most acquainted with the case, he or she is usually entrusted with the Opposition case and the preparations prior to making the decision. This second member of the Opposition Division is usually called the rapporteur. A third member will usually be the minute's writer in the event of Oral Proceedings.

According to Art. 101(1), if the opposition is admissible, the Opposition Division shall examine, in accordance with the Implementing Regulations, whether at least one ground for opposition under Art. 100 prejudices the maintenance of the European patent. During this examination, the Opposition Division shall invite the parties, as often as necessary, to file observations on communications from another party or issued by itself.

In accordance with Rule 79(1) the Opposition Division shall communicate the notice of opposition to the proprietor of the patent and shall give him the opportunity to file his observations and to amend, where appropriate, the description, claims and drawings within a period to be specified. In return, patentee will usually file a response outlining his defense. If several notices of opposition have been filed the patent proprietor may respond to several opponents by one statement only, or he may also file separate statements responding to each of the opponents.

If several notices of opposition have been filed, the Opposition Division shall communicate them to the other opponents in accordance with Rule 79(2).

3 書面審理

　特許異議申立書が提出されると、方式審査を経て異議部に送られる。異議部は欧州特許庁の審査官3人から構成され、そのうち少なくとも2人は、その申立てに関する特許付与手続に関与していない者である（第19条(2)）。異議部の第一構成員（通常、最も経験豊富な者であり、特許付与前にその事件に係る出願を担当した審査官ではない者）が審査長になる。当然のことながら、出願を審査した審査官がその内容に最も精通しているので、その審査官が、通常、異議申立事件につきその審査の準備を委ねられる。異議部の第二構成員は、通常、担当審査官と称される。第三構成員は、通常、口頭審理で記録官になる。

　第101条(1)の規定によれば、特許異議の申立てが受理された場合、異議部は、施行規則に従って、第100条に定める特許異議申立理由の少なくとも1つが欧州特許の維持を妨げるか否かを審査する。この審査期間中に、異議部は、当事者らに対し、必要に応じて何度でも、他の当事者からの又は異議部自身が発した通知について意見書を提出する機会を与える。

　規則79(1)によれば、異議部は、特許権者に対し、特許異議申立書を送付し、相当の期間を指定して、意見書を提出し、該当する場合は、明細書、クレーム及び図面について補正をする機会を与える。それを受けて、特許権者は、通常、抗弁を記載した応答書を提出する。特許異議の申立てが複数された場合は、特許権者は、1つの書面のみによって複数の申立人に対して応答することもできるし、又は各申立人に対して別々に応答することもできる。

　特許異議の申立てが複数されたときは、異議部は、規則79(2)に従い、その特許異議申立書を他の申立人に送付する。

Following Rule 79(3) the Opposition Division shall communicate any observations and amendments filed by the proprietor of the patent to the other parties, and shall invite them, if it considers this expedient, to reply within a period to be specified.

Accordingly, it is the opponent's turn to once again respond, and so forth. Usually two to three written statements are forwarded by each side. While the opponent may certainly react to patentee's response, in principle he may not take a "second shot" in the sense that he introduces new material and even new grounds of opposition, unless this is motivated by the patentee's response.

EPO case law in an attempt to expedite Opposition Proceedings and to avoid piecemeal argumentation for tactical reasons, has imposed rather strict procedural limitations in this respect. That is, in principle, the grounds of Opposition forwarded and substantiated in the initial notice of Opposition and the evidence contained therein, set the legal and factual framework for the entire Opposition Proceedings (G 9/91 and G 10/91).

Additional grounds (n.b. EPO's interpretation of "grounds" above) need not be considered by the Opposition Division. However, it is at the discretion of the Opposition Division to do so under Article 114(1) and Rule 81 EPC. According to the Enlarged Board of Appeal, however, exercising this discretion must be limited to exceptional circumstances, where there are *prima facie* strong reasons that speak in favor of the relevance of the respective grounds of opposition and against the maintenance of the patent in its entirety (G 10/91).

Similarly, claims that were not attacked in the original notice of Opposition are not the subject of Opposition Proceedings. While dependent claims may still be examined by the Opposition Division in the case where their patentability is *prima facie* in question on the basis of the available material, independent claims may not.

規則79(3)によれば、異議部は、特許権者によって意見書及び補正書が提出されたときは、それらについて他の当事者に通知し、適切であると認めるときは、それらの者に対し、相当の期間を指定して、当該通知に応答する機会を与える。

　したがって、今度は申立人が応答する番である。通常、それぞれの側が二又は三の書面を送付する。申立人は特許権者の応答に対応することができるが、原則として、特許権者の応答によってその必要が生じない限りは、新たな事項や新たな特許異議申立理由を追加することができない意味において「セカンドショット」を撃つことができない。

　欧州特許庁のケースローは、特許異議申立手続を迅速化し、戦術的な理由による断片的な議論を回避しようとする観点から厳密な手続的制限を課している。すなわち、原則として、特許異議申立書が提出された時に立証された特許異議申立理由及びそこに含まれる証拠により、特許異議申立手続全体の法的、かつ、事実的な枠組みが定められるのである（G 9/91及びG 10/91）。

　異議部は、追加の異議理由（上記「理由」に関する欧州特許庁の解釈に注意）を考慮する必要はない。一方、第114条(1)及び規則81によれば、追加の理由を考慮するかどうかは異議部の裁量である。ただし、拡大審判部によれば、この裁量権の行使は、特許全体の維持に反する各異議申立理由の妥当性を支持する明らかに強い理由があるという例外的な状況に限定される（G 10/91）。

　同様に、特許異議申立書において攻撃されなかったクレームは、特許異議申立手続の対象ではない。異議部は、入手可能な資料に基づいてその特許性に明らかな疑義がある場合には、従属クレームであれば審査することができるが、独立クレームを審査することはできない。

Prior art that was not introduced within the nine months Opposition period may also be disregarded by the EPO for belated filing (T 1002/92). Accepting documents that were filed later is, again, purely at the discretion of the Opposition Division, and this discretion has to be exercised on the basis of a *prima facie* analysis of the relevance of the late filed documents.

These strict procedural rules show that opposition proceedings are contentious Revocation Proceedings rather than a continuation of the pre-grant examination procedure. The principle that the EPO examines the facts of its own motion as laid down in Article 114(1) EPC is thereby basically sacrificed for procedural reasons.

In Opposition Proceedings, the EPO, therefore, basically no longer acts as a patent office but, rather, as a court. In fact, G 9/91 rendered it clear that nowadays the European Opposition is to be considered as a truly contentious proceeding, wherein the conflicting interests of the patentee and the opponent(s) have to be decided upon. It is therefore also not surprising that the EPO's practice of Rule 84(2) EPC, which prescribes that the Opposition Proceedings may be continued even if opponent withdraws, is such that the withdrawal of the opponent (or all opponents in the case of more than one opponent) marks the end of the proceedings unless there is a clear cut lack of novelty.

The written proceedings may extend over a period of 2 to 3 years. The Opposition Division may then issue a decision on the basis of the written statements only. However, in the vast majority of cases, the decision will be made following an Oral Hearing.

4   Oral Proceedings

In their basic layout, the European Opposition Proceedings are written proceedings. Oral Proceedings are not compulsory. However, Opposition Proceed-

欧州特許庁は、9月の異議申立期間内に提出されず、遅れて提出された先行技術を無視することができる（T 1002/92）。この場合もやはり、遅れて提出された書類を受理するか否かは異議部の裁量であり、この裁量権は、遅れて提出された書類の妥当性を疎明分析して行使されなければならない。

これらの厳格な手続規則は、特許異議申立手続が特許付与前の審査手続の続審ではなく、係争的な取消手続であることを示している。よって、欧州特許庁が職権により事実を審査するという第114条(1)に規定されている原則は、手続的な理由により基本的には犠牲になっている。

よって、特許異議申立手続において、欧州特許庁は、基本的にはもはや特許庁として機能するのではなく、裁判所のように機能する。実際、G 9/91において、特許異議の申立ては、現在では、特許権者及び申立人の対立する利害について決定しなければならない真に係争的な手続と考えるべきであることが明確になった。規則84(2)は、申立人が特許異議申立書を取り下げた場合であっても、特許異議申立手続を続行することができることを規定しているが、新規性が明確に欠如しない限り、申立人（又は、申立人が複数の場合には申立人全員）の取下げが手続の終了を告げるというのが欧州特許庁の実務であることも驚くべきことではない。

書面審理は、2～3年の期間に及ぶこともある。その後、異議部は、提出された書面のみに基づいて決定をすることができる。しかしながら、その決定は、ほとんどの場合、口頭審理の後に行われる。

4　口頭審理

特許異議の申立ては基本的には書面審理による。口頭審理は必須ではない。しかし、特許異議申立手続がこの基本に従うことはほとんどない。第116条(1)

ings rarely follow this basic layout. It is a rather common practice for both the opponent and the patentee to routinely request Oral Proceedings under Article 116(1) EPC. Once such a request has been filed, the EPO has no discretion; it must summon for Oral Proceedings.

The summons to Oral Proceedings must be sent by the EPO at least two months in advance of the Oral Proceedings (Rule 115). Nowadays, however, such summons is usually issued many months earlier.

There is, however, also a legal reason why the EPO issues the summons to Oral Proceedings rather timely. This reason is Rule 116 EPC, which yet again shows the EPO's preference of procedural efficiency over the aim of ultimate quality of examination:

> *"(1) When issuing the summons, the European Patent Office shall draw attention to the points which in its opinion need to be discussed for the purposes of the decision to be taken. At the same time a final date for making written submissions in preparation for the oral proceedings shall be fixed. Rule 132 shall not apply. New facts and evidence presented after that date need not be considered, unless admitted on the grounds that the subject of the proceedings has changed.*
>
> *(2) If the applicant or patent proprietor has been notified of the grounds prejudicing the grant or maintenance of the patent, he may be invited to submit, by the date specified in paragraph 1, second sentence, documents which meet the requirements of the Convention. Paragraph 1, third and fourth sentences, shall apply mutatis mutandis".*

Rule 116 EPC, of course, also aims at setting the framework for fair play amongst the parties by forcing them to present their case early and, thus, allowing for the sufficient preparation on the part of the EPO and the other parties before the Oral Proceedings.

の規定により口頭審理を請求することは、申立人及び特許権者の双方にとって一般的である。このような請求がなされると、欧州特許庁には裁量権がなく、口頭審理を召喚しなければならない。

規則115により、欧州特許庁は、口頭審理の少なくとも２月前に口頭審理召喚状を送付する。現在では、このような召喚状は、通常、数カ月前に発行されている。

一方、欧州特許庁が口頭審理召喚状を適時に発行する法的理由も存在する。この理由は規則116（下記参照）にあり、審査の最終的な質の目的よりも手続の効率を欧州特許庁が優先することを示している。

(1) 召喚状を発するに際し、欧州特許庁は、その見解において、決定をするために討議する必要がある論点について注意を喚起する。同時に、口頭審理の準備として提出すべき書類の最終提出期日を定める。規則132は適用しない。当該日後に提出される新たな事実及び証拠は考慮されない。ただし、手続の対象が変更になったという理由で受理されるときはこの限りではない。

(2) 出願人又は特許権者は、特許の付与又は維持を妨げる理由について通知を受けた場合は、条約の要件を満たす書類を(1)の第二文で指定された日までに提出するよう求められる。(1)の第三文及び第四文を準用する。

当然のことながら、規則116は、事件を早期に提示することを促し、口頭審理前に欧州特許庁及び他の当事者側の十分な準備を可能にすることによって、当事者間の公正な取扱いに関する枠組みを定めることも目的とする。

A further issue is the language of the proceedings. Most of all oppositions are lodged in the German or English language. The majority of opponents thus plead and speak in these languages though the language of the proceedings (the language used by the Opposition Division) may be different. The language of the proceedings is the language in which the attacked patent was issued (predominantly English). For the Oral Hearing (only), the EPO will provide a translation service at its own expense if this is requested by the parties or the Opposition Division. There will be simultaneous translation of what is said in the proceedings. These translations can be followed by earphones.

The Oral Hearing is open to the public. The actual Oral Proceedings is much like a court case. Usually the Chairman gives a short introduction into the case and then the opponent is given the opportunity to present his case. The patentee may, of course, reply, and so forth. It is thereby not rare that members of the Opposition Division address specific questions to the parties.

The burden of proof is firstly with the opponent. As the opponent is the party that initiated the Opposition Proceedings it is up to him to show that his allegations are probable. If he complies with this requirement, for example by forwarding compelling experimental evidence, the burden of proof may shift to the patent proprietor.

Once the arguments are exchanged, the Opposition Division will interrupt the Oral Proceedings and retreat for internal discussion. In most cases, the Chairman upon reopening the proceedings will then issue a decision or, less often, continue with the discussion. It is also not rare that in Oral Proceedings the case is dealt with in a step-by-step fashion, whereby formalities and the individual grounds of opposition, i.e. in most cases novelty and inventive step, are dealt with and decided upon individually, one after the other.

As a basis of their decision, the Opposition Division must adhere to the text, i.e. the requests forwarded by the patentee. The Opposition Division can only decide

さらなる問題は手続言語である。特許異議の申立てのほとんどは、ドイツ語又は英語でなされている。このように、申立人の大多数は、これらの言語で弁論及び対話をするが、手続言語（異議部が用いる言語）が異なる場合がある。手続言語は、申立てに係る特許が付与された言語（主に英語）である。口頭審理の場合に限り、当事者又は異議部の請求により、欧州特許庁は、特許庁の費用で通訳サービスを提供する。口頭審理の内容は同時通訳される。これらの通訳は、イヤホンで聴取することができる。

　口頭審理は、公衆に公開される。実際の口頭審理は裁判事件に類似する。通常、審査長が事件の簡単な概要を述べ、その後、説明の機会が申立人に与えられる。当然のことながら、特許権者は応答をすることができる。異議部の構成員が、当事者らに対して具体的な質問を行うことも珍しくはない。

　立証責任は、最初は、申立人にある。申立人は特許異議申立手続を開始した当事者であるため、自らの主張に相当の理由があることを示すのは申立人である。例えば、有力な実験証拠を提出することによって申立人がこの要件を満たせば、立証責任が特許権者に転換される。

　双方の議論が交換されると、異議部は口頭審理を中断し、内部での議論に入る。ほとんどの場合、審判長は、口頭審理を再開させた後にその決定をする。あるいは、あまり頻繁ではないが中断前の議論を続けさせることもある。口頭審理では、事件が段階的に処理されることが珍しくはなく、方式及び特許異議申立理由（新規性及び進歩性に係るものがほとんど）が順に個別に処理されて決定される。

　異議部は、特許権者によって提出された書面による請求に基づいて決定をしなければならない。異議部は、これらの請求が欧州特許条約の要件を満たすか

whether or not these requests are in conformity with the EPC (Article 113(2) EPC). Accordingly, even if the Opposition Division is of the opinion that a slight change could render the claims proposed by patentee patentable, they may not effect this change themselves. If patentee is not willing to effect this change or fails to notice respective hints given by the Opposition Division, the Opposition Division has no choice but to revoke the patent.

5 Amendments

In Opposition Proceedings, the patent proprietor is entitled to amend his patent. These amendments are subject to Article 123(2) and (3) EPC, and impose the following restrictions:

- the European patent may not be amended in such a way that it contains subject matter which extends beyond the content of the application as filed, and

- the claims of the European patent may not be amended during Opposition Proceedings so that they extend the scope of protection.

If the patent proprietor wishes an amendment to the claims, he may use the entire original application text as a basis. He is not limited to what is already contained in the claims. He is free to insert features from the description into the claims, provided that their scope is not extended thereby.

Rule 80 EPC concerns amendments to a patent granted by the EPO and under opposition. It is expressed in permissive language to allow the patent proprietor to amend whenever *"the amendments are occasioned by grounds for opposition specified in EPC Article 100"*. Decisions of the EPO Boards of Appeal in the past have restricted the scope for amendments during opposition to amendments necessary to overcome the particular attacks from the opponent. The opposition pro-

否かについてのみ審理し決定をすることができる（第113条(2)）。したがって、特許権者が提案したクレームをわずかに修正すれば特許性があると異議部が考える場合であっても、異議部はこの修正を行うことができない。特許権者がこの修正を望まないか、又は異議部から与えられた示唆に気づかない場合、異議部は特許を取り消すしかない。

5　補正

特許異議申立手続において、特許権者は、自らの特許について補正をすることができる。これらの補正は、第123条(2)及び(3)の規定に従わなければならず、以下の制限が課される。

- 欧州特許は、その出願の出願時の内容を超える対象を含めるように補正をしてはならない。

- 欧州特許のクレームは、特許異議申立手続において、その保護範囲を拡張するように補正をしてはならない。

特許権者がクレームの補正をすることを望む場合、当初の出願書類全体を根拠として用いることができる。特許権者は、クレームにすでに含まれている事項に限定されない。特許権者は、クレームの範囲を拡張しないことを条件に明細書からクレームに特徴を加えることができる。

規則80は、欧州特許庁が付与した特許であって、特許異議の申立てに係る特許の補正に関する。規則80には、許容的な文言で、「当該補正が第100条に掲げられた特許異議申立理由に起因するときはいつでも」、特許権者による補正が認められると記載されている。欧州特許庁の拡大審判部による過去の審決では、特許異議申立手続での補正範囲は、申立人からの特定の攻撃を克服するのに必要な補正に限定されていた。特許異議申立手続は、申立人が提起した問題

cess is not to be regarded as an opportunity for a patent proprietor to make a general review and revision of the text of his patent, unrelated to the issues raised by the opponent. The mere addition of new claims to the granted claims is inadmissible since such amendment cannot be seen as meeting the grounds for opposition. However, Rule 80 EPC gives the proprietor permission to make any amendment which can be justified as a response to a "theoretical" ground of opposition *"even if the respective ground has not been invoked by the opponent"*. Thus, if the proprietor is aware of potential, but not yet actual grounds for opposition to his patent, he should be able to rely on this rule for permission to make remedial amendments to his patent, even though the actual opponent has not raised the same attack. For example, in opposition proceedings admissibly opened on the grounds of patentability, the patent proprietor may submit amendments to remove added subject-matter.

6 Intervention of the Assumed Infringer

Art. 105(1) enables any third party to intervene in opposition proceedings after the opposition period has expired, if the third party proves that proceedings for infringement of the same patent have been instituted against him, or following a request of the proprietor of the patent to cease alleged infringement, the third party has instituted proceedings for a ruling that he is not infringing the patent. According to Art. 105(2) the EPO will treat an admissible intervention as an opposition. In accordance with Rule 89(1) EPC, the notice of intervention should be filed within three months of the date on which proceedings referred to in Art. 105 EPC are instituted. The filing of the notice of intervention requires the payment of the opposition fee.

Intervention is permissible as long as opposition or appeal proceedings are pending. A third party can become a party to the proceedings during the period for filing an appeal only if a party to the proceedings in which the decision was given files an appeal pursuant to Art. 107; otherwise the decision of the Opposi-

に関係なく、特許権者が自ら特許明細書を再検討して是正するための機会とみなされるべきではない。特許付与されたクレームに新たなクレームを単に追加するような補正は、特許異議申立理由に対処するものとはみなされないので認められない。しかしながら、規則80は、「その理由は申立人により申し立てられていなくても」、「理論上の」特許異議申立理由に対する応答として正当化され得る補正を特許権者が行うことを認めている。よって、実際に申し立てられた特許異議申立理由ではないが潜在的な特許異議申立理由を特許権者が自ら認識している場合には、申立人がその理由を基に実際に攻撃しなかった場合であっても、特許権者は、この規則に基づいて、自己の特許に対して救済的な補正を行うことができるはずである。例えば、特許性に関する理由で開始された特許異議申立手続では、特許権者は、新規事項を取り除くために補正書を提出することができるであろう。

6 　侵害者とされた者の参加

　第105条(1)の規定により、いかなる第三者も、同一の特許についての侵害訴訟がその者に対して開始されたこと、又は特許権者がその者に被疑侵害を停止するよう請求した後に、その者が特許権を侵害していない旨の裁判所の判決を求める手続を開始したことを証明するときは、異議申立期間が経過した後、特許異議申立手続に参加することができる。第105条(2)の規定により、欧州特許庁は、受理された参加を、特許異議の申立てとして取り扱う。規則89(1)による参加の申請書は、第105条にいう手続が開始された日から3月以内に提出しなければならない。参加の申請書の提出には、特許異議申立手数料の納付が必要とされる。

　特許異議申立手続又は審判手続が係属している限り、参加は認められる。第三者は、その決定に係る手続の当事者が第107条の規定により審判を請求するときに限り、その審判を請求することができる期間内に、当該手続の当事者になることができ、審判請求がなければ、審判請求期間の終了時に、異議部の決

tion Division will become final on expiry of the appeal period (G 4/91 and G 1/94).

A properly filed and admissible intervention is treated as an opposition, which may be based on any ground of opposition under Art. 100 (G 1/94). This means that, when intervening at any stage of first-instance proceedings, the intervener enjoys essentially the same rights as any other party to the proceedings. If the intervener introduces new facts and evidence which appear to be crucial, the proceedings may need to be prolonged to enable them to be adequately considered.

7 Conclusion of the Opposition Procedure

At the end of the opposition procedure the Opposition Division may reject the opposition, revoke the patent or maintain the patent in an amended form (Art. 101(2)(3)).

The decision of the Opposition Division may be appealed by the party or parties adversely affected by it by filing an appeal with the EPO within two months after the notification of the respective decision. The appeal is forwarded to the Appeal Board that issues a final decision.

The effect of decisions issued by the Opposition Division (with no appeal filed) and those issued by the Appeal Board is set forth in Art. 68 that defines that the European patent application and the resulting patent shall be deemed not to have had, from the outset, the effects specified in Articles 64 and 67, to the extent that the patent has been revoked or limited in opposition limitation or revocation proceedings.

Beyond this, however, the decision has no effect. That is, in particular, it does not prevent the unsuccessful opponent from filing national revocation actions on exactly the same grounds and with exactly the same prior art as he did before the

定が確定する（G 4/91及びG 1/94）。

　適切に提出され、かつ、受理可能な参加の申請は、第100条に掲げるいずれかの理由に基づく特許異議の申立てとして取り扱われる（G 1/94）。つまり、参加人は、第一審の手続のどの段階で参加した場合でも手続の他の当事者と本質的に同じ権利を享受するのである。重要と思われる新たな事実及び証拠を参加人が追加した場合、それらを適切に考慮するために、手続の延長が必要となることがある。

7　特許異議申立手続の終結

　特許異議申立手続の終了時に、異議部は、異議申立てを棄却するか、特許を取り消すか、又は特許を補正された形式で維持することができる（第101条(2)(3)）。

　異議部の決定によって不利益を受けた当事者は、各決定の通知後2月以内に審判請求書を欧州特許庁に提出することにより、異議部の決定に対して審判を請求することができる。審判請求書は、最終決定を発行する審判部に送付される。

　異議部が発行した決定の効果（審判の請求がされなかった場合）及び審判部が発行した決定の効果は、第68条に規定されている。つまり、欧州特許出願及びその結果として生ずる欧州特許は、第64条及び第67条に定められる効果については、特許異議の申立て、限定又は取消しの手続において特許が取り消され又は限定された範囲においてはじめから存在しなかったものとみなされる。

　決定はこれ以上の効果を伴わない。すなわち、不利な決定を受けた申立人は、欧州特許庁に提出した理由及び先行技術とまったく同一の理由及び先行技術に基づいて、国内の取消訴訟を提起することを妨げられない。欧州特許庁の

EPO. Decisions issued in EPO Opposition Proceedings do not have a binding effect on the parties; the matter is not *res judicata* for national revocation courts.

Accordingly, the unsuccessful opponent has a second, though laborious and expensive chance to reach his goal nationally.

For the unsuccessful patentee, however, there is no second chance. The patent is gone and cannot be revived nationally.

特許異議申立手続で発行された決定は、当事者を拘束しない。その事件は、国内の取消裁判の既判事項にはならないのである。

　したがって、不利な決定を受けた申立人には、手間がかかり費用も要するが、国内でその目的を果たす２回目の機会がある。

　一方、不利な決定を受けた特許権者には２回目の機会がない。特許は消滅し、国内で回復させることはできない。

Chapter 15

Appeals

審 判

Morten Garberg

MEMO

▶ 審判部は、欧州特許庁の他の機関から独立しており、審判部の規則を独自に有しているという点で、日本特許庁の審判部に類似します（§1）。

▶ 欧州特許庁の第一審手続の最終決定により不利益を受けたいずれの者（出願人、異議申立人、特許権者）も審判を請求することができます（§2）。**異議申立人**が不服を申し立てることができる点で日本の実務と異なります。

▶ 審判請求書の提出期限と審判請求の理由を記載した書面の提出期限が**別々に設定**されています（§2.1及び§2.2）。

▶ 欧州特許庁の審判が純粋な法律審ではない点、日本に類似するでしょう。審判請求の理由を記載した書面を提出する際に、当事者は、補正されたクレームを新たに提出することができます（§3）。付属の審判部規則第12条を参照してください。新たな証拠が手続的に許可されるかどうかは審判部の裁量により審判部ごとにばらつきがあります（§3）。

▶ 異議申立手続の第二審（控訴審）の場合、当事者（特許権者又は申立人）が審判請求人又は審判被請求人のどちらに分類されるかで、審判請求の結果に影響します（§4.1）。（補正された形式で特許が維持される）中間決定の場合は、双方が審判請求をすることが多いです。審判手続においても、第三者による意見の提出（情報提供）や参加制度があります（§4.2及び§4.3）。

▶ 審判手続には、書面審理と口頭審理があります（§5.1）。**査定系審判でも口頭審理**が行われ、口頭審理の終わりに審判部の決定が口頭で告げられます（§5.2）。当事者系審判の場合は、書面審理のなかで何回かの書面交換が行われ、その後に口頭審理があります（§5.3）。査定系審判でも当事者系審判でも、**裁判所への不服申立てというルートはありませんので、審判部の決定が最終決定**です。

▶ 欧州特許庁は、イギリスやアメリカのようなコモンローに基づいていませんので、審判部は拘束力あるケースロー制度の原理に基づいて機能していません。個々の審判部は、基本的に、別の審判部の審決に拘束されません（§7）。

▶ 拡大審判部は技術審判部等に追加される審級ではなく、法律上の論点に関する付託を処理し、再審理の申請について決定をするという2つの特別の役割を持ちます（§8）。

Introduction

In proceedings before the EPO, a party has the right to appeal against a first instance decision which has gone against him.

Broadly speaking, there are two types of appeal cases which are common.

The first is referred to as *ex parte* appeals; these are appeal cases solely between a party to proceedings at the EPO and the EPO itself. A typical example of such an appeal would be a case where a patent application has been refused by an examining division, and the applicant considers that the reasoning given is not correct or fair.

The second type is referred to as *inter partes* appeals; these are appeals in cases where there are two or more adversarial parties, typically this would relate to an EPO opposition case.

1   The Boards of Appeal

From an organizational perspective, the boards of appeal are separate from other departments of the European patent office. According to the EPO organizational structure, the EPO is divided into five directorates-general (DG), where DG 1 is responsible for e.g. first instance examination and opposition proceedings and DG 3 is responsible for appeals. The boards of appeal are based in Munich, where all appeal hearings take place.

The work done by the boards of appeal is done by the so-called members of the boards of appeal. These are EPO employees who have a time-limited contract of usually five years (which can be extended), and who have either a technical degree or a legal degree. The members of the boards of appeal are typically chosen amongst the best and most experienced examiners, and external recruitment

はじめに

欧州特許庁の手続においては、当事者は、不服のある第一審の決定に対して審判を請求する権利を有する。

大まかにいえば、よくある不服審判事件として2つのタイプがある。

第一のタイプは、査定系審判といわれる。これは欧州特許庁における手続の当事者と特許庁とに関係する場合の不服審判である。このような審判の典型例は、特許出願が審査部により拒絶され、その理由付けが適切でないか、又は公平でないと出願人が考える場合である。

第二のタイプは当事者系審判といわれる。これは二以上の対立する当事者が存在する場合の不服審判であり、通常、欧州特許庁の特許異議申立事件と関連する。

1　審判部

組織論的な側面からいうと、審判部は、欧州特許庁の他の組織から分離されている。欧州特許庁の組織構造によると、欧州特許庁は5つの総局（DG）に分けられる。DG 1 は、第一審としての審査及び特許異議申立手続を担当し、DG 3 は審判手続を担当する。審判部はミュンヘンに本拠を置き、審判の口頭審理はすべてここで行われる。

審判部が行う業務は、いわゆる審判部の構成員により行われる。これらの者は、通常5年（延長可能）に限定された雇用契約により雇用された欧州特許庁の被雇用者で、技術の学位又は法律の学位を有している。審判部の構成員は、最良、かつ、最も経験を積んだ審査官から選ばれるのが通常であるが、外部からの採用もある。審判部の構成員は、欧州特許法の事実上の判事であり、欧州

also takes place. It is generally considered that the members of the boards of appeal are effectively judges of European patent law and they operate with significant independence from the EPO. They only work on appeal cases.

The boards of appeal are divided up into a number of specific boards. There are at present 28 technical boards of appeal, each of which is populated by a number of technical members and a number of legal members. The technical members have a relevant science degree, and the legal members have a degree in law. There is also a legal board of appeal and an enlarged board of appeal, populated by certain members of the boards of appeal who also sit on the technical boards of appeal. We will return to the function of the enlarged board of appeal later.

When an appeal is filed, it is assigned to a board of appeal, usually to one of the technical boards. The assignment to a particular technical board is done on the basis of the IPC class of the application or the patent to which the appeal relates; this ensures that the appeal is handled by a board with the appropriate technical knowledge. There is a pre-existing business distribution scheme which is published by the EPO each year which defines which boards are responsible for which IPC classes.

If an appeal relates exclusively to a legal issue, it will be referred to the legal board of appeal rather than to a technical board of appeal.

For a given case, the responsible technical board of appeal will assign a panel of three members to hear and decide on the case. The panel consists of three members (with the option for expansion if needed); at least two technically-qualified members and one legally qualified member are present. In contrast, a legal board of appeal would consist of three legally-qualified members.

Within the three-man panel, one member is assigned as the chairman. It is the chairman's responsibility to conduct the proceedings fairly. Typically, each board only has one chairman so that he will sit in on every case assigned to this

特許庁から独立して業務を行うと一般的には考えられている。これらの者は審判事件のみを扱っている。

審判部は特定された数々の審判部門に分かれている。現在、28の部門に分かれた技術審判部があり、各々に複数の技術構成員と複数の法律構成員が配置されている。技術構成員は該当する技術の学位を持っており、法律構成員は法律の学位を持っている。また、1つの法律審判部及び1つの拡大審判部がある。拡大審判部には、審判部の特定の構成員であり、技術審判部にも籍をおく者が配置されている。拡大審判部の役割については後で再び説明する。

審判が請求されると、通常は、1つの技術審判部に割り当てられる。特定の技術審判部への割り当ては、審判に係る出願又は特許のIPC分類に基づいて行われる。これにより、審判は適切な技術的知識を持った技術審判部により処理されることになる。既存の業務区分計画表があり欧州特許庁により毎年出版されており、どの技術審判部がどのIPC分類を担当するかが特定されている。

審判が法律問題にのみ関係する場合は、技術審判部ではなく法律審判部に付託される。

ある事件を、担当する技術審判部は、3人の構成員からなる合議体をその事件に割り当て審理し決定させる。合議体は（必要に応じて拡大する場合もあるが）3人の構成員からなり、少なくとも2人の技術構成員と1人の法律構成員が存在する。これとは対照的に、法律審判部は3人の法律構成員からなる。

3人の合議体では、1人の構成員が審判長として任命される。手続を公平に処理することは審判長の任務である。各部門には通常1人の審判長が存在し、この部門に割り当てられたすべての事件に出席する。審判長に加え第一の構成

board. In addition to the chairman, there will be a first member assigned; he will typically be a technically qualified member, and he will be principally responsible for studying the written arguments and evidence of the case, briefing his two colleagues in advance of the hearing and for writing the reasons for the decision. Each board will have several technically qualified members, so that they rotate and each take part in fewer cases per year than the chairman. The third member of the panel is typically the legal member, whose task it is to focus on legal aspects of the case. As can be expected, the extent to which complex legal issues come up varies much from case to case, and of course the technical members are very experienced in substantive patent law. Therefore, the legal member is not always so heavily involved in the decision-making process. It is a legal requirement that there is a legally-qualified member present in each appeal hearing.

2 Initiating an Appeal

An appeal can be filed against any final decision of an EPO first instance by any party who is adversely affected by that decision. A party is adversely affected if his main request was not granted to him by the EPO. Thus, in EPO opposition proceedings a patentee can appeal if his patent was revoked or if it was maintained on the basis of an auxiliary request. Similarly, an opponent can appeal if he had requested complete revocation and the EPO decided to maintain the patent in any form. It can therefore happen that an opposition case has an intermediate outcome which is appealed both by the opponent and by the patentee.

If an appeal is filed from an opposition case and there is only one appellant, then the non-appealing party to the opposition is still a party in the appeal proceedings where he is referred to as a respondent.

There are two essential steps that are required to initiate an appeal, namely

員が任命される。第一の構成員は通常、技術構成員であり、主に答弁書及び証拠を検討し、その合議体の他の2人の構成員に聴聞（口頭審理）に先立ち概要を伝え、決定の理由を記載する任務を有する。各技術審判部には複数の技術構成員がいるため、これらの者が持ち回り制で担当し、各人は年間、審判長よりも少ない事件に関与する。合議体の第三の構成員は通常、法律構成員であり、その任務は事件の法的側面に重点的に取り組むことである。予期されるように、複雑な法律問題が生じる程度は、事件により大きく変動し、技術構成員は当然、実体特許法には非常に精通している。したがって、法律構成員は、判断過程に常に大きく関与するわけではない。法律上の要件から各聴聞には法律職構成員が出席することになっている。

2　審判の開始

　欧州特許庁の第一審の最終決定により不利益を受けたいずれの者も、この最終決定に対して審判を請求することができる。ある者のメインリクエストが欧州特許庁により認められなかった場合は、その者は不利益を受けたといえる。欧州特許庁の特許異議申立手続においては、特許権者は自身の特許が取り消されたか、補助リクエストに基づいて自身の特許が維持された場合は、審判を請求することができる。同様に異議申立人が特許の全取消しを請求したにもかかわらず、欧州特許庁がいずれかの形式で特許を維持することを決定した場合は、異議申立人は審判を請求することができる。よって、特許異議申立事件は異議申立人と特許権者の双方により不服が申し立てられる中間結果になることもある。

　特許異議の申立てに係る審判が請求され、審判請求人が1人だけの場合は、審判を請求していない当事者は依然として審判手続の当事者であり、審判被請求人と呼ばれる。

　審判を開始するために必要な2つの不可欠なステップがある。すなわち、(i)

the filing of (i) a notice of appeal and (ii) the grounds of appeal.

2.1 The Notice of Appeal

The notice of appeal consists of a statement that an adversely affected party wishes to appeal against a certain first instance decision. It must be accompanied by the appeal fee. The notice of appeal must be filed within two months of notification of the written decision which is being appealed. This deadline is not extensible.

2.2 The Grounds of Appeal

The grounds of appeal consist of a reasoned statement explaining why the decision under appeal is wrong and why it should be overturned. According to the rules of procedure of the boards of appeal, an appellant must set out his full case in his grounds of appeal. The deadline for filing the grounds of appeal is four months after notification of the written decision which is being appealed. This deadline is also not extensible.

3 Subject and Scope of the Appeal

In some EPC member states, e.g. the UK, the purpose of an appeal is to provide a review of the legal correctness of the first instance decision. Therefore, in British appeal proceedings, the appellant is essentially restricted to presenting arguments relating to the application of the law by the first instance Judge. However, arguments which relate to factual matters would not be accepted and generally new evidence cannot be filed. Other EPC member states, e.g. Germany, take a different approach and effectively allow an appellant to re-run his case so that it is possible to also argue that the first instance decision is wrong due to a factual error, and the filing of new evidence might also be possible.

審判請求書の提出、及び、(ii)審判請求の理由を記載した書面（以下、理由記載書）の提出である。

2.1 審判請求書

審判請求書は、不利益を受けた当事者が、第一審の決定に対して審判を請求することを望む陳述から構成される。これには審判請求費用を伴うことが必要である。審判請求書は、不服申立ての基礎となる書面による決定の通知から2月以内に提出する必要がある。この期限は延長できない。

2.2 理由記載書

理由記載書は、審判の対象である決定が誤っている理由、及びこれが覆されるべき理由を説明する根拠を記載した書面である。審判部手続規則によると、審判請求人は審判請求の理由において、その主張のすべてを詳述する必要がある。理由記載書の提出期限は、審判請求に係る書面による決定の通知から4月以内である。この期限も延長できない。

3 不服申立ての対象と範囲

イギリスなど一部の欧州特許条約の締約国では、不服申立ての目的は第一審の決定の法的正当性の再検討を行うことである。よってイギリスの訴訟手続では、請求人は実質的に、第一審の判事による法律の適用に関する主張を提出することに制限される。事実問題に関連する主張は受理されず、一般的に新たな証拠は提出できない。ドイツなど他の欧州特許条約の締約国は異なるアプローチをとっており、請求人が事件を再びやり直すことを事実上認めているため、事実誤認により第一審の決定が誤っていることを主張することも可能であり、新たな証拠の提出も可能となる場合がある。

The European Patent Convention itself does not expressly define which types of arguments an appellant should be allowed to rely on and as such there is a somewhat diverging practice between different EPO appeal boards. Generally speaking, the EPO boards of appeal are relatively generous and flexible when it comes to accepting new material in appeal proceedings. Thus, it is often possible for an applicant or a patentee to file new amended claims during an appeal, or in general for parties to file new arguments or new evidence. It is always possible in an appeal to challenge the correctness of factual findings by the first instance.

This characteristic of EPO appeal proceedings, coupled with the relatively low cost results in a rather large number of appeals is being filed each year.

4   Parties to the Proceedings

As mentioned above, the parties to an EPO appeal may include one or more appellants and one or more respondents. As will be discussed below, whether a party is an appellant or a respondent can make a difference.

By definition, an appellant is any party who files an admissible appeal in time.

A respondent is any party who is not an appellant but was a party to the proceedings resulting in the decision under appeal.

4.1   Relevance of Party Status: Prohibition of *Reformatio in Peius*

Whether a party is classified as an appellant or a respondent can have an impact on the legal flexibility of that party during appeal proceedings. This is because of a well-established legal principle referred to as the prohibition of *reformatio in peius*. This principle excludes the possibility that the sole appellant in

欧州特許条約は、いずれのタイプの主張が審判請求の根拠となるのかを明示的に規定しておらず、欧州特許庁審判部の部門間においては若干異なる実務になっている。一般的にいえば、欧州特許庁審判部は、新たな資料を審判手続で受理することについては比較的寛大であり、柔軟性を有する。審判請求人又は特許権者は、審判手続の過程で、補正されたクレームを新たに提出することができる場合があり、一般的には、当事者らは、新たな議論を展開したり、新たな証拠を提出できる場合がある。第一審による事実認定の正当性に異議を述べることも審判では常に可能である。

こうした特徴から、比較的安い審判手続費用と相俟って、欧州特許庁には毎年かなり多くの件数の審判請求が申し立てられている。

4　手続の当事者

上記のように、欧州特許庁における審判手続の当事者らには、一以上の審判請求人と一以上の審判被請求人とが含まれることがある。以下に考察するように、当事者が審判請求人となるか、審判被請求人となるかにより違いが生じる。

審判請求人とは、許可され得る審判請求を提出するいずれかの当事者と定義される。

審判被請求人とは、審判請求人ではないが、審判に係る決定の手続の当事者であったいずれかの当事者である。

4.1　当事者適格の関連性：不利益変更の禁止

当事者が審判請求人に分類されるか、審判被請求人に分類されるかは、審判手続過程で当該当事者の法的な柔軟性に影響する。これは「不利益変更の禁止」と呼ばれる確立した法原則によるものである。この原則は、欧州特許庁の審判手続で唯一の請求人が、審判の結果、より困窮する状況になることを排除

EPO proceedings can be left worse off as a result of the appeal. Put differently, it means that if an appellant is the only appellant, then he is guaranteed an overall outcome which is at least as good as the outcome of the first instance decision.

As will be appreciated, this principle is only relevant in *inter partes* proceedings, and where the outcome of the first instance was an intermediate result maintaining the patent in amended form on the basis of an auxiliary request.

In this situation, if both parties appeal, the outcome of the appeal is entirely open and could be anywhere in the range from maintenance of the patent as granted to complete revocation.

However, if only the opponent had appealed, then the opponent would be guaranteed that the patent could not be maintained with any claims which are broader than those which were left at the end of the first instance proceedings. Conversely, if the patentee was the sole appellant, patentee would be guaranteed to keep those claims and so the sole subject of the appeal would be to decide whether broader claims could be allowed.

In order to avoid this restriction, in opposition cases where the result is an intermediate one so that neither party wins, it is typical for both parties to appeal.

4.2 Third Party Observations

Anyone who is not party to the proceedings can still contribute by making third party observations. These observations can be submitted anonymously, and can contain arguments and evidence relating to the ongoing appeal. Those can then be taken over by the parties to the appeal, or by the appeal board itself.

4.3 Intervention of the Assumed Infringer

As discussed in the preceding chapter on opposition proceedings, a party

する。言い換えると、これは、審判請求人が唯一の審判請求人である場合、この者は第一審の決定の結果と少なくとも同然な全体としての結果を保証されることを意味する。

上記からわかるように、この原則は、第一審の結果が補助リクエストに基づいて補正された形式で特許を維持するという中間結果であった場合の当事者間の手続についてのみ関連する。

この状況では、両当事者が審判請求する場合は、審判請求の結果は全体として未確定であり、付与された形式での特許の維持からその全取消しの範囲までのいずれも起こり得ることとなる。

一方、異議申立人のみが審判を請求した場合には、異議申立人は第一審手続の最後の段階で残されていたクレームより広いクレームを有する特許が維持されないことを保証される。逆に特許権者が唯一の審判請求人であった場合は、特許権者はこれらのクレームを維持することが保証されるため、審判請求の唯一の主題は、より広いクレームが認められるか否かを決定することである。

この制限を回避するために、いずれの当事者も勝訴しないという中間結果に終わる特許異議申立事件では、両当事者が審判請求をするのが常である。

4.2　第三者による意見書

手続の当事者ではない者は、何人も、第三者による意見書を提出することにより依然として手続に関与することができる。当該意見書は匿名で提出でき、係属中の審判に関する主張と証拠をそれに含めてもよい。当該意見書は審判手続の当事者ら又は審判部自身により考慮され得る。

4.3　被疑侵害者の参加

特許異議申立手続について前章で考察したように、欧州特許条約の締約国に

who has been sued for infringement in an EPC member state may join an ongoing opposition against that patent, even if he did not oppose in time. It is also possible for the alleged infringer to join during an ongoing appeal relating to an opposition case.

5 How Appeal Proceedings are Conducted

5.1 Written and Oral Proceedings

In both *ex parte* and *inter partes* appeals, there will typically be an initial phase of written argument exchange (written proceedings) followed by a hearing (oral proceedings). The decision will typically be announced at the end of the hearing, and written reasoning for the decision will follow later. In more detail:

5.2 *Ex Parte* Appeals

In *ex parte* appeals, there is only one party to the appeal. Typically, the filing of the grounds of appeal will be followed by a relatively long period of inactivity until the board of appeal issues a summons to oral proceedings. The hearing date is decided by the board of appeal and the appellant is informed of this in advance in writing. The board of appeal has the option of providing intermediate written communications to the appellant, and they may also provide a preliminary opinion on the case in advance of the hearing. Such communications serve to highlight any issues which the board of appeal primarily considers to be key points on which the appellant so far has not managed to ensure compliance with the EPC.

Oral proceedings will only take place if the appellant has requested a hearing (which is a routine measure). Typically, a hearing request will be conditional meaning that the appellant makes it clear that no hearing is wanted or needed if the EPO appeal board is minded to reverse the decision under appeal. Then a written decision in the appellant's favour can be issued without the need for a

おいて侵害訴訟で訴えられた当事者は、異議申立期間内に特許異議の申立てをしなかったとしても、係属中の特許異議申立手続に参加することができる。被疑侵害者は、特許異議申立事件に係る審判手続が係属中であれば、その手続にも参加することができる。

5 審判手続はどのように行われるか

5.1 書面及び口頭審理

査定系及び当事者系審判の双方では、書面による議論のやりとり（書面審理）の段階が最初にあり、その後に口頭審理が行われるのが通常である。決定は、通常、口頭審理の最後に告げられ、決定の理由は後に書面で告げられる。詳細は以下のとおりである。

5.2 査定系審判

査定系審判では、一当事者のみが審判手続に存在する。理由記載書を提出した後は、口頭審理召喚状を審判部（これより先、特定部門の「技術審判部」を「審判部」と表記する）が発行するまではなんの動きもない比較的長い期間があるのが通常である。口頭審理の期日は審判部が決定し、事前に書面で審判請求人に通知される。審判部は審判請求人に対して書面により中間通知を行うこともでき、この通知では口頭審理に先立ち、事件に関する予備的見解を提示することができる。当該通知は、審判請求人に対して、欧州特許条約に定める要件を満たしていない要点について審判部が仮見解を強調する役割を果たす。

口頭審理は、審判請求人が口頭審理を請求した場合にのみ行われる（その請求はお決まりの措置である）。口頭審理の請求は、審判部が審判に係る決定を覆すことを意図している場合には口頭審理を望まない、又は必要としないことを請求人が明確にすることを意味する条件語句である。よって、審判請求人に有利な書面による決定は、口頭審理を行うことなく発行される。

hearing to take place.

If a hearing does take place, this will not be open to the public. The hearing will take place in a closed hearing room; it is usually be set for one day, starting first thing in the morning and concluding once the discussion is complete. The hearing will be attended by the members of the boards of appeal responsible for deciding the case as well as the applicant's European patent attorney and optionally some representatives from the applicant (e.g. technical experts, the inventor or an in-house patent attorney). Usually an *ex parte* appeal hearing might take 1-5 hours. At the end of the hearing, a decision will almost always be announced. Possible outcomes include the dismissal of the appeal (in which case the examining division's refusal of the appeal is finally confirmed), a decision to allow the appeal and overturn the contested decision (in which case a patent would be granted) or the case could be partially decided on some issues only and then remitted to the first instance to continue examination.

Generally speaking, it is often difficult to persuade an appeal board that an EPO examining division was overly tough, and so quite a lot of *ex parte* appeals are not successful. Of course, the chance of success is strongly dependent on the case in question. So if the examiner did make a mistake, this can be corrected by filing an appeal, and if the applicant is able to cure deficiencies in the application by bringing new arguments, evidence or amendments this may also lead to success.

A written decision is issued at a later point in time, typically 1 to 2 months after the hearing. This will contain the detailed reasons why the board of appeal decided the way it did.

The boards of appeal are the highest EPO instance, which means that no further appeal is possible and that the decisions issued are final.

口頭審理は、一般には公開されずに行われる。口頭審理は閉鎖された口頭審理室で行われることになる。朝一番に開始し、協議が完結すると終結するという1日の期日が設定されるのが通常である。口頭審理には判断を下す任務を有する審判部の構成員、並びに審判請求人の代理人である欧州弁理士、そして任意で出願人を代表する者（例えば、技術者、発明者、社内弁理士）が出席する。査定系審判の口頭審理は1～5時間かかるのが通常である。ほとんどの場合、口頭審理の最後に決定が告げられる。口頭審理の結果として、審判請求の棄却（審査部による出願の拒絶が最終的に確認される）、審判請求を認めて争われている決定を覆す決定（特許査定がされる）、事件を一部の争点についてのみ部分的に決定し、審査を続けるために第一審に差し戻す決定がある。

　一般的にいえば、審査部が極端に厳しかった点について審判部を説得することは困難である。よって、査定系審判で成功することはほとんどない。もちろん、成功率は係争中の事件に大きく左右される。よって審査官が誤っていた場合は、これは審判請求をすることにより是正され、審判請求人が新たに議論を展開したり、証拠を提出したり、又は補正をすることにより出願の不備が是正できる場合は、これにより成功に至る場合もある。

　口頭審理の後で文書により決定が発行される。通常は口頭審理から1～2月後である。当該決定には審判部がその決定に至るにあたっての詳細な理由が含まれる。

　審判部は欧州特許庁において最も高い審級である。よって、これ以上の不服申立ては不可能であり、発行された決定は最終的である。

5.3 *Inter Partes* Appeals

In *inter partes* appeals, the proceedings are somewhat more complicated. As mentioned above, the filing of the notice of appeal and grounds of appeal initiates appeal proceedings. Once the EPO receives the grounds of appeal, this will be forwarded to the other parties. The other parties will be set a deadline (usually four months) for the filing of a response to the grounds of appeal. This deadline is theoretically extensible, although the practice varies from board to board as to whether or not such discretionary extensions are given.

The response to the grounds of appeal is a very important brief, because the rules of procedure of the boards of appeal specify that the grounds of appeal and/or the response to the grounds of appeal shall set out a party's full case. In other words, this means that a party is not free to amend his case by adding new claim amendments, arguments or evidence at a later point in time. If a party nevertheless does wish to amend his case later, any new amendments, arguments or evidence will be admitted only on a discretionary basis, the decision on admission being dependent on the surrounding circumstances (e.g. relevance of the new material, the increase in complexity it causes, procedural fairness, timing of the filing and reasons for the lateness).

Once the EPO receives the response to the grounds of appeal, this will also be forwarded to all the other parties to the proceedings. Typically, no deadline will be set for further written submissions although the other parties are free to make further written submissions if they want to.

Eventually, time will come for oral proceedings to be held. As in *ex parte* cases, oral proceedings are held only at the request of the parties. However, in opposition appeal cases the patentee will typically request a hearing if the patent cannot be maintained as granted, while the opponents will request a hearing if the patent cannot be completely revoked. In this scenario, a hearing is inevitable.

5.3 当事者系審判

当事者系審判では手続は若干複雑である。上述したように、審判請求書及び理由記載書の提出により審判手続が開始される。欧州特許庁が理由記載書を受理すると、これが他方当事者らに送付される。他方当事者らには、理由記載書に対して答弁書を提出する期間（通常は4月）が設定される。この期限は理論的には延長可能であるが、延長がされるか否かに関しての実務は、審判部の裁量により、審判部ごとに異なる。

答弁書は非常に重要である。審判部手続規則によれば、理由記載書、答弁書又はその両方により当事者の全ケースが提示されるべきだからである。言い換えれば、クレームの補正、議論又は証拠を新たに追加することにより、後の時点で事件を修正する自由が当事者にはないのである。それにもかかわらず、当事者が後に自身のケースを改めることを望む場合は、新たな補正、主張又は証拠のいずれも審判部の裁量によってのみ手続的に許可され得るのであり、この決定は、取り巻く状況（新たな資料の関連性、これによる複雑化、手続的公正、提出のタイミング、遅延の理由等）により左右される。

欧州特許庁は答弁書を受理すると、手続の他方当事者のすべてにそれを送付する。これらの他方当事者は、さらに書面を提出することもできるが、こうした書面提出のための期限は通常設定されない。

やがて、口頭審理が行われる時期が到来する。査定系事件でもそうであるように、口頭審理は当事者らの請求があった場合にのみ行われる。しかし特許異議申立てに係る審判事件では、特許権者は、通常、特許が付与された形式で維持されない場合に口頭審理を請求し、他方で申立人らは、特許を完全に取り消すことができない場合に口頭審理を請求する。このシナリオでは、口頭審理は避けられない。

When the appeal board is ready for the hearing to be held, it will notify the parties by issuing a summons to oral proceedings at least two months before the intended hearing date. The board of appeal will have the option to include e.g. with the summons a preliminary opinion which sets out the board's preliminary view of the case and highlights key issues for discussion during the hearing. Whether or not such a preliminary opinion is provided is discretionary and here practice varies significantly from board to board and member to member. It is however not at all unusual for the board to decide not to issue any communication to the parties other than the summons which includes only practical details about where and when the hearing will take place.

An *inter partes* hearing at the EPO is public meaning that anyone can attend. Naturally, the members of the boards of appeal responsible for deciding the case will be present. Each party to the proceedings will also have been invited, and will usually be represented by their European patent attorney, optionally accompanied by one or more representatives from their client company (e.g. technical experts, in-house patent attorneys etc.).

The chairman of the board of appeal will be responsible for conducting the proceedings and it will be his decision in which order the various topics on the agenda are to be discussed. It is also the chairman who decides when the parties are allowed to address the board. Typically, the debate is structured by discussing one topic at a time. Usually, the chairman will focus on the decision under appeal and will require the appellant to explain why he believes that this decision should be overturned. The other parties to the proceedings will of course also have an opportunity to present their point of view and to explain why the decision should stand, and they may also present other arguments to support their overall case.

Generally speaking, the case presentation is done by the parties' respective European Patent Attorneys. Although there are provisions for witnesses to be heard and for expert testimonies to be given, these are not often used.

審判部が口頭審理を行う準備ができている場合は、予定された口頭審理期日の少なくとも2月前に、口頭審理召喚状を発行して当事者らに通知する。この際、審判部は、例えば、審判部による事件の予備的見解を提示して口頭審理における審議の主な争点を強調する仮見解を召喚状に含めるという選択肢を有する。かかる仮見解が出されるか否かは任意であり、ここでの実務は審判部門により、そして構成員により大きく異なる。口頭審理が行われる日時・場所に関する実務的詳細のみを含む召喚状以外の通知を審判部が当事者らに発行しないことはまったく異例ではない。

　欧州特許庁における当事者間の口頭審理は公開して行われる。よって、いずれの者もこの口頭審理に出席することができる。もちろん判断を下す任務を有する審判部の構成員は出席することとなる。手続の各当事者も口頭審理に召喚されており、通常は欧州弁理士により代理され、依頼人の会社の1人又は複数人の代表者（例えば、技術専門家、社内弁理士等）を任意に伴う場合がある。

　審判長は手続を遂行する任務を有し、審理事項の種々の主題を審理する順序は審判長が決定する。当事者らがいつその審判部に対して論説できるかを決定するのも審判長である。通常、審議は一度に1つの主題を審理することで構成される。通常、審判長は審判に係る決定に集中し、審判請求人に対しこの決定が覆されるべき理由を説明するよう求める。審判手続の他方当事者はもちろん自身の視点を提示し、決定が有効である理由を説明する機会を有し、自身の立場全体を裏付ける他の議論を展開することもできる。

　一般的にいえば、当事者らの各々の欧州弁理士により、その事件が提示される。証人が聴取され、鑑定が行われるという規定もあるが、これらは頻繁に利用されるものではない。

Once a certain topic has been discussed and all parties have had a reasonable chance to present their views on that topic, the board will typically choose to deliberate on that topic. For the deliberation, everyone except the members of the board will leave the room and the board will reach a decision on the points which were discussed. When the hearing resumes, the board will usually announce its decision on that point to the parties and the chairman will then decide how the debate is going to continue.

Broadly speaking, the board will usually focus on the main request and auxiliary requests of the patentee, and will assess these one at a time starting with the main request (i.e. the highest ranking request, which will usually have the broadest claims). The examination of a particular request will come to an end either when one argument against the validity of those claims is found by the board to be justified, or when all arguments against the validity of the claims have been discussed and found to be unfounded. If the claims are found not to be valid, the discussion will move on to the next request on file. If the claims under discussion are found to be valid, then the patent will be maintained on the basis of those amended claims.

It is generally difficult for patentee to amend his claims during the oral proceedings (unlike in the first instance, where this is not so uncommon). Therefore, in EPO appeal proceedings it is very important for patentee to consider his fall-back positions at an early stage and file appropriate auxiliary requests.

Inter partes appeal hearings are very variable in length, this depending very greatly on the complexity of the case and the number of parties involved. Typically, if there are more than three parties involved or if the case is very complex, the hearing will be set for two consecutive days. A normal opposition appeal will only be set for one hearing day.

At the end of the oral proceedings, the board of appeal will typically announce a final decision. Broadly speaking, the board of appeal can decide to revoke the

特定の議題について議論され、かつ、当該議題について見解を述べる適切な機会がすべての当事者らに与えられると、審判部は、当該議題を審議することを通常は選択する。審議をするにあたっては、審判部の構成員を除くすべての者が部屋を立ち去り、審判部は議論された点に関しての決定に至る。口頭審理が再開すると、審判部は当事者らに対して当該論点に関する決定を告げるのが通常であり、審判長は討論をどのように続けるかを決める。

大まかにいって、審判部は、通常、特許権者のメインリクエストと補助リクエストに注力し、これらをメインリクエスト（最高ランク付けの請求であり、最も広いクレームを有することが一般的である）から開始して1つずつ判断する。特定の請求についての審理は、そのクレームの有効性に対して反論がなされ、その反論が審判部により妥当であると認定される場合、あるいはクレームの有効性に対してなされたすべての反論が審理され、根拠なしと認定される場合に終結する。クレームが有効であると認定されない場合は、提出されている次の請求に審理が移る。そこで議論されているクレームが有効であると認定されると、補正されたクレームに基づいて特許が維持される。

口頭審理において特許権者が自身のクレームを補正することは概して難しく、この点において第一審とは異なる。よって欧州特許庁の審判手続においては、最悪の場合の代案を初期の段階で考慮して適切な補助リクエストを提出することが特許権者にとって非常に重要である。

口頭審理にかかる時間は、当事者系審判の場合は、事件の複雑性と関与する当事者の数に大きく左右され、非常にばらつきがある。4以上の当事者が関与する場合、又は事件が非常に複雑な場合、通常、口頭審理は2日間連続して設定される。通常の審判事件では、その口頭審理のために1日の期日が指定される。

審判部は、通常は、口頭審理の最後に最終決定を告げる。大まかにいうと、審判部は、特許を取り消すか、補正された形式で特許を維持するか、又は付与

patent, to maintain it in amended form or to maintain the patent as granted. They also have the option to only decide one aspect of the case and then to remit the case to the first instance for further examination. This means that EPO opposition proceedings would resume. The willingness to remit cases is rather variable from board to board; a typical scenario where a case might well be remitted is where the first instance decision only decides on certain EPC requirements, and where the appeal board subsequently finds that decision to be wrong. For example, if a first instance decision says that all requests lack novelty but makes no comment on inventive step, then the case is very likely to be remitted if the appellant can convince the board that the claims are novel. This is because there is a general principle that a party to proceedings before the EPO must have the possibility to have his case considered by two instances. However, the appeal boards do also understand that EPO opposition and appeal proceedings already take a very long time and that a decision to remit the case will significantly prolong these proceedings. In an average case, a remittal might cause a delay of 3-4 years in proceedings that are already lengthy.

While it is not so meaningful to provide statistics on the outcome of appeal proceedings, it can generally be said that the result at the end of the appeal is often different than that at the end of the opposition. Sometimes this is because the appeal board thinks that the first instance decision was not correct, and sometimes this is because the case has changed (in that new evidence, arguments or amendments are presented). Also for this reason, the filing of an appeal at the end of an opposition case is a relatively routine measure for many users of the EPO system.

A written decision is issued at a later point in time, typically 1 to 2 months after the hearing. This will contain the detailed reasons why the board of appeal decided the way it did.

All decisions of the boards of appeal are published online and each is assigned a case number which has the format T XXX/YY for the technical board of appeal

された形式で特許を維持するかを決定することができる。審判部はさらに、事件の1つの側面のみを決定し、さらなる審理のために事件を第一審に差し戻す選択肢を有する。これは、欧州特許庁での特許異議申立手続が再開することを意味する。事件を差し戻す程度は審判部の間に若干ばらつきがある。事件が差し戻されるのも無理はないという典型的なシナリオは、第一審の決定が特定の欧州特許条約の要件のみを判断している場合、そしてその後、審判部がその決定を誤っていると認定する場合である。例えば、すべての請求が新規性を欠いていると第一審の判断が述べているが、進歩性に関していかなる見解も述べておらず、クレームに記載された発明が新規であることについて審判請求人が審判部を説得することができる場合には、差し戻される可能性が非常に高い。欧州特許庁における手続の当事者は、自身の事件が2つの審級による審理を受ける権利を有するという一般原則によるものである。一方で、欧州特許庁の特許異議申立て及び審判手続にすでに非常に長い時間がかかっており、事件を差し戻す決定が当該手続を大いに長引かせるものであることを審判部は認識している。平均的な事件では、差戻しがされると、すでに長引いている手続に3〜4年の遅延が生じる。

審判手続の結果に関する統計を提示することはあまり意味がないが、概して、審判後の結果は特許異議申立後の結果とは異なることが多いといえる。その理由は、第一審の決定が正しくないと審判部が考えることがあり、また（新たな証拠、主張又は補正が提示されるため）状況が変わることもあるからである。このような理由もあって、特許異議申立事件の後に審判を請求することは、欧州特許庁制度を利用する多くの者にとっては比較的あたりまえの方策である。

書面による決定は、口頭審理の後で発行される。通常は口頭審理から1〜2月後である。書面による決定には審判部がその決定に至るにあたっての詳細な理由が含まれる。

審判部の決定（審決）はすべてがオンラインで公表され、技術審判部の決定についてはT XXX/YYという様式、法律審判部の決定についてはJ XXX/

decisions and J XXX/YY for the decisions of the legal board of appeal. YY represents the year in which the appeal was filed and the integers XXX represent a serial number. The most important decisions are published in the EPO Official Journal, and the EPO also publishes a case law book which summarizes the most important decisions which have an impact on current EPO practice.

6 Time and Cost of Proceedings

6.1 Time to Completion

An EPO appeal typically takes 2-4 years to complete. Appeals are usually handled by the responsible board based on the order in which the appeals were filed. The duration of an appeal is therefore strongly dependent on the workload of the board to which the appeal is assigned, and so it can vary from one technical field to another.

6.2 Acceleration

Acceleration of appeal proceedings can be requested. While the EPO will consider any request, it is only if there is ongoing infringement litigation in an EPC member state that there is a high likelihood that the board of appeal will put that case at the front of its queue of cases. Acceleration can have quite an impact on speed, and will allow the appeal to be resolved much more quickly. If acceleration is granted from the start of the appeal, the case might be resolved within a year or so. If acceleration is granted while the appeal is ongoing, the appeal board will typically immediately schedule a hearing for the first available date. A request for acceleration can be filed by one of the parties or e.g. by a judge in a national court where the national litigation may be stayed to await the outcome of the EPO case.

YYという様式の事件番号が各決定に付与される。YYは審判が請求された年を表し、XXXという整数は整理番号を表している。最も重要な決定は欧州特許庁の公報で公表され、欧州特許庁は、欧州特許庁の現在の実務に影響する重要な審決をまとめたケースローと題する本も発行している。

6　審判手続に関する時間と費用

6.1　完了までの時間

欧州特許庁における審判は、普通、完了するまでに2～4年かかる。審判は、通常、審判が請求された順序で担当する審判部により処理される。審判の期間は審判を担当する審判部の作業量に大きく左右されるため、技術分野ごとに変わり得る。

6.2　早期審理

審判手続の早期審理を請求することができる。欧州特許庁ではすべての早期審理請求が考慮されるが、欧州特許条約の締約国で係属中の侵害訴訟がある場合にのみ、審判部が案件処理順序のいちばん前にその事件を置く可能性が高い。早期審理は早さにかなり影響し、審判をかなり早く解決することができる。早期審理が審判の最初から認められると、事件は1年くらいで解決する場合がある。審判が係属中に早期審理が認められると、審判部は、通常、最も早い可能日に口頭審理を即座に予定する。早期審理の請求は、事件の一当事者によってなされてもよく、あるいは欧州特許庁の事件の結果を待つために国内訴訟を中断する国内裁判所の判事によってされてもよい。

6.3 Costs

The costs for an EPO appeal are the official fee (€ 1860) plus the costs for the European Patent Attorney handling the case.

Legal costs for an EPO *inter partes* appeal are usually strictly handled by requiring each party to pay their own costs. There is typically no possibility for the winner to collect costs from the loser, contrary to the situation in many national courts in EPC members states, e.g. Germany and the UK. Although there is a provision for the award of costs in EPO proceedings, this is used extremely rarely.

Overall, costs of an EPO appeal are moderate or even low when compared to e.g. the costs of national patent litigation in key EPC member states such as Germany and the UK.

7 Binding Effect of Previous Decisions

Common law jurisdictions such as the UK operate with a system of binding precedent. This means that, when a court is deciding on a given case, it must take into account and follow earlier decisions on the same legal point from the same court or from higher courts.

However, the EPO does not operate on this basis. Thus, an individual board of appeal has a high degree of freedom as regards how it decides a case before it.

Specifically, an earlier decision of a technical board of appeal or a legal board of appeal is not binding on an appeal board for which reason a deviation from certain principles previously established is possible.

6.3 費用

欧州特許庁の審判にかかる費用には、庁費用（1860ユーロ）に加え、欧州特許弁理士による事件処理費用が含まれる。

欧州特許庁における当事者系審判の審判手続費用は、通常、各当事者が自身の費用を支払うように求められ管理されている。ドイツ、イギリスなどの締約国の国内裁判所における状況とは反対に、勝った者が負けた者から費用を回収する可能性は通常ゼロである。欧州特許庁手続における費用の分担について法規定はあるが、極めて稀にしか利用されない。

全体として、審判の費用は、例えば、ドイツやイギリスなどの主な締約国の国内特許訴訟の費用と比べると高くはなく、むしろ低いものである。

7　先の審決の拘束力

イギリスなどコモンローの法域では拘束力あるケースローの制度が作用する。これはある事件を裁判所が判断する際に、同一の裁判所又は上級審から同一の法律上論点に関する先の判決を考慮に入れ、これに従う必要があることを意味する。

一方で、欧州特許庁は、このケースロー制度に基づき機能しない。よって、事件についてどのように判断するかに関して各々の審判部門は高い自由度を持っている。

具体的にいうと、技術審判部又は法律審判部の先の審決は審判部門を拘束せず、そのため、先に確立された一定の原則から逸脱した理由も可能である。

In practice, it is fair to say that the EPO boards of appeal do aim at the establishment of mainstream case law which is the result of continuous refinement of principles and practices established through previous decisions. Therefore, quoting from earlier decisions can often be persuasive.

As will be discussed in the section below, the enlarged board of appeal also issues decisions and opinions. These decisions are also not strictly binding on boards of appeal in other cases, although the boards of appeal have less flexibility to decide the case in a manner which is in direct contradiction with a key principle from an earlier decision or opinion of the enlarged board of appeal. In such a situation, the board of appeal would be required to submit a further referral to the enlarged board of appeal for reconsideration of the legal issue at hand.

8 The Enlarged Board of Appeal

The enlarged board of appeal is made up by members of the boards of appeal. Typically, the members of the enlarged board are the most senior members of the boards of appeal and many are chairmen of their individual technical boards.

The enlarged board of appeal is not a further appeal instance in addition to e.g. the technical boards of appeal. The enlarged board instead has two other specific roles, namely to address specific referrals on points of law and to decide on so-called petitions for review.

8.1 Decisions of the Enlarged Board of Appeal

From time to time, e.g. in proceedings before the boards of appeal, a legal issue will come up which the responsible board of appeal considers difficult to resolve on its own. This difficulty might result from the fact that the same issue has been resolved differently in various earlier decisions, or because it is a particularly complex legal issue. In those cases, the board of appeal may choose to refer a

実際上、欧州特許庁の審判部は、先の審決を通して確立された原則と実務を継続して洗練させることにより主流のケースローを確立させることを狙っているというのが適切である。よって、先の審決を引用することで説得力を得ることが多い。

以下のセクションで考察するように、拡大審判部もまた決定や見解を出す。これらの決定は他の事件における審判部の各部門を厳密には拘束しない。しかし、拡大審判部の先の審決や見解から生じた主な原則に直接反する態様で判断する柔軟性は審判部にはほとんどない。このような状況にあっては、審判部は法律問題の再審理を求めて拡大審判部にさらに付託する必要があるだろう。

8　拡大審判部

拡大審判部は、審判部の構成員から構成される。通常、拡大審判部の構成員は審判部の最も年配の構成員であり、多くは個々の技術審判部門の審判長である。

拡大審判部は技術審判部等に追加される審級ではない。その代わり拡大審判部には、2つの特別の役割がある。法律上の論点に関する特定の付託を処理すること、及び再審理の申請について決定をすることである。

8.1　拡大審判部の決定

例えば審判部の手続では、時々、担当する審判部門が自身では解決することが難しいと考える法律問題が浮上する。この難しさは、同一の争点が以前の種々の決定では異なって解決されてきたという事実からきている場合があり、また特に法律問題であるという理由もある。これらの事件では、当該審判部門は法律問題を拡大審判部に付託することを選択できる。

question of law to the enlarged board of appeal.

When such a referral is made, appeal proceedings are temporarily interrupted and proceedings before the enlarged board initiated. The proceedings before the enlarged board will be aimed at answering the legal question which has been posed by the referring board, and in deciding how to answer the questions the enlarged board will take into account submissions by the parties to the proceedings as well as submissions by other interested parties such as e.g. non-governmental organizations, bar associations or industry associations. These proceedings could last several years and will result in a written opinion or decision providing the answer to the questions that have been posed. The case will then go back to the referring appeal board which will complete the case applying the answers that have been provided.

Decisions of the enlarged board of appeal are also published and are assigned a case number with the format G XXX/YY, where YY is the year of the referral and XXX is a serial number.

8.2 Petitions for Review

In addition to providing decisions on interesting points of law, the enlarged board of appeal is also responsible for reviewing and deciding on so-called petitions for review. It is mentioned above that a decision of the board of appeal is a final decision and that there is no further EPO instance. The petition for review process provides for the possibility that a case can be continued even after a final decision by a board of appeal; however, this is possible only in very rare circumstances. Specifically, this system is meant to provide a safeguard against procedural mistakes or gross unfairness in connection with a completed appeal, and effectively allows for a retrial if a party can prove that such a serious mistake took place. As will be evident, this provision of the law is meant to provide a possibility for a retrial only in exceptional circumstances, for which reason the number of successful petitions for review is predictably small.

このような付託が行われると、審判手続は一時的に中断し、拡大審判部における手続が開始される。拡大審判部における手続は、付託部門により提起された法律問題に回答することを目的とし、この問題にどのように回答するかを決定する際に、拡大審判部は、審判手続の当事者らによる提出物、並びに非政府組織、弁護士会、企業団体など他の利害関係人による提出物も考慮する。この手続は数年続き、書面による見解や提起された法律問題に回答する決定が出される。その後、当該事件は付託審判部門に戻され、拡大審判部からの回答を適用することによりその事件は完了する。

　拡大審判部の決定もまた公表され、G XXX/YY という様式の事件番号が付される（YY は付託の年度であり、XXX は整理番号である）。

8.2　再審理の申請

　法律上の興味深い論点に関する決定に加え、拡大審判部は、いわゆる再審理の申請を検討して決定する任務を有する。上述したように、審判部の決定は最終的であり、欧州特許庁にはこれ以上の審級はない。再審理の申請によれば、審判部による最終決定の後であっても事件が係属する可能性が出てくる。一方、これは非常に稀な状況においてのみ起こり得る。特にこの制度は、完了した審判手続をめぐって手続上の誤りや全体的な不公平がある場合に対する対抗手段を与えることを意味し、このような誤りが生じたことを当事者が立証できる場合は、再審理の余地が有効に与えられる。この法規定が意味するところは、例外的な状況においてのみ再審理が可能であることであり、よって、再審理の申請が認められる数は少ないと予想される。

Chapter *16*

Central Limitation and Revocation Procedure

一元的な限定・取消手続

David Lethem

MEMO

- ▶ 一元的取消しの手続制度によれば、特許権者は**自身の欧州特許を取り消す**ことについて、欧州特許庁に対して取消請求をすることができます。これは、日本の特許実務には存在しない制度です。

- ▶ 一元的限定の手続制度は、その目的から日本特許庁の訂正審判制度に多少は類似するかもしれません（§1）。欧州特許が付与された後、特許権者は、特許の保護範囲を限定する目的で、主にクレームを減縮補正することができます。

- ▶ 欧州特許の取消し又は限定の効果は遡及効を有します（第68条参照）。

- ▶ 一元的限定請求がされると、補正されたクレームが欧州特許条約における通常の**形式的要件**（明確性、開示十分性、新規事項の追加禁止といった要件）をすべて満たしているかどうかが審査されます（§2）。

- ▶ 一元的限定請求は欧州特許が付与された後であればいつでも請求可能ですが、日本の実務（特許法第126条第2項）と同様に、欧州特許庁において特許異議申立手続が係属中の場合は除かれます（§3）。一元的取消しについても、特許異議申立手続が係属している場合は請求することができません（§3）。

- ▶ 一元的限定及び一元的取消しは、その請求書を欧州特許庁に提出しますが、いずれにおいても**請求の理由は必要とされません**（§

4）。

▶ 一元的限定・取消請求に関する手続及び決定は、（審判部でなく）**審査部**が担当します（§5）。一元的限定の手続においては、日本特許庁の訂正審判制度（第126条第7項）と異なり、**引例との関係で特許要件を審査することはありません**（§5）。

▶ 欧州特許条約では、一元的限定手続を利用することで、**締約国ごとに異なるクレーム限定を請求する**ことができます（§6）。

▶ 限定請求が認められるには、限定された特許の正文書を確認し、公報掲載手数料を納付し、欧州特許庁の公用語による**翻訳文を提出**しなければなりません（§7）。

▶ 限定請求が認められない場合は、日本と同様に不服申立てをすることができますが、不服申立ては**技術審判部**に対して行います（§8）。

Overview

Central limitation and central revocation procedures were introduced into European patent law in December 2007 as part of the EPC2000 package. These procedures respectively enable the proprietor of a European patent to request limitation of the patent claims or complete revocation of the patent. Operation of these procedures has been without legal controversy evidenced by the fact that there have been no decisions from the Technical Boards of Appeal on their operation in the intervening several years.

Central limitation provides a convenient and cost-effective way for a patent proprietor to restrict the scope of their patent after it has been granted. In the early years of the EPC, patent proprietors seeking to limit their patent centrally at the EPO could self-oppose, provided that this was done within 9 months of grant. However, self-opposition was outlawed by the EPO Enlarged Board of Appeal Decision (G 9/93). The national patent offices of some EPC contracting states (notably those of the UK, Germany, the Netherlands, France, Italy and Spain) permit post-grant claim limitation, but a claim limitation conducted by a national patent office is only effective in that contracting state. Following this path is both expensive and inconvenient as it requires coordinating parallel limitation procedures with each national patent office. The introduction of a central limitation procedure was therefore a welcome addition to the options available to patent proprietors.

The reader will appreciate that the EPO central limitation procedure is conceptually similar to the procedure based upon Article 126(1)(i) of the Japanese Patent Act. One similarity between the EPO and JPO limitation procedures is that any accepted limitation has retroactive effect.

The EPO central limitation and revocation procedures are relatively speedy. If a request for central limitation is clearly allowable, the time taken for the entire procedure is approximately three to six months. If, however, the limitation gives

概要

　一元的な限定及び取消手続は、EPC2000による改正の一環として2007年12月に欧州特許法に導入された。欧州特許の特許権者は、これらの手続を用いれば、特許されたクレームを限定するか、特許を完全に取り消すことについて請求をすることができる。これらの手続は、法的な争いなくこれまで運用されてきた。このことは、どの部門の技術審判部からも運用に関する審決がこの数年間にわたり出されていないことからも明らかである。

　一元的限定の手続制度により、特許権者は簡便、かつ、経済的に、特許が付与された後に、その権利範囲を減縮することができる。欧州特許条約の創設初期の頃は、欧州特許庁にて欧州特許を一元的に限定しようとする特許権者は、特許付与後9月以内に手続を行うことを条件として、自己の特許に対し異議を申し立てることができた。しかし、このような自己異議申立ては拡大審判部の審決（G 9/93）により違法とされた。一部の締約国（特に、イギリス、ドイツ、オランダ、フランス、イタリア、スペイン）の国内特許庁は、特許付与後にクレームを限定することを認めているが、国内特許庁によるクレームの限定はその締約国内でしか効力を持たない。このルートを採ると、各国内特許庁に対して、平行する限定手続を連係させる必要があるため、費用が高額になり、かつ、利便性が悪い。このため、一元的限定手続の導入は歓迎すべきものであり、特許権者が採り得る新たな選択肢となった。

　読者の方もおわかりであろうが、欧州特許庁の一元的限定手続は、日本特許法第126条第1項第1号の規定に基づく手続と概念的に類似する。欧州特許庁と日本特許庁の各限定手続の類似点の1つは、限定が認められると遡及効を有するということである。

　欧州特許庁における一元的な限定・取消しの手続は比較的迅速に行われる。一元的限定請求については、明らかに認められ得るものである場合、その手続全体に要する時間はおよそ3〜6月である。一方、請求した限定について疑義

rise to objections, then the procedure can take a year or more. The procedure for central revocation is simpler than the central limitation procedure, and typically takes from two to four months.

1   Why Limit or Revoke a Granted Patent?

The most common reason for limiting the scope of a granted patent is to ensure that its claims are novel and inventive over prior art that was not considered by the EPO Examiner during examination. National prior rights (national applications that are pending but unpublished at the effective priority date of a patent) are one example of this type of prior art, as EPO Examiners rarely cite such prior art during EPO examination proceedings. This is because national prior rights do not constitute prior art under the European Patent Convention. National prior rights do, however, belong to the state of the art in their national jurisdiction, hence it is necessary to ensure that the claims in each EPC contracting state are valid over any local national prior rights. The threat of national prior rights is set to become more significant when the Unitary Patent (European patent with unitary effect) enters into force, as it is possible for a single national prior right to invalidate an entire Unitary Patent. The central limitation procedure may be used in the future to prevent the total revocation of a Unitary Patent on the basis of a national prior right.

A patent proprietor may also amend the granted claims in order to establish novelty and an inventive step over the more usual type of pre-published prior art, particularly documents which first come to the proprietor's attention post-grant.

Alternatively, a patent proprietor might choose to limit the claims as granted so that they are more closely tailored to the product or process of an infringing party. Although this sacrifices claim scope, it decreases the likelihood that the infringing party will be able to respond to an infringement action by citing invalidating prior art when counterclaiming for revocation during litigation. Limiting the

がある場合は、手続が1年以上に及ぶこともある。一元的取消手続は一元的限定手続よりも簡易であり、通常2～4月かかる。

1　特許付与後に限定又は取消しを行う理由

　特許が付与された後にその範囲を限定する動機として最も一般的なものは、欧州特許庁の審査官により審査段階で考慮されなかった先行技術に対してクレームの新規性や進歩性を確保することである。この種の先行技術の例としては、先の国内の権利（特許の有効な優先日において係属中であり、かつ、未公開である国内出願）が挙げられる。なぜなら、欧州特許庁の審査官は、欧州特許庁での出願手続中にこの類の先行技術をめったに引用しないからだ。先の国内の権利が欧州特許条約下では先行技術を構成しないためである。一方、先の国内の権利はその国内の管轄下では技術水準に属するため、各締約国におけるクレームを、各国内の先の国内の権利に対して有効なものにしておく必要がある。単一効特許（単一効を有する欧州特許）が施行されることになれば、たった1つの先の国内の権利によって単一効特許全体が無効にされるおそれがあるため、先の国内の権利の脅威はさらに大きなものとなる。将来、一元的限定手続は、先の国内の権利に基づいて単一効特許が完全に取り消されることを防ぐために利用されよう。

　特許権者は、出願時には公開されていた一般的なタイプの先行技術文献、特に特許付与後にはじめて特許権者が気づいた文献に対して新規性及び進歩性を確保する目的で、特許されたクレームを補正することもできる。

　あるいは、特許権者は侵害者の製品又は方法にさらに近づくように特許されたクレームを限定することもできる。これによりクレームの範囲を犠牲にすることになるが、侵害訴訟において、特許取消しを求める反訴の際に、特許無効化につながる先行技術を引用することで侵害者が当該訴訟に対抗し得る可能性は低くなる。したがって、このようなかたちでクレームを限定することは、特

claims in this way may therefore be a useful strategy when preparing to sue for patent infringement.

The reasons for requesting central revocation at the EPO are few, since it is possible to passively abandon a patent across Europe by neglecting to pay renewal fees if, for example, the patent is either no longer required or is found to be incurably invalid. However, central revocation at the EPO affords a quicker and more decisive option than allowing a patent to become abandoned through inaction. Moreover, central revocation via the EPO has retroactive effect, meaning that the patent is deemed never to have existed. Central revocation might therefore be a potential bargaining point when negotiating with third parties.

2 What can and cannot be Limited by Amendment?

As central limitation is concerned with the protective scope of a patent, it is primarily concerned with the claims. The description can only be amended if this is necessary to ensure that it is consistent with claims that are amended as a result of the central limitation procedure.

Not all claim amendments are acceptable. First and foremost, the claims resulting from an amendment must comply with all of the usual formal requirements of the European Patent Convention such as clarity, sufficiency and prohibition against adding subject-matter. It is also necessary that the claim amendments must effect a limitation. This means that it must be impossible to imagine an embodiment which falls within the scope of the limited claims but which did not fall within the scope of the claims as granted. Claim amendments that simply 'tidy up' or attempt to clarify the claims will be rejected; so too will amendments that merely introduce extra dependent claims. This however does not preclude amendments being made solely to limit the scope of dependent claims (Guide-

許侵害訴訟に備える際の有用な戦略となり得る。

　欧州特許庁における一元的取消しについては、これを請求する理由はほとんど見当たらない。なぜなら、例えばその特許がもはや不要であるか、又はその特許に解消不可能な無効事由があることが見つかった場合には、更新手数料をあえて納付しないことで欧州全体に及ぶ特許を消極的に放棄することができるからである。ただし、欧州特許庁での一元的取消しは、不作為のまま特許の放棄を待つことに比べ、より迅速でより決定的な選択肢である。また、欧州特許庁経由の一元的取消しは遡及効を有するため、当該特許は最初から存在しなかったものとみなされることになる。したがって、一元的取消しは第三者との交渉の際に交換条件となり得る。

2　補正によって限定できるもの、できないもの

　一元的限定は特許の保護範囲に関するものなので、主にクレームが対象となる。明細書については、一元的限定手続の結果、補正されたクレームと整合性をとるために必要な場合にのみ補正をすることが可能である。

　クレームの補正はすべてが認められるとは限らない。まず第一に、補正されたクレームは、欧州特許条約における通常の形式的要件（明確性、開示十分性、新規事項の追加禁止といった要件）をすべて満たしていなければならない。また、クレームの補正は限定の効果をもたらすものでなければならない。つまり、限定後のクレームの範囲内ではあるが、特許が付与された（元の）クレームの範囲からは外れる実施形態が想定されてはならない。クレームを単に「整理」するとか明確化を図ろうとする補正は却下される。従属クレームを追加するだけの補正も同様である。ただしこれは、従属クレームの範囲の限定のみを目的として補正をすることを妨げるものではない（審査基準 D-X 4.3）。

lines D-X 4.3).

3   When can Amendments be Made?

Central limitation can be requested at any time after the grant of a European patent, with one important exception. Central limitation cannot be requested if EPO opposition proceedings are pending (Article 105a(2) EPC). This situation is therefore similar to that in Japan by virtue of Article 126(2) of the Japanese Patent Act. If an opposition is filed against a patent that is already the subject of pending limitation proceedings, the limitation proceedings are terminated and the limitation fee is refunded (Rule 93(2) EPC).

A valid request for central revocation cannot be filed if opposition proceedings are pending (Article 105a(2) EPC). However, a proprietor is able to terminate the opposition proceedings in a relatively quick fashion by filing a statement at the EPO disapproving the granted text without filing a replacement text in its place. Filing a statement of this kind leads to the rapid revocation of the opposed patent by the EPO.

Central limitation proceedings do not take precedence over national proceedings, such as revocation proceedings, that are taking place in contracting states where the patent is in force. However, as central limitation has retroactive effect, many jurisdictions will stay their national proceedings pending the outcome of the central limitation procedure.

4   How is a Request for Central Limitation or Revocation Made?

Central limitation and central revocation are commenced by filing a request in writing at the EPO together with payment of the appropriate fee. As of Septem-

3 補正が可能な時期

　一元的限定請求は、欧州特許が付与された後であればいつでも請求可能であるが、1つだけ重要な例外がある。欧州特許庁において特許異議申立手続が係属中の場合は、一元的限定請求を行うことができない（第105a条(2)）。このような状況は日本でも同様であり、日本特許法第126条第2項がこれに該当する。係属中の限定手続の対象となっている特許に対して特許異議の申立てがされた場合は、その限定手続は終了し、限定請求手数料が返還される（規則93(2)）。

　一元的取消しについても、特許異議申立手続が係属している場合は、有効な取消請求をすることはできない（第105a条(2)）。特許権者は、一方で、特許が付与された正文書を不承認とする陳述を、その正文書を差し替えることなく欧州特許庁に提出することで、比較的早くに特許異議申立手続を終わらせることができる。このような種類の陳述書を提出することにより、欧州特許庁による異議申立対象の特許の取消手続が迅速化される。

　一元的限定手続は、その特許が効力を有する締約国内の国内手続（例えば、取消手続等の国内手続）に優先するものではない。ただし、一元的限定は遡及効を有するので、多くの管轄では一元的限定手続の結果が出るまで国内手続を停止させるであろう。

4 一元的な限定又は取消しの請求をする方法

　一元的限定及び一元的取消しの手続は、その請求書を欧州特許庁に提出し、併せて適切な手数料を納付することで開始される。2016年9月現在、一元的限

ber 2016, the fee for requesting central limitation is € 1,165 and the fee for requesting central revocation is € 525.

In the case of both limitation and revocation, the request must indicate the patent number, the patent proprietor and the contracting states in which the patent is in force (Rule 92(2) EPC). If the patent is owned by different proprietors in different contracting states, the requesting party must provide evidence that they are authorised to act on behalf of all proprietors (Rule 92(2)(c) EPC). The requestor must include the amended claims, together with amended description pages where appropriate, if central limitation is sought. There is no requirement to give the reason for requesting central limitation or revocation (Guidelines D-X 4.2). In particular, when filing a request for central limitation, there is no requirement to identify the prior art which the restricted claims are intended to distinguish from.

5 How does the EPO Examine a Request for Central Limitation or Revocation?

In accordance with Rule 91 EPC, the Examining Divisions of the EPO are responsible for processing and deciding upon requests for central limitation and revocation. The first stage in both the central limitation and revocation procedures is an initial examination to ensure that the request meets the basic formal requirements outlined in the previous section. The EPO will contact the requestor if the request is formally deficient, and will set a time limit in which any deficiencies must be rectified. Failure to rectify the deficiencies within the time limit will result in the request being deemed inadmissible. The Examining Division will also check that no opposition proceedings are pending, since opposition proceedings supersede both central limitation and revocation proceedings. If opposition proceedings are pending, then the request will be rejected and the limitation fee refunded.

定請求の手数料は1,165ユーロであり、一元的取消請求の手数料は525ユーロである。

　限定及び取消しのいずれの場合においても、請求書面には特許番号、特許権者、及び当該特許が有効となっている締約国を記載しなければならない（規則92(2)）。締約国ごとに特許権者が異なる場合、請求人は全特許権者の代理権を有する旨の証拠を示さなければならない（規則92(2)(c)）。一元的限定請求の場合、補正されたクレームと、必要に応じて補正された明細書のページを添付しなければならない。一元的限定請求と一元的取消請求のいずれにおいても、請求の理由は必要とされない（審査基準 D-X 4.2）。一元的限定請求をする際に、減縮されたクレームにより差別化を図ろうとする先行技術を特定して示す必要はない。

5　一元的な限定又は取消しの請求はどのように審査されるのか

　一元的な限定及び取消請求に関する手続及び決定は、規則91に従い、欧州特許庁の審査部が担当する。一元的な限定及び取消手続のいずれにおいても、まず第一段階として、先に述べたように基本的な方式要件を請求が満たしているか確認するため、最初の審査が行われる。請求に方式上の不備がある場合、欧州特許庁は請求人にその旨を通知し、すべての不備を是正するように期限を設定する。期限内に不備を是正できなかった場合、その請求は受理することができないと判断される。また、一元的な限定及び取消手続のいずれに対しても特許異議申立手続が優先されるため、審査部は特許異議申立手続が係属しているか否かの確認を行う。特許異議申立手続が係属していれば、請求は却下され、限定手数料が返還される。

Once the Examining Division is satisfied that the request is admissible, it will begin the second stage of the procedure. For central revocation, this entails the EPO informing the requestor that their request is allowed. At the same time, the Examining Division indicate the date when the revocation decision will be published (Rule 95(1) EPC).

The second stage of the central limitation procedure involves a review of the proposed amendments. They are firstly examined to check that they represent a limitation of the existing claims, which means that the scope of at least one independent or dependent claim has been restricted. It should be borne in mind that this is not necessarily assessed with respect to the claims as granted, as the claims might already have been limited through a previous central limitation procedure. As central limitation has retroactive effect, claims that have been limited by a previous central limitation procedure become the granted claims and are therefore the claims against which 'limitation' is assessed.

The amendments proposed by the requestor are also examined to ensure that they comply with the clarity, sufficiency and added subject-matter provisions of the European Patent Convention. It will also be checked that the amendments do not result in the broadening of the patent's scope in any way. It is necessary to explain where basis is provided in the application as originally filed for the limited claims when filing a request for limitation in order to show that the limited claims do not add subject-matter. The Examiner will not assess substantive patentability requirements, such as novelty and inventive step when examining a request for limitation. This represents a significant difference from Japanese practice, according to which the JPO will assess the patentability of a claim amended by post-grant limitation procedure in accordance with Article 126(7) of the Japanese Patent Act.

If the Examiner does not consider the limitation request to be allowable during this second stage of the procedure, for example if the claims are considered to add subject-matter, a Communication will be issued inviting the requestor

審査部により請求が受理できるものと判断されると、手続の第二段階が開始される。一元的取消しの場合、この段階で欧州特許庁は、請求を認める旨を請求人に通知する。同時に、審査部は、その決定が欧州特許公報に掲載される日を示す（規則95(1)）。

一元的限定手続の第二段階では、提出された補正について検討がされる。まず、その補正が現行クレームの限定となっているか、つまり、少なくとも１つの独立クレーム又は従属クレームの範囲が減縮されているかを確認する審査が行われる。このとき、先の一元的限定手続ですでにクレームが限定されている場合もあるので、必ずしも特許が付与されたクレームが限定の判断基準になるわけではないという点に留意すべきである。一元的限定は遡及効を有するので、先の一元的限定手続で限定されたクレームが特許が付与されたクレームとなり、そのクレームを基準として「限定」の判断が行われることになる。

請求人により提出された補正については、欧州特許条約における明確性、開示十分性、及び新規事項に関する各規定の要件を満たしているかについて審査が行われる。また、その補正がなんらかのかたちで特許請求の範囲を拡張していないかの確認も行われる。限定請求をする際には、限定後のクレームに新規事項の追加がされていないことを示すために、当初の出願書類のどこに当該クレームの根拠が記載されているのかを説明する必要がある。限定請求の審査の際、審査官は、新規性や進歩性といった実体的な特許要件の判断は行わない。この点は日本の実務とは大きく異なる。特許法第126条第７項の規定によれば、日本特許庁では登録後の訂正審判において訂正されたクレームについて特許性の判断が行われる。

この第二段階の手続において限定請求が認められないものと判断した場合（例えば、補正によりクレームが新規事項を追加するものとみなされた場合）は、審査官は、請求人に対して、拒絶の理由を通知し、応答する機会を与える。ここ

to address the objections raised. Failure to overcome the objections at this first attempt may result in the request for limitation being rejected (Rule 95(4) EPC). The requestor is only entitled by right to one opportunity to address objections which are raised. The EPO will occasionally give the requestor an opportunity to address any remaining objections, but this is generally only if such objections have arisen as a result of the requestor's response to the first Communication. Since the requestor is afforded limited opportunities to address objections raised by the Examiner, it is prudent to include a precautionary request for oral proceedings, either when filing the limitation request or when responding to a Communication raising objections against the proposed claims.

The examination of limitation requests is an *ex parte* procedure, meaning that the request for limitation cannot be contested by a third party in the same way as validity can be contested in opposition proceedings. Third parties can, however, file observations in order to draw the attention of the Examining Division to reasons why the request for limitation should not be allowed. As with third party observations filed in other EPO proceedings, such observations can be filed anonymously.

6 Obtaining Different Claims for Separate Contracting States

The EPC permits a proprietor to file different sets of claims for different contracting states if the proprietor can show that this is appropriate due to the existence of national prior rights, which would be relevant to the validity of the claims in one or more designated contracting states (Rule 138 EPC). The central limitation procedure can be used to request different limitations to the claims for different contracting states.

If the patent proprietor requests the EPO to limit the claims for only a limited selection of contracting states, or wishes to request different limitations for dif-

で、1回目の応答を試みてその拒絶理由を解消できない場合、限定請求は却下される（規則95(4)）。提起された拒絶理由について請求人に与えられる応答の機会は一度だけである。欧州特許庁は他の拒絶理由について請求人に応答の機会を与えることもあるが、これは通常、最初の通知に対して請求人が応答した結果、他の拒絶理由が生じた場合に限られる。審査官の提起する拒絶理由に対して請求人が応答できる機会は限られているので、限定請求の提出時か、あるいは提出したクレームに対して提起された拒絶理由に応答する際に、口頭審理の請求を予備的な請求として含めておくことが賢明である。

限定請求の審査は査定系の手続である。つまり、特許異議申立手続では第三者が特許の有効性を争うことができるのに対して、限定請求については第三者が争うことはできない。ただし第三者は、限定請求を認めるべきでない理由について審査部に注意喚起するために意見書を提出することができる。この意見書は、欧州特許庁の他の手続で第三者により提出される意見書と同様、匿名で提出することができる。

6　各締約国ごとに異なるクレームの取得

指定された1つ又は複数の締約国においてクレームの有効性に関連する先の国内の権利が存在することに起因してそれが妥当であると特許権者が示すことができれば、特許権者は、締約国ごとに異なる一式のクレームを提出することができる（規則138）。一元的限定手続を利用すれば締約国ごとに異なるクレームの限定を請求することができる。

特許権者が、欧州特許庁に対して、ある一定の選択した締約国についてのみクレームを限定するよう請求する場合、あるいは締約国ごとに異なる限定を請

ferent contracting states, then this has to be explained when making a request for central limitation. In this case, it is necessary to file a copy of the relevant national prior right(s) pursuant to Rule 138 EPC to evidence that different claims for different states are warranted.

7 Successful Request

If a request for revocation meets the formal requirements previously outlined, then the requestor is informed of both the positive outcome and the date upon which the revocation will be published by the EPO (Rule 95(1) EPC).

For successful limitation requests, however, there is an additional stage before the outcome is published by the EPO. This additional stage allows the requestor to check the documents which the EPO intends to publish as the limited patent (Rule 95(3) EPC). It is permissible to correct simple typographic errors at this stage, but it is not permissible to make substantive amendments to the text. It is also necessary to pay a publication fee and to file translations of the claims into the two official languages of the EPO that are not the language of the proceedings.

8 Unsuccessful Request

As with Japanese practice, an unsuccessful request for limitation can be appealed. Appeals against adverse central limitation decisions at the EPO are processed by a Technical Board of Appeal. This is a relatively expensive procedure, and currently very slow due to a significant backlog of cases pending with the Appeal Boards. A more practical approach would be to file a new limitation request which cures, as far as possible, the deficiencies identified by the Examining Division in the earlier refused request.

求したいと希望する場合、一元的限定請求の請求時にそのことを説明しなければならない。この場合、国ごとに異なるクレームの正当性を証明するために、規則138に従い、関連する先の国内の権利の写しを提出する必要がある。

7 　請求が認められる場合

取消請求の場合、その請求が前述の方式要件を満たしていれば、その肯定的結果及び当該取消しが欧州特許公報に掲載される日が請求人に通知される（規則95(1)）。

限定請求が認められるには、欧州特許公報にその旨が掲載される前に、もうひとつ別の段階が設けられている。当該段階で、請求人は、限定された特許として欧州特許庁が特許公報に掲載する文書を確認することができる（規則95(3)）。この段階で単純な誤字等を修正することは差し支えないが、実体的な補正を行うことはできない。また、特許公報への掲載手数料を納付し、その手続言語以外の欧州特許庁の2つの公用語によるクレームの翻訳文を提出しなければならない。

8 　請求が認められない場合

限定請求が認められない場合に不服申立てをすることができるのは日本の実務と同様である。欧州特許庁の一元的限定に係る不利な決定に対して提起された不服申立ては、技術審判部により処理される。これは比較的高額な手続であり、処理待ちの事件が審判部に多数係属している現状から、その進行が非常に遅くなっている。限定請求が却下された際には、先に拒絶された請求において審査部によって指摘された不備を可能な限り解消して新たな限定請求をするほうがより現実的なアプローチであろう。

Part IV

National and EU Law Related to EPC

欧州特許条約に関連する国内法と欧州法

Legal Text

Article 64 Rights conferred by a European patent

(1) A European patent shall, subject to the provisions of paragraph 2, confer on its proprietor from the date on which the mention of its grant is published in the European Patent Bulletin, in each Contracting State in respect of which it is granted, the same rights as would be conferred by a national patent granted in that State.

(2) If the subject-matter of the European patent is a process, the protection conferred by the patent shall extend to the products directly obtained by such process.

(3) Any infringement of a European patent shall be dealt with by national law.

Article 65 Translation of the European patent

(1) Any Contracting State may, if the European patent as granted, amended or limited by the European Patent Office is not drawn up in one of its official languages, prescribe that the proprietor of the patent shall supply to its central industrial property office a translation of the patent as granted, amended or limited in one of its official languages at his option or, where that State has prescribed the use of one specific official language, in that language. The period for supplying the translation shall end three months after the date on which the mention of the grant, maintenance in amended form or limitation of the European patent is published in the European Patent Bulletin, unless the State concerned prescribes a longer period.

(2) Any Contracting State which has adopted provisions pursuant to paragraph 1 may prescribe that the proprietor of the patent must pay all or part

法規

第64条　欧州特許により与えられる権利

(1)　欧州特許は、(2)の規定に従うことを条件として、その付与の旨が欧州特許公報に掲載された日から、それが付与された各締約国において、当該締約国で付与された国内特許によって与えられる権利と同一の権利をその特許権者に与える。

(2)　欧州特許の対象が方法である場合には、特許によって与えられる保護はその方法によって直接得られた物に及ぶ。

(3)　欧州特許権の侵害は国内法によって処理される。

第65条　欧州特許明細書の翻訳文

(1)　いかなる締約国も、欧州特許庁により付与され、補正され、又は限定された欧州特許が当該締約国の公用語のいずれか1つで作成されていない場合には、特許権者に対し、当該特許権者の選択により当該締約国の公用語のいずれか1つによる欧州特許の翻訳文（当該締約国が特定の公用語の使用を定めている場合にはその公用語による翻訳文）を、当該締約国の中央産業財産権官庁に提出すべきことを定めることができる。翻訳文を提出するための期間は、当該締約国により長い期間を定めていない限り、欧州特許が付与された旨又は補正若しくは限定された形式で特許が維持された旨が欧州特許公報に掲載された日から3月までとする。

(2)　(1)に従う規定を採用した締約国は、当該締約国が定める期間内に、翻訳文の公表にかかる費用の全部又は一部を特許権者が納付すべき旨を定める

of the costs of publication of such translation within a period laid down by that State.

(3) Any Contracting State may prescribe that in the event of failure to observe the provisions adopted in accordance with paragraphs 1 and 2, the European patent shall be deemed to be void ab initio in that State.

Article 138 Revocation of European patents

(1) Subject to Article 139, a European patent may be revoked with effect for a Contracting State only on the grounds that:

    (a) the subject-matter of the European patent is not patentable under Articles 52 to 57;

    (b) the European patent does not disclose the invention in a manner sufficiently clear and complete for it to be carried out by a person skilled in the art;

    (c) the subject-matter of the European patent extends beyond the content of the application as filed or, if the patent was granted on a divisional application or on a new application filed under Article 61, beyond the content of the earlier application as filed;

    (d) the protection conferred by the European patent has been extended; or

    (e) the proprietor of the European patent is not entitled under Article 60, paragraph 1.

(2) If the grounds for revocation affect the European patent only in part, the

ことができる。

(3) 締約国は、(1)及び(2)に従って採用した規定が遵守されないときは、当該締約国において欧州特許権ははじめから存在しなかったものとみなすことができる。

第138条　欧州特許の取消し

(1) 第139条の規定に従うことを条件として、欧州特許は、締約国の法律により次の事由に基づいてのみ当該締約国の領域にわたる効力をもって取り消すことができる。

　(a)　欧州特許の対象が第52条から第57条の規定により特許を受けることができないとき

　(b)　欧州特許が、その技術分野の専門家が実施することができる程度に明確かつ十分に、その発明を開示していないとき

　(c)　欧州特許の対象がその出願の出願時の内容を超えているとき、又は、欧州特許が分割出願について若しくは第61条に規定する新たな出願について付与された場合において先の出願の出願時の内容を超えているとき

　(d)　欧州特許によって付与された保護が拡張されているとき

　(e)　特許権者が第60条(1)に規定する権利を有していないとき

(2) 取消しの理由が欧州特許の一部に関わるときは、それに対応するクレー

patent shall be limited by a corresponding amendment of the claims and revoked in part.

(3) In proceedings before the competent court or authority relating to the validity of the European patent, the proprietor of the patent shall have the right to limit the patent by amending the claims. The patent as thus limited shall form the basis for the proceedings.

Article 139 Prior rights and rights arising on the same date

(1) In any designated Contracting State a European patent application and a European patent shall have with regard to a national patent application and a national patent the same prior right effect as a national patent application and a national patent.

(2) A national patent application and a national patent in a Contracting State shall have with regard to a European patent designating that Contracting State the same prior right effect as if the European patent were a national patent.

(3) Any Contracting State may prescribe whether and on what terms an invention disclosed in both a European patent application or patent and a national application or patent having the same date of filing or, where priority is claimed, the same date of priority, may be protected simultaneously by both applications or patents.

Article 141 Renewal fees for European patents

(1) Renewal fees for a European patent may only be imposed for the years which follow that referred to in Article 86, paragraph 2.

(2) Any renewal fees falling due within two months of the publication in the

ムの補正によって当該特許を限定し又は部分的に取り消す。

(3) 欧州特許の有効性に関して管轄権を持つ裁判所又は当局における手続において、特許権者は、クレームの補正をすることにより、特許を限定する権利を有する。その後の手続は、限定された特許に基づくものとする。

第139条　先の権利及び同日に発生する権利

(1) 指定されたいずれの締約国においても、欧州特許出願及び欧州特許は、国内特許出願及び国内特許に関して、先の権利として、国内特許出願及び国内特許と同一の効力を有する。

(2) ある締約国における国内特許出願及び国内特許は、その締約国を指定している欧州特許に関して、その欧州特許が国内特許であるものとすれば先の権利と同一の効力を有する。

(3) いかなる締約国も、同一の出願日（優先権が主張されている場合は同一の優先日）を有する欧州特許出願又は欧州特許及び国内特許出願又は国内特許の双方に開示された発明を双方の出願又は特許により同時に保護し得るか、及びいかなる条件の下で保護し得るかを規定することができる。

第141条　欧州特許の更新手数料

(1) 欧州特許についての更新手数料は、第86条(2)の年に続く年についてのみ課すことができる。

(2) 欧州特許を付与する旨が欧州特許公報に掲載されてから2月以内に納付

European Patent Bulletin of the mention of the grant of the European patent shall be deemed to have been validly paid if they are paid within that period. Any additional fee provided for under national law shall not be charged.

期限がくる更新手数料は、その期間内に当該更新手数料が納付されたときは、その更新手数料は有効に納付されたものとみなされる。国内法に規定するいかなる追加の手数料も請求することはできない。

Chapter 17

EPC and National Law

欧州特許条約と国内法

Klemens Stratmann

1 Rights Conferred by European Patents

As of the date of grant, a European patent shall confer on its proprietor in each contracting state in respect of which it is granted the same rights as would be conferred by a national patent granted in that state (Article 64(1) EPC). Moreover, the national law must comply with Article 64(2) EPC stipulating that, if the subject-matter of the European patent is a process, the protection conferred by the patent shall extend to the products directly obtained by such process.

This provision is of great practical significance.

Example: A European patent application describes a new and inventive catalyst for making polyethylene and proceeds to grant on the basis of claims which exclusively concern the catalyst as such. If a competitor of the proprietor uses this catalyst in Japan for the preparation of polyethylene and delivers this polyethylene to an EPC contracting state, these actions do not infringe the patent.

However, the addition of process claims or use claims prior to grant could have provided a suitable basis for asserting an infringement of the patent. A proper use claim would for instance read:

Use of catalyst X for making polyethylene.

A suitable process claim would be

Process for the manufacture of polyethylene comprising the step of polymerizing ethylene in the presence of catalyst X.

Since the polyethylene delivered to Europe is the product directly obtained by such use (process), Article 64(2) EPC thus provides valuable protection.

1 欧州特許により与えられる権利

欧州特許は、その付与の日をもって、各締約国において、当該締約国で付与された国内特許により与えられる権利と同一の権利を、その特許権者に与える（第64条(1)）。国内法は、「欧州特許の対象が方法である場合には、特許によって与えられる保護はその方法によって直接得られた物に及ぶ」と規定する第64条(2)を遵守する必要がある。

当該規定は実務上非常に意義がある。

例： 欧州特許出願には、ポリエチレンを製造する新規で、かつ、進歩性のある触媒が記載されており、このような触媒のみを対象とするクレームに基づき、欧州特許が付与されている。特許権者の競業者がこの触媒をポリエチレンを生成するために日本で使用し、このポリエチレンを欧州特許条約の締約国に供給する場合、これらの行為は当該特許の特許性を侵害しない。

一方、特許の付与に先立ち方法クレーム又は使用クレームを追加していた場合、特許の侵害を主張する適切な根拠を与えられたであろう。適切な用途クレームは例えば以下のように記載される。

「ポリエチレンを製造するための触媒Xの使用」

適切な方法クレームは以下のようになる。

「触媒Xの存在下でエチレンを重合させるステップを含む、ポリエチレンの製造方法」

欧州に供給されたポリエチレンは、当該使用（方法）により直接得られた物であるため、第64条(2)により、特許権者には有益な保護が与えられる。

However, the EPC does not contain any provisions specifying what actions constitute an infringement, how an infringement can be asserted and what claims result therefrom if the infringer is held to be liable by a national court. The EPC only states that any infringement of a European patent shall be dealt with by national law (Article 64(3) EPC).

2 Validation and Translation Requirement

The European patent does not represent a unitary patent. Once the decision to grant a European patent takes effect, i.e. on the date the grant is published in the European Patent Bulletin (Article 97(3) EPC) it falls apart into a bundle of national patent rights. Each of these national patent rights is subject to the respective national jurisdiction. There are, however, two important exceptions to this principle where the EPO retains its jurisdiction over the European patent as a whole, namely opposition proceedings pursuant to Article 99 EPC (see Chapter 3.1) and the central request for limitation or revocation pursuant to Article 105(a) EPC) (see Chapter 16).

In some EPC contracting states such as the United Kingdom (UK), France (FR), or Germany (DE), no further steps are to be taken after grant in order to validate the corresponding national right. In these countries, the timely payment of national annuities which have fallen due will suffice to maintain the national right until it expires 20 years from the application date. In other contracting states national rights will only come into existence if certain legal requirements are met. These typically include the submission of a translation of the claims and if applicable also of the description into the official language of the respective state as well as the appointment of a national representative or at least the indication of an address of service.

Any contracting state may, if the European patent as granted, amended (after opposition proceedings) or limited by the EPO is not drawn up in one of its offi-

しかし、欧州特許条約には、いかなる行為が侵害を構成するのか、侵害をどのように主張できるのか、及び国内裁判所が侵害者に法的責任があると認定することで、いかなる請求が生じるのかを特定する規定がない。欧州特許条約は、欧州特許の侵害が国内法令により処理されることを述べているに過ぎない（第64条(3)）。

2 国内有効化及び翻訳要件

欧州特許は統一特許を意味していない。欧州特許を付与する決定の効力が生じると（すなわち、欧州特許を付与する旨が欧州特許公報に掲載された日に）（第97条(3)）、欧州特許は国内特許の権利の束となる。国内特許の権利の各々は、各国内裁判管轄に服する。しかしこの原則には、欧州特許庁が全体として欧州特許に管轄権を保有する2つの重要な例外がある。すなわち第99条に規定する特許異議の申立て（第14章を参照）と、一元的な限定又は取消請求（第105条(a)）である（第16章を参照）。

イギリス、フランス、ドイツなど欧州特許条約の一部の締約国は、欧州特許が付与された後に、対応する国内の権利を有効化するにあたって次のステップを必要としない。これらの国々では、支払期日が到来した国内の年金を適切な時期に支払うことで、出願日から20年の期間が満了するまで国内の権利を維持することができる。他の締約国では、特定の法的要件を満たす場合にのみ国内の権利が生じる。これには、通常、その締約国の公用語によるクレームの翻訳文の提出、必要に応じて明細書の翻訳文の提出が含まれ、国内代理人の選任又は少なくとも送達の住所の表示が含まれる。

いずれの締約国も、欧州特許庁により付与され、（特許異議申立手続後）補正され、又は限定された欧州特許が公用語の1つで作成されていない場合、当該

cial languages, prescribe that the proprietor of the patent shall supply to its central industrial property office a translation of the patent in one of the official languages. The period for supplying the translation shall end three months after the date on which the mention of grant, maintenance in amended form or limitation of the European patent is published in the European Patent Bulletin (Article 65(1) EPC). Currently, only two states make use of the possibility provided in Article 65(1) EPC to prescribe longer periods, namely San Marino (6 months) and Iceland (4 months). If the translation of the European patent is not provided to the national patent office within the prescribed time limit, the patent is deemed to be void *ab initio* in that state.

The EPO publishes and updates on its website a summary of applicable national provisions; see <https://www.epo.org/law-practice/legal-texts/national-law.html>. Furthermore, the EPO issues at regular intervals a booklet entitled *"National Law Relating to the EPC"* with which the EPO aims to provide European patent applicants and proprietors with a concise guide to the most important provisions and requirements of the relevant national law in the EPC contracting states.

From these publications it can be gathered which measures, if any, are necessary to validate a European patent in the respective state and the applicable terms.

For many years, the translation requirement had been the main reason for the very high costs associated with a European patent and the main obstacle for patent proprietors to validate a European patent in a greater number of states. Aiming at reducing the translation costs, several EPC contracting states concluded in London on 17 October 2000 the *"Agreement on the Application of Article 65 of the Convention on the Grant of European Patents"*, frequently referred to as the *"London Agreement"*. The London Agreement entered into force for 14 states on 1st May 2008 and after the accession of further EPC contracting states, is now valid in 21 states. The Agreement provides that contracting states that have an offi-

特許権者に対して、公用語の1つによる当該特許の翻訳文を工業所有権中央官庁に提出するよう規定することができる。翻訳文を提出するための期間は、欧州特許の付与、補正された形式での欧州特許の維持又は欧州特許の限定についての旨が欧州特許公報に掲載された日から3月後に終了する（第65条(1)）。現在、2つの国のみが第65条(1)で規定する可能性を利用して、より長い期間を定めている。サンマリノ（6月）とアイスランド（4月）である。指定された期間内に国内特許庁に欧州特許の翻訳文が提出されなかった場合は、当該特許は当該締約国においてはじめから存在しなかったものとみなされる。

欧州特許庁は、適用可能な国内規定の概要をウェブサイトで公示し、更新している（〈https://www.epo.org/law-practice/legal-texts/national-law.html〉参照）。また、欧州特許庁は『EPCに関する国内法令』という名称の小冊子を定期的に発行している。これにより、欧州特許庁は、欧州特許条約の締約国における関連する国内法令のうち最も重要な規定及び要件について簡潔な指針を欧州特許出願人及び特許権者に与えることを意図している。

これらの刊行物により、各国で適用可能な条件で欧州特許を有効化するために必要な方策がある場合は、これがいかなる方策であるかを収集することができる。

翻訳文の要件は、長年にわたって、欧州特許に関連する高額な費用の主な原因であり、特許権者が多くの締約国で欧州特許を有効化する際の主な障害ともなっていた。翻訳費用を削減することを目指して、「欧州特許の付与に関する条約第65条の適用に関する協定」（「ロンドン協定」といわれる）が2000年10月17日にロンドンで多数の締約国により締結された。ロンドン協定は、2008年5月1日に14カ国について発効し、さらなる締約国の加入があって、現在は21カ国で有効である。ロンドン協定は、欧州特許庁の公用語（すなわち、英語、フランス語、ドイツ語）と共通する公用語を有する締約国は、これらの国々の公用語の1つによる欧州特許の翻訳文を要求しないと規定している。他の締約国で

cial language in common with an official language of the EPO, i.e. English, French or German, no longer require translations of European patents into one of their official languages. Other contracting states have to choose one of the official EPO languages as a "prescribed language", into which European patents have to be translated in order to enter into force in their country. They, however, keep the right to require a translation of the claims in one of their official languages.

The current implementation of the London Agreement is shown in the following table.

Country	Code	Entry into force of London Agreement	Translation required[3]	
			Description	Claims
Albania	AL	1.9.2013	No	No
Austria	AT	–	Yes	Yes
Belgium	BE	–	Yes	Yes
Bulgaria	BG	–	Yes	Yes
Croatia	HR	1.5.2008	Yes (Croatian)[1]	Yes
Cyprus	CY	–	Yes	Yes
Czech Republic	CZ	–	Yes	Yes
Denmark	DK	1.5.2008	Yes (English, Danish)[1]	Yes
Estonia	EE	–	Yes	Yes
Finland	FI	1.11.2011	Yes (English, Finnish)[1]	Yes
France	FR	1.5.2008	No	No
Germany	DE	1.5.2008	No	No
Greece	GR	–	Yes	Yes
Hungary	HU	1.1.2011	Yes (English, Hungarian)[1]	Yes
Iceland	IS	1.5.2008	Yes (English, Icelandic)[1]	Yes
Ireland	IE	1.3.2014	No	No
Italy	IT	–	Yes	Yes
Latvia	LV	1.5.2008	No[2]	Yes
Liechtenstein	LI	1.5.2008	No	No
Lithuania	LT	1.5.2009	No[2]	Yes
Luxembourg	LU	1.5.2008	No	No

は、国内有効化にあたり、欧州特許庁の公用語の1つを「規定された翻訳言語」として選択する必要がある。これら締約国は、クレームについては、これらの国々の公用語による翻訳文を要求する権利を留保している。

ロンドン協定の現在の履行を、以下の表に示している。

国名	コード	ロンドン協定の発効	必要とされる翻訳文[3]	
			明細書	クレーム
アルバニア	AL	2013年9月1日	不要	不要
オーストリア	AT	-	要	要
ベルギー	BE	-	要	要
ブルガリア	BG	-	要	要
クロアチア	HR	2008年5月1日	要（クロアチア語）[1]	要
キプロス	CY	-	要	要
チェコ共和国	CZ	-	要	要
デンマーク	DK	2008年5月1日	要（英語、デンマーク語）[1]	要
エストニア	EE	-	要	要
フィンランド	FI	2011年11月1日	要（英語、フィンランド語）[1]	要
フランス	FR	2008年5月1日	不要	不要
ドイツ	DE	2008年5月1日	不要	不要
ギリシャ	GR	-	要	要
ハンガリー	HU	2011年1月1日	要（英語、ハンガリー語）[1]	要
アイスランド	IS	2008年5月1日	要（英語、アイスランド語）[1]	要
アイルランド	IE	2014年3月1日	不要	不要
イタリア	IT	-	要	要
ラトビア	LV	2008年5月1日	不要[2]	要
リヒテンシュタイン	LI	2008年5月1日	不要	不要
リトアニア	LT	2009年5月1日	不要[2]	要
ルクセンブルク	LU	2008年5月1日	不要	不要

Country	Code	Entry into force of London Agreement	Translation required[3]	
			Description	Claims
Former Yugoslav Republic of Macedonia	MK	1.2.2012	No[2]	Yes
Malta	MT	–	Yes	Yes
Monaco	MC	1.5.2008	No	No
Netherlands	NL	1.5.2008	Yes (English, Dutch)[1]	Yes
Norway	NO	1.1.2015	Yes (English, Norwegian)[1]	Yes
Poland	PL	–	Yes	Yes
Portugal	PT	–	Yes	Yes
Romania	RO	–	Yes	Yes
San Marino	SM	–	Yes	Yes
Serbia	RS	–	Yes	Yes
Slovak Republic	SK	–	Yes	Yes
Slovenia	SI	1.5.2008	No[2]	Yes
Spain	ES	–	Yes	Yes
Sweden	SE	1.5.2008	Yes (English, Swedish)[1]	Yes
Switzerland	CH	1.5.2008	No	No
Turkey	TR	–	Yes	Yes
United Kingdom	GB/UK	1.5.2008	No	No

1) These states dispense with further translation requirements if the European patent has been granted in English, or translated into English and supplied under the conditions provided for in Article 65(1) EPC (Article 1(2) of the London Agreement). In Denmark, Finland, Hungary, Iceland, the Netherlands, Norway and Sweden, the European patent may also be supplied in the national language.
2) These states dispense with translation requirements for the description (Article 1(2) of the London Agreement).
3) If not stated otherwise, a translation into the official language of the state concerned is required.

The EPO does not publish any statistics showing to what extent EP patents are validated in the individual contracting states. Straathof and van Veldhuizen investigated in 2010 the average validation rates for the EPC contracting state in 2005 <http://www.voxeu.org/article/another-reason-eu-patent-declining-validation-rates>. These essentially correlate with the share of this state in the

国名	コード	ロンドン協定の発効	必要とされる翻訳文[3] 明細書	クレーム
マケドニア旧ユーゴスラビア共和国	MK	2012年2月1日	不要[2]	要
マルタ	MT	-	要	要
モナコ	MC	2008年5月1日	不要	不要
オランダ	NL	2008年5月1日	要（英語、オランダ語）[1]	要
ノルウェー	NO	2015年1月1日	要（英語、ノルウェー語）[1]	要
ポーランド	PL	-	要	要
ポルトガル	PT	-	要	要
ルーマニア	RO	-	要	要
サンマリノ	SM	-	要	要
セルビア	RS	-	要	要
スロバキア共和国	SK	-	要	要
スロベニア	SI	2008年5月1日	不要[2]	要
スペイン	ES	-	要	要
スウェーデン	SE	2008年5月1日	要（英語、スウェーデン語）[1]	要
スイス	CH	2008年5月1日	不要	不要
トルコ	TR	-	要	要
イギリス	GB/UK	2008年5月1日	不要	不要

1) これらの締約国は、欧州特許が英語で付与された場合、又は英語に翻訳され、かつ、第65条(1)に規定する条件により提出された場合は、それ以上の翻訳文の要件を省略する（ロンドン協定第1条(2)）。デンマーク、フィンランド、ハンガリー、アイスランド、オランダ、ノルウェー、スウェーデンにおいては、その国の言語でも翻訳文を提出することができる。

2) これらの締約国は、明細書の翻訳文の要件を省略する（ロンドン協定第1条(2)）。

3) 他の規定がない限り、当該国の公用語による翻訳文が要求される。

　欧州特許庁は、個々の締約国で欧州特許がどの程度有効化されているかを示す統計を発表していない。Straathof and van Veldhuizen は、2005年の欧州特許条約の締約国に関して平均有効化率を2010年に調査した〈http://www.voxeu.org/article/another-reason-eu-patent-declining-validation-rates〉。これらは実質的に全締約国の国内総生産（GDP）に占めるこの締約国のシェアと関連してい

gross domestic product (GDP) of all EPC contracting states. Thus, unsurprisingly, the likelihood of validation in a particular state increases with its economic relevance. This explains why (in 2005) 92% of all European patents were validated in Germany and about 80% in the United Kingdom and France, while the validation rates for Italy and Spain dropped already to about 50% and 33%, respectively. This is shown in the following graph:

Straathof, van Veldhuizen also observed that in the period from 1985 to 2008 smaller countries experienced a substantial decrease in validation shares, while the shares of large economies have remained approximately constant. Whether the London agreement has stopped or reversed this trend is currently unknown.

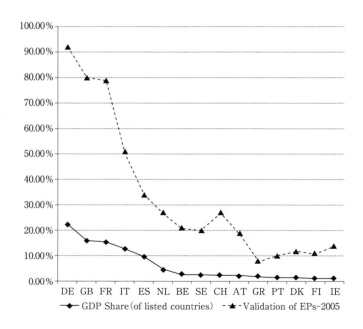

る。そして当然に特定の締約国で有効化する見込みは、経済的関連性とともに増加する。これにより、2005年に全欧州特許の92％がドイツで有効化されており、約80％がイギリスとフランスで有効化されている一方で、イタリアとスペインでは有効化率が各々約50％と33％に下がっている理由が説明できる。これは、以下のグラフで表される。

Straathof, van Veldhuizen は、1985年から2008年の間に小国は有効化シェアの大幅な減少を経験したが、経済大国のシェアはほぼ一定を保っていたことに気づいた。ロンドン協定がこの傾向を止めたか維持したかは現在のところ不明である。

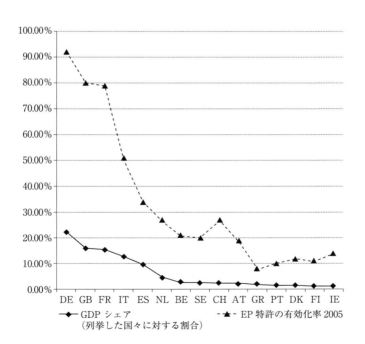

3 The Prohibition of Double Patenting

It is an accepted principle in most patent systems that two patents cannot be granted to the same applicant for one invention. The EPC leaves it to the contracting state to permit or prohibit simultaneous protection of the same invention by means of a national patent and the national part of a European patent. According to Article 139(3) EPC, any contracting state may prescribe whether and on what terms an invention disclosed in both a European patent application or patent and a national application or patent having the same date of filing or, where priority is claimed, the same date of priority, may be protected simultaneously by both applications/patents.

Most EPC contracting states have made use of this possibility and enacted laws prohibiting double protection. However, double protection is permitted in AT, DK, FI, HU, IS, NO, PL and SE. If double protection is not allowed, the national patent loses its effect to the extent to which the scope of the claims overlaps with the scope of the claims of the EP patent.

In some countries the national patent ceases (at least partially) to have effect from the date on which

a) the period for filing the notice of opposition to the European patent has expired without such notice being filed; or

b) the opposition proceedings are finally closed, the European patent having been maintained.

In the United Kingdom the Comptroller may revoke the national patent after the dates provided in a) or b).

In a further group of countries, including France, Germany, Spain and Italy, the prohibition of double protection also applies

3 ダブルパテントの禁止

　1つの発明につき同一の出願人に対して2つの特許が付与されないことはほとんどの特許制度ですでに認められた原則である。欧州特許条約は、締約国が国内特許及び欧州特許の国内部分を介して同一発明につき同時に保護することを認めるか禁止するかを締約国に委ねている。第139条(3)によると、いずれの締約国も、同じ出願日、若しくは優先権が主張されている場合は同じ優先日を有する欧州特許出願又は欧州特許及び国内出願又は国内特許の双方に開示された発明を双方の出願／特許により同時に保護し得るか及びいかなる条件の下で保護し得るかを規定することができる。

　ほとんどの締約国はこの可能性を活用しており、二重の保護を禁止する法律を成立させた。一方、オーストリア、デンマーク、フィンランド、ハンガリー、アイスランド、ノルウェー、ポーランド、及びスウェーデンでは二重の保護が認められている。二重の保護が認められない場合は、国内特許はクレームの範囲が欧州特許のクレームの範囲と重複する程度でその効果を失う。

　一部の締約国では、国内特許は以下のいずれかの日から（少なくとも部分的には）その効力を失う。

a)　異議申立書が提出されることなく欧州特許に対する異議申立期間が満了した日

b)　特許異議申立手続が最終的に完結した日（欧州特許が維持されている場合）

　イギリスでは、a)又はb)に規定する日以後に長官が国内特許を取り消すことができる。

　二重の保護の禁止は、フランス、ドイツ、スペイン、イタリアを含む一群の国にも適用される。

C) if the national patent is granted if such date falls after that provided for in a) or b).

Then, the national patent will not take effect if its scope fully overlaps with that of the corresponding EP patent, or only in part if its scope does not fully overlap.

If hence a European patent application claims the priority of a national patent application deposited in an EPC contracting state, applicants should carefully examine whether double patenting issues can arise and, if so, what measures are to be taken in order to prevent a national patent from (partially) losing its effect. If this is undesired, it is as a rule recommendable to withdraw the designation of a corresponding EPC contracting state prior to grant.

4 Annuities

The national patent offices may only impose renewal fees for a European patent for the years which follow the year in which the mention of the grant of the European patent is published in the European Patent Bulletin (Articles 141(1) and 86(2) EPC).

> Example: The European Patent Bulletin publishes on 3 June 2011 the mention of grant of a European patent application having 2 June 2008 as filing date. The renewal fee for the third year (due on 30 June 2010) and the renewal fee for the fourth year (due on 30 June 2011) are to be paid at the EPO. The renewal fee for the fifth and all following years are to be paid at the national patent offices.
>
> In this example, the fourth patent year has already commenced to run on 3 June 2011. Therefore, the mention of grant is published in the fourth patent year with the consequence that the renewal fee for the fourth year

c) 国内特許が付与される場合であって、かかる日付がa)又はb)に規定する日後に当たる場合

そのため、国内特許の範囲が対応する欧州特許の範囲と完全に重複する場合、又は、完全には重複しないが部分的にのみ重複する場合は、国内特許の効力を生じさせない。

よって、締約国になされた国内特許出願に基づき欧州特許出願が優先権を主張する場合は、出願人はダブルパテントの問題を生じさせるか否かを注意深く検討すべきであり、もし生じさせるのであれば、国内特許がその効果を（部分的にでも）失うことを防ぐには、どのような方策が採られるべきかを検討すべきである。これが好ましくないのであれば、特許付与前に、対応する締約国の指定を取り下げることが一般には推奨される。

4　年金

締約国の特許庁は、欧州特許が付与された旨が欧州特許公報に掲載された年に続く年についてのみ、欧州特許の更新手数料を課すことができる（第141条(1)及び第86条(2)）。

例：　2008年6月2日の出願日を有する欧州特許出願について特許が付与された旨が、2011年6月3日付で欧州特許公報に掲載される。第3年目の更新手数料（2010年6月30日が納付期限）及び第4年目の更新手数料（2011年6月30日が納付期限）は、欧州特許庁に支払う必要がある。第5年目及びその翌年以降のすべての更新手数料は、国内特許庁に支払う必要がある。

この例では、第4年目の特許年度は2011年6月3日にすでに開始している。よって、特許が付与された旨が掲載されたのは、第4年目の特許年度に当たる。第4年度についての更新手数料は依然として欧州特許庁に支払

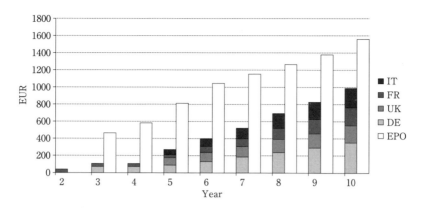

is still to be paid at the EPO.

The renewal fees to be paid to the national offices are much lower than those fixed by the EPO. Even if the total amount of renewal fees incurring at the national offices of those contracting states (DE, UK, FR and IT) having the highest validation rates is considered, there is still a substantial gap to the amount charged by the EPO as can be seen from the graph above.

5 National Jurisdiction and Applicability of EPC and EP Case Law

As of grant, in each state where the European patent was validated, the corresponding national part is subject to the jurisdiction of the national courts with the exception discussed below in Section 6. The EPC prescribes the national courts in Article 138, which grounds may be relied on to revoke a European patent with effect for a contracting state:

(a) the subject-matter of the European patent is not patentable under Articles 52 to 57;

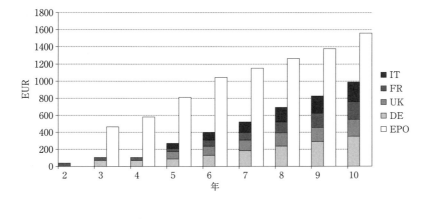

われる。

　国内官庁に支払うべき更新手数料は、欧州特許庁が設定した費用よりかなり安価である。有効化率が最も高い締約国（ドイツ、イギリス、フランス、イタリア）の国内官庁でかかる費用の総額を考慮すると、上のグラフからわかるように、欧州特許庁が請求する額との間には大きなギャップが依然として存在する。

5　国内裁判管轄、並びに欧州特許条約及びケースローの適用可能性

　欧州特許が有効化された各締約国において、その特許の国内部分は、以下セクション6で考察する例外があるものの、特許が付与された時点から国内裁判所の管轄に服する。ただし、欧州特許条約は、第138条で国内裁判所による欧州特許の取消しを規定している。第138条には、締約国の領域にわたる効力をもって欧州特許を取り消すことができる取消理由が列挙されている。

(a)　欧州特許の対象が第52条から第57条の規定により特許を受けることができないとき

(b) the European patent does not disclose the invention in a manner sufficiently clear and complete for it to be carried out by a person skilled in the art;

(c) the subject-matter of the European patent extends beyond the content of the application as filed or, if the patent was granted on a divisional application or on a new application filed under Article 61, beyond the content of the earlier application as filed;

(d) the protection conferred by the European patent has been extended; or

(e) the proprietor of the European patent is not entitled under Article 60, paragraph 1.

Item (a) includes the common revocation grounds of lacking novelty, lack of inventive step and exclusion from patentability. Items (a), (b) and (c) hence define the same grounds as can be invoked under Article 100 EPC when lodging an opposition to a European patent.

Grounds (d) and (e), however, are only applicable in national revocation proceedings. Ground (d) applies if, contrary to Article 123(3) EPC, the protection conferred by the European patent has been extended due to amendments conducted in opposition or limitation proceedings. For questions of entitlement, as referred to in ground (e), the EPO is also not competent.

The national law and practice of the EPC contracting states ensures the full applicability of Article 138. Pursuant to Article 138(2), (3), the proprietor of the patent shall also have the right to limit the patent by amending the claims if the grounds for revocation affect the European patent only in part.

In view of the link to the national law provided in Article 138, the practically very significant question arises of whether, and to what extent, the national

(b) 欧州特許が、その技術分野の専門家が実施することができる程度に明確かつ十分に、その発明を開示していないとき

(c) 欧州特許の対象がその出願の出願時の内容を超えている、又は欧州特許が分割出願について若しくは第61条に規定する新たな出願について付与された場合において、先の出願の出願時の内容を超えているとき

(d) 欧州特許によって付与された保護が拡張されているとき

(e) 欧州特許の所有者が第60条(1)に規定する権利を有していないとき

上記(a)には、新規性の欠如、進歩性の欠如及び特許性からの除外という一般的な取消理由が含まれる。上記(a)、(b)、(c)は、欧州特許に対する異議の申立てを行う際に使われる第100条に規定される理由と同一の理由を定義している。

一方、上記(d)及び(e)は、国内取消手続でのみ適用され得る。上記(d)は、欧州特許により与えられる保護が、特許異議申立手続又は限定手続で行われた補正により第123条(3)に反して拡張される場合に適用される。上記(e)で言及されるように、欧州特許庁は権利享受の問題に関して管轄権を持たない。

締約国の国内法令及び実務は、第138条の適用を完全に確保している。第138条(2)及び(3)によると、特許権者は、取消理由が欧州特許に部分的にのみ影響を与える場合に、クレームを補正することにより、特許を限定する権利を有する。

第138条に規定する国内法令との関連を考慮すると、国内裁判所が取消理由に関連して特許の有効性を判断する際に、欧州特許庁審判部のケースローを遵

courts follow the case law of the EPO Boards of Appeal when examining a patent in respect of the invoked revocation grounds.

The interpretation of the EPC by the Legal and Technical Boards of the Appeal and the Enlarged Board of Appeal is not binding for the national courts. This had the consequence that, after the entry into force of the EPC on 7 October 1977, the national courts continued their practice for many years with only few adaptations to the practice of the EPO. The resulting discrepancies between national decisions concerning the same European patent were perceived by users as a major drawback of the European patent system. Only in the last decade have the national courts, especially the judges in the UK, Germany and the Netherlands, strived for a greater harmonization with the EPO practice.

The German Federal Court of Justice highlights for instance in *Walzenformgebungsmaschine* (OJ EPO 11/2010, 622) that

> *the German courts are required to consider decisions rendered by organs of the European Patent Office and courts in other EPC contracting states and pertaining to a largely similar issue and, where appropriate, address the reasons leading to a diverging result in the earlier decision. Insofar as points of law are concerned, this also applies, for instance, to the question of whether the subject-matter of a property right was obvious in the light of prior art.*

The Federal Court of Justice emphasizes that this approach is necessary both from the point of view of legal certainty as well as in the interest of harmonizing the case law in EPC contracting states.

Likewise, the House of Lords, which is the highest court in the UK, held in *Kirin-Amgen Inc v Hoechst Marion Roussel Ltd* ([2004] UKHL 46) that:

> *the United Kingdom should apply the same law as the EPO and the other*

守するか否か、そしてどの程度遵守するか、という実務上非常に重要な問題が生じる。

法律審判部及び技術審判部並びに拡大審判部による欧州特許法の解釈は、国内裁判所を拘束しない。その結果、1977年10月7日付で欧州特許条約が発効した後、国内裁判所は、その実務を欧州特許庁の実務に若干適合させるのみで長年の実務を継続させた。同一の欧州特許に関する国内の判断の結果として生じる不一致を、欧州特許制度の利用者は主な欠点として感じていた。国内裁判所（特に、イギリス、ドイツ、オランダの裁判官）が、欧州特許庁の実務とのより深いハーモナイゼーションを獲得しようとしたのはここ10年のことである。

ドイツ連邦裁判所は、例えば *Walzenformgebungsmaschine*（欧州特許庁公報2010年11月号、622頁）で以下の点を強調している。

> 「ドイツ裁判所は、欧州特許庁の機関及び他の欧州特許条約の締約国の裁判所により、ほとんど類似する問題に関して下された決定を検討し、必要に応じて、以前の決定で判断の分かれる結果となった理由に対応する必要がある。法律上の争点に関する限り、これは例えば所有権の対象が先行技術から見て自明であるか否かの問題にも適用される。」

連邦裁判所は、このアプローチが法的安定性の観点、並びに締約国のケースローとのハーモナイゼーションのためにも必要であることを強調している。

同様に、イギリスにおける最高裁判所に当たる上院は、*Kirin-Amgen Inc v Hoechst Marion Roussel Ltd*（[2004] UKHL 46）において以下のように判示した。

> 「イギリスは、欧州特許条約の目的において何が新しいかを判断する際

Member States when deciding what counts as new for the purposes of the EPC.

Although the decisions of the Boards of Appeal of the EPO are not binding on the UK courts, these decisions have been described by the House of Lords as being of *"great persuasive authority"* both because they are from *"expert courts"*, and furthermore because *"it would be highly undesirable for the provisions of the EPC to be construed differently in the EPO from the way they are interpreted in the national courts of a Contracting State"*.

To some more limited extent, French courts usually take the reasoning of the EPO decisions into account when deciding on the validity of a patent. In this regard, the Paris Court of First Instance held in *Actavis v. Merck* (TGI, 3rd ch. 1st sect., 28 Sept. 2010) that:

> *The French courts are not bound by the decisions of the EPO which is not a court so that these decisions even issued by the Enlarged Board of Appeal are merely indications of the analysis made by the EPO to grant European patents.*

Despite the trend towards harmonization, major differences continue to exist between the respective national practice of the EPC contracting states and that of the EPO. The national courts in the majority of EPC contracting states including the German and British courts seem to be more lenient regarding the allowability of amendments and reject the strict added matter test developed by the EPO, which often seems to require a literal disclosure of the desired amendment (see Chapter 12).

When judging the admissibility of amendments in light of the disclosure of the application as filed, the German Federal Court of Justice has repeatedly held, e.g. in "Spleißkammer" (X ZB 9/89 of 23. January 1989) and "Kommunikationskanal" (X ZR 107/12 of 11 February 2014) that it would generally not be inad-

に、欧州特許庁及び他の締約国と同様の法律を適用すべきである。」

　欧州特許庁拡大審判部の決定はイギリス裁判所を拘束しないが、これらの決定は「非常に説得力ある権威」であると上院により述べられている。なぜならこれらの決定は、「専門裁判所」からなされたものであり、さらに「欧州特許条約の規定が欧州特許庁で締約国の国内裁判所で解釈される手法とは異なった手法で解釈されるのは好ましくないから」という理由による。

　フランスの裁判所は特許の有効性を決定する際に、通常、もう少し限定された程度で、欧州特許庁の決定の論法を考慮する。パリ第一審裁判所は、*Actavis v. Merck*（TGI, 3rd ch. 1st sect., 2010年9月28日）において以下のように判示した。

　　「フランスの裁判所は、裁判所ではない欧州特許庁の決定には拘束されないため、拡大審判部により出された決定であっても、それは欧州特許を付与する欧州特許庁によりなされた分析の指摘に過ぎない。」

　ハーモナイゼーションの傾向にかかわらず、欧州特許条約の各締約国の国内実務と欧州特許庁の実務とには依然として大きな違いがある。ドイツとイギリスの裁判所を含む大多数の締約国の国内裁判所は、補正を認めることについてより寛大であり、欧州特許庁により構築された新規事項追加のテストで所望の補正につき文言による開示を要求している傾向にある厳格なテスト（第12章参照）を排除しているように思われる。

　補正が認められるか否かを当初の出願書類の開示の観点から判断することにつき、ドイツ連邦裁判所は、実施形態から複数の特徴の一部のみを独立クレームに組み込むことは一般的に認められないと繰り返し判示している。例えば、"Spleißkammer"（X ZB 9/89、1989年1月23日）及び"Kommunikationskanal"

missible to incorporate only some of a plurality of features of an embodiment into the independent claims. If features of an embodiment either jointly or individually contribute to the success achieved with the invention, and serve to specify the protected invention, it is essentially permissible that the patent be limited by incorporating such features, individually or in their entirety, into the claim.

If, in proceedings before the EPO, an amendment involves a singling-out of features from a combination of features disclosed in one working example, the yardstick for the admissibility of the amendment is however whether the skilled person could recognize without any doubt that those (singled-out) features/characteristics were not so closely related to the other features/characteristics of the working example and that they apply directly and unambiguously to the more general context (see e.g. T 962/98).

Meanwhile, in a recent UK case, the Court of Appeal held that the generalization of the description of a part of a brake calliper as *"hockey-stick shaped"* in the application as filed to *"asymmetric shaped"* in the granted patent was an allowable amendment (*AP Racing Ltd v Alcon Components Ltd* [2014] EWCA Civ 40). This seems to be more lenient than the approach of the Boards of Appeal of the EPO. For example, in T 653/03, it was held that the replacement of the specific term *"diesel engine"* disclosed in the application as filed with the undisclosed general term *"combustion engine"* was not allowable.

Another practically important area where the national courts do not, or do not entirely, follow the EPO is the assessment of inventive step, and especially the application of the problem-solution approach developed by the EPO.

The first step of the problem-solution approach involves the determination of the so-called "closest prior art". By contrast, according to the jurisprudence of the German Federal Court of Justice (BGH GRUR 2009, 1039 – *Fischbissanzeiger*), the choice of a specific starting point requires a particular justification. Accordingly, inventive step is typically assessed by the German courts in light of

（X ZR 107/12、2014年2月11日）を参照されたい。実施形態の特徴が、発明によって達成される成功に共同して又は個々に貢献し、かつ、保護される発明を特定するのに役立つものであれば、かかる特徴を個々に又は全体としてクレームに組み込むことで特許が限定されることは、実質的に認められる。

　欧州特許庁に対する手続において、1つの実施例で開示された特徴の組合せから特徴を抽出する補正をする場合は、これら（抽出された）特性／特徴が、実施例の他の特性／特徴とは密接に関連しておらず、より一般的な内容に直接的かつ一義的に適用されるということを、当業者が疑いの余地なく認識できるか否かが補正を認める基準となる（例えば、T 962/98参照）。

　最近のイギリスの事件で、控訴裁判所は、ブレーキ部品について明細書で当初の「ホッケー用スティックの形状」として記載されたものを、付与された特許で「非対称の形状」と一般化する補正は認められると判示した（*AP Racing Ltd v Alcon Components Ltd*［2014］EWCA Civ 40）。これは欧州特許庁の拡大審判部のアプローチより寛大であると思われる。例えば、T 653/03では、当初の出願で開示された特定の用語「ディーゼルエンジン」を開示されていない包括的用語である「燃焼機関」で置き換えることは認められないと判示された。

　国内裁判所が欧州特許庁の実務に従っていない（あるいは完全に従っていない）他の重要な領域として、進歩性の判断がある。特に欧州特許庁により開拓された課題解決アプローチの適用である。

　課題解決アプローチの第一段階は、いわゆる「最も近い先行技術」の判断を伴う。一方で、ドイツ連邦裁判所の法理（BGH GRUR 2009, 1039 - *Fischbissanzeiger*）によると、特定の出発点を選択するには特別の正当な理由が必要である。したがって、ドイツ裁判所は、可能な出発点として、複数の文献を考慮して進歩性を判断するのが通常である。他方、連邦裁判所は最近の多

several documents as possible starting points. On the other hand, the Federal Court of Justice emphasized in a number of recent decisions that, in order to conclude lack of inventive step, it is insufficient for the nullity plaintiff to show that the technical problem was recognizable. Beyond this, the prior art must furnish an inducement, motivation, hint or other cause to seek the solution of the technical problem in the same way as the invention (*Betrieb einer Sicherheitseinrichtung*, BGH GRUR 2009, 746). Since this test links the question of obviousness with the technical success accomplished by the invention, it will frequently lead to similar results as the problem-solution approach of the EPO. At the same time, the inventive step assessment by the German courts does not only rely on an objectively defined problem, but considers equally other reasons which may induce a skilled person to modify the existing art, such as simplification, saving of cost and energy reduction or the like. These practically important causes for technical developments are often not considered by the problem-solution approach and can have the consequence that a European patent is declared null and void in Germany even if it was previously held to be valid by the EPO.

The practice of the British courts is even further apart from that of the EPO. A set of rules regarding the approach taken by the United Kingdom courts was laid out by the Court of Appeal in *Windsurfing International Inc. v Tabur Marine (GB) Ltd.* [1985] RPC 59, in determining the requirements for inventive step. This test has been slightly reworked in the more recent Court of Appeal case *Pozzoli Spa v BDMO SA & Anor* [2007] EWCA Civ 588 (22 June 2007) as follows:

1. (a) Identify the notional "person skilled in the art", (b) Identify the relevant common general knowledge of that person;

2. Identify the inventive concept of the claim in question or if that cannot readily be done, construe it;

3. Identify what, if any, differences exist between the matter cited as form-

数の判決のなかで、進歩性の欠如を結論付けるためには、技術的課題が認識できることを無効訴訟の原告が示すことでは不十分であることを強調した。その域を越えて、先行技術は発明と同じようにして技術的課題についての解決手段を求めるための誘因、動機付け、ヒント又はその他の要因を備えている必要がある（*Betrieb einer Sicherheitseinrichtung*, BGH GRUR 2009, 746）。このテストは、自明性の問題と、発明により達成される技術的成功を関連付けるため、欧州特許庁の課題解決アプローチと同様の結果を導くことが多い。ドイツ裁判所による進歩性の判断は、客観的な課題に基づくだけでなく、単純化、コスト削減、エネルギー削減等の他の理由で当業者を促して既存の技術を変更させ得るものを等しく考慮する。技術開発のこれら実務上重要な根拠は、課題解決アプローチでは考慮されないことが多く、欧州特許庁により欧州特許が有効と判断されていたとしても、当該欧州特許はドイツでは無効と宣言される結果となる場合がある。

イギリス裁判所の実務は、欧州特許庁の実務とはさらにかけ離れている。イギリス裁判所が採用するアプローチに関する規則が、*Windsurfing International Inc. v Tabur Marine（GB）Ltd.* [1985] RPC 59において、進歩性の要件を判断するに際して、控訴裁判所により整備された。このテストは、より最近の控訴裁判所の事件である*Pozzoli Spa v BDMO SA & Anor* [2007] EWCA Civ 588（2007年6月22日）により、以下のように若干修正された。

1. (a)抽象的な「当業者」を特定し、(b)かかる者の関連する技術常識を特定する。

2. 争点となるクレームに記載され発明の概念を特定する（それが容易でなければ解釈する）。

3. 「技術水準」を構成するとして引用された対象と、クレームに記載され

ing part of the "state of the art" and the inventive concept of the claim or the claim as construed;

4. Viewed without any knowledge of the alleged invention as claimed, do those differences constitute steps which would have been obvious to the person skilled in the art or do they require any degree of invention?

It follows from this approach that, in contrast to the problem-solution approach applied by the EPO, the UK practice does not involve a mosaicing of documents (combination of prior art teachings). The information and teaching provided by secondary documents is rather considered in step 1(b), where the common general knowledge of the person skilled in the art is identified. It is easily understood that this approach can lead to decisions diverging from those rendered by the EPO.

6 Precedence of EPO Opposition Proceedings over National Invalidation Proceedings

The national jurisdiction as of grant of a European patent does not necessarily mean that the respective national part can be immediately attacked in invalidation proceedings. In order to avoid diverging decisions and to relieve the national courts, several EPC states have stipulated that EPO opposition proceedings take precedence over national invalidation proceedings. According to section 81(2) of the German Patent Act, an action for declaration of nullity of a patent may not be brought as long as an opposition may still be filed or opposition proceedings are pending.

Similar provisions are found in the national laws of France.

On the contrary, in Italy and Spain there is no provision that prevents the starting of an action for declaration of nullity of a patent in the period during

た又はクレームから解釈された発明の概念との間の相違点を特定する。

4．クレームに記載された発明を知ることなくして、これらの相違は、当業者にとって自明となり得るステップを構成するか、あるいはある程度の発明を要求するか？

このアプローチに従えば、欧州特許庁で適用される課題解決アプローチとは対照的に、イギリス実務は文献の寄せ集め（先行技術の教示の組合せ）を伴わない。二次的な文献により提供される情報及び教示は、むしろステップ1(b)で考慮され、ここでは当業者の技術常識が特定される。このアプローチによると欧州特許庁が下した決定とは異なる決定となり得ることが容易に理解できる。

6 国内無効手続に対する欧州特許庁異議申立手続の優先性

欧州特許の付与の時点での国内裁判管轄は、欧州特許の各国内部分が国内の無効手続で直ちに攻撃され得ることを必ずしも意味しない。不一致となる判断を避けて国内裁判所の負担を除くために、欧州特許条約の締約国のなかには、欧州特許庁の特許異議申立手続が、国内無効手続に優先することを規定している国々がある。ドイツ特許法第81条(2)によると、特許異議の申立てをすることができるか又は特許異議申立手続が係属中である限り、特許の無効の確認の訴えを提起することはできない。

類似の規定は、フランスの国内法令にも見つけることができる。

これに対して、イタリアとスペインでは、特許異議の申立てをすることができるか又は特許異議申立手続が係属中である期間中に、特許の無効確認の訴え

which an opposition may be filed or opposition proceedings are pending.

Another notable exception is the UK, where the courts assess whether or not to stay proceedings in line with the principles set out by the Court of Appeal in *IPcom v HTC Europe* ([2013] EWCA Civ 1496). In this decision, the Court of Appeal held that a stay of national proceedings is the default option, but can be refused at the discretion of the court. Some of the factors considered in reaching this decision are:

- the length of time that it will take for the proceedings to reach a conclusion,

- whether there is evidence that commercial certainty would be achieved at an earlier date in UK proceedings, and

- whether the refusal of a stay will irrevocably deprive a party of a benefit which would be available if the proceedings were stayed.

- Also in the Netherlands it is at the discretion of the judges as to whether nullity proceedings are stayed or not.

の開始を阻止する規定はない。

　他の特筆すべき例外はイギリスであり、裁判所は、*IPcom v HTC Europe*（[2013] EWCA Civ 1496）において控訴裁判所が定めた原則に沿って、手続を中断するか否かを判断する。この判決で控訴裁判所は、国内手続の中断はデフォルトであるが、裁判所の裁量で却下できる旨を判示した。この判断に至る際に考慮された要因は以下のとおりである。

- 上記手続において結論に至るまでの時間。

- 事業の確実性がイギリス訴訟で早期に達成されるであろうという証拠があるか否か。

- 訴訟の中断を却下することにより、訴訟が中断されていたならば得られたであろう利益を当事者から決定的に奪うか否か。

- オランダでも、無効訴訟手続を中断させるか否かは裁判官の裁量による。

Chapter 18

The European Patent within the Future EU Patent Package

今後の EU 特許パッケージの 枠組みにおける欧州特許

Thorsten Bausch

MEMO

▶ 単一効特許、統一特許裁判所、及び EU 特許パッケージ全体に関して、さらに詳細な情報は、Hoffmann Eitle 刊行物である *EU Patent Package Handbook*（英語版のみ）をご参照ください。弊所の下記ウェブサイトからも無料の e-book としてダウンロード可能です。

〈http://www.hoffmanneitle.com/information/publication/The-EU-Patent-Package-Handbook-A-Practitioners-Guide/115/〉

▶ 本章では、欧州単一効特許の創設に関する規則を「単一効特許規則」と略記し、翻訳言語要件について定める規則を「翻訳言語規則」と略記します。

Introduction

At the date of finishing this article (August 2016), it seems possible that a new type of patent, the so-called *European Patent with Unitary Effect*, will come into existence in the not too distant future, even though it is difficult to predict when exactly this will happen. In this Chapter, we will be using the abbreviation EP-UE since it indicates that the EP-UE is based on a granted European patent (EP). Just like any other European patent, the EP-UE is filed at, prosecuted, and eventually granted by the European Patent Office (EPO).

1   Legal Basis

At the end of 2012, agreement was reached on the legal instruments constituting the so-called EU Patent Package. These legal instruments are the Regulations[1] creating the European Patent with Unitary Effect (EP-UE) and setting forth the translation requirements, and the Unified Patent Court Agreement (UPCA)[2] as an international agreement. The EP-UE Regulation makes use of an option provided in the European Patent Convention to validate European patents supra nationally.

Although the Regulations are already in force, they will apply only if and when the Unified Patent Court Agreement (UPCA) also enters into force. The UPCA was *signed* on February 19, 2013 by 25 EU Member States, but it must still be *ratified* according to the respective constitutional requirements of the signatory states. The UPCA will enter into force if 3 plus 10 countries ratified it, the three

---

[1] Regulation (EU) No. 1257/2012 of December 17, 2012 implementing enhanced cooperation in the area of the creation of unitary patent protection (the EP-UE Regulation) and Regulation (EU) No. 1260/2012 of December 17, 2012 implementing enhanced cooperation in the area of the creation of unitary patent protection with regard to the applicable translation arrangements (the Translation Regulation).
[2] Agreement on a Unified Patent Court of February 19, 2013 (UPCA).

はじめに

本稿執筆終了時点（2016年8月）の見通しによると、新しいタイプの特許「欧州単一効特許」が、その発足時期は正確に予測できないが、近い将来に発足することになろう。欧州単一効特許は、付与された欧州特許に基づく特許であり、本章では「単一効特許」と略記する。他の既存の欧州特許と同様、単一効特許においても、出願、審査及び特許付与に至るまでの手続は欧州特許庁にて行われる。

1 法的根拠

2012年末に、いわゆるEU特許パッケージを構成する一連の法令に関して合意が成立した。一連の法令とはすなわち、欧州単一効特許（単一効特許）の創設に関する規則及び翻訳言語要件について定める規則の2つの規則[1]、並びに、国家間協定としての統一特許裁判所協定（UPCA）[2]である。単一効特許規則は、欧州特許条約によって与えられたオプションを利用して欧州特許を超国家的に有効化するものである。

単一効特許規則と翻訳言語規則はすでに発効しているが、その適用には統一特許裁判所協定が発効することが条件とされ、その発効時点からの適用となる。統一特許裁判所協定は、2013年2月19日に25カ国のEU加盟国により署名されたが、各署名国の憲法上の要請に従って批准される必要がある。統一特許裁判所協定の発効については3カ国+10カ国による批准が条件であって、3カ

---

[1] 単一効特許保護の創設の分野における強化された協力を実施する2012年12月17日の規則（EU）No. 1257/2012（単一効特許規則）及び単一効特許保護の創設の分野における強化された協力を実施する適用翻訳言語の取決めに関する2012年12月17日の規則（EU）No. 1260/2012（翻訳言語規則）

[2] 2013年2月19日の統一特許裁判所協定

countries being Germany, the United Kingdom, and France, and the other ten being any of the further 22 signatory states. Currently, ten states have ratified the UPCA (AT, FR, BE, SE, DK, LU, MT, PT, FI and BG). The ratification of Germany (DE) is no problem of principle, but the ratification of the UK (GB) is now very doubtful, following the outcome of the referendum about Great Britain's membership in the EU, which will result in GB leaving the EU (so-called Brexit). The Court of Justice of the European Union (CJEU) has opined in C 01/09 that the UPC must be a court within the institutional and judicial framework of the European Union and, hence, be part of the judicial system provided for in Article 19(1) of the EU Treaty. As a consequence, the UPC must be able to refer questions of law to the CJEU and has to accept the supremacy of decisions by the CJEU. It has been concluded from these principles that the UPC can only be open to EU Member States, which are bound by EU law. Whether an exception could be made for ex-EU member states that acknowledge supremacy of CJEU jurisprudence, is currently being considered by some practitioners, but the overriding political problem is whether the new UK government really wants to accept that and join the EU patent package now, given that the UK as a whole will leave the EU in a few years. Assuming that the UK will most likely no longer want to join the "EU Patent Package" and to ratify the UPCA, the entry into force of the EU Patent Package will be significantly delayed, since several aspects of the European Patent Package will first have to be re-negotiated, including the seat of the central division of the UPC. Nevertheless, the political will of the remaining EU Member States participating in the enhanced cooperation on patents to enact the UPCA still appears unbroken and thus it may be useful to consider the new provisions of the European Patent Package in this book.

2 How to Obtain an EP-UE

How can a European Patent with Unitary Effect (EP-UE) be obtained? Basically by the following three steps:

国とはドイツ、イギリス、フランスであり、10カ国とは残り22の署名国の内いずれかの国である。現在、10カ国がすでに同協定を批准している（オーストリア、フランス、ベルギー、スウェーデン、デンマーク、ルクセンブルク、マルタ、ポルトガル、フィンランド、ブルガリア）。ドイツによる批准は原則として問題がないとみられるが、イギリスのEU離脱を問う国民投票の結果（いわゆる、Brexit）を受けて、イギリスによる同協定の批准は現在非常に疑わしい。欧州連合司法裁判所は、C 01/09において、統一特許裁判所について意見を述べている。すなわち、統一特許裁判所は、EUの枠組みでの組織的であって司法上の裁判所でなければならず、EUのリスボン条約第19条第1項に規定される司法上の体系の一部であるとされる。その結果、統一裁判所は、法律問題を欧州連合司法裁判所に付託することができなければならず、欧州連合司法裁判所による決定を最高法規として受け入れなければならない。このような原則から、統一特許裁判所は、EU法によって拘束されるEU加盟国に対してのみ開かれている。過去にEU加盟国であった国であって欧州連合司法裁判所の最高法規の法体系を認める国は例外的に扱われるべきと議論する実務家がいるが、新たなイギリス政府がEU特許パッケージを受け入れ、それに参加することを本当に望むのかという大きな政治的問題がある。これは、イギリスが全体としてEUを離脱することを考慮した場合である。イギリスがEU特許パッケージに参加し統一裁判所協定を批准する意欲がないという推定の下では、欧州特許パッケージの発効はかなり遅れるだろう。統一特許裁判所の中央部の設立地等を含むEU特許パッケージの側面について再交渉する必要があるからだ。とにかく、特許統一裁判所を制定する強化された協力に参加している残りのEU加盟国では、その政治的意思は絶えることがなく、EU特許パッケージの新たな規定を本書において考慮することは有用であろう。

2　単一効特許の取得方法

では、欧州単一効特許（単一効特許）とはどのような手順で取得できるのか。基本的には次の3つのステップを踏めばよい。

- applying and prosecuting to grant a European patent at the European Patent Office (EPO), designating all member states participating in the EU patent package;

- requesting the EPO to have the European patent registered as an EP-UE within one month after grant of the European patent; and

- submitting a translation of the entire patent together with the request for registration as an EP-UE, i.e. apparently also within the above one month time limit, for a transitional period of at least six, and possibly up to twelve years.

From the date the EP-UE Regulation becomes applicable, i.e. the date of entering into force of the UPCA, any European patent which at that time is still within the one-month period after grant can be registered as an EP-UE. This means, EP-UEs can be registered from day one since they are prosecuted as "normal" European patents.

3 The Territorial Scope of an EP-UE

The territorial scope of the EP-UE will be determined by the EU Member States' (a) participation in the enhanced cooperation to create the EP-UE Regulation and (b) ratification of the UPCA. Here we will be referring to countries fulfilling both conditions as EP-UE Member States. The UK will most probably not become an EP-UE Member State following the Brexit decision, but it will in any case remain a member of the European Patent Organisation (EPO), so that classic EP bundle patents will continue to be available for the UK.

The request for enhanced cooperation (a) has been signed by 25 countries so far (all EU Member States except Croatia and Spain).

- 欧州特許出願をして、特許付与に至るまでの手続を欧州特許庁にて行う。その際、EU特許パッケージ参加加盟国のすべてを指定する。

- 欧州特許が付与された後1月以内に、欧州特許庁に対し当該特許を単一効特許として登録する旨の請求を行う。

- 単一効特許の登録請求と同時に（すなわち、上記1月の期間に）、特許全文の翻訳文を提出する（少なくとも6年、最長でおそらく12年の移行期間の措置である）。

単一効特許規則が適用可能となる日（すなわち、統一特許裁判所協定が発効する日）以降、欧州特許のうちその時点で特許付与後1月以内にあるものは、いずれも単一効特許として登録することができる。つまり、「通常の」欧州特許として手続が進められたものであるので、初日から単一効特許として登録可能となる。

3　単一効特許の地域的範囲

単一効特許の地域的範囲がどのような範囲になるかは、EU加盟国による、(a)単一効特許規則の創設に係る強化された協力への参加と、(b)統一特許裁判所協定の批准によって決まる。ここでは、この2つの条件を両方とも満たしている国を「単一効特許加盟国」と呼ぶことにする。Brexit決定を受けて、イギリスはおそらく単一効特許加盟国とはならないだろう。とはいっても、イギリスは欧州特許機構の締約国として残存するので、これまでどおり、権利の束としての欧州特許をイギリスで取得することが可能である。

(a)強化された協力に関する要請については、これまでのところ25カ国（クロアチアとスペインを除く全EU加盟国）が署名している。

The requirements for ratifying the UPCA (b) differ considerably within the signatory states. Therefore it can be expected that if and when the UPCA enters into force, the initial territory where the UPCA enters into force will not be constituted by all states, and some states will be subsequently joining from time-to-time.

For example, Spain and Poland have indicated that they will not join the agreement in the foreseeable future, the Czech republic has announced that it will wait with the ratification until really reliable machine translations into Czech will be available, and Croatia has to date neither signed the UPCA nor indicated that it will join the enhanced co-operation for establishing the EP-UE. Also CY, GR, SK and SI seem to want to stay out for now, and whether there is a future for GB as a UPCA member state is completely unclear.

In those subsequently joining states the UPCA will enter into force only upon their respective ratification. To be more precise, the UPCA will enter into force in the initial and any subsequently joining states after a short transitional period, namely on the first day of the fourth month after depositing the instrument of ratification.

A granted European patent having been registered as an EP-UE will have effect in all of those countries where the UPCA had entered into force at the time of registration as an EP-UE. Let us assume the UPCA initially enters into force only in 13 states: a European patent which is registered immediately thereafter will cover only the territory of those 13 states. The territorial scope of an EP-UE once registered will also not be subsequently extended when the UPCA is ratified in further states. Only European patents that are later registered as EP-UEs, i.e. after the UPCA has entered into force in the further states, will enjoy the enlarged territory.

For all EU Member States which either did not participate in the enhanced cooperation or where the UPCA has not yet entered into force (Non-EP-UE Mem-

第 18 章：今後の EU 特許パッケージの枠組みにおける欧州特許　617

(b)統一特許裁判所協定の批准に関しては、各署名国で批准手続が大幅に異なる。このことから、たとえ統一特許裁判所協定が発効したとしても、最初の段階では、すべての加盟国で同協定が有効になるわけではなく、一部の国は同協定に後から随時参加することになろう。

　例えば、スペインとポーランドは当面の間は同協定に参加しないという意向を示しており、チェコ共和国は信頼性の高いチェコ語への機械翻訳が利用可能になるまで批准を見合わせると公表している。またクロアチアは現在に至るまで、同協定の署名も、単一効特許創設に関する強化された協力への参加の意思表明も行っていない。また、キプロス、ギリシャ、スロバキア及びスロベニアは、現在のところ、参加を望んでいないようである。そして、将来イギリスが統一特許裁判所協定の加盟国となるかについては、まったく不明である。

　このような後続の参加国においては、各国内で批准されてはじめて統一特許裁判所協定が発効することになる。具体的にいうと、同協定は初期段階の参加国と、短い移行期間を経た後の（すなわち、批准書の寄託から4月目の月の初日からの）後続の参加国において発効する。

　特許付与後に単一効特許として登録された欧州特許は、その単一効特許登録の時点で統一特許裁判所協定が発効しているすべての国において効力を有することになる。例えば、同協定がまず13カ国でのみ発効するとしよう。その場合、同協定発効の直後に登録された欧州特許は、それら13カ国の地域のみをカバーする。その後に他の国で統一特許裁判所協定が批准されたとしても、いったん登録された単一効特許の地域的範囲は、後続の国に拡大されることはない。後から単一効特許として登録された欧州特許、つまり、後続の国における統一特許裁判所協定の発効後に登録された単一効特許だけが、拡大された地域での利益を享受する。

　強化された協力に参加していない、あるいは統一特許裁判所協定がまだ発効していない EU 加盟国（非単一効特許加盟国）についてはすべて、従来と同様

18

ber States), the European patent will still have to be validated nationally as before. The same will apply permanently with regard to all EPC Member States that are not EU Member States, such as Turkey, Switzerland, Norway and - in the future, following the Brexit - the UK, since non-EU Member States are, according to the prevailing legal view, excluded from participating in an enhanced cooperation under EU law.

National validation will therefore remain available to complement the registration as EP-UE. This means that applicants will have a choice in the future for many EU member states whether they want an EP-UE or rather a classic European bundle patent[3].

The determination of the territorial scope as of the time of registration as an EP-UE must lead to two considerations. First, in some cases it might be advantageous to delay the grant of a European patent to ensure a broader territorial scope. Should it be foreseeable when the Examining Division gives notice of its intention to grant the European patent that the UPCA will soon enter into force in further relevant EU Member States, the patentee may save renewal fees and possibly translation costs if it delays the grant so as to ensure that when the European patent is registered as an EP-UE, the UPCA will already have entered into force in those countries. Secondly, the time when the registration as an EP-UE is effected will not be in the hands of the patentee. It will depend on the speed of the registration process. If a country where the patent shall have effect is about to join the EP-UE territory (become a EP-UE Member State), but it is not clear whether this will happen before or after the patent's registration as an EP-UE, the patentee may have to initiate a national validation as a safety measure. This again may speak in favor of delaying the grant if a desired country is about to become an EP-UE Member State.

---

[3] If a European patent has been registered as an EP-UE, an additional national validation in any country within the territorial scope of the EP-UE will be ineffective.

に、国ごとに欧州特許を有効化しなければならない。このことは、欧州特許条約の締約国であるがEUに加盟していないすべての国について永久に当てはまり、トルコ、スイス、ノルウェーなどがこれに該当し、Brexitを受けて将来はイギリスにも当てはまろう。これらの国はEU法における強化された協力に参加できないからである。

したがって、国内有効化のルートは、今後も単一効特許登録を補完するものとして利用可能である。つまり出願人は、多くのEU加盟国について、単一効特許にするか、従来のいわゆる権利の束としての欧州特許にするか[3]、将来にわたって選択することができる。

単一効特許の地域的範囲はその登録の時点で決まることから、2つの点に留意する必要がある。1つ目は、より広い地域的範囲を確保するために、欧州特許の特許付与を遅らせるほうが有利な場合があるという点である。仮に、欧州特許を付与する意図があることを審査部が通知した時点で、より有意義なEU加盟国で統一特許裁判所協定が間もなく発効するという見通しがあるとする。その場合、特許付与を遅らせることで、当該欧州特許の単一効特許登録の時期が該当国での同協定の発効後となるように調整できれば、特許権者は更新手数料だけでなく、場合によっては翻訳費用も節約することができる。2つ目は、単一効特許の登録が確定する時期は、特許権者がコントロールできるわけではないという点である。確定時期は、登録手続の進み具合によって左右される。もし特許を有効化したい国が、近々単一効特許地域に加わる（単一効特許加盟国になる）予定ではあるものの、その加盟時期が単一効特許登録より先になるか後になるか定かではないという場合、安全策として国内有効化手続を開始したほうがよいこともあり得る。この場合も、もし希望国が近々単一効特許加盟国になるという見込みがあるならば、特許付与を遅らせたほうがよいということになるだろう。

---

[3] 欧州特許を単一効特許として登録した場合、単一効特許の地域的範囲内のいずれかの国でさらに国内有効化を図ることはできない。

4 Unitary Effect

With the supra national validation of a European patent as an EP-UE by registration at the EPO, the EP-UE will become a "unitary right". Upon registration of unitary effect, the EP-UE shall have unitary character retroactively as of the date of publication of mention of grant in the EPO Official Bulletin in all EP-UE Member States at the time of registration. Unlike nationally validated European patents, EP-UEs will have the same legal fate in all covered EP-UE Member States. The EP-UE can only be invalidated, limited or allowed to lapse with regard to its entire territory. It can also be assigned only for its entire territory. Licenses can, however, be limited to certain territories.

For patentees, one advantage of this unitary effect will be that renewal fees will have to be paid only at one patent office, the EPO, and not at each national patent office. On the other hand, the practice of letting less important national EP parts later lapse to reduce renewal fees will not be available for the EP-UE. Also, with regard to their particularly valuable patents, patentees may dislike the simplified invalidation by a central action before the Unified Patent Court (UPC) instead of national invalidation proceedings in all relevant countries, as is currently the case with European patents after expiry of the nine-month opposition period. National invalidation is cumbersome and expensive for a competitor and bears the risk that the patent will remain in force at least in some countries.

A further aspect is the applicable property law. Property laws are relevant for a number of questions such as the rights of co owners as well as the requirements for assigning, licensing, and providing a patent as security. The European Patent Convention (EPC) does not set forth comprehensive provisions on the EP as a property. Instead it refers to the property laws of the countries in which the patent will have effect after grant. Upon grant, a European patent is treated like a national patent such that the respective national property laws apply to each of its national parts. However, since the EP-UE is a unitary right, this solution of apply-

4　単一効

　欧州特許庁にて欧州特許を単一効特許として登録して超国家的に有効化することで、単一効特許は「単一の権利」となる。単一効特許の登録がなされると、欧州特許庁の特許公報に特許が付与された旨が掲載された日から、登録時におけるすべての単一効特許加盟国において、その単一効特許は遡及的に単一であることになる。各国ごとに有効化される欧州特許とは異なり、単一効特許の場合は、その効力が及ぶすべての単一効特許加盟国において同一の法律効果を生じることになる。単一効特許の無効化、限定、消滅は、全対象域において一律になされる。譲渡の場合も、その効果は一律に全地域に及ぶ。ただしライセンスについては、特定の地域に限定して行うことができる。

　特許権者にとって、この単一効の利点の1つは、更新手数料を各国の国内特許庁ごとに納付するのではなく、1つの特許庁（欧州特許庁）に納付するだけで済むということであろう。一方、現在の実務として、欧州特許の国内権利分のうち重要性の低いものを後に失効させることで更新手数料を節減するという方法があるが、単一効特許にはこの方法を用いることができない。また、特許権者としては、特に重要な特許については、統一特許裁判所にてセントラル・アクションにより特許が無効化され得るという簡素化された無効化手続を嫌うであろう。既存の欧州特許の場合、9月の異議申立期間終了後は、すべての該当国で国ごとに無効訴訟が行われ、国ごとの無効化は、相手方にとっては煩雑で費用のかかる手続であり、しかも、少なくとも一部の国では特許の効力が存続し続けるかもしれないというリスクを伴う。

　もうひとつの側面は、適用可能な財産法についてである。財産法は、共有者の権利や、特許の譲渡、実施許諾、担保設定の際の要件といった多くの問題に関わってくる。欧州特許条約には財産権としての欧州特許に関する包括規定が定められていない。代わりとして、特許付与後にその効果が発生する国の財産法についての記載はある。特許付与後、欧州特許は国内特許と同等に扱われ、各国内の権利については、その国の国内財産法がそれぞれ適用される。しかし、単一効特許は単一の権利であるため、このように各国の国内権利ごとに異なる財産法を適用するという手段を単一効特許に用いることはできない。EU

ing a different property law to each of its national parts could not be maintained for the EP-UE. The drafters of the EU Patent Package had to find a different solution which sets forth one specific property law being applicable to the entire unitary right. They resolved this not by creating a specific property law only for EP-UEs, but by setting forth conflict-of-law rules which select the national property law that is applicable to an EP-UE. According to these conflict-of-law rules, simply put, the property law of the EP-UE Member State shall apply where the applicant had its residence or its (principal) place of business at the filing date of the European patent application. Should the applicant have no residence or place of business in any EP-UE Member State, German property law shall apply as default. For the many applicants from Asia and the USA, German property law will therefore become more relevant.

5 Translations

To register an EP-UE, a translation of the entire patent will be required during a transitional period of at least six, and at most 12 years. The transitional period shall end when an independent committee has established that machine translations into all official languages of the EU Member States have attained a sufficiently good quality. The EPO is working to improve such translations in cooperation with Google.

During the transitional period, the following provisions apply: (1) If the European patent was prosecuted and granted in German or French, an English translation will be required[4]. (2) If the European patent was prosecuted in English (which is predominantly the case – about 80% of EP's are in English), the appli-

---

[4] It is open to speculation whether these language requirements will remain the same in the negotiations to take place following the Brexit decision. The current language regime was one of the main reasons why Spain did not want to join the enhanced cooperation on patents.

特許パッケージの起草時には、ある特定の財産法で単一の権利全体をカバーできるような、別の方法を探すことが必要となった。この課題の実際の解決策となったのは、単一効特許用に特化した財産法を作るのではなく、国際私法原則によって単一効特許に適用可能な国内財産法を選択するというものであった。簡単にいうと、国際私法原則に従い、単一効特許には、出願人が欧州特許出願の出願日において居所又は（主たる）事業所を有する単一効特許加盟国の財産法が適用されることになる。出願人がいずれの単一効特許加盟国にも居所又は事業所を有していない場合は、ドイツ財産法が既定適用となる。したがって、アジアやアメリカの多くの出願人にとっては、ドイツ財産法がより大きく関わるものとなるであろう。

5　翻訳

単一効特許の登録を行うためには、少なくとも6年、最長12年の移行期間中は、特許の全文翻訳が必要となる。この移行期間は、独立した委員会の評価により、EU加盟国すべての公用語への機械翻訳が十分に高品質な水準に達したと認められたときに終了する。欧州特許庁はGoogleと連携しつつ、このような機械翻訳の改良に取り組んでいる。

移行期間中においては、以下の条件が適用される：(1)欧州特許の手続及び特許付与の言語がドイツ語又はフランス語であった場合、英語による翻訳文が求められる[4]。(2)欧州特許の手続言語が英語であった場合（大半がこれに該当し、欧州特許の約80％は英語によるものである）、出願人は欧州連合の他の公用語のう

---

[4]　Brexit決定を受けて行われる交渉において、同じ言語要件となるかは推測の域を出ない。特許についての強化された協力にスペインが参加しなかった理由は現在の言語体制にある。

cants will have to provide a translation into any other official language of the European Union. This even includes the languages of those EU Member States which the EP-UE will not cover – at least in the foreseeable future -, such as Spanish, or Polish.

The decision as to which language to choose for the translation will mainly be a commercial one. If the European patent is to be additionally validated also in Spain or Poland, a national validation in these countries will require a translation of the patent into the official languages of these countries anyway. Such a translation could then also be used for registering the EP-UE.

The correctness of the EP-UE translation does not have legal relevance; it is for information purposes only. This is different from the translations required for some national validations.

Moreover, a translation of the EP-UE may be required when enforcing it, namely if the proceedings are conducted in a language other than the language of the granted patent and the submitted translation. This will apply also beyond the transition period.

6   Renewal Fees

The renewal fees for the future EP-UE have meanwhile been determined and will be approximately equivalent to the cumulated renewal fees of the TOP4 states (DE, FR, GB, NL).

It is thus clear that applicants who were used to only validate their European patents in the three most important member states (DE, GB, FR) will have to pay significantly more than now when they want to acquire an EP-UE. This applies to about 50% of all applicants. A further 40% of the applicants have so far validated their European patents in DE, FR, GB, IT and ES. They will also likely experience

ちのいずれか1つの言語による翻訳文を提出する必要がある。このような言語には、スペイン語やポーランド語など、（少なくとも今後しばらくの間）単一効特許が適用されないEU加盟国の言語も含まれる。

翻訳言語としてどの言語を選択するかは、主に営利上の判断によるものとなろう。もし欧州特許を有効化する国としてスペイン又はポーランドも加える予定があるならば、同国の国内有効化手続を行う際に、いずれにせよその国の公用語による特許の翻訳文が必要となるので、この翻訳文を単一効特許の登録用として利用することができる。

単一効特許の翻訳文の精度は法的には問題とならない。この翻訳文は情報提供のみを目的とするものである。この点は、いくつかの締約国で必要とされる国内有効化手続に必要な翻訳文とは異なる。

また、例えば単一効特許の権利を行使する際（具体的には、特許付与時の言語や提出した翻訳文の言語とは異なる別の言語で権利行使の手続を行う場合）には、さらに単一効特許の翻訳が必要になることもある。これは、移行期間終了後も同様である。

6　更新手数料

今後発生する単一効特許の更新手数料については決定がされており、TOP4（ドイツ、フランス、イギリス、オランダ）の更新手数料の累計額におおよそ相当する額となる。

このことからわかるように、これまで重要な3カ国（ドイツ、イギリス、フランス）のみを対象に欧州特許の有効化を行っていた出願人は、単一効特許を取得しようとする場合、今までよりも高額な手数料を支払わざるを得なくなる。全出願人のうち約50％がこのケースに該当する。さらに40％の出願人は、従来の手続においてドイツ、フランス、イギリス、イタリア、スペインにおい

no savings in renewal fees, since for Spain a national validation will still be necessary and the NL fees that go into the EP-UE renewal fees are much higher than the IT renewal fees used to be. Another disadvantage of the EP-UE is that it is not possible to drop individual designations as in the past. On the other hand, the territory of the EP-UE will be much larger than the combined territory of DE, GB, FR and NL.

The sum of the total renewal fees over 20 years is expected to be 35,555 EUR.

7 For Whom will an EP-UE Commercially Make Sense?

Patentees faced with the decision of whether to register their European patents as EP-UEs will have to consider the advantages and disadvantages. Unfortunately, this is quite a complex assessment, even more so following the "Brexit" decision by the UK referendum, and many factors can play a role. The following considerations cannot therefore be comprehensive, but they should provide the reader with some initial ideas.

7.1 Cost of an EP-UE Compared to National Validation

If one were to compare the costs of an EP-UE to the costs of validating a patent nationally in all EP-UE Member States, the EP-UE would certainly be more cost efficient. However, this is an overly simplistic view since in practice European patents are validated only in selected countries and most patentees are under such budget constraints that they will mainly consider how the EP-UE compares to their established validation strategy. For such a comparison, the following may be considered:

て欧州特許の有効化を行っている。スペインについては今後も依然として国内有効化手続が必要であり、かつ、単一効特許の更新手数料で考慮されるオランダの料金はイタリアの料金よりはるかに高額であることから、これらの出願人にとってもやはり更新手数料の節減効果はほとんど得られないと思われる。単一効特許のもうひとつの不利な点は、加盟国の指定国を個々に取り下げることができないことである。その一方で、単一効特許の領域は、ドイツ、フランス、イギリス、オランダを統合した地域よりも、はるかに広い。

20年にわたる更新手数料総額は、3万5555ユーロになると見込まれる。

7 誰にとって単一効特許は採算に合うのか

特許権者は、欧州特許を単一効特許として登録するか否か決めるにあたって、いくつかのメリットとデメリットを考え合わせる必要がある。ただ残念ながらこの評価作業は非常に難しく、またイギリスの国民投票によって決定されたBrexitを受けてさらに難しくなっている。これには、多くの要因が関与する。その意味で、以下の考察は網羅的なものとはいえないが、読者の方にとって検討を始める際の手がかりにはなるはずである。

7.1 単一効特許ルートと国内有効化ルートの費用の比較

仮に、すべての単一効特許加盟国で特許の国内有効化手続を各々に行った場合の費用と、単一効特許登録した場合にかかる費用とを比べるならば、たしかに単一効特許のほうが費用効率は高いであろう。ただし、これはあまりにも単純すぎる例である。実際には欧州特許の国内有効化は選択した国についてのみ行われるものであり、大部分の特許権者は予算の制約を受けるため、既定の権利有効化戦略と比べて単一効特許がどの程度見合うものになるかを重視するであろう。このような比較を行う際の検討事項としては、以下のようなものが挙げられる。

7.2 Renewal Fees

The renewal fees for the EP-UE will be at around the TOP4 level (see above). Whether this is more or less than the costs of a national validation will depend on the countries where the European patent would otherwise be validated. For example, the accumulated renewal fees of the new EP-UE until the end of its 20-year lifetime will be about 10,000 € higher than the accumulated renewal fees for DE, FR and GB. However, the average lifetime of an EP is currently only about 11 years, so that the disadvantage will be much less pronounced.

A further factor to be considered are the savings which can be achieved in administrative costs and fees for paying multiple renewal fees versus one renewal fee for an EP-UE.

7.3 Translation Costs

At least in the transitional period in which the request for a registration as an EP-UE must be submitted together with a translation of the European patent, translation costs will also remain relevant. To compare the translation costs for a complete translation of a patent for EP-UE registration with the translation costs otherwise incurred for national validations, even more factors must be taken into account. The translation costs will also depend on the number of pages to be translated and the differing costs depending on the language.

Again, for patentees who otherwise would only validate in the TOP3 states, i.e. Germany, the UK, and France, the translation costs incurred for an EP-UE will certainly be higher than for national validations. In all these countries no translation is required for national validation. If the patent is, however, to be validated also in Spain, the translation costs for an EP-UE will be identical to those for a EP patent plus a complete national validation. To validate a European patent in Spain, so as to complement the registration as an EP-UE, a translation into Spanish will

7.2 更新手数料

単一効特許の更新手数料は、おおよそ「TOP4」水準である（上記参照）。この水準が国内有効化ルートの場合の費用を上回るか下回るかは、もし国内ルートを採るならどの国で権利有効化を行うかによって変わってくる。例えば、新ルートである単一効特許において20年の存続期間満了までに発生する更新手数料の累計額は、ドイツ、フランス及びイギリスの3カ国の更新手数料の累計額より約1万ユーロ高額になる。ただし、欧州特許の平均存続期間は現時点では約11年程度のものなので、この点はそれほど目立つデメリットにはならないであろう。

もうひとつ考慮すべき点は、複数国で更新手数料を支払う場合と、単一効特許1件分の更新手数料のみを支払う場合とでは、維持管理に伴う費用や手数料の面でどちらが節約になるかである。

7.3 翻訳費用

少なくとも移行期間中、つまり単一効特許の登録請求と同時に欧州特許の翻訳文の提出が必要な期間中は、翻訳にかかる費用を忘れてはならない。単一効特許登録用の全文翻訳に係る翻訳費用と、国ごとの国内有効化の際に生じる翻訳費用とを比較するためには、多くの要素を考え合わせる必要がある。翻訳費用の額は、翻訳対象となるページ数や、翻訳言語ごとの料金の違いといった要因によっても差が出てくる。

繰り返すが、特許権者がドイツ、イギリス、フランスの上位3カ国のみで有効化を望むときは、単一効特許ルートの翻訳費用は、国内有効化ルートの翻訳費用より確実に高額になる。これらの国々では国内有効化手続において翻訳文の提出が必要とされていないからだ。一方、これに加えてスペインでもその特許を有効化するのであれば、単一効特許ルートの翻訳費用は、欧州特許の翻訳費用に国内有効化に必要な一式の翻訳費用を加えた額に等しい。単一効特許として登録する際に、その補完として欧州特許をスペインでも有効化するには、

be required which can be used also for registering the EP-UE. If the validation pattern should be Germany, UK, France and The Netherlands, the translation costs for the EP-UE will again be higher than for national validations since for a national validation in The Netherlands only a translation of the claims is required. For the UK, no extra translation will be necessary, since the claims of an EP patent must be in English language or be translated into English anyway.

On the other hand, if a patentee wants take advantage of the entire territorial scope of the EP-UE, this would infer a significant reduction in translation costs compared to the regular national validations.

7.4 Enforcement Costs

Enforcement costs may be regarded as being less important since only a small fraction of patents will be litigated. It should be noted, however, that the litigation costs will be generally higher at the newly established UPC than they are now in Germany, though probably lower than in the UK in these days. This will, however, largely depend on the value of the matter in dispute. Thus, our statement is applicable for lower or "normal" values (up to about 3 million €), but not for very high values (such as 30 or 50 million €), as they are sometimes applicable in pharma or telecom cases.

8 The Other Side of the Equation: The Covered Territory

If a patentee should determine after considering the above that, compared to its established validation strategy, a EP-UE will be more expensive, it should also consider before abandoning the idea of registering an EP-UE that additional protection in further countries will be obtained. In which additional countries protec-

その有効化手続にスペイン語の翻訳文が必要となるが、この翻訳文は単一効特許登録用として利用できる。権利有効化の際の選定パターンが「ドイツ、イギリス、フランス、及びオランダ」である場合、オランダの国内有効化手続の際に求められる翻訳はクレームの翻訳文のみであるため、先の例と同様に単一効特許ルートの翻訳費用は国内有効化ルートの翻訳費用よりも高額である。イギリスについては、欧州特許のクレームが英語であるか英語に翻訳されているであろうから、翻訳文は必要とされない。

一方、単一効特許の地域的範囲の全域を活用したいと特許権者が望む場合には、単一効特許ルートを採ることで、通常の国内有効化ルートに比べて翻訳費用は大幅に削減できる。

7.4　特許権行使にかかる費用

特許の案件のうち訴訟にまで至るケースは少ないので、特許権行使の費用に関してはそれほど重視されることはないだろう。ただし訴訟費用に関していえば、新たに設置される統一特許裁判所における費用額は、現在のドイツで発生する費用額と比べるとおおむね高くなるようだが、イギリスにおける最近の費用額よりはおそらく低くなると思われる。ただし、この件については訴訟物の価格に大きく依存する。したがって、ここで述べることが当てはまるのは、訴訟物の価格が低額か、「通常の」価格（約300万ユーロまで）の場合であって、製薬関係や電気通信関係の訴訟事件で時折見られるような、訴額が非常に高いケース（例えば3000万〜5000万ユーロ）には当てはまらない。

8　もうひとつの側面：保護対象となる地域

もし特許権者が上記事項を検討したうえで、既定の権利有効化戦略と比べて単一効特許のほうが高くつくと判断したとする。その場合でも、単一効特許登録の選択肢を捨てる前に、より多くの国々で追加的な保護が得られるという点も考えに入れたほうがよい。保護がどの追加国まで及ぶかは、単一効特許の登

tion will be provided will depend on when the EP-UE is registered. As set out above, initially the EP-UE may only cover 13 or so EP-UE Member States. It will take a while until all 25 signatory states have ratified the UPCA.

A patentee should consider whether the additional territorial scope is worth the additional costs of the EP-UE and whether it can find the money in its budget to obtain the additional protective scope which it has not deemed necessary up to that point.

As can be seen in the figure shown below[5], the EP-UE will upon ratification in all countries that have signed the UPCA cover in addition to the three biggest markets a large number of comparatively small economies, many of which are in Eastern Europe. These countries are presently developing and thus may become more important in the future.

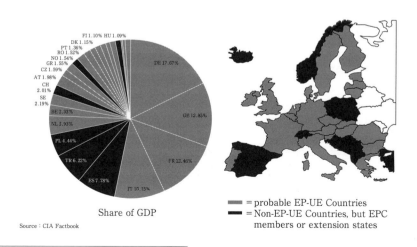

Share of GDP
Source: CIA Factbook

▬ = probable EP-UE Countries
▬ = Non-EP-UE Countries, but EPC members or extension states

---

[5] This figure and the last one were drawn before the UK referendum. In a few years, the UK will most probably leave the EU. In this case and as of then, the UK should also be colored in black.

録をいつ行うかによって異なる。すでに述べたように、単一効特許によってカバーできるのは、最初の段階では13カ国程度の単一効特許加盟国のみであろう。25カ国すべての署名国が統一特許裁判所協定の批准を終えるまでには、もうしばらく時間がかかるであろう。

特許権者は、単一効特許にすることで増える地域的範囲が、その際の追加費用分に値するものかどうか、また、その保護地域についてはその時点まで必要性を認めていなかったという点を考慮して、これを追加取得するための予算をとることができるかどうか検討すべきである。

以下の図[5]に示すとおり、統一特許裁判所協定の全署名国がこれを批准すれば、単一効特許による保護範囲は、大きな市場を持つ上位3カ国だけでなく比較的経済規模の小さい数多くの国々（その多くは東欧諸国）にも及ぶことになる。現在これらの国々は経済成長を続けており、おそらく将来は重要性が増してくるものと思われる。

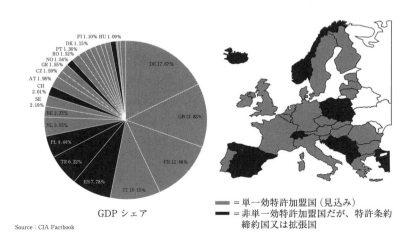

GDPシェア

Source：CIA Factbook

▨ ＝単一効特許加盟国（見込み）
■ ＝非単一効特許加盟国だが、特許条約締約国又は拡張国

---

[5] この図は、イギリスで国民投票が行われる前に作成されたものである。国民投票の結果を受けて、数年後にイギリスがEUから脱退することがほぼ確実になった。EU脱退以後は、イギリスは黒色でマークされることになる。

9 Further Factors

Further factors to be considered are that an EP-UE will simplify the internal and external administrative processes compared to registering several national patents, not only with regard to renewal fees, but also in cases of transfers, name changes, etc.

The other side of the coin is less flexibility. With a portfolio of nationally validated European patents, a patentee will have the possibility to flexibly decide from time to time to reduce the number of countries in which the patent is to be maintained, in the extreme to one country, if the patent is later regarded to be less important, but not entirely dispensable. An EP-UE can, however, only be maintained or allowed to lapse in its entirety.

10 Conclusion: EP-UE, European Patent or National Patent?

Which of the three options to obtain patent protection in the EP-UE Member States is the best will have to be a case by case decision. In view of the probably higher enforcement costs and uncertainty as to the Unified Patent Court's (UPC's) future practice, some applicants may at least initially avoid the EP-UE and instead stick with the existing EP bundle patent and opt out from the UPC, or they may even be looking more closely at national patents in addition to or in lieu of filing a European patent application. The UPC will eventually have jurisdiction not only for EP-UEs, but also for nationally validated European patents in UPCA member states. However, during a transitional period of at least seven years, it will be possible for patentees to "opt out" from the UPC. This means that national courts will remain solely competent for enforcement or invalidation actions.

In sectors where infringements are necessarily Europe wide, excluding an

9　その他

その他の判断要因として挙げられるのは、単一効特許のほうが、複数の国内特許登録を行う場合に比べて内外の維持管理に係る手続が簡単になるという点である。このような手続の例としては、更新手数料に関する手続のほか、権利移転や名義変更の際の手続などがある。

ただし裏を返せば、柔軟性に欠けるということになる。欧州特許を各国ごとに国内有効化して保有していれば、例えば後になってその欧州特許の重要度が下がったものの完全にそれを捨てることはできないという状況になった場合に、特許権者の柔軟な判断により、逐次その特許を維持する国の数を減らすことができ、極端にいえば１カ国にしてしまうこともできる。一方、単一効特許の場合には、全体を維持するか全体を消滅させるかの二者択一となる。

10　結論：単一効特許、欧州特許、 それとも国内特許か

単一効特許加盟国で権利保護を求める際に３つの選択肢のうちのどれがベストかという点については、ケース・バイ・ケースの判断になる。おそらく権利行使に係る費用が増えることや、統一特許裁判所における将来の実務面が不透明である状況を考えると、出願人は、少なくとも最初の段階では単一効特許を避けて既存の「束」としての欧州特許で通し、統一特許裁判所の管轄権からオプトアウトする策を採るほうがよいかもしれない。あるいは、欧州特許出願に加えて、若しくはそれに代えて、各国ルートで国内特許を取得するという選択肢も検討してみる余地がある。統一特許裁判所は、最終的には単一効特許だけでなく、統一裁判所協定加盟国で国内有効化した欧州特許についても管轄することになる。ただし少なくとも７年の移行期間中は、特許権者の選択により同裁判所の管轄権からオプトアウトすることが可能である。この場合、国内裁判所が依然として権利行使に係る訴訟や無効訴訟について唯一管轄権を有する。

侵害が必然的に欧州全土にわたるような分野では、競合相手にとって、重要

important market like Germany is in many cases not commercially feasible for a competitor; thus a national German patent or an EP patent validated in just DE, GB or FR may be entirely sufficient. The German government has been trying to make national German applications more attractive by allowing the initial filing of applications in English or French. A translation will only have to be filed after twelve months, and not later than 15 months from the priority date. A request for examination will not have to be submitted until after seven years from the application date and this will allow postponement of payment of a considerable share of the costs.

市場（ドイツ等）を除外することは多くの場合、商業面から見て現実的ではない。この点を考えると、ドイツの国内特許を取得するか、あるいは欧州特許をドイツ、イギリス又はフランスのみで有効化すれば、おそらくそれで十分であろう。ドイツ政府は、ドイツへの直接出願をより魅力的なものにしようと、英語又はフランス語で最初に出願を行うことを認めている。翻訳文は出願日から12月以内、優先日から15月以内に提出すればよい。出願審査の請求は、出願日から7年が経過するまで行われなくてもよく、諸費用のなかでもかなりシェアの高い費用の支払いを先送りすることができる。

Annex

Rules of Procedure of the Boards of Appeal of the EPO

欧州特許庁の審判部の手続規則

Rules of Procedure of the Boards of Appeal of the EPO

Article 11   Remission to the department of first instance

A Board shall remit a case to the department of first instance if fundamental deficiencies are apparent in the first instance proceedings, unless special reasons present themselves for doing otherwise.

Article 12   Basis of Proceedings

(1) Appeal proceedings shall be based on

   (a) the notice of appeal and statement of grounds of appeal filed pursuant to Article 108 EPC;

   (b) in cases where there is more than one party, any written reply of the other party or parties to be filed within four months of notification of the grounds of appeal;

   (c) any communication sent by the Board and any answer thereto filed pursuant to directions of the Board.

(2) The statement of grounds of appeal and the reply shall contain a party's complete case. They shall set out clearly and concisely the reasons why it is requested that the decision under appeal be reversed, amended or upheld, and should specify expressly all the facts, arguments and evidence relied on. All documents referred to shall be

   (a) attached as annexes insofar as they have not already been filed in the course of the grant, opposition or appeal proceedings or produced by the Office in said proceedings;

欧州特許庁の審判部の手続規則

第11条　第一審部門への差戻し

　　審判部は、第一審手続に基本的不備があったことが明らかであるときは、事件を第一審部門に差し戻す。ただし、差戻しをしない特別の理由が存在する場合はこの限りでない。

第12条　手続の原則

(1)　審判手続は以下に基づくものとする。

　(a)　欧州特許条約第108条の規定に従い提出された審判請求書及び審判請求の理由を記載した書面

　(b)　二以上の当事者が存在する場合は、他の当事者又は他の複数当事者によって提出された答弁書であって、審判請求の理由の送達から4月以内に提出されたもの

　(c)　審判部から送付された通知及びこれに対する応答であって審判部の命令に従い提出されたもの

(2)　審判請求の理由を記載した書面及び答弁書は、一の当事者の主張一式を含むものとする。これらの書面には、審判により決定が覆され、補正され、維持されることを請求する理由を明確かつ簡潔に記載し、根拠となるすべての事実、主張及び証拠を明記するものとする。参照されるすべての書面は以下のとおりとする。

　(a)　特許付与手続、特許異議申立手続、又は審判手続において提出されなかった、又は、当該手続において特許庁により作成されなかった場合は、添付書類として添付されたもの。

(b) filed in any event to the extent that the Board so directs in a particular case.

(3) Subject to Articles 113 and 116 EPC the Board may decide the case at any time after filing of the statement of grounds of appeal or, in cases where there is more than one party, after the expiry of the time limit in (1) (b).

(4) Without prejudice to the power of the Board to hold inadmissible facts, evidence or requests which could have been presented or were not admitted in the first instance proceedings, everything presented by the parties under (1) shall be taken into account by the Board if and to the extent it relates to the case under appeal and meets the requirements in (2).

(5) Extension of time limits may exceptionally be allowed in the Board's discretion following receipt of a written and reasoned request.

Article 13 Amendment to a party's case

(1) Any amendment to a party's case after it has filed its grounds of appeal or reply may be admitted and considered at the Board's discretion. The discretion shall be exercised in view of inter alia the complexity of the new subject matter submitted, the current state of the proceedings and the need for procedural economy.

(2) Other parties shall be entitled to submit their observations on any amendment not held inadmissible by the Board ex officio.

(3) Amendments sought to be made after oral proceedings have been arranged shall not be admitted if they raise issues which the Board or the other party or parties cannot reasonably be expected to deal with without adjournment of the oral proceedings.

(b) 審判部が特定の事件で命令する限りにおいて提出されたすべての書類。

(3) 欧州特許条約第113条及び第116条の規定に従うことを条件として、審判部は、審判請求の理由を記載した書面が提出された後いつでも、又は、二以上の当事者が存在する場合は(1)(b)の期間満了後いつでも、事件の判断を下すことができる。

(4) 第一審手続で提出できたはずであるか、又は第一審手続で許可されなかった事実、証拠又は請求を排除する審判部の権限を害することなく、(1)に基づき当事者らにより提出されたすべての書面は、審判請求の対象である事件に関連する限りにおいて、かつ、その範囲内で、並びに、(2)の要件を満たす場合は、審判部により考慮されるものとする。

(5) 期限の延長は、審判部の裁量により、理由を記載した書面による請求の受領の後、例外的に認められる。

第13条　当事者の主張の訂正

(1) 一の当事者が審判請求の理由を記載した書面又は答弁書を提出した後は、当事者の主張の補正は、審判部の裁量によってのみ受理され、かつ、考慮される。裁量は、特に、提出された新たな主題の複雑性、手続の現状、及び審判手続経済の必要性を考慮して行使される。

(2) 他の当事者らは、審判部が職権で補正を不受理としないことに対して意見を述べる権利を有する。

(3) 口頭審理が設定された後になされる補正は、審判部又は他の（一又は複数の）当事者にとって、口頭審理を延期することなくして処理することが合理的に予測できない論点が当該補正により提起されるときは、許可されない。

Article 14 Interventions

Articles 12 and 13 shall apply mutatis mutandis to interventions commenced while an appeal is pending.

Article 15 Oral Proceedings

(1) If oral proceedings are to take place, the Board may send a communication drawing attention to matters which seem to be of special significance, or to the fact that questions appear no longer to be contentious, or containing other observations that may help concentration on essentials during the oral proceedings.

(2) A change of date for oral proceedings may exceptionally be allowed in the Board's discretion following receipt of a written and reasoned request made as far in advance of the appointed date as possible.

(3) The Board shall not be obliged to delay any step in the proceedings, including its decision, by reason only of the absence at the oral proceedings of any party duly summoned who may then be treated as relying only on its written case.

(4) The Chairman presides over the oral proceedings and ensures their fair, orderly and efficient conduct.

(5) When a case is ready for decision during oral proceedings, the Chairman shall state the final requests of the parties and declare the debate closed. No submissions may be made by the parties after the closure of the debate unless the Board decides to re-open the debate.

(6) The Board shall ensure that each case is ready for decision at the conclusion of the oral proceedings, unless there are special reasons to the

第14条　参加

第12条及び第13条は、審判が係属中に参加が開始されたときに準用する。

第15条　口頭審理

(1) 口頭審理が行われる場合、審判部は、特別に重要と思われる事項又は論点はもはや争点ではないと思われる事実を喚起する通知、あるいは口頭審理の骨子に専念するための助けとなる見解を含んだ通知を送付することができる。

(2) 口頭審理の期日の変更は、審判部の裁量により、指定された期日よりも可能な限り前に、理由を記載した書面による請求があれば、その請求の受領の後、例外的に認められる。

(3) 審判部は、適法に口頭審理に召喚されたいずれかの当事者が口頭審理に欠席することのみを理由として、審決を含むいかなる審判手続をも遅延させる義務を持たないものとする。当該当事者は、その後は書面審理にのみ依拠して取り扱われる。

(4) 審判長は口頭審理を司り、公平で秩序ある、効率的な進行を確保する。

(5) 口頭審理において審決をしようとするときは、審判長は、当事者らの最終的な請求を述べて、議論の終わりを宣言する。議論の終了後は、当事者らはいかなる申出も行うことができない。ただし、審判部が議論を再開することを決定した場合はこの限りでない。

(6) 審判部は、口頭審理の終結に際し、各事件が審決をする状態にあることを確保する。ただし、これに反する特別の理由がある場合はこの限りでな

contrary. Before the oral proceedings are closed, the decision may be announced orally by the Chairman.

Article 17 Communications to the parties

(1) In the written phase of proceedings, replies to requests and directions on matters of procedure shall be given by means of communications.

(2) If a Board deems it expedient to communicate with the parties regarding a possible appreciation of substantive or legal matters, such communication shall be made in such a way as not to imply that the Board is in any way bound by it.

Article 20 Deviations from an earlier decision of any Board or from the Guidelines

(1) Should a Board consider it necessary to deviate from an interpretation or explanation of the Convention given in an earlier decision of any Board, the grounds for this deviation shall be given, unless such grounds are in accordance with an earlier opinion or decision of the Enlarged Board of Appeal. The President of the European Patent Office shall be informed of the Board's decision.

(2) If, in its decision, a Board gives a different interpretation of the Convention to that provided for in the Guidelines, it shall state the grounds for its action if it considers that this decision will be more readily understood in the light of such grounds.

Article 21 Deviation from an earlier decision or opinion of the Enlarged Board of Appeal

Should a Board consider it necessary to deviate from an interpretation

い。審決は、口頭審理が終了する前に審判長が口頭で告げることができる。

第17条　当事者らとの通信

(1)　書面審理においては、請求に対する回答及び手続事項に関する命令は、通信手段によってなされるものとする。

(2)　審判部が、重要事項又は法律事項を理解するにあたって当事者らと通信することが便宜であると判断する場合、かかる通信は、これに審判部が拘束されることを意味しない態様でなされるものとする。

第20条　別の審判部による先の審決又は審査基準との不整合

(1)　先の審決により別の審判部でなされた条約の解釈又は説明から逸脱することが避けられないと考えるときは、審判部はその理由を提示する。ただし、かかる理由が拡大審判部による先の見解又は決定に従っている場合はこの限りでない。審判部の決定は欧州特許庁長官に報告される。

(2)　審判部は、審査基準に記載されているものと異なる条約の解釈を審決において提示する場合であって、理由を述べることで審決がより容易に理解できると考えるときは、その理由を述べる。

第21条　拡大審判部による先の審決又は見解との不整合

　　拡大審判部による先の見解又は審決に含まれる条約の解釈又は説明から

or explanation of the Convention contained in an earlier opinion or decision of the Enlarged Board of Appeal, the question shall be referred to the Enlarged Board of Appeal.

Article 22 Referral of a question to the Enlarged Board of Appeal

(1) If a point is to be referred to the Enlarged Board of Appeal, a decision to this effect shall be taken by the Board concerned.

(2) The decision shall contain the items specified in Rule 102, sub-paragraphs (a), (b), (c), (d) and (f), and the point which the Board refers to the Enlarged Board of Appeal. The context in which the point originated shall also be stated.

(3) The decision shall be communicated to the parties.

逸脱することが避けられないと審判部が考えるときは、論題は拡大審判部に付託される。

第22条　拡大審判部への論題の付託

(1)　論点が拡大審判部に付託されるときは、この趣旨での審決は関与した審判部によりなされる。

(2)　当該審決には、規則102条(a)、(b)、(c)、(d)、及び(f)に規定された事項、及び、審判部が拡大審判部に付託する論点が含まれる。当該論点を生じさせるに至った背景も記載される。

(3)　当該審決は当事者らに通知される。

Authors / 執筆者

Martin Bachelin
Disclosure Concepts and Novelty

GERMAN AND EUROPEAN PATENT ATTORNEY

Specialisation: Examination, opposition and appeal proceedings before the European and German Patent Offices and the Federal Patent Court in the fields of organic and pharmaceutical chemistry as well as polymer chemistry.

Career: Studied chemistry at the University of Regensburg; diploma thesis at the University of Lausanne in the field of organometallic chemistry. Scholarship of the Technical University of Munich for his doctoral thesis on the determination of oligonucleotide structures in solution; research on the association of ions in non-aqueous solutions at the University of Leeds via an Erasmus Scholarship. With Hoffmann · Eitle since 1997.

Stephan Disser
Disclosure Concepts and Novelty

GERMAN AND EUROPEAN PATENT ATTORNNY

Specialisation: Examination, opposition and appeal proceedings before the European and German Patent Offices in the field of organic, pharmaceutical, catalyst, polymer and food chemistry, as well as material science; legal opinions. Special expertise in the field of dust filtration media, catalysts, polymers, silicon wafers, tissue paper and absorbent articles.

Career: Studied chemistry at the University of Frankfurt/Main; diploma thesis in 1995 in the field of semiconductor wafers. Doctoral thesis on mesoporous materials and their use in heterogeneous catalysis in 1999. Scholarship from the Chemical Industry Trust. With Hoffmann · Eitle since 1999.

Declan Mulhern

Inventive Step

IRISH, BRITISH AND EUROPEAN PATENT ATTORNEY

Specialisation: Drafting and prosecuting patent applications internationally as well as handling opposition and appeal proceedings before the European Patent Office. Expertise is primarily in the field of chemistry, with a particular focus on pharmaceuticals, personal care products, foodstuffs, dyes, biological assays and general inorganic chemistry.

Career: Studied chemistry at Dublin City University (DCU) and Friedrich Schiller Universität, Jena. Awarded a Ph.D. in chemistry by DCU (2003) for developing new synthetic routes to ruthenium-polypyridyl complexes for use as water-splitting catalysts or sensitisers in solar cells. Certificate in Intellectual Property Law from the University of London (2011). Industrial experience as a chemical engineer at Mitani Sangyo, Tokyo (1997-1999) and as a research scientist at Daiichi Pure Chemicals (now Sekisui Medical), Ibaraki (2003-2007). With Hoffmann · Eitle since 2007.

Jan-Hendrik Spilgies

Prior Art

GERMAN AND EUROPEAN PATENT ATTORNEY

Specialisation: Examination, opposition, appeal and nullity proceedings before the European and German Patent Offices as well as the Federal Patent Court, among others in the fields of pharmaceuticals (including active principles and formulations), polymers and paper chemistry. Furnishing legal opinions on issues of validity and infringement of patents; national and international litigation activities, in particular in the field of pharmaceuticals.

Career: Studied chemistry at the University of Cologne; diploma thesis in physical chemistry (1992). Doctoral thesis in the field of colloid and interface chemistry and the determination of structures in microemulsions (1996); industry research projects in the field of process engineering (extractive distillation and catalyst research, in Germany) and pharmacology (pharmaceutical technology, in the USA). With Hoffmann · Eitle since 1996.

Joachim Renken

Sufficiency of Disclosure

GERMAN AND EUROPEAN PATENT ATTORNEY

Specialisation: Examination, opposition and appeal proceedings before the European and German Patent Offices, as well as the Federal Patent Court; nullity actions before the Federal Patent Court and Federal Supreme Court; litigation and legal opinions. Particular expertise in biotechnology, organic chemistry, food science and cosmetics. Litigation experience with patents involving pharmaceuticals, DNA chips and fine chemicals.

Career: Studied chemistry at the Universities of Aachen and Heidelberg. Diploma and doctoral thesis in biophysical and bioanalytical chemistry at the University of Heidelberg. Practical experience in the field of surface chemistry, protein chemistry and bioanalytical devices. Erasmus Scholarship at the University of Montpellier (France). With Hoffmann · Eitle since 1996.

Andreas Stefferl

Patentable Subject-Matter I

GERMAN AND EUROPEAN PATENT ATTORNY

Specialisation: Opinion work; examination, opposition and appeal proceedings before the European and German Patent Offices and before the Federal Patent Court, mainly in the field of biotechnological inventions.

Career: Studied biology at the University of Vienna and Victoria University of Manchester, UK. Diploma thesis in the field of neurobiology in 1995. Doctoral thesis at the Max-Planck-Institutes for Psychiatry and Neurobiology in the fields of neuroimmunology and neuroendocrinology of inflammatory diseases of the central nervous system, in particular multiple sclerosis. Doctoral thesis in 2000. Postdoctoral associate at the University of Vienna in 2000. Research analyst in a rating agency from 2001 to 2002. Investment manager at a venture capital firm specialised in biotechnology startup companies until 2003. With Hoffmann · Eitle since 2003.

Michele Baccelli

Patentable Subject-Matter II

ITALIAN AND EUROPEAN PATENT ATTORNEY

Specialisation: Examination, appeal and opposition proceedings before the European Patent Office, especially in the areas of telecommunications, software patents, electronics/circuit technologies. Assisting clients in nullity and litigation proceedings, also cross country. Counseling in licensing negotiations, particularly in relation to technical aspects of small to large patent portfolios.

Career: Studied electrical engineering from the University of L'Aquila, Italy, specializing in electromagnetic compatibility. Research focusing on electromagnetic software simulators. Visiting researcher at University of Kentucky (USA). From 1999 to 2002, with SONY International Europe in Munich, later Sony Ericsson, working initially as mobile phones development engineer and then as project manager, leading product and new technologies projects. From 2003 to 2008, patent examiner at the EPO, handling examination cases also as chairman, especially in the area of telecommunications. With Hoffmann · Eitle since 2008.

Rainer E. Zangs

Patentable Subject-Matter II

GERMAN AND EUROPEAN PATENT ATTORNEY

Specialisation: Examination, opposition and appeal proceedings before the German Patent and Trademark Office, the Federal Patent Court and the European Patent Office, nullity actions and litigation, especially in the area of semiconductor and circuit technologies, telecommunication and medical devices.

Career: Studied general electrical engineering at the Technical University of Aachen (RWTH), particularly in the field of telecommunications, computer science, micro-electronics and theoretical electronic engineering, graduating in 1985. Participated in a research project of the Ministry of Research and Technology (BMFT) of the Federal Republic of Germany from 1983 to 1986. Practical experience as an engineer with Philips GmbH in Aachen. With Hoffmann · Eitle since 1987.

Leonard L. Werner-Jones

Filing of EP Applications

GERMAN AND EUROPEAN PATENT ATTORNEY

Specialisation: Examination, opposition and appeal proceedings before the European and German Patent Offices and the Federal Patent Court. Preparation of litigation and legal opinions. Expertise in biotechnology, in particular neurobiology, immunology, cell biology, molecular biology and genetic engineering.

Career: Studied biology at Dartmouth College, Hanover, NH/USA; B.A. in 1991. Doctoral thesis at the Max-Planck-Institute of Neurobiology in Martinsried/Munich in 1998. Post-doctoral scientist and faculty member at the University of California/San Diego (UCSD) researching nerve regeneration following spinal cord injury (1999-2004). Author of over 30 international scientific publications. Scholarships and research grants from US-NIH, US-VA, US-NARSAD, DAAD, Max-Planck-Society and Hoffmann-La Roche. With Hoffmann · Eitle since 2004.

Matthias Wolf

Claims

GERMAN AND EUROPEAN ATTORNEY

Specialisation: Examination, opposition and appeal proceedings before the European and German Patent Offices and the Federal Patent Court relating to chemical and pharmaceutical patents, opinion work and litigation. Particular expertise in photochemistry, pharmaceuticals, agrochemicals, polymer and fluoropolymer chemistry, textile chemistry, lithographic printing technology, and magnetic materials.

Career: Studied chemistry at the University of Göttingen with a focus on physical chemistry, graduated in 1988. Doctoral thesis on the kinetics and dynamics of gas phase radical reactions in combustion processes (1992) at the MPI für Strömungsforschung, Göttingen. Postdoctoral fellowship awarded by the German Research Association (DFG); research at the Sandia National Laboratories, Livermore, CA in the field of atmospheric pollution mechanisms. Postdoctoral research at the ETH Lausanne in the area of heterogeneous reactions in the upper atmosphere. With Hoffmann · Eitle since 1995.

James M. Ogle

Priority

BRITISH AND EUROPEAN PATENT ATTORNEY

Specialisation: Oppositions and appeals before the European Patent Office; patent prosecution before the EPO and UK-IPO and coordinating the prosecution of patent portfolios worldwide; drafting and advising on new patent applications. Opinion work, including freedom to operate and patentability opinions; due diligence. Experience across the life sciences (biotechnology and pharmaceuticals), including molecular biology, biochemistry, medical inventions, diagnostic methods and products, research tools. Particular expertise in the area of RNA and other nucleic acid-based technologies, e.g. RNAi, antisense, nucleic acid modifications.

Career: Studied biochemistry at the Universities of Regensburg and Oxford. PhD on the structure and function of the ribosome with Venki Ramakrishnan at the University of Cambridge closely connected with Ramakrishnan's Nobel Prize for Chemistry 2009. Fellow of Trinity College, Cambridge; scholar of the Boehringer Ingelheim Foundation, the UK Medical Research Council, the Studienstiftung des Deutschen Volkes and under the Bavarian Act for Promoting Highly Gifted Students. Joined Hoffmann · Eitle in 2004. Trained and worked with a leading IP law firm in London (2006-2012).

Georg Siegert

European Search

GERMAN AND EUROPEAL PATENT ATTORNEY

Specialisation: Examination, opposition and appeal proceedings before the German Patent and Trademark Office, the Federal Patent Court and the European Patent Office, nullity suits and litigation proceedings, especially in the area of mobile communications, computers and semiconductor technology.

Career: Studied physics at the University of Ulm and the Université de Paris VII, emphasis on theoretical physics and solid state physics. Maître en Physique in 1986. Dipl.-Phys. in 1989. Doctoral thesis at the University of the Federal Armed Forces, Munich, in cooperation with industrial R&D at Siemens AG, on sub-micron transistors. Doctorate awarded in 1994. With Hoffmann · Eitle since 1994.

Christiane Stein-Dräger

Substantive Examination

GERMAN AND EUROPEAN PATENT ATTORNEY

Specialisation: Chemical Patents, in particular examination, opposition and appeal proceedings before the European and German Patent Offices and the Federal Patent Court as well as legal opinions on patent infringement and validity questions. Particular expertise in the fields of polymer chemistry, liquid crystals, photochemistry and applied organic chemistry, with an emphasis on cosmetics, washing and detergent compositions, foodstuffs and textile chemistry.

Career: Studied chemistry (inorganic, organic and physical chemistry) at the Technical University of Munich from 1977-1986. Graduated in 1983, doctoral thesis in organic and macromolecular chemistry on the decomposition of polymerisation initiators and synthesis of fluorinated organic compounds. With Hoffmann · Eitle since 1990.

Morten Garberg

Amendments
Appeals

BRITISH AND EUROPEAN PATENT ATTORNEY

Specialisation: Examination, opposition and appeal proceedings before the European Patent Office. Opinions regarding validity, infringement and freedom to operate under British law. In the fields of chemistry, including pharmaceutical chemistry, polymer chemistry and food chemistry. Particular expertise and experience in EPO opposition cases (ca. 15-20 hearings per year). Involved in the coordination of multi-jurisdiction litigation, and providing hands-on advice during litigation. Listed as one of only 30 recommended individuals Europe-wide for EPO work in the 2015 edition of the IAM 1000 guide.

Career: Studied chemistry (inorganic, organic and physical chemistry) at Oxford University (Keble College) 1998-2002. He graduated with a Master's honours degree in 2002, having carried out a final year research project and written a thesis in the field of inorganic chemical crystallography. He obtained the Certificate in Intellectual Property Law from Queen Mary College, University of London. Morten has been with Hoffmann · Eitle since 2002.

Matthias Kindler

Remedies

GERMAN AND EUROPEAN PATENT ATTORNEY

Specialisation: Chemical patents, principally litigation, legal opinions, opposition and appeal proceedings before the European and German Patent Offices and the Federal Patent Court, nullity actions before the Federal Supreme Court, as well as patent application proceedings. Numerous cases in SPC matters before the German Federal Patent Court, the Federal Supreme Court (Idarubicin, Sumatriptan, Pantoprazol, Anti-helicobacter preparation, Doxorubicin sulfate) and the European Court of Justice (C-392/97 - Farmitalia Carlo Erba s.r.l., C-31/03 - Pharmacia Italia). Particular expertise in the field of pharmaceuticals, cosmetics, washing and detergent compositions, foodstuffs, polymers and electrochemistry.

Career: Studied chemistry at the University of Regensburg, graduated in 1981. Doctoral thesis in 1985 in the field of electrochemistry and battery development. Industrial experience in the research, development, and production of semiconductors (with Siemens AG), and printing inks (M. Huber GmbH). With Hoffmann · Eitle since 1987.

Veit-Peter Frank

Opposition Procedure

GERMAN AND EUROPEAN PATENT ATTORNEY

Specialisation: Examination, opposition and appeal proceedings before the German Patent and Trademark Office, the Federal Patent Court and the European Patent Office; nullity actions, litigation and preliminary injunction proceedings, especially in the area of mobile communications, digital and analogue circuits and systems and antenna technology.

Career: Studied electrical engineering at the Technical University of Aachen (RWTH), with emphasis on the fields of telecommunications, high frequency technology, control engineering and circuit design, graduating in 1988. Scholarship from the Technical University of Aachen for post-graduate studies and research in the field of digital telecommunications at the Imperial College, London. Awarded an M.Sc. by the University of London in 1989. With Hoffmann · Eitle since 1990.

David Lethem

Central Limitation and Revocation Procedure

BRITISH AND EUROPEAN PATENT ATTORNEY

Specialisation: Contentious proceedings before the Opposition Divisions and Appeal Boards of the European Patent Office across the entire spectrum of chemical and pharmaceutical inventions, in addition to patent application proceedings before the EPO and the UK Intellectual Property Office. Particular expertise in the area of refrigerant compositions, bio-active ingredients for foodstuffs and photochemistry. Involved in Decision G 1/99 concerning the issue of reformatio in peius in the EPO.

Career: Studied natural sciences at Cambridge University with an emphasis on organic chemistry including reaction mechanisms and organic synthesis, organometallic chemistry including molecular conformation and catalytic activity, and biochemistry including gene expression and genetic recombination. From 1983 to 1987 patent experience in a British patent law firm. With Hoffmann · Eitle since 1987.

Klemens Stratmann

EPC and National Law

GERMAN AND EUROPEAN PATENT ATTORNEY

Specialisation: Examination, opposition and appeal proceedings before the European and German Patent Offices and the Federal Patent Court in chemical and pharmaceutical patents; litigation and legal opinions; numerous proceedings in Supplementary Protection Certificate matters. Particular expertise in paper chemistry, photochemistry, organic chemistry, especially in the pharmaceutical and agrochemical fields, and nanomaterials.

Career: Studied chemistry at the Technical University in Karlsruhe with emphasis on organic synthesis, graduated in 1989. Doctoral thesis in biosynthesis reactions in plants (1992); research at the University of Hawaii in the area of the isolation and structural elucidation of anti-cancer drugs from marine plants until 1994. Scholarships from the State Graduate Sponsorship Program and the German Research Association (DFG). With Hoffmann · Eitle since 1994.

Thorsten Bausch

The European Patent within the Future EU Patent Package

GERMAN AND EUROPEAN PATENT ATTORNEY

Specialisation: Chemical Patents, with a particular focus on cross-border and national litigation, legal opinions. Opposition and appeal proceedings before the European and German Patent Offices and the Federal Patent Court; nullity actions before the Federal Court of Justice; patent prosecution. Particular expertise in the fields of pharmaceuticals, immunology, polymers and construction chemistry. Litigation experience with pharmaceutical patents concerning (among others) donepezil, oxycodone, anastrozole, tramadol, pantoprazole, sildenafil, cyclosporin A, lamotrigin, fulvestrant, calcipotriol, valsartan, memantine as well as with patents covering diagnostic immunoassays and retroreflective sheetings. Involved in Decision G 1/99 concerning the prohibition of the reformatio in peius in the EPO and in Decision "Polifeprosan/MIT" of the European Court of Justice in an SPC matter.

Career: Studied chemistry at the University of Würzburg, the Technical University of Munich, and at the Massachusetts Institute of Technology. Faculty Award of the University of Würzburg 1984; scholarships from the Studienstiftung des Deutschen Volkes, the Chemical Industry Trust, and the Ernest Solvay Foundation. Graduated in 1990, doctoral thesis 1992. With Hoffmann · Eitle since 1992.

Editors / 編者

Mieko Matsuzawa

EUROPEAN PATENT ATTORNEY

Specialisation: Examination, opposition and appeal proceedings before the European Patent Office in the fields of materials science and engineering (including semiconductor, ceramics, metal and biological materials), bioelectronics and biomedical devices.

Career: Studied bioengineering at Tokyo Institute of Technology (Tokyo). Ph.D. from Johns Hopkins University (USA). Doctoral thesis in an interdisciplinary field of materials science and neuroscience. Post-doctoral scientist at Max-Planck Institute (Mainz). Research fellow at RIKEN, (Wako, Japan), worked on defense project in the USA. Patent experience in a Japanese law firm (Tokyo). J.D. from Franklin Pierce Law Center (USA). Passed the U.S. Patent Bar Examination while working as a trainee in a US law firm in Washington, D.C (the registration expired in 2008). Passed NY and Washington D.C. Bar examinations. With Hoffmann · Eitle since 2007.

Joachim Renken

GERMAN AND EUROPEAN PATENT ATTORNEY

Specialisation: Examination, opposition and appeal proceedings before the European and German Patent Offices, as well as the Federal Patent Court; nullity actions before the Federal Patent Court and Federal Supreme Court; litigation and legal opinions. Particular expertise in biotechnology, organic chemistry, food science and cosmetics. Litigation experience with patents involving pharmaceuticals, DNA chips and fine chemicals.

Career: Studied chemistry at the Universities of Aachen and Heidelberg. Diploma and doctoral thesis in biophysical and bioanalytical chemistry at the University of Heidelberg. Practical experience in the field of surface chemistry, protein chemistry and bioanalytical devices. Erasmus Scholarship at the University of Montpellier (France). With Hoffmann · Eitle since 1996.

Assistant Editors / 編集助手   Izumi Shikama & Mari Eichler

Our Office / 事務所紹介

Hoffmann Eitle

With approximately 400 employees at six locations across Germany and Europe (Munich, London, Düsseldorf, Hamburg, Milano and Madrid), Hoffmann Eitle is one of the largest and most successful firms specialized in intellectual property. The firm has patent attorneys specialized in the technical fields covering chemistry, biotechnology, materials science, mechanical engineering, electrical engineering and information technology as well as German attorneys-at-law specialized in the areas of trademarks & designs and patent litiga-tion & licensing. One of the strengths is the interdisciplinary cooperation between the patent attorneys and German attorneys-at-law. The main office is located in Munich.

In 1892, engineer Emil Hoffmann laid the foundation of the firm in Berlin. In 1925, after completing his chemistry studies, Emil Hoffmann's son Erich joined the firm as a partner, and father and son worked together until Emil's death in 1944. That same year, the office building was completely destroyed in an Allied air raid. Just before the Soviet army marched into Berlin, Erich Hoffmann fled with his family to Munich where he rebuilt the firm after the war. In 1954, engineer Werner Eitle joined the firm as a trainee, and in 1960 became a partner of Erich Hoffmann. The third partner, joining the firm five years later, was Erich Hoffmann's son Klaus. The firm and the professional partnership continued to grow without merger or acquisition. The vast majority of the present partners have been with the firm for their entire professional career. The reputation of the firm is ensured by highly qualified IP professionals, supported by a team of technically accomplished, experienced and reliable staff members.

編著者紹介

ホフマン アイトレ（Hoffmann Eitle）

1892年にベルリンで設立。知的財産権を専門的に取り扱う欧州屈指の特許法律事務所として、長い歴史と豊富な実績をもつ。化学、バイオテクノロジー、材料科学、機械工学、電気電子工学からITに至る技術分野において高度の専門知識を有する弁理士と、商標、意匠、特許訴訟、ライセンシングの分野を専門的に取り扱うドイツ弁護士とを多数擁し、多種多様な事案に対応して柔軟に取り組める体制を有している。現在は、ミュンヘンを拠点として欧州に6つのオフィスを構え、弁理士、弁護士、それらを支えるスタッフ含め総勢400名余が在籍し、高品質なサポート及びサービスを提供している。

［対訳］実務家のための欧州特許条約

2016年11月8日　第1版第1刷発行

編著者——ホフマン アイトレ
発行者——串崎　浩
発行所——株式会社 日本評論社
　　　　　〒170-8474 東京都豊島区南大塚 3-12-4
　　　　　電話 03-3987-8621　　FAX 03-3987-8590
　　　　　振替 00100-3-316　　https://www.nippyo.co.jp/
印刷所——精文堂印刷
製本所——牧製本印刷
装　幀——Agentur2 GmbH + ギンゾウ工房
検印省略　© Hoffmann Eitle 2016
ISBN978-4-535-52192-6　　Printed in Japan

JCOPY〈(社) 出版者著作権管理機構 委託出版物〉
本書の無断複写は著作権法上での例外を除き禁じられています。複写される場合は、そのつど事前に、(社) 出版者著作権管理機構（電話03-3513-6969、FAX 03-3513-6979、e-mail: info@jcopy.or.jp）の許諾を得てください。また、本書を代行業者等の第三者に依頼してスキャニング等の行為によりデジタル化することは、個人の家庭内の利用であっても、一切認められておりません。